Competition Law in Switzerland

Pranvera Këllezi

Competition Law in Switzerland

Law and Practice in a European Context

Springer

Pranvera Këllezi
Geneva, Switzerland

ISBN 978-3-031-45116-4 ISBN 978-3-031-45117-1 (eBook)
https://doi.org/10.1007/978-3-031-45117-1

This Springer imprint is published by the registered company Springer Nature Switzerland AG
The registered company address is: Gewerbestrasse 11, 6330 Cham, Switzerland

Paper in this product is recyclable.

Preface

Why Pay Attention to Competition Law in Switzerland?

Delving into Swiss competition law reveals a rich and complex set of regulatory changes that have reshaped the business environment for companies over the years. In 2003, direct sanctions for breaches of competition law were introduced, complementing an EU-style competition law adopted in the mid-1990s and the creation of the Competition Commission, an independent authority composed of lawyers and economists with extensive powers. Fines were quickly extended to foreign companies, with the BMW fine being one of the largest ever imposed for banning parallel imports between the EU and Switzerland. At the same time as removing barriers to trade with the EU, the Swiss Supreme Court also abolished any constraints on the extraterritorial application of competition law. This move allows the Swiss Cartel Act to exert its influence globally.

Fines have changed a lot of things, not only in terms of the number of enforcement decisions, but also in terms of length and their justification. Fines had to be defended and the arguments of the parties had to be given their due place. In 2007, the Federal Administrative Court replaced the ACCI, an expert body dealing with appeals, and since then there have been no economists in the appeal courts. Simple economic assessments have been replaced by complex legal reasoning justifying why we should abandon assessment of economic facts. At the same time as economic assessment and reasoning began to vanish, the length of the Federal Administrative Court's proceedings and decisions increased significantly. The Federal Supreme Court has managed to keep its rulings short, but not simple. This has done little to improve legal certainty for business.

The Forest and the Trees

The risk for practitioners is twofold: not being able to see the forest for the trees and, conversely, not being able to see the trees for the forest. The big picture and the relevant details are important in assessing regulatory risk, a process that is ultimately subjective and follows the risk appetite of the organisation. In writing this book, I have been mindful that, in practice, too much detail about fact-specific case law or academic arguments can cloud the main assessment process. I have therefore chosen to strike a balance between the two, presenting what seems relevant to me and to a hypothetical mindful practitioner. Of course, this is also a subjective exercise, and this will give the book its individual character.

Who Should Read and Use This Book?
The book can be read by anyone. Practitioners and in-house counsels will find a wealth of information to guide them in risk assessment. This book is better used as a toolbox in which professionals can find information, sensitive points or strategic guidance that will enable them to assess the risk of conduct, make decisions on how to deal with a case or what to consider during an assessment or investigation. Academics will appreciate discovering a body of law and reasoning that can feed their curiosity and raise questions for further research. Through its varied and sometimes surprising reasoning, judge-made law is an expression of Switzerland's potential for innovation in legal reasoning, which extends beyond its economy. The book is not intended to provide legal advice in specific cases, and companies and professionals are well advised to make their own assessment. This applies particularly to the conduct of investigations and procedural issues.

Why in English?
Reflecting the composition of the Swiss economy, about 80% of the decisions are in German, the rest in French and a few in Italian. Language is still an obstacle for foreign practitioners and Swiss alike, making the process of decoding this large number of decisions and judgments inefficient. While working as an in-house counsel and later as an attorney at law, the need to find the right information in the forest and present it in French and English became increasingly urgent. This book is a contribution to the understanding of the Swiss competition law in another widely used language.

Staying up to Date
Keeping abreast of developments in competition law is stimulating. In Switzerland, a few days before the manuscript was due to be submitted, the Federal Council published a draft law on the revision of the Cartel Act. Where relevant, I have mentioned the provisions affected by the changes without commenting on the prospects of the individual proposals. The need to keep up to date remains unchanged. Everything changes, everything stays the same.

My Journey in the Field
My journey into competition law began as a student in 1998. Writing a doctoral thesis on competition law in 2000 was a process of discovery and deep immersion in EU and Swiss competition law, while an LLM in Bruges helped to unpack the EU side of the coin. This was followed by a period of intensive involvement with trade associations and companies that must apply EU and Swiss competition law, as an in-house counsel and as an attorney. While practising business law in Geneva, I have

been a member of the Swiss Competition Commission since 2016. You would think the task would be easier, and it is, but the more you know the details, the more you see the need to simplify it for the outside world. The views expressed are personal.

Geneva, Switzerland

Pranvera Këllezi

Contents

About the Author

Pranvera Këllezi is a Commissioner of the Swiss Federal Competition Commission and a practising lawyer in Geneva, where she advises companies on Swiss and European competition law and its impact on business, as well as on commercial law, data protection, corporate governance and economic regulation. She has more than 20 years of experience in advising on regulations that have a direct impact on the strategy and activities of companies. She holds a PhD from the Faculty of Law of the University of Geneva, an LL.M. in European Law from the College of Europe in Bruges and a Board Director Diploma from IMD, Lausanne.

Abbreviations

ACCI	Appeals Commission for Competition Issues, until 2009 (Rekurskommission für Wettbewerbsfragen/Commission de recours pour les questions de Concurrence/ Commissione di ricorso in materia di concorrenza)
ACL	Federal Act on Administrative Criminal Law of 22 March 1974 (RS 313.0)
APA or Administrative Procedure Act	Federal Act on Administrative Procedure (RS 172.021)
BBl	Swiss Federal Journal (Feuille fédérale/Foglio federale (FF)/Bundesblatt)
B2B	Business to business
B2C	Business to consumers
bn	Billion
c./ca.	Circa
Cartel Act or CartA	Federal Act on Cartels and other Restraints of Competition (RS 251)
CASO or Cartel Act Sanctions Ordinance	Ordinance on Sanctions imposed for Unlawful Restraints of Competition (RS 251.5)
CC	Swiss Civil Code (RS 210)
cf.	Compare
CFI	Court of First Instance of the ECJ (before 1 December 2009)
CH	Switzerland
CHF	Swiss franc
CH-EU Agreement on Competition	Agreement between the European Union and the Swiss Confederation concerning cooperation on the application of their competition laws (OJ L 347, 3.12.2014, p. 3; RS 0.251.268.1)

CH-EU Air Transport Agreement	Agreement between the European Community and the Swiss Confederation on Air Transport (OJ L 114, 30.4.2002, p. 73; RS 0.748.127.192.68)
CH-DE Agreement on Competition	Agreement between the Department of Economic Affairs, Education and Research of the Swiss Confederation and the Federal Ministry of Economics and Climate Protection of the Federal Republic of Germany on Cooperation and Coordination of Competition Authorities of 1 November 2022, FF 2023 313 (Abkommen zwischen dem Departement für Wirtschaft, Bildung und Forschung der Schweizerischen Eidgenossenschaft und dem Bundesministerium für Wirt-schaft und Klimaschutz der Bundesrepublik Deutschland über Zusammenarbeit und Koordinierung der Wettbewerbsbehörden vom 1. November 2022, BBl 2023 313.)
CJEU	Court of Justice of the European Union (after 1 December 2009)
CO	Federal Act on the Amendment of the Swiss Civil Code, Part Five: The Code of Obligations (RS 220)
COMCO	Swiss Competition Commission, Bern
COMCO-Secretariat or Secretariat	Secretariat of the Swiss Competition Commission, Bern
Consolidated Jurisdictional Notice	Commission Consolidated Jurisdictional Notice under Council Regulation 139/2004 on the control of concentrations between undertakings, OJ C95, 16.04.2008, p. 1
CrimC	Swiss Criminal Code of 21 December 1937 (RS 311.0)
CPC	Swiss Civil Procedure Code of 19 December 2008 (RS 272)
CrimPC	Swiss Criminal Procedure Code (RS 312.0)
CR_n	Concentration Ratio measuring the percentage market share held by *n* largest undertakings
Cst	Federal Constitution of the Swiss Confederation of 18 April 1999 (RS 101)
DE	Germany
De minimis Notice	Commission Notice on agreements of minor importance which do not appreciably restrict competition under Article 101(1) of the Treaty on the Functioning of the European Union (de minimis), OJ C 291, 30.08.2014, p. 1
DEBA	Swiss Federal Act on Debt Enforcement and Bankruptcy (RS 281.1)
Directive 2014/104	Directive 2014/104 of the European Parliament and of the Council of 26 November 2014 on certain rules governing actions for damages under national law for infringements

	of the competition law provisions of the Member States and of the European Union, OJ L 349, 5.12.2014, p. 1
Draft law of 23 May 2023	Draft law of 23 May 2023 amending the Cartel Act
e.g. or eg	For example
EAER	Federal Department of Economic Affairs, Education and Research
EC	European Community
ECHR	European Convention for Human Rights of 4 November 1950 of the Council of Europe
ECJ	European Court of Justice (before 1 December 2009)
ECtHR	European Court of Human Rights
EEA	European Economic Area
EU	European Union
Explanatory note on instruments of investigation	COMCO Secretariat, Explanatory note of 6 January 2016 on Selected Instruments of Investigation
Explanatory note on leniency program	COMCO Secretariat, Explanatory note and form of the Secretariat of 8 September 2014, Leniency program (voluntary report)
Explanatory note on merger notification	COMCO, Merger notification, notification form and explanatory note of 21 October 2014
Explanatory note on relative market power	Explanatory note of the COMCO Secretariat of 6 December 2021 regarding relative market power
Explanatory note on the notifications of a restriction on competition	COMCO, Explanatory note and form of 21 October 2014, Notification of a restriction on competition
Explanatory note to the Verticals Notice	Explanatory Note of the Competition Commission to the Notice on the assessment of vertical agreements of 12 December 2022
FAC	Swiss Federal Administrative Court, St. Gallen (Bundesverwaltungsgericht/Tribunal administratif fédéral/ Tribunale amministrativo federale/Tribunal administrative federal)
FCC	Federal Criminal Court, Bellinzona, Canton of Ticino
FCP	Federal Act of 4 December 1947 on Federal Civil Procedure (RS 273)
FF	Swiss Federal Journal (Feuille fédérale/Foglio federale/ Bundesblatt (BBl))
ff	And following
FINMA	Swiss Financial Market Supervisory Authority

FoIA or Freedom of Information Act	Federal Act on Freedom of Information in the Administration of 17 December 2004 (SR 152.3)
FSC	Swiss Federal Supreme Court, Lausanne (Bundesgericht/Tribunal fédéral/Tribunale federale/Tribunal federal)
FSC (I-Civil)	The First Civil Law Division, Swiss Federal Supreme Court
FSC (II-Public)	The Second Public Law Division, Swiss Federal Supreme Court
GC	General Court of the CJEU (after 1 December 2009)
GDP	Gross Domestic Product
Guidance on abusive exclusionary conduct	EU Commission, Guidance on the Commission's enforcement priorities in applying Article 82 of the EC Treaty to abusive exclusionary conduct by dominant undertakings (OJ C 45, 24.2.2009, p. 7)
Guidelines on the effect on trade concept	Commission Notice—Guidelines on the effect on trade concept contained in Articles 81 and 82 of the Treaty (OJ C 101, 27.04.2004, p. 81)
Guidelines on vertical restraints or EU Vertical Guidelines	Guidelines on vertical restraints (OJ C 248, 30.6.2022, p. 1)
Guidelines on the setting of fines	Guidelines on the method of setting fines imposed pursuant to Article 23(2)(a) of Regulation No 1/2003, OJ C 210, 1.9.2006, p. 2
HCCH 1970 Evidence Convention	The Convention of 18 March 1970 on the Taking of Evidence Abroad in Civil or Commercial Matters (RS 0.274.132)
HHI	Herfindahl-Hirschman Index
HMT	Hypothetical monopolist test
i.e.	Id est (that is)
Id./Idem	The same as previously mentioned
IP	Intellectual property
kg	Kilogram
LPC	Law and Policy on Competition (RPW/DPC), official publication of Swiss competition authorities
Lugano Convention 2007	Convention on jurisdiction and the recognition and enforcement of judgments in civil and commercial matters, OJ L 339, 21.12.2007, p. 3 (RS 0.275.12)
m	Million
m^2	Square metre
MCO or Merger Control Ordinance	Ordinance on the Control of Concentrations of Undertakings (RS 251.4)
MFN	Most Favoured Nation
min	Minutes

NAAT-rule	The non-appreciable affectation of trade rule
Note on decision-making process	Note of 21 October 2019 of the COMCO: Decision-making process of the Competition Commission in cartel investigations within the meaning of Article 27 ff Cartel Act
Note on preliminary investigations	COMCO Secretariat, Note of 19 February 2020: the conduct of the preliminary investigation explained in simple terms
Notice on amicable agreements	COMCO Secretariat's notice of 28 February 2018 on amicable agreements
Notice on ancillary restraints	Commission Notice on restrictions directly related and necessary to concentrations (OJ C 56, 5.03.2005, p. 24)
Notice on calculation schemes	Notice on the conditions for the admissibility of agreements on the use of calculation schemes under the Cartel Act, Decision of the Competition Commission of 4 May 1998
Notice on concentrations from the Secretariat	Notice of the Secretariat of the COMCO of 25 March 2009, Practice regarding the notification and assessment of concentrations
Notice on effect on trade	Commission Guidelines on the effect on trade concept contained in Articles 81 and 82 of the Treaty (OJ C 101, 27.4.2004, p. 81)
Notice on sports equipment	Notice on the Homologation and Sponsoring of Sports Equipment, Decision of the Competition Commission of 15 December 1997
Notice on the relevant market	Commission Notice on the definition of relevant market for the purposes of Community competition law (OJ C 372, 9.12.1997, p. 5)
OECD	Organisation for Economic Co-operation and Development
OJ	Official Journal of the European Union
p./pp.	Page(s)
para/paras	Paragraph(s)
PILA	Federal Act on Private International Law (RS 291)
PSA	Price Supervision Act of 20 December 1985 (RS 942.20)
pt/pts	Point(s)
R&D	Research and development
Regulation 4064/89	Council Regulation (EEC) No 4064/89 of 21 December 1989 on the control of concentrations between undertakings, OJ L 395, 30/12/1989 p. 1 (no longer in force in the EU)
Regulation 1/2003	Council Regulation 1/2003 of 16 December 2002 on the implementation of the rules on competition laid down in Articles 81 and 82 of the Treaty, OJ L1, 4.1.2003, p. 1

Regulation 139/2004	Council Regulation 139/2004 of 20 January 2004 on the control of concentrations between undertakings, OJ L 24, 29.01.2004, p. 1
Regulation 2022/720 or EU-VBER	Commission Regulation 2022/720 of 10 May 2022 on the application of Article 101(3) of the Treaty on the Functioning of the European Union to categories of vertical agreements and concerted practices, OJ L 134, 11.5.2022, p. 4
Regulation 2659/2000	Commission Regulation 2659/2000 of 29 November 2000 on the application of Article 81(3) of the Treaty to categories of research and development agreements, OJ L 304, 5.12.2000, p. 7
Regulation 316/2014	Commission Regulation 316/2014 of 21 March 2014 on the application of Article 101(3) of the Treaty on the Functioning of the European Union to categories of technology transfer agreements, OJ L 93, 28.03.2014, p. 17
Regulation 773/2004	Commission Regulation 773/2004 of 7 April 2004 relating to the conduct of proceedings by the Commission pursuant to Articles 81 and 82 of the EC Treaty, OJ L 123, 27.4.2004, p. 18
Remarks on CASO	COMCO Secretariat, Remarks on the Ordinance on Fines
RMP	Relative market power
RPM	Resale price maintenance
RS or SR	Classified compilation of Swiss federal acts & ordinances (Systematische Sammlung des Bundesrechts/Recueil systématique du droit fédéral/Raccolta sistematica del diritto federale/Collecziun sistematica)
Secretariat or Comco-Secretariat	Secretariat of the Swiss Competition Commission, Bern
SLC	Substantial lessening of competition
SME Notice	Notice on agreements with limited market impact, Decision of the Competition Commission of 19 December 2005
SMEs	Small and medium size enterprises
SMP	Significant market power
SR or RS	Classified compilation of Swiss federal acts & ordinances (Systematische Sammlung des Bundesrechts/Recueil systématique du droit fédéral/Raccolta sistematica del diritto federale/Collecziun sistematica)
SSNIP	Small but Significant and Non-transitory Increase in Price
TCA	Telecommunications Act (RS 784.10)
TEC	Treaty Establishing the European Community
TFEU	Treaty on the Functioning of the European Union

UCA	Federal Act against Unfair Competition (RS 241)
UK	United Kingdom
US/USA	United States of America
v	Versus
Verticals Notice	COMCO's Notice on the Assessment of Vertical Agreements of 12 December 2022

Chapter 1
Enactment, Scope of Application, and Enforcement of the Cartel Act

1.1 Introduction

Competition law enforcement started very early in Switzerland, before the creation of COMCO in 1996. The cases were based on Article 28 of the Civil Code, which protects the right of personality, including its economic dimension, and on the previous Cartel Act of 1962, [1] and were mainly driven by the demand of wholesalers, retailers and discounters for access to cheap consumer products such as tobacco, beer or spirits. [2] The Cartel Act of 1962 established a Competition Commission, but it only issued opinions and recommendations after conducting investigations, and it was up to the Federal Council to file an application with the Federal Supreme Court and to seek prohibition and other measures against cartels.

The Cartel Act of 1995 [3] established a Competition Commission (COMCO) with decision-making powers and a Secretariat with administrative powers to conduct investigations and take measures to prohibit unlawful practices and to carry out *ex ante* merger control. This allowed public enforcement to develop rapidly. In parallel, private enforcement also developed but remains modest compared to the positive development of public enforcement. The 1995 Cartel Act is the focus of this book.

An English translation of the Cartel Act and its main ordinances, as well as some notices, [4] can be found on the website of the Swiss Competition Commission. [5] Not

[1] RO 1964 49.

[2] See for instance FSC, judgment of 22 December 1965, *Walch contre Navazza,* ATF 91 II 489; FSC, jugement of 15 février 1966, *Alex Martin contre l'Association suisse des fabricants de cigarettes*, ATF/BGE 92 II 1; FSC, judgemnt of 16 September 1970, *Denner v Schweizer Bierbrauerverein*, ATF 96 I 297; FSC, judgment of 18 September 1973, *Verband des Schweizerischen Spirituosengewerbes gegen Angehrn & Co*, ATF 99 II 228.

[3] Federal Act on Cartels and other Restraints of Competition (CartA; RS 251).

[4] https://www.weko.admin.ch/weko/en/home/rechtliches_dokumentation.html.

[5] https://www.weko.admin.ch/weko/fr/home.html.

P. Këllezi, *Competition Law in Switzerland*,
https://doi.org/10.1007/978-3-031-45117-1_1

all notices are translated into English, but they are all available in the three official languages: German, French and Italian. [6] The decisions of the Swiss Competition Commission are published in the official publication of the Swiss Competition Commission and are available to the public online. [7] Courts are required to notify the Competition Commission of their decisions in competition matters, which are also published in the official publication of the Competition Commission.

The context in which the 1995 Carte Act was enacted and its scope are discussed below.

1.2 Context of the Enactment of the Cartel Act in 1995

The Swiss Cartel Act aims to "prevent the harmful economic or social effects of cartels and other restraints of competition and, by doing so, to promote competition in the interests of a liberal market economy". [8]

At the time of its adoption, the Cartel Act was part of a comprehensive programme to revitalise the market economy in Switzerland. The Cartel Act was enacted following the rejection of the referendum on EEA membership in 1992 and, like other laws enacted in this context, aimed at compatibility with European Union law in order to facilitate the integration of the EU's internal market. The Agreement between the EU and Switzerland recognises "that the competition enforcement systems of the Union and of Switzerland are based on the same principles and provide for similar rules". [9]

The Federal Supreme Court (FSC) regularly refers to EU competition law and has stated that the Cartel Act seeks to ensure material compatibility in order to increase legal certainty for companies: [10] the Cartel Act should be "equally strict and not

[6] https://www.weko.admin.ch/weko/fr/home/rechtliches_dokumentation.html.

[7] Law and Policy on Competition (LPC/RPW/DPC), official publication of Swiss competition authorities, available at https://www.weko.admin.ch/weko/fr/home/praxis/droit-et-politique-de-la-concurrence-en-pratique%2D%2Ddpc-.html.

[8] Article 1 CartA.

[9] Agreement between the European Union and the Swiss Confederation concerning cooperation on the application of their competition laws, OJ L 347, 3.12.2014, p. 3; RS 0.251.268.1, Recital 3.

[10] FSC, judgment of 28 June 2016, 2C_180/2014, ATF/BGE 143 II 297 *Gaba*, para 6.2.3: "[I]t is clear from the parliamentary debate that the Swiss regulation with regard to Article 5 (4) of the Cartel Act should be the same as that of the European Union, i.e. equally strict and not stricter: a regulation that differs materially from that of the EU would lead to legal uncertainty. In this respect, the parallelism of the regulations allows that 'for the purpose of legal certainty, recourse can also be made to what the EU has excluded or permitted in its regulation in the form of vertical agreements'. However, the legislator does not expressly refer to European competition law in relation to vertical agreements as applicable under Swiss law. And such European competition law is not simply comparative law - in the sense of an element of interpretation to be taken into account. The reason for this is that comparative legal interpretation would allow the outcome that follows to be disregarded, which is precisely what the legislator did not want with regard to Article 5 (4) of the

stricter", but this has not been the case as there are areas where the Cartel Act is stricter than EU competition law, what is known in common language as a "Swiss finish". Material compatibility means that EU competition law is only relevant to the extent that the market situation and the effects of the restrictions on competition are comparable in the respective markets, which justifies a stricter approach, for example in terms of limiting territorial protection.

The competition law of the EU is of great importance for the interpretation of the Swiss Cartel Act. The case law on Article 102 TFUE is for instance considered to be a valid precedent for defining the meaning and limits of abuse under Article 7 CartA. The general clause of Article 7(1) CartA was therefore considered as a clear legal basis to cover a margin squeeze practice for the purpose of imposing a fine of more than CHF 180 million, as the same practice was considered abusive under Article 102 TFEU (see Sect. 5.3.2).

The aim of our book will be to draw parallels between the Cartel Act and EU competition law and, in particular, to point out where the laws differ, whether as a system, in the way they are applied or in the outcome.

1.3 Scope of Application

1.3.1 Application to Undertakings

The Cartel Act applies to private or public undertakings that are parties to cartels or to other agreements affecting competition, which exercise market power or which participate in concentrations of undertakings. [11] The Cartel Act defines them as all buyers or suppliers of goods or services active in commerce regardless of their legal or organisational form. [12]

All businesses organised as commercial companies with legal personality are private undertakings. Foundations and associations whose activity consists in purchasing or offering goods or services on the market are also considered private

Cartel Act. Although not technically identical, it wanted a materially identical regulation between Article 5 (4) Cartel Act and EU competition law with regard to vertical agreements - despite the lack of a dynamic reference. When interpreting European competition law, the European methodological doctrine must be taken into account. Despite all the required parallelism, it must not be forgotten that this can only be assumed if the fundamental concepts, the case law and the system of European competition law with regard to vertical agreements have not fundamentally changed since 2003. It must also be borne in mind that 'the quality of an competition regime can only be assessed in relation to the country, economy or economic area considered'. In this respect, the economic markets affected by the respective legal systems should be comparable: in particular, vertical agreements on absolute territorial protection have very different effects in smaller countries than in large countries or unified internal market areas such as the EU." (free translation, references omitted)

[11] Article 2(1) CartA.

[12] Article 2(1bis) CartA.

undertakings. Natural persons offering goods or services as self-employed persons (not as employees) are likewise subject to the Cartel Act as undertakings.

Associations are not mentioned in Article 4(1) CartA on agreements. There are no rules similar to the specific provisions for associations in Article 23(2) and (4) Regulation 1/2003. Decisions of associations are considered as agreements between the members of the associations to the extent that the latter are undertakings within the meaning of Article 2(1) and (1bis) CartA. An association is an undertaking if it itself carries out an economic activity consisting of buying or selling on the market.

Public undertakings with separate legal personality are clearly considered undertakings and are subject to the Cartel Act. This is the case with Swisscom or Swiss Post. The status of other public entities or organisations, such as public authorities or administrative units without legal personality, has been more controversial and Article 2(1bis) CartA was enacted to resolve this issue. By referring to the status of buyer or supplier of products in the market, regardless of their legal or organisational form, it has created a basis for including public authorities [13] or administrative units without legal personality [14] in the scope of application as undertakings.

The reference to the status of buyers and purchasers in relation to the activities of undertakings is similar to the EU concept of economic activity, but the Cartel Act has a broader reach than the concept of economic activity in the TFEU, which also aims to divide competences between the EU and the member states. [15] The Cartel Act applies without restriction to the activities of the cantons within the scope of their competences, unless competition is excluded or regulated by law. To distinguish whether an activity is an economic activity as opposed to a non-economic activity related to the task of public authorities, public services or regulated activities, Article 3(2) CartA on the relationship with regulation is therefore equally or even more important.

The concept of undertaking is distinct from the formal requirements for being the addressee of a decision, which are discussed in Sect. 7.2.1.

The reference to the 'exercise of market power' by undertakings refers to dominant undertakings or undertakings with relative market power, but it is not necessary at the stage of the material scope of application of Article 2 CartA to examine to what extent an undertaking has market power or whether it exercises

---

[13] COMCO, decision of 6 October 2008 *Tarifverträge Zusatzversicherung Kanton Luzern*, LPC 2008/4, p. 544, para 27, where the cantonal public hospitals controlled by a canton were considered as a group of companies and the canton as an undertaking.

[14] COMCO Secretariat, final report of 7 August 2007, *Beschaffung von Leichten Transport- und Schulungshelikoptern (LTSH) durch armasuisse*, LPC 2007/4, p. 517, paras 21 and 46. Armasuisse is a unit of the Federal Administration that purchases training vehicles and helicopters for the Swiss Military. Armasuisse was considered as an undertaking but did not enjoy a dominant position and the investigation was therefore closed. Cf. ECJ, judgment of 11 July 2006, *FENIN*, C-205/03 P, ECLI:EU:C:2006:453, paras 26 and 27, where it is the subsequent use of the goods purchased which determines whether there is an economic activity.

[15] See Hatzopoulos (2011).

such power.[16] A certain influence on the market is presumed as soon as the Secretariat of COMCO has decided to open an in-depth investigation on the basis of Article 27 CartA. The assessment of market power must be carried out when applying Article 4(2) CartA to such undertakings.

1.3.2 Territorial Jurisdiction and Extra-territorial Application of the Cartel Act

According to its Article 2(2), the Cartel Act "applies to practices that have an effect in Switzerland, even if they originate in another country." The provision therefore explicitly refers to the so-called 'effects doctrine'.

The question of whether effects in Switzerland should be qualified with a certain intensity was not clear until the Swiss Federal Supreme Court (FSC) had to rule on export bans in Switzerland by introducing a formal assessment for absolute territorial protection clauses covered by Article 5(4). CartA. It held that the examination of a specific intensity of such effects in Switzerland is neither necessary nor permissible under Article 2(2) CartA.[17] This means that the mere possibility that an agreement or unilateral conduct may have effects in Switzerland is enough to assert jurisdiction.[18]

The first difference with the EU courts' position on the 'effects doctrine' is that the latter require a sufficient probability[19] that the agreement will have "immediate, substantial and foreseeable effect in the European Union".[20] The Cartel Act contains

[16] FAC, judgment of 16 February 2021, B-2798/2018 *Naxoo/Supermédia,* para 5.1.2.

[17] FSC, judgment of 28 June 2016, 2C_180/2014, ATF/BGE 143 II 297 *Gaba*, para 3.7.

[18] Idem, para 3.4. See also Këllezi (2017), p. 185.

[19] GC, judgment of 12 June 2014, *Intel*, case T-286/09, ECLI:EU:T:2022:19, paras 256 et 257, referring to *Javico*, 28 April 1998, case C-306/96, paras 16 and 18; actual effects are not required, but a sufficient probability that the agreement at issue is capable of having a more than insignificant influence in the EU.

[20] GC, 12 June 2014, *Intel*, T-286/09, ECLI:EU:T:2022:19, para 243; CFI, 25 March 1999, *Gencor*, T-102/96, ECLI:EU:T:1999:65, para 90: "Application of the Regulation is justified under public international law when it is foreseeable that a proposed concentration will have an immediate and substantial effect in the Community". See also CJEU, 6 September 2017, *Intel*, C 413/14 P, ECLI: EU:C:2017:632, paras 44 ff, and the explanation of the attorney general in *Intel* (case C 413/14 P), paras 299 and 300: "That does not mean, however, that any effect, no matter how weak or indirect, could trigger the application of EU competition rules. In a globalised economy, conduct that takes place anywhere in the world, for example in China, will almost inevitably have some sort of effect in the European Union. Yet, the application of Articles 101 and 102 TFEU cannot be based on a link or effect that is too remote or purely hypothetical. I consider it to be particularly important that jurisdiction is asserted with restraint in relation to behaviour that has not, strictly speaking, taken place within the territory of the European Union. Indeed, to comply with a certain form of comity and, by the same token, to ensure that undertakings can operate in a foreseeable legal environment, it is only with a great deal of caution that the effect of the conduct complained of can be used as the

neither an ‘implementation doctrine’ nor a ‘qualified effects’ criterion, in contrast to EU competition law.

The second difference is that the FSC ruling leaves no discretion to the enforcement authorities or judges. Any examination of the specific intensity of the effects in Switzerland of an agreement or conduct that takes place outside Switzerland is unlawful.

Consequently, the effects of conduct outside Switzerland are only to be assessed under the substantive provisions of the Cartel Act, such as Articles 5 or 7 of the Cartel Act, and not under Article 2(2) CartA. For example, the parties may argue before the COMCO Secretariat or a judge that their agreement has only trivial or insignificant effects in Switzerland (‘cas bagatelle’) when assessing Article 5 CartA.

The impact of the FSC ruling on the extraterritoriality of Swiss Cartel Act on foreign companies is enormous. This is particularly true for distribution agreements that contain export prohibitions outside the allocated territory. Articles 2(2) and 5(4) of the Cartel Act applied to an agreement between an American company and its distributors in the USA prohibiting the latter from selling outside the USA (see examples at the end of Sect. 4.3.2.1). It would also apply for example to an agreement between an Australian manufacturer and its distributor in New Zealand containing export bans, even if Switzerland was not the target of the export ban or was not even mentioned in the distribution agreement.

In the case of merger control, the requirements of effects in Switzerland are fulfilled if the turnover thresholds of Article 9(1) CartA are met. [21] The COMCO applies the same reasoning as for the notification obligation of a dominant company under Article 9 (4) Cartel Act: there is a notification obligation even if the target company is active in a foreign geographic market and has no activities in Switzerland, and there is no need to investigate the effects on the Swiss market under Article 2 (2) Cartel Act. [22]

1.3.3 *Interface with Other Regulation*

The application of the Cartel Act is excluded if another law regulates the effects of an activity on competition. The Cartel Act specifically mentions intellectual property and legislation relating to public services or sectoral regulation. Both types of

yardstick for asserting jurisdiction. That is all the more important today. There are over 100 national or supranational authorities worldwide that claim jurisdiction over anticompetitive practices”.

[21] FSC, judgment of 24 April 2001, *Rhône-Poulenc SA et Merck & Co. Inc (Merial)*, ATF/BGE 127 III 219, para 3.b).

[22] See for instance COMCO, final report of 12 April 2007 *Swisscom AG/Fastweb S.p.A.*, LPC 2007/2, p. 312, para 20.

exclusion are interpreted narrowly in view of the constitutional foundations of the market economy, [23] leaving a wide scope for the application of the Cartel Act.

According to Article 3(1) CartA, "statutory provisions that do not allow for competition in a market for certain goods or services take precedence over the provisions of this Act. Such statutory provisions include in particular: a. provisions that establish an official market or price system; and b. provisions that grant special rights to specific undertakings to enable them to fulfil public duties." Exclusion from the scope of application is only possible if there is a clear legal basis that requires or permits conduct that restricts competition. The Cartel Act is still applicable to the extent that the reserved regulation leave room for competition. [24] Article 3(1) reserves only legislation that has an effect on competition, and only these can contradict the Cartel Act and therefore exclude its application. For example, the delimitation of a geographical area of production is an indispensable condition for the protection of PDOs and PGIs. The resulting exclusion of producers outside this area is inherent in the PDO and PGI system and therefore the Cartel Act does not apply to such geographical delimitation. [25]

Regulations that do not have the objective of affecting competition by regulating the market or prices do not exclude the application of the Cartel Act. In the latter case, both such regulations and the Cartel Act apply in parallel. However, they are taken into account as an external factor in the competition assessment under the Cartel Act. [26] For example, the regulation of advertising for medicinal products and the rules on the doctor-patient relationship do not aim to regulate competition on the market, but to regulate aspects of health policy. They were not considered to be reserved norms within the meaning of Article 3(1) of the Cartel Act, which would exclude its application. [27]

The strict interpretation of the exclusions was used by COMCO at a very early stage to open the electricity transmission network to competition at a time when the liberalisation of the market was rejected in a referendum. In its decision, COMCO took the view that the Article 3(2) exemption did not apply, which was upheld by the FSC. EEF was ordered to grant access to its transmission network. Twenty years later, COMCO opened the gas market by excluding Article 3(2) of CartA and granting access under Article 7(2)(a) of CartA (see Sect. 5.3.3.1).

According to its Article 3(2), the Cartel Act does not apply to "effects on competition that result exclusively from the legislation governing intellectual property. However, import restrictions based on intellectual property rights shall be assessed under this Act". The FAC held that the first sentence of Article 3(2) of

[23] FSC, judgment of 17 June 2003, 2A.520/2002, *EEF*, ATF/BGE 129 II 497, para 3.3.3; FSC, judgment of 2 November 2022, 2C_596/2019, *SIX DCC*, para 2.2.3; FSC, judgement of 9 May 2023, 2C_395/2021, *Naxoo*, para 7.1. See Article 94 (4) and 96 (1) Cst.

[24] FSC, judgment of 2 November 2022, 2C_596/2019, *SIX DCC*, para 2.2.3.

[25] FSC, judgment of 5 October 2015, 2C_1004/2014, *Interprofession du Gruyère*, para 6.2.

[26] FSC, judgment of 4 February 2021, 2C_149/2018, *Pfizer*, ATF/BGE 147 II 72, para 2.4.1.

[27] Idem, para 3.3.8.

the Cartel Act does not provide for an exception to the scope of the Cartel Act for intellectual property. This is because no clear distinction can be made between the legitimate exercise of intellectual property rights and unlawful restrictions of competition. Such a distinction can only be made in the context of the substantive assessment of a situation on the basis of Article 5 or 7 of the Cartel Act. [28]

The second sentence of Article 3(2) CartA was introduced in 2004 together with Article 5(4) CartA on vertical restraints and direct sanctions. In this respect, previous case law already provided for a narrow interpretation of the scope of intellectual property rights, opening the way for parallel imports and the application of the Cartel Act: in 1996, the FSC established the principle of international exhaustion of trademarks, [29] in 1998 it confirmed the international exhaustion of copyright protected products, [30] and in 1999, the FSC ruled on national exhaustion of patented goods, but held that the Cartel Act remained applicable. [31] Thus, existing case law makes it difficult, if not impossible, for the owner of the intellectual property to restrict parallel imports by using either intellectual property law protection or contractual protection, as the latter would fall within the scope of the Cartel Act.

At the federal level, there is a Price Supervisor, [32] who is primarily responsible for regulated industries and companies with market power. The Price Supervision Act focuses on abusive prices resulting from agreements or imposed by companies with market power. Abuse occurs, as defined in the PrSG, when "the price level is not the result of effective competition". [33] The Price Supervisor attends the meetings of the COMCO. Proceedings under the Cartel Act take precedence, unless the Competition Commission and the Price Supervisor jointly decide otherwise. [34]

1.4 Choice Between Public and Private Enforcement

The Cartel Act provides for two parallel avenues of action for injured parties, one before the Competition Commission and the other before the civil courts. Historically, competition claims have been dealt with primarily by the civil courts, and this route remains open, but public enforcement has gained prominence with the creation of the Competition Commission as an administrative body with the power to initiate *ex officio* investigations. As will be explained in Sect. 1.4 below, COMCO and its Secretariat have broad discretionary powers to initiate and conduct investigations, with no right of appeal for complainants. The question therefore arises as to what

[28] FAC, judgment of 18 December 2018, B-831/2011, *SIX DCC*, para 87.

[29] FSC, judgment of 23 October 1996, *Chanel*, ATF/BGE 122 III 469.

[30] FSC, judgment of 20 July 1998, *Nintendo*, ATF/BGE 124 III 321.

[31] FSC, judgment of 7 December 1999, *Kodak*, ATF 126 III 129.

[32] Price Supervision Act of 20 December 1985 (PSA).

[33] Article 12(1) PSA.

[34] Article 3(3) PSA.

criteria are used to determine whether an investigation will be pursued through the public enforcement route.

Administrative proceedings under the Cartel Act protect primarily the public interest in a functioning market, not private interests. [35] COMCO and its Secretariat have wide discretion in deciding whether or not to open a preliminary or full investigation, which is why there is no right of appeal against the rejection of a complaint under the Cartel Act (Sect. 1.5.5). The COMCO and its Secretariat can choose which cases to pursue. In cases where the COMCO and its Secretariat decide not to open an investigation or not to pursue an investigation, the aggrieved parties may bring an action against the other undertaking before the civil courts. It is then up to the complainant to decide whether or not to proceed before the civil courts. Private enforcement by civil courts thus serves to protect the private interest in having a remedy in competition matters:

> The Cartel Act provides for parallel civil law (Articles 12 ff of the Cartel Act) and administrative law (Articles 18 ff of the Cartel Act) proceedings for the enforcement of substantive claims. This co-existence, which is provided for by law, means that the public law route is primarily directed towards the public interest in a functioning competition; if, on the other hand, primarily private interests are at stake, the civil law route is to be taken, in which interim measures are also possible [. . .]. Even if third parties who are hindered in the exercise of competition do not have a right to an injunction in connection with a request for precautionary measures or the opening of an investigation [by the COMCO], they are not without legal protection, but can take action under civil law [. . .]. [36]

The distinction is important in the context of interim measures. Interim measures can be ordered by the COMCO or the civil courts. The choice between administrative and civil proceedings depends on whether the anti-competitive practice is likely to harm the public interest in protecting effective competition or primarily the private interests of an undertaking that is the victim of the practice. [37] In particular, for public enforcement by COMCO, the relevant question will be whether the alleged anticompetitive practice causes a disadvantage to the functioning of effective competition that cannot be easily remedied. [38] It is not sufficient that the affected undertaking suffers a disadvantage. The aggrieved undertaking cannot therefore freely choose between public and private enforcement, and the COMCO may refer the claimant undertaking to the civil judge if it considers that only private interests are involved. [39]

Civil courts cannot dismiss the claim as inadmissible on discretionary grounds, but only after examining the merits of the case. As the conditions for interim measures that can be issued by the COMCO are stricter, private enforcement may be more appropriate in clear-cut cases. Civil courts are also quicker to react.

---

[35] FSC, judgment of 12 December 2008, case 2C_292/2008, ATF/BGE 135 II 60, para 3.1.2.

[36] FSC, judgment of 13 July 2004, case 2A.74/2004, ATF/BGE 130 II 521, para 2.9.

[37] FSC, judgment of 19 December 2003, case 2A.417/2003, *Sellita Watch Co SA c. ETA SA Manufacture Horlogère Suisse*, ATF/BGE 130 II 149, para 2.4.

[38] Idem, para 3.4.1.

[39] Idem, para 4.

1.5 Public Enforcement of the Cartel Act

1.5.1 Enforcement by the Swiss Competition Authority

The Swiss competition authorities are the Competition Commission (COMCO) and its Secretariat. In a nutshell, the Competition Commission is the body that takes decisions, and the Secretariat is the body that conducts investigations. Both are independent of Parliament and act independently of the Federal Council (the government).

1.5.1.1 The Competition Commission

The Competition Commission consists of eleven to fifteen legal and economic experts appointed by the Federal Council. [40] The majority are independent experts; the rest are legal or economic experts representing the business and consumer organisations. They are appointed on a part-time basis and spend the majority of their time in other professional activities. There are currently twelve members.

The Competition Commission takes the final decision on an infringement, including the measures imposed on undertakings and fines, upon a draft decision submitted by the Secretariat. It also approves the amicable settlements concluded between the COMCO Secretariat and the parties under investigation (Sect. 7.3). The Secretariat conducts investigations independently form the COMCO, except for a few procedural decisions which are endorsed by the President.

In the domain of merger control, the COMCO has the power to open an in-depth investigation and to take all decisions until the final clearance or prohibition. Investigations are handled by the Secretariat on its behalf.

The COMCO has other advocacy powers to issue recommendations and opinions to other federal or cantonal authorities. [41] This is done regularly during the legislative process at federal level that would have an impact on the functioning of the market or economic regulation.

1.5.1.2 The Secretariat of the Competition Commission

The Secretariat of the COMCO is the investigative body of the COMCO. It conducts the investigations and prepares a draft decision, which at the same time constitutes a proposal for the measures and fines to be adopted by COMCO. It is also with the Secretariat that the undertakings discuss an amicable settlement and submit a leniency application or a merger notification. The Secretariat has considerable procedural powers and discretion in deciding whether or not to open a case, as

[40] Article 18 CartA.

[41] Article 46 CartA.

well as great influence over the final outcome of the proceedings. The executive management of the Secretariat, i.e. the Director and the four Vice-Directors, are appointed by the Federal Council [42] and therefore do not report to the COMCO and are not subordinate to it. COMCO only formally appoints the rest of the Secretariat's staff, based on an initial selection by the executive management of the Secretariat.

Article 23 (1) CartA provides that the Secretariat prepares the business of the COMCO, conducts any investigations and, together with a member of the COMCO presidium, issues any necessary procedural decisions. It submits proposals to the COMCO, in particular a draft decision, and implements its decisions. It deals directly with the parties involved, third parties and any authorities. The powers of investigation are presented in the following sections, but Article 23(2) CartA also provides one of the most useful tools for undertakings, namely the possibility of requesting the opinion of the COMCO Secretariat on a current restriction of competition or to assess the risks of a business project. This can be done on behalf of an undertaking or a group of undertakings or without disclosing the parties, but the request must specify as much as possible the facts of the case or the project, since the opinion is fact specific. The informal opinion does not bind COMCO, nor does it bind or preclude the Secretariat itself from opening an investigation. However, it has proved to be a very useful tool for businesses.

1.5.2 Exclusive Public Enforcement in Merger Control

COMCO is competent for *ex ante* merger control. Civil courts are not involved. The Secretariat is responsible for investigations, but all clearance or prohibition decisions are taken by COMCO. The rights of third parties are limited in that only the undertakings concerned have the status of party and therefore the rights of a party during the procedure. As a result, only the companies concerned can appeal against a COMCO decision to prohibit or accept a concentration of undertakings with conditions and obligations, and not competitors.

The procedure is described in more detail in Chap. 6.

1.5.3 Duty to Provide Information

Article 42 of the Cartel Act provides for a comprehensive obligation to provide information to the COMCO Secretariat during a preliminary or in-depth investigation of restrictive practices or during an ex-ante control of concentrations.

Parties to agreements, undertakings with market power, undertakings involved in concentrations and affected third parties must provide the COMCO Secretariat with

---

[42] Article 24 CartA.

all the information and documents necessary for its investigations. The term "affected third parties" is interpreted broadly to include all undertakings operating in the same relevant market or having a contractual or other relationship with the undertakings under investigation.

Undertakings refusing or failing to provide information are liable to a fine of up to CHF 100,000, while individuals intentionally failing to provide information are liable to a fine of up to CHF 20,000 (see Sect. 7.4 on other administrative and criminal sanctions).

Foreign companies that meet these conditions may also be asked to provide information. A simple request which cannot be served on a subsidiary or branch based in Switzerland, because there is none, is sent directly to the foreign address of the company, which may respond voluntarily. In a case where a company subject to an investigation could not provide information due to blocking statutes in its country, the COMCO sent a formal request to the foreign country of incorporation based on the 1970 Hague Convention on Evidence.[43] The formal request states that the COMCO considers itself to be a judicial authority in civil or commercial matters[44] and can therefore use this instrument to request a foreign country to serve its request for information on companies located there. The French Ministry of Justice considered the COMCO to be a judicial authority in civil or commercial matters and accepted the request.

1.5.4 *Preliminary Investigation of Restraints of Competition*

The Secretariat may conduct preliminary investigations *ex officio*, at the request of undertakings or following a complaint from third parties.[45] The Secretariat is authorised to initiate, conduct and close a preliminary investigation on its own initiative, without having to seek the approval of COMCO or a member of the COMCO Presidency. In other words, at this stage, the Secretariat has full discretion to open and conduct the investigation.

If the preliminary investigation confirms the suspicion of an unlawful agreement within the meaning of Article 5(3) and (4) CartA or an abuse of a dominant position, the COMCO Secretariat will generally open an investigation. If the suspicion concerns an unlawful practice not subject to a fine, i.e. an agreement not covered by Article 5(3) and (4) CartA or an abuse of relative market power, the COMCO Secretariat may close the preliminary investigation if the undertakings agree to adapt or put an end to their restrictive agreements or practices. In this case, the COMCO

---

[43] Article 3(a) HCCH 1970 Evidence Convention.

[44] COMCO, Commission rogatoire du 17 décembre 2013 au sens des articles 1 et 3 de la Convention sur l'obtention des preuves à l'étranger en matière civile ou commerciale (Convention de la Haye du 18 mars 1970) dans l'enquête LIBOR/TIBOR/EURIBOR, LPC 2014/2, p. 450.

[45] Article 26 (1) CartA.

Secretariat closes the preliminary investigation. Otherwise, the Secretariat opens an in-depth investigation. [46]

During the preliminary investigation, the Secretariat has the power, but not the obligation, to propose measures to the undertakings to eliminate or prevent restrictions of competition. [47] The undertakings can use this window of opportunity to change their behaviour to bring the investigation to an end. They can also decide to be proactive and change their behaviour voluntarily. The closure of the procedure does not bind the Secretariat and the COMCO in the sense that the Secretariat can reopen a procedure, in particular if the market situation changes, or other facts are brought to its attention.

During the preliminary investigation stage, the undertakings under investigation do not have the right of access to the file, [48] but the Secretariat may decide to disclose certain pieces of evidence to the parties under investigation if it considers it useful for the conduct of the investigation.

The Secretariat has wide discretion when it comes to initiating and conducting preliminary inquiries. Complainants do not have the right to initiate a preliminary investigation and therefore cannot appeal against the rejection of their complaint or the COMCO Secretariat's failure to act.

1.5.5 In-depth Investigation of Restraints of Competition

During the preliminary investigation, a complainant, leniency applicant or whistleblower may provide evidence that there are indications of a restriction of competition in the form of an agreement or abuse of a dominant position or relative market power.

If there are indications of an unlawful restraint of competition, the Secretariat, in consultation with a member of the COMCO Presidency, opens an in-depth investigation. [49] In any event, the Secretariat must open an in-depth investigation if requested to do so by the COMCO or the Department of Economic Affairs of the Federal Council. [50]

Articles 6 and 48 APA determine whether an undertaking or person has the status of a party to the proceedings, with rights of access to the file and the right to be heard. Undertakings that are the subject of an investigation, such as parties to an agreement,

---

[46] COMCO Secretariat, Note of 19 February 2020: the conduct of the preliminary investigation explained in simple terms (Note on preliminary investigations), paras 13ff.

[47] Article 26 (2) CartA.

[48] Article 26 (3) CartA.

[49] Article 27 (1) CartA.

[50] Article 27 (2) CartA. The Federal Department of Economic Affairs, Education and Research (EAER) is a department of the Federal Government and is headed by one of the seven members of the Federal Council.

undertakings with a dominant or relative market position, automatically have the status of party to the proceedings because their rights or obligations are likely to be affected by the COMCO decision (Article 6 APA).

The circle of persons who may participate in the procedure is wider, as Article 43 CartA provides that third parties may participate in the investigation. Among these third parties, some that meet the conditions of Articles 6 and 48 APA have the status of a party, while others that do not meet these conditions do not have that status.

Third parties must be specifically affected by the decision of the COMCO and have a legitimate interest in the outcome of the investigation in order to be granted party status. These parties have the same rights as the undertakings under investigation, including access to the file and the right to comment on the Secretariat's draft decision.

On the other hand, third parties such as trade associations and consumer protection organisations mentioned in Article 43 CartA may participate in the investigation but do not have party status. The same could apply to complainants or undertakings that are prevented from entering the market or from competing as a result of restrictions of competition. This means that they do not have access to the file, but can comment on the draft decision prepared by the COMCO Secretariat or otherwise present their views to the COMCO in writing or, if invited, orally.

The Secretariat and the COMCO have wide discretion when it comes to initiating and conducting in-depth inquiries. Complainants do not have the right to initiate an investigation and therefore cannot appeal against the rejection of their complaint or the COMCO Secretariat's failure to open an in-depth investigation. A decision not to open an investigation or to reject a complaint is not considered to be a formal decision that is subject to appeal, and there is no obligation to give an explanation as to why there are no grounds for action. This differs significantly from the complainant's status under EU law. [51]

Unlike preliminary investigations, the Secretariat cannot close an in-depth investigation on its own; only COMCO can terminate an in-depth investigation by adopting a decision to close the investigation or to prohibit the infringement. In the decision to close the investigation, COMCO states in its reasoning that the agreement or unilateral practice is lawful either because it does not restrict competition or because it is justified on economic or business grounds. In the decision finding an unlawful restriction of competition, COMCO orders in the operative part the prohibition of the restriction of competition, the measures necessary to put an end to the restriction or approval of an amicable settlement (see Sect. 7.3), and the fines pursuant to Article 49a Cartel Act. The closure of an in-depth investigation is therefore much more demanding than the closure of a preliminary investigation, where the Secretariat has full discretion.

Formally, COMCO is given supervisory powers and determines the order of priority in which investigations are dealt with. [52] In reality, the Secretariat has a wide

---

[51] Cf. Articles 5–9 of Regulation 773/2004.

[52] Article 27 (3) CartA.

margin of discretion in the order in which in-depth investigations are conducted, as this is closely linked to the use of its resources.

1.5.6 Inspections, Searches and Seizure of Documents

The Secretariat may ask a member of the COMCO Presidency to order searches and the seizure of evidence [53] in a search warrant. At the same time, a decision is taken to open an in-depth investigation, if this has not already been done. Searches and seizures are carried out by the Secretariat. Searches and seizures of documents are coercive measures and as such are carried out in accordance with Articles 45–50 ACL, [54] which apply by analogy. Appeals against searches and seizure of documents or the lifting of the escrow on legally privileged documents are filed with the Federal Criminal Court (FCC).

The Secretariat has produced an explanatory note which contains a wealth of information on searches. [55] We will only mention some of the relevant information here.

A copy of the warrant is given to the company representative present when the search begins. [56] The search may begin before the lawyers arrive, but the documents to be seized will be put aside until their arrival, if any, so that they can examine at the documents and ask for them to be sealed. [57]

All types of premises can be searched, both the business premises of a company under investigation or a third party, and the private homes of agents and employees of the company. Within the premises, the search team can search any part of the premises, such as desks, safes and lockers, gardens, car parks and vehicles. Part of the premises can be sealed and made inaccessible for a certain period of time, and anyone who breaks, removes or breaks an official seal risks imprisonment for up to 3 years or a fine. [58]

All types of documents or other records, such as photographs and videos on paper or other media, can be searched. Today, searches focus mainly on electronic data and any data that can be accessed from within the premises can be searched and seized.

The attorney-client privilege covers and protects all documents, correspondence, letters or e-mails, own records, legal assessments prior to litigation, notes of meetings, strategy documents and drafts of contracts or settlements communicated to or

[53] Article 42 CartA

[54] Federal Act on Administrative Criminal Law of 22 March 1974 (ACL; RS 313.0).

[55] COMCO Secretariat, Explanatory note of 6 January 2016 on Selected Instruments of Investigation (Explanatory note on instruments of investigation). The note can be found in English at https://www.weko.admin.ch/weko/en/home/rechtliches_dokumentation/communications.html.

[56] Explanatory note on instruments of investigation, para 5.

[57] Explanatory note on instruments of investigation, paras 8 and 9.

[58] Article 290 CP.

received by lawyers registered in a Swiss canton and lawyers authorised to practise law in an EU or EFTA member state. [59] Legal privilege does not apply to communications with lawyers based in other countries or with corporate or in-house counsel. [60] If the representatives of the company being searched object to the seizure of such documents, they must appeal in writing or orally against the search and seizure by the end of the search, and the document will be sealed and kept separate. [61] It is up to the COMCO Secretariat to file an unsealing request with the Appeals Chamber of the Federal Criminal Court. Before doing so, the Secretariat asks the company whether it wishes to continue with the appeal or whether it wishes to cooperate by carrying out a kind of informal unsealing of documents. If the company does not agree to an informal sealing, the Appeals Chamber of the Federal Criminal Court will first examine the legality of the search and, if the search is confirmed, will separate privileged documents that will not be disclosed to the Secretariat from other documents that can be unsealed and handed over to the Secretariat. [62]

The employees or representatives of the company being searched have a duty to submit to the search, i.e. to passively endure the search and not to prevent or obstruct it, including the duty to grant access to the rooms, containers and computer systems being searched by opening doors and safes and disclosing passwords. [63] Failure to comply with this duty will be considered an aggravating circumstance and will result in higher fines. Otherwise, companies have no duty to cooperate actively, unless they decide to apply for leniency (see Sect. 7.2.4), [64] in which case they must cooperate fully and actively, for example by indicating where the evidence is located in the filing system, computer system or premises. Active cooperation will be taken into account as a mitigating circumstance even if no leniency application is filed.

The COMCO Secretariat does not conduct searches on behalf of other competition authorities, except in the air transport sector in support of or on behalf of the European Commission pursuant to Article 11(1) of the EU-Swiss Air Transport Agreement [65] and the corresponding Article 42a of the Cartel Act. The CH-EU Cooperation Agreement and the CH-DE Agreement on the application of competition laws [66] have no comparable provision. However, the EU Commission and COMCO can exchange information on their ongoing investigations and carry out

[59] EFTA member states include Iceland, Liechtenstein, Norway and Switzerland.

[60] Explanatory note on instruments of investigation, para 22.

[61] Explanatory note on instruments of investigation, para 26.

[62] Explanatory note on instruments of investigation, paras 34 and 35. See for a recent case, FSC, judgement of 1 December 2021, causes 2C_295/2021 et 2C_307/2021.

[63] Explanatory note on instruments of investigation, paras 18–20.

[64] The intention to apply for leniency can also be made during a search.

[65] Agreement between the European Community and the Swiss Confederation on Air Transport, OJ L 114 30.4.2002, p. 73; RS 0.748.127.192.68.

[66] Agreement between the European Union and the Swiss Confederation concerning cooperation on the application of their competition laws, OJ L 347, 3.12.2014, p. 3; RS 0.251.268.1.

separate but simultaneous searches, which has happened twice recently (see Sect. 1.5.12 below).[67]

During the search, the Secretariat team may interview representatives of the parties, such as the board of directors or senior management, and employees who are considered as third parties. The main rules for interviewing are set out in the next section.

1.5.7 Questioning of Witnesses and Parties

Pursuant to Article 42(1) CartA, the Secretariat and the COMCO may hear third parties as witnesses and question the parties.[68] The difference between a witness and a party is important, as the former has a duty to testify and tell the truth, while parties have the right to remain silent.[69] The current legal or de facto organs of the company, such as directors or members of management, are considered parties and may therefore refuse to answer general or specific questions. Former directors and management, and current employees of the company are considered third parties and must respond as witnesses.

The FSC recently confirmed that a former CEO of a company is a third party and can therefore be summoned and heard as a witness without restriction.[70] The FSC disagreed with the FAC, which had limited the hearing of the former CEO to factual information that would not have a direct impact on the company under investigation. The FSC stated that the *nemo tenetur* principle is not intended to protect legal persons from incriminating statements, but only to ensure an effective defence.

---

[67] Press release of 8 March 2023, "COMCO investigates possible collusions in the fragrance market", announcing that "dawn raids were conducted at various locations. These were carried out in consultation with other competition authorities, namely the European Commission, the US Department of Justice Antitrust Division and the UK Competition and Markets Authority." Available at https://www.weko.admin.ch/weko/en/home/medien/press-releases/nsb-news.msg-id-93502.html. Accessed 22 May 2023. Press release of 15 September 2022, "Investigation on use of patents". Available at https://www.weko.admin.ch/weko/en/home/medien/press-releases/nsb-news.msg-id-90320.html. Accessed 22 May 2023. See also Reuters, "Swiss competition watchdog probes Novartis over patent use", 15 September 2022. Available at https://www.reuters.com/business/healthcare-pharmaceuticals/swiss-competition-commission-investigating-pharmaceutical-firm-over-patent-use-2022-09-15/. Accessed 22 May 2023.

[68] Article 64 FCP applies by analogy.

[69] Explanatory note on instruments of investigation, paras 55–71.

[70] FSC, judgment of 8 March 2021, cause 2C_383/2020, ATF/BGE 147 II 144.

1.5.8 Draft Decision of the Secretariat

The COMCO Secretariat prepares a draft decision at the end of its investigation. The draft decision is much more comprehensive than the statement of objections in the EU, [71] as it contains all the relevant facts, the legal assessment together with the operative part of the decision, and this constitutes a "request from the Secretariat" presented to the COMCO within the meaning of Article 30(1) CartA.

The draft decision will be sent to the parties to the investigation, who may submit written observations, together with a time limit within which they may request investigative measures and a hearing by the COMCO. [72] The parties' observations will be communicated to the other parties for their observations, without prejudice to business secrets.

The Secretariat will consider the comments and the investigative measures requested by the parties and, if necessary, modify its draft decision in the light of those observations and the results of the additional investigative measures, and resubmit the modified draft decision to the parties for their comments. [73]

If the Secretariat considers that the draft decision does not need to be modified, it will submit the draft decision, together with the parties' observations, to the COMCO for decision. From that moment on, the COMCO is competent to decide on the parties' requests and other investigative measures. [74]

The investigation is considered concluded when the case is submitted to the COMCO, and therefore the COMCO will generally not carry out any further investigative measures. However, the COMCO has the power, *ex officio* or at the request of the parties, to carry out other investigative measures if it considers them necessary. It will generally delegate such measures to the Secretariat. If the COMCO considers that substantial investigative measures are necessary, it may also refer the file back to the Secretariat with a request to carry out further investigations. [75] However, this has rarely been the case.

---

[71] Cf. Articles 27(1) and 25(3)(d) Regulation 1/2003 and 1(2) Regulation 773/2004. Formally, the Cartel Act does not provide for a document similar to the preliminary assessment referred to in Articles 9(1) Regulation 1/2003 and 2(1) Regulation 773/2004.

[72] COMCO, Note of 21 October 2019: Decision-making process of the Competition Commission in cartel investigations within the meaning of Art. 27 ff Cartel Act (Note on decision-making process), para 10.

[73] Note on decision-making process, para 12.

[74] Note on decision-making process, para 15.

[75] Note on decision-making process, para 17.

1.5.9 Hearings

The rules and conduct before and during the hearings are set out in a COMCO notice. [76] The undertakings under investigation and other third parties may be heard by the COMCO if they so require. [77] Other participants without party status may be invited to attend the hearings but have no right to be heard or to attend them. [78]

The representatives of the undertakings or their lawyers may present oral arguments. At the end, COMCO members may ask questions related to their oral arguments, but generally there will be no questioning about specific facts or evidence. Prior to 2019, hearings before the COMCO were a mixture of oral arguments and questioning of the parties on the main facts, followed in certain cases by an exchange between the parties and the COMCO. This is no longer the case, and the COMCO's involvement in the hearing is now generally limited to seeking clarification about the parties' oral arguments.

1.5.10 Interim Measures

COMCO may take interim measures on its own initiative or at the request of an undertaking, even if the Cartel Act does not expressly provide for such measures. Competition law applies the conditions for ordering interim measures in administrative proceedings, i.e. a disadvantage to the functioning of the effective competition that cannot be easily remedied, a particular urgency that goes beyond the general endeavour to implement legal requirements as quickly as possible, and the proportionality of the order. [79] Interim measures are based on a mere summary examination of the factual and legal situation. The forecast of the outcome in the main proceedings may be considered if it is clear. If factual or legal ambiguities remain, the case-law requires the authorities to exercise restraint, because in this case the necessary basis for the decision must first be obtained in the main proceedings. If the outcome of the proceedings appears doubtful, there are higher requirements for accepting the need to eliminate the disadvantage for the duration of the proceedings, the urgency and the proportionality of the order. [80]

The courts have recently upheld several of COMCO's decisions on interim measures on abuse of dominance cases. The two most recent decisions, which we present below, show that COMCO has a broad discretion to order interim measures

[76] Note on decision-making process, Section C.4.

[77] Article 30(2) CartA.

[78] Note on decision-making process, paras 23–27.

[79] FSC, judgment of 19 December 2003, 2A.417/2003, *Sellita Watch Co SA c. ETA SA Manufacture Horlogère Suisse*, ATF/BGE 130 II 149, para 2.3.

[80] FSC, judgment of 13 March 2001, 2A.530/2000, *Swisscom c. TDC Switzerland*, ATF/BGE 127 II 132, paras 3 and 4

even in what may appear to be very atypical cases of abuse of dominance. By means of interim measures, COMCO prevented Swisscom from expanding its FTTH network based on a single-fibre model, as this new technology would no longer allow it to grant so-called Layer 1 access to third parties.[81] Until a decision is made on the main issue, Swisscom must refrain from expanding its new fibre-optic network, which was considerably cheaper than the existent four-fibre model. Layer 1 access was provided using a more expensive technology based on the four-fibre model. In the new single-fibre model, Swisscom would not be able to rent to third parties a single continuous physical line between the central office and the subscriber's premises. Instead, Swisscom would have offered third parties a so-called Layer 3 offer, in which it takes over the transmission of information between the connection centre and the local loop as a service. The FSC first confirmed that the absence of an obligation to grant access to the optical fibre network under the Telecommunications Act[82] does not exclude the application of the Cartel Act. Second, the FSC confirmed the conditions for interim measures established by the FAC and COMCO. There was a serious risk that effective competition would be impaired because, in the event of a change in the network architecture, not only the complaining competitor but also all other telecommunications companies would be prevented from providing independent telecommunications services to end customers.[83] The obligation to ensure independent physical Layer 1 access for competitors when building a new optical fibre network, which is equivalent to an obligation to maintain the current optical fibre technology in order to ensure access to the optical fibre network for competitors, was not considered disproportionate in terms of costs for Swisscom. Furthermore, the regional, social or other socio-political considerations, which in this case amounted to a delay in the extension of fibre optic Internet access to remote and underserved areas, were not considered relevant, as consumer interests are taken into account in the assessment of effective competition.[84] The FSC upheld the FAC's conclusion that failing to provide Layer 1 access could also prove to be a potential infringement of the Cartel Act. This case shows that the FAC and the FSC have de facto lowered the threshold for intervention by means of interim measures.

In 2020,[85] the FAC refused to withdraw the suspensive effect of a COMCO' decision on provisional measures of the previous year, which ordered the Swatch Group to continue to supply only SMEs with a maximum number of mechanical movements, which implied that it would not supply the major watch brands, leaving

[81] FSC, judgment of 29 November 2022, 2C_876/2021, *Netzbaustrategie – Anordnung vorsorglicher Massnahmen.*

[82] See in particular Article 11 of the TCA, which has unbundled the last mile of the copper local loop.

[83] FSC, judgment of 29 November 2022, 2C_876/2021, *Netzbaustrategie – Anordnung vorsorglicher Massnahmen*, para 7.5.2.

[84] Idem, para 8.3.

[85] FAC judgment of 13 May 2020, B-409/2020, *Swatch Group Lieferstopp/Ablauf Lieferverpflichtung (withdrawal of suspensive effect)*, LPC 2021/1, p. 401.

the latter dissatisfied with a decision that reduced their supply options to Swatch's competitors. COMCO's decision followed the expiry of an amicable agreement concluded in 2013 [86] between COMCO and the Swatch Group governing the latter's gradual withdrawal from the supply of movements to the watchmaking industry: Swatch's duty to deal would have lapsed at the end of 2019. Six months later, [87] COMCO closed the investigation against the Swatch Group because the increase in production capacity in the market was sufficient to meet demand, mainly due to the increase in capacity of Swatch's main competitor. The initial production capacity forecasts of the COMCO 2013 decision were not achieved due to the declining demand for watches, which was not due to Swatch's market dominance or the lack of investment by other companies. Although the impact of the interim measures was limited, this decision raised the question of the highly regulatory nature of interim measures and whether this is an appropriate tool in competition law.

1.5.11 Prohibition Order, Sanctions and Measures

The COMCO decides on whether to close the in-depth investigation or to declare the existence of a restriction of competition, such as an unlawful agreement or an abuse of a dominant position or relative market power. In the latter case, it decides on the appropriate measures and, if applicable, on sanctions and on the approval of the amicable settlement. [88] Only the measures and sanctions are included in the operative part. [89] The unlawful restrictions of competition are set out in the statement of reasons. An order to pay the costs is also included in the operative part of the decision.

The measures and sanctions can only be taken against the undertakings that are party to an agreement or abusive conduct, and not against undertakings that have merely supported or helped those undertakings. The wholesalers and the operator of a software database that allowed the transmission of price recommendations from pharmaceutical companies to pharmacies could not be ordered to refrain from assisting pharmaceutical companies and pharmacies in the future. [90]

---

[86] COMCO decision of 21 October 2013, *Swatch Group Lieferstopp*, LPC 2014/1, p. 215.

[87] COMCO decision of 13 July 2020, *Swatch Group Lieferstopp/Ablauf Lieferverpflichtung*, LPC 2021/1, p. 306.

[88] Article 30 CartA.

[89] FSC, judgment of 11 April 2011, 2C_343/2010 and 2C_344/2010 ATF/BGE 137 II 199, para 6.2.

[90] FSC, judgment of 8 December 2021, 2C_148/2018, ATF/BGE 148 II 182. The order of the operative part of the judgment was the following: "The wholesalers Galexis, Unione Farmaceutica Distribuzione, Voigt and Amedis-UE, as well as e-mediat, are no longer allowed to carry out any supporting activities (e.g. forwarding, processing, publication of price recommendations, etc.) in relation to these public price recommendations." (free translation)

1.5.12 Investigative Measures in International Agreements

Switzerland has signed two cooperation agreements on competition law. The EU-Swiss Agreement on Competition entered into force on 1 December 2014. It was accompanied by an exchange of notes concerning the notification of acts of public authority relating to competition policy. [91] The second agreement with Germany was signed on 1 November 2022 and entered into force on 1 September 2023. [92] The two agreements are similar, and the most relevant information for practitioners is summarised below:

- The competition authorities may exchange information for the purpose of coordinating investigations and the timing of inspections, and they may freely exchange non-confidential information, including outside the scope of an investigation.
- COMCO may exchange confidential information without the consent of an undertaking only in the context of formal investigations into the same facts. Article 42b CartA [93] sets out the conditions for the transmission of confidential information.
- The competition authorities may serve the acts of public authority on behalf of the other authority, except that service within an EU Member State is subject to its consent. An act of public authority is any decision involving the imposition of

[91] Echange de notes du 17 mai 2013 entre le Conseil fédéral suisse et la Commission européenne concernant la notification d'actes de puissance publique relevant de la politique de la concurrence, RS 0.251.268.11.

[92] Abkommen zwischen dem Departement für Wirtschaft, Bildung und Forschung der Schweizerischen Eidgenossenschaft und dem Bundesministerium für Wirtschaft und Klimaschutz der Bundesrepublik Deutschland über Zusammenarbeit und Koordinierung der Wettbewerbsbehörden vom 1. November 2022, BBl 2023 313. See also Botschaft zur Genehmigung des Abkommens zwischen dem Departement für Wirtschaft, Bildung und Forschung der Schweizerischen Eidgenossenschaft und dem Bundesministerium für Wirtschaft und Klimaschutz der Bundesrepublik Deutschland über Zusammenarbeit und Koordinierung der Wettbewerbsbehörden vom 11. January 2023, BBl 2023 311.

[93] Art. 42b CartA on disclosure of data to foreign competition authorities reads as follows: "1) Data may only be disclosed to a foreign competition authority based on an act, an international agreement or with the consent of the undertaking concerned. 2) Without the consent of the undertaking concerned, the competition authorities may disclose confidential data, in particular business secrets, to a foreign competition authority on the basis of an international agreement only if: a. the behaviour under investigation in the recipient state is also unlawful under Swiss law; b. both competition authorities are investigating the same or related behaviour or transactions; c. foreign competition authority uses the data only for the purpose of applying provisions of competition law or as evidence in relation to the subject matter of the investigation for which the competition authority requested the information; d. the data is not used in criminal or civil proceedings; e. the foreign procedural law safeguards party rights and official secrecy; and f. the confidential data is not disclosed to the foreign competition authority in the context of an amicable settlement (Art. 29) or when assisting in the discovery and elimination of the restraint of competition (Art. 49a para. 2). 3) The competition authorities shall notify the undertaking concerned and invite it to state its views before transmitting the data to the foreign competition authority."

sanctions, the obligation to comply with a given practice or the prohibition of a given practice or requiring the addressees to transmit certain information. A letter initiating an investigation or a non-binding request for information do not constitute acts of public authority.
- Leniency and immunity applications cannot be communicated without the consent of the applicant (see Sect. 7.2.4).
- Privileged information cannot be communicated.
- Neither competition authority can carry out searches or inspections on behalf of the other. Therefore, COMCO does not carry out searches on behalf of the EU Commission or the Bundeskartellamt on the basis of these two agreements.

The CH-EU Air Transport agreement too provides for an extended exchange of information between the EU Commission and the COMCO. Article 42a CartA contains specific provisions in this respect. [94] As explained in Sect. 1.5.6 above, the EU-Swiss Air Transport Agreement also allows COMCO to carry out searches on behalf of the EU Commission.

In view of the exchange of notes between the EU and Switzerland and the special provisions of the CH-DE Agreement on Competition, there is no need for a special authorisation under Article 271 CP for the Federal Council to notify acts of public authorities in Switzerland and for the companies to provide information in response to requests from the EU Commission and the German Federal Cartel Office.

In the case of requests for information or for investigation measures from competition authorities in other countries, companies based in Switzerland must apply to the EAER for the authorisation required under Article 271 of the Swiss Criminal Code [95] before providing information to a foreign competition authority.

[94] Art. 42a CartA on investigations in proceedings under the Swiss/EC Air Transport Agreement states the following: "1) The Competition Commission is the Swiss authority responsible for co-operation with the institutions of the European Community under Article 11 of the Agreement between the European Community and the Swiss Confederation of 21 June 1999 on Air Transport. 2) If an undertaking opposes a review in proceedings under Article 11 of the Agreement, investigative measures pursuant to Article 42 may be undertaken at the request of the European Commission. Article 44 applies."

[95] Art. 271 CrimC on unlawful activities on behalf of a foreign state reads as follows: "1. Any person who carries out activities on behalf of a foreign state on Swiss territory without lawful authority, where such activities are the responsibility of a public authority or public official, any person who carries out such activities for a foreign party or organisation, any person who facilitates such activities, shall be liable to a custodial sentence not exceeding three years or to a monetary penalty, or in serious cases to a custodial sentence of not less than one year. 2. Any person who abducts another by using violence, false pretences or threats and takes him abroad in order to hand him over to a foreign authority, party or other organisation or to expose him to a danger to life or limb shall be liable to a custodial sentence of not less than one year. 3. Any person who makes preparations for such an abduction shall be liable to a custodial sentence or to a monetary penalty."

However, non-binding requests for information are not acts of public authority and therefore do not require prior authorisation. [96]

1.6 Private Enforcement by Civil Courts

The Cartel Act contains a chapter on civil enforcement concerning the claims that can be brought before the courts. There are no special procedural rules or presumptions on damages similar to those introduced in the EU by Directive 2014/104. The general conditions for awarding damages, which are generally applicable to claims for damages under the Code of Obligations, are briefly described below. Private enforcement is only moderately used by companies due to the uncertainty of the outcome and the high costs involved. Public enforcement is an alternative for complainants, although civil proceedings are faster. In some sectors, such as the automotive sector, companies use private enforcement for claims related to the termination of distribution contracts, [97] as COMCO has indicated that it will not intervene in such cases. In other areas, such as abuse of relative market power, it is expected that COMCO will refer complainants to civil courts after deciding some benchmark cases.

1.6.1 Competent Courts and Procedure

Civil procedure is unified at federal level by the Civil Procedure Code (hereafter CPC). The organisation of the courts is a cantonal matter, but the CPC requires that cartel law disputes be heard by a single cantonal instance, [98] which means that there is only one level of appeal to the FSC.

Violations of the Cartel Act are unlawful acts that give rise to tort actions. The CPC provides for alternative jurisdictions and actions may be brought in the court of the domicile or seat of the injured party or the defendant, or in the court of the place where the act occurred or had its effect. [99]

---

[96] See EAER, Note on competition questionnaires sent by the European Commission to Swiss companies, available at https://www.weko.admin.ch/weko/en/home/rechtliches_dokumentation/internationale_abkommen.html. Accessed 29 May 2023.

[97] See for instance FSC, judgment of 18 January 2022, 4A_229/2021, ATF 148 III 77. The case concerned an action by a spare parts wholesaler against a car manufacturer which refused to supply spare parts directly to the wholesaler. The FSC sided with the manufacturer and held that there was no illegal agreement within the meaning of Articles 4 and 5 of the Cartel Act. The wholesaler's claim under Articles 12 and 13 of the Cartel Act was dismissed.

[98] Article 5(1)(b) CPC.

[99] Article 36 CPC.

The plaintiff must present all evidence and prayers for relief, and the court cannot award a party more or different relief than the party requested or less than the opposing party conceded. The rules of procedure are laid down in the CPC.

1.6.2 Actions for Restrictions of Competition

The Cartel Act lists the types of claims that may be brought in the event of a restriction of competition, i.e. an unlawful agreement within the meaning of Article 5 CartA or an abuse of a dominant position or relative market power within the meaning of Article 7 CartA.

A person who is prevented from entering or competing in a market as a result of an unlawful restraint of competition is entitled to seek the removal or cessation of the restraint, damages and satisfaction in accordance with the Code of Obligations, and the surrender of unlawfully obtained profits in accordance with the provisions on agency without authority. [100] The courts may declare all or part of a contract null and void or order the person responsible for the restraint of competition to conclude a contract with the person so restrained on market or industry standard terms and conditions. [101]

Any undertaking that is hindered in its activities by an unlawful agreement or an abusive practice has the right to bring an action. Consumers and employees do not appear to have standing, nor do trade associations if they do not act as undertakings in the market. The draft law of 23 May 2023 amending Article 12 of the Cartel Act [102] intends to correct this situation by proposing to grant standing to all persons "whose economic interests are threatened or affected by an unlawful restriction of competition", which would include consumers, local authorities or trade associations, even if they do not act as undertakings in the market.

A plaintiff can therefore bring an action and ask the court to order the cessation of the restraint of competition and to order certain conduct for the future. An action for a declaratory judgment is also possible, but it is subsidiary in the sense that it is not open where an action for performance or for modification of a legal relationship is possible. [103] The FSC has confirmed the possibility of negative declaratory relief in international matters. In the same judgment, it left the question open for domestic situations. [104]

---

[100] Article 12 CartA.

[101] Article 13 CartA.

[102] See Federal Council, Press release of 24 May 2023, "Loi sur les cartels: le Conseil fédéral adopte le message concernant la révision partielle", available at https://www.admin.ch/gov/fr/accueil/documentation/communiques/communiques-conseil-federal.msg-id-95384.html. Accessed 25 May 2023.

[103] Article 88 CPC.

[104] FSC, judgement of 14 March 2018, 4A_417/2017, *Swatch*.

The Cartel Act expressly provides for actions for damages, compensation for non-material damage and restitution of unjustly obtained profits in accordance with the provisions on agency without authority. [105] Article 12 (1) (b) CartA refers to Articles 41 ff CO, which is a formal reference to other legal norms. This means that the plaintiff in an action for damages must prove that the conditions on the existence of damage, natural and adequate causality and fault are met. Article 12 (2) (b) CartA on moral (non-material) damages refers to Article 49 CO, and Article 12 (2) (c) CartA on the disgorgement of unlawful gains refers to Article 423 CO.

The four conditions of liability in tort [106] are the existence of damage, an unlawful conduct, a causal link between the damage and the wrongful act, and fault:

– *Damage*. The damage recognised by the law is the involuntary reduction of net assets, which is the difference between the current amount of the injured party's assets and the amount they would have been if the harmful event had not occurred. [107] The loss may take the form of a decrease in assets, an increase in liabilities, a non-increase in assets, or a non-decrease in liabilities. [108] This definition excludes the payment to the injured party of an amount in excess of the loss suffered. [109] Under Swiss law, losses resulting from the loss of a chance or of an opportunity are not legally recognised and are therefore not compensated. [110] Finally, purely economic losses are compensated only if the harmful conduct violates a norm intended to protect the injured party. [111] Although the main objective of the Cartel Act is the protection of competition, it also aims at the protection of the individual freedom of competitors, which is also reflected in Articles 12 ff Cartel Act, and therefore purely economic damages should in principle be compensated.

  It is up to the plaintiff to prove both the existence of the damage and its amount. [112] According to the FSC, the facts must be stated with sufficient precision to enable the other party to substantiate its claim or to prove the contrary. [113] If the opposing party disputes the plaintiff's factual allegations, the plaintiff may be required to set out the relevant facts in detail and not only in their essential features.

[105] Article 12 CartA.

[106] Article 41 CO.

[107] FSC, judgment of 1 October 2001, 4C.299/2000 ATF/BGE 128 III 22, para 2(aa); FSC, judgement of 19 January 2001, ATF/BGE 127 III 73, para 4a; FSC, judgment of 18 July 2000, ATF/BGE 126 III 388, para 11a.

[108] FSC, judgement of 26 September 1996, ATF/BGE 122 IV 279 para 2a; FSC, judgment of 3 February 1995, ATF/BGE 121 IV 104, para 2c).

[109] FSC, judgement of 1 March 2005, ATF/BGE 131 III 360, para 6.1.

[110] FSC, judgement of 13 June 2007, 4A_61/2007 ATF/BGE 133 III 462, para 4.4.3.

[111] FSC, judgement of 18 April 2007, 4C.386/2006, ATF/BGE 133 III 323, para 5.1.

[112] Article 42 (1) CO.

[113] FSC, judgment of 30 May 2001, ATF/BGE 127 III 365, para 2b.

The judge may, at his discretion, estimate the value of the damage if it is difficult or impossible to determine. [114] The court's discretion is a matter of factual assessment that cannot be reviewed by the SFC. [115] In order to benefit from the discretionary determination of damages by the court, [116] the claimant must provide the court with all the elements necessary to establish the existence of damages and their fair assessment. [117] Consequently, Article 42 (2) CO does not exempt the plaintiff from proving all the elements on which his claim for damages is based.

- *Causation.* Natural causation is a question of fact: the injured party must prove that the alleged damage would not have occurred in the absence of the unlawful agreement or the abuse of a dominant position or relative market power (the unlawful act). In other words, the unlawful agreement or abuse must be a necessary condition for the damage to occur. In L'Etivaz, the SFC was very strict and annulled the damages awarded by the cantonal court for lack of a natural causal link between the unlawful act and the alleged damage. [118] With regard to adequate causation, which is a question of law, the plaintiff must prove that the unlawful agreement or abusive conduct is likely, in the ordinary course of events and life experience, to cause the alleged damage.

  Particular attention should be paid to the existence of facts that could interrupt the causal link and prevent an adequate causal link from being established, if such facts are considered to be predominant in the occurrence of the damage (e.g. exogenous market events).
- *Fault.* The claimant must prove fault on the part of the infringing undertaking and must therefore allege and prove the elements constituting fault in a precise manner.
- *Unlawful conduct.* The unlawful conduct consists of an unlawful agreement or abuse of a dominant position or relative market power. In the event of follow-on actions, the pleading may benefit from reference to all relevant facts established by COMCO, FAC or FSC.

The conditions for compensation for non-material (moral) damage under Article 49 CO are the same as those for damages. We are not aware of any case in which moral damages have been awarded for a violation of the Cartel Act. The amounts awarded for moral damages are generally low. The FSC has examined the amounts awarded for non-material damages in the past and concluded that in cases involving the loss of a parent or bodily injury that causes lasting physical damage that clearly causes

[114] Article 42(2) CO.

[115] FSC, judgment of 1 February 2010, 4A_546/2009, para 5.

[116] Article 42 (2) CO.

[117] FSC, judgment of 23 February 2005, 4C.412/2004, para 3.2.

[118] FSC, judgment of 23 May 2013, 4A_449/2012, *L'Etivaz*, para 10 (unpublished).

the injured party significant mental suffering, the victims have only been awarded amounts between CHF 15,000 and CHF 25,000. [119]

Actions for the removal or cessation of the restraint are not time-barred. However, actions for damages or compensation for tortious acts are time-barred and a relative limitation period of 3 years applies to claims arising from an unlawful restriction of competition. This is not sufficient as administrative procedures often take longer than 3 years. [120] The draft law of 23 May 2023 amending Article 12 of the Cartel Act intends to correct this situation by proposing to suspend the limitation period during the in-depth investigation and until a final decision has been taken before the FSC. Direct and indirect victims are covered and the suspension of the limitation period applies to all companies in a group. The proposed provision reads as follows:

Art. 12a Limitation period

1) The limitation period for claims arising from unlawful restriction of competition shall not commence or, if it has commenced, shall be suspended from the opening of an investigation into this restriction of competition until a final decision has been taken.
2) Paragraph 1 applies mutatis mutandis if the European Commission initiates proceedings on the basis of Article 11 paragraph 1 of the Agreement of 21 June 1994 between the Swiss Confederation and the European Community on Air Transport

1.6.3 Follow-on Actions

Swiss law does not regulate the effect on the civil courts of a COMCO finding of an unlawful agreement or abuse of dominance or of relative market power. This is a disputed point. In other areas, the decisions of other authorities do not bind the civil judge. [121] Regardless of whether the civil court is formally bound by a final COMCO decision, the latter will have a significant influence on the civil court. [122] For reasons

[119] FSC, judgment of 11 April 2012, 4A_741/2011, ATF/BGE 138 III 337, para 6.3.5.

[120] Message concernant la révision partielle de la loi sur les cartels, p. 40. Available at https://www.newsd.admin.ch/newsd/message/attachments/78850.pdf. Accessed 29 May 2023.

[121] Article 53 CO, which governs the relationship with criminal law, states that the court is not bound by the provisions on criminal responsibility or by an acquittal by the criminal court when determining fault or lack of fault and capacity or lack of capacity, or when determining and assessing compensation.

[122] Cf. Article 9(1) Directive 2014/104 which provides that "Member States shall ensure that an infringement of competition law found by a final decision of a national competition authority or by a review court is deemed to be irrefutably established for the purposes of an action for damages brought before their national courts under Article 101 or 102 TFEU or under national competition law."

of expediency, the civil court will not deviate from COMCO's finding of an unlawful agreement or abuse of dominance—as confirmed by the FAC and possibly the FSC—without serious reasons.

As the damage is not the subject of the COMCO investigation, the civil court is in no way bound by the decision of the COMCO. However, certain established facts may be helpful in calculating the damage and in discussing the other conditions of liability under Article 41 CO, such as fault.

The draft law submitted to Parliament in May 2023 suspends the limitation period during investigations (see Sect. 1.6.2 above) but does not regulate the binding effect of COMCO decisions or provide for presumptions of damages similar to those provided for in Directive 2014/104.

1.6.4 Opinion of the COMCO

If the legality of a restraint of competition is challenged in civil proceedings, the case is referred to the COMCO for an expert opinion, which is not binding on the court. [123] COMCO opinions are generally, but not always, followed. In *L'Etivaz*, for example, the court did not follow the COMCO's definition of the relevant market and therefore found a dominant position and abuse, unlike the COMCO (see Sect. 5.3.3.1). [124] In super-provisional and interim measures, the judge is not obliged to ask for an opinion. A civil court judge may, at any stage of the proceedings and independently of Article 15, request the opinion of the COMCO pursuant to Article 47(1) CartA. The judge may also contact the Secretariat of the COMCO informally at any time if he or she wishes to obtain further information on cartel law in general. [125]

1.6.5 Interim Measures

In the case of interim measures, the application may be lodged either with the court with jurisdiction to hear the main action or the court of the place where the measure is to be enforced. [126] The applicant must show that a right to which he is entitled has been infringed or is likely to be infringed and that the infringement threatens to cause

[123] Article 15(1) CartA.

[124] FSC, judgment of 23 May 2013, 4A_449/2012, ATF/BGE 139 II 316 *L'Etivaz*.

[125] Note on relations between the civil courts and the Competition Commission applicable from 1 July 1996, para 4 and 5. Available at file:///C:/Users/Pranvera%20Kellezi/Downloads/Note%20sur%20les%20relations%20avec%20les%20tribunaux%20civils.pdf. Accessed 29 May 2023.

[126] Article 13 CPC.

him damage which cannot easily be repaired. [127] In cases of special urgency, in particular where there is a risk that the enforcement of the measure will be frustrated, the court may order the interim measure immediately and without hearing the opposing party. [128] If an undertaking fears that an interim or other measure may be applied for against it without being heard, it may state its position in advance by lodging a protective letter with the court, which will not be served on the future applicant. [129] The protective letter will only be served on the opposing party if he initiates the relevant proceedings. The protective letter is valid for 6 months but may be renewed or extended.

1.6.6 Nullity of Unlawful Agreements

An unlawful agreement within the meaning of Article 5 CartA is void in accordance with Article 20 CO. [130] Only the terms of a contract that are unlawful are void unless there is cause to assume that the contract would not have been concluded without them. [131]

There is no need for a decision of the COMCO or a court decision to establish or declare the nullity of an agreement or a contractual clause. Article 13 CartA stating that the courts may, at the plaintiff's request, rule that any contracts are null and void in whole or in part, may be confusing in this respect.

The Cartel Act does not regulate whether the unlawful clause or contract is void *ex tunc* (from the beginning) or *ex nunc* (when one of the parties raises the issue or the court decides). This question must therefore be answered in the light of the case law under Article 20 CO, which is not conclusive. Both *ex tunc* and *ex nunc* nullity may be applied, depending on the circumstances and the effects on the parties, in particular on the victim or injured party.

[127] Article 261 CPC.

[128] Article 265(1) CPC.

[129] Article 270 CPC.

[130] FSC, judgement of 12 June 2008, 4A_16/2008 ATF/BGE 134 III 438, para 2.2. In this case the FSC dealt with the civil consequences of a consortium agreement in which one of the parties refused to pay the agreed amount to the other party to the consortium on the grounds that the consortium was unlawful under Article 5 of the Cartel Act and therefore void. The lower courts confirmed the obligation to pay even in the hypothesis of an agreement declared unlawful under Article 5 of the Cartel Act. The FSC upheld the obligation to pay because nullity does not necessarily preclude the recovery of amounts due under the unlawful contract.

[131] Article 20(2) CO.

1.6.7 Private International Law

According to Article 137 (1) PILA on restraints of competition, claims based on a restraint of competition are governed by the law of the state in whose market the restraint has direct effects on the injured party. Article 137(2) PILA limits the award of damages by Swiss courts to the amount that would have been awarded for a restraint of competition under Swiss law, even if the claims are based on a restraint of competition governed by foreign law.

Actions are brought in the court of the defendant's domicile, unless the PILA provides for a specific jurisdiction for the claim. [132] For interim measures, the courts of the place where the measure is to be enforced also have jurisdiction. [133]

In 2018, [134] the FSC opened the possibility for Swiss companies facing a claim under foreign competition law abroad to file an application for a negative declaratory decision in Switzerland. The company's interest in securing a forum in Switzerland by filing an action for a declaration was confirmed in international matters, subject to cases of abuse of rights. As Switzerland is not known for the slowness of its procedures, there is no reason to fear the practice of "torpedo actions". The case was decided on the basis of Swiss procedural law as *lex fori*, rather than *lex causea*, which would have been UK law by virtue of Article 137 (1) PILA. The Swiss action was brought by Swatch, which was threatened with a claim under EU competition law in the United Kingdom, then a member of the EU, following the termination of a contract for the supply of spare parts. Swatch asked the court to declare that Swatch had no obligation to supply the defendant with spare parts for its products and that it did not owe the defendant anything, in particular no damages, as a result of the termination of the supply of spare parts for the plaintiffs' products to the defendant.

Recognition of foreign decisions on civil and commercial matters is based on the Lugano Convention 2007 for judgment issued in the EU and EFTA countries and on Articles 25–27 PILA for judgment rendered by competent authorities in other countries. Enforcement is done according to the debt collection procedure based on DEBA for judgments ordering to pay a sum of money and according to Article 335 ff CPC for other judgments ordering cessation or performance.

The recognition and enforcement of judgments of Swiss courts in the EU and EFTA countries is based on the 2007 Lugano Convention. Recognition and enforcement of Swiss judgments in other countries is governed by the law of the country in which enforcement is sought.

[132] Article 2 PILA.

[133] Article 10 (b) PILA.

[134] FSC, judgement of 14 March 2018, case 4A_417/2017, *Swatch*.

1.7 Exceptional Authorisation by the Federal Council

Agreements that have been declared unlawful and unilateral conduct that has been considered as abusive by the COMCO [135] or civil courts [136] may be authorised by the Federal Council for compelling public interest reasons. The same procedure is available for mergers that have been prohibited by the COMCO. [137]

It is possible to apply to the Federal Council for an exemption on public interest grounds after the COMCO has issued a decision on the unlawful agreement or abusive conduct of a dominant undertaking or an undertaking with significant market power. Very few cases have reached the Federal Council in this way, and to date it has not granted any exemptions on compelling public interest grounds.

List of Documents

CH-EU Agreement on Competition, Agreement between the European Union and the Swiss Confederation concerning cooperation on the application of their competition laws, OJ L 347, 3.12.2014, p. 3; RS 0.251.268.1.

COMCO Secretariat, Explanatory note of 6 January 2016 on Selected Instruments of Investigation (Explanatory note on instruments of investigation).

COMCO, Note of 21 October 2019: Decision-making process of the Competition Commission in cartel investigations within the meaning of Art. 27 ff Cartel Act (Note on decision-making process)

Commission Regulation 773/2004 of 7 April 2004 relating to the conduct of proceedings by the Commission pursuant to Articles 81 and 82 of the EC Treaty, OJ L 123, 27.4.2004, p. 18

Council Regulation 1/2003 of 16 December 2002 on the implementation of the rules on competition laid down in Articles 81 and 82 of the Treaty, OJ 2003 L 1, p. 1

Directive 2014/104 of the European Parliament and of the Council of 26 November 2014 on certain rules governing actions for damages under national law for infringements of the competition law provisions of the Member States and of the European Union, OJ 2014 L 349, p. 1

[135] According to Article 8 CartA, "agreements affecting competition and behaviour by dominant undertakings that have been declared unlawful by the competent authority may be authorised by the Federal Council at the request of the undertakings involved if, in exceptional cases, they are necessary for compelling public interest reasons."

[136] According to Article 15 (2) CartA, "if a restraint of competition that is as such unlawful is claimed to be necessary for compelling public interest reasons, the matter shall be decided by the Federal Council."

[137] According to Article 11 CartA, "a concentration of undertakings that has been prohibited in accordance with Article 10 may be authorised by the Federal Council at the request of the undertakings involved if, in exceptional cases, it is necessary for compelling public interest reasons."

Federal Act of 4 December 1947 on Federal Civil Procedure (FCP; RS 273)
Federal Act on Administrative Criminal Law of 22 March 1974 (ACL; RS 313.0)
Federal Act on Administrative Procedure (APA; RS 172.021)
Federal Act on Cartels and other Restraints of Competition (CartA; RS 251)
Federal Act on Private International Law (PILA; RS 291)
Federal Act on the Amendment of the Swiss Civil Code, Part Five: The Code of Obligations (CO; RS 220)
Lugano Convention 2007, Convention on jurisdiction and the recognition and enforcement of judgments in civil and commercial matters, OJ L 339, 21.12.2007, p. 3 RS 0.275.12.
Message concernant la révision partielle de la loi sur les cartels, p. 40. Available at https://www.newsd.admin.ch/newsd/message/attachments/78850.pdf. Accessed 29 May 2023.
Swiss Civil Code (CC; RS 210)
Swiss Civil Procedure Code of 19 December 2008 (CPC; RS 272)
Swiss Criminal Code of 21 December 1937 (CrimC; RS 311.0)

References

Hatzopoulos V (2011) The concept of 'economic activity' in the EU treaty: from ideological dead-ends to workable judicial concepts. Research paper in law 06/2011, College of Europe. https://www.coleurope.eu/sites/default/files/research-paper/researchpaper_6_2011_hatzopoulos_0.pdf. Accessed 28 May 2023
Këllezi P (2017) Switzerland: prohibition of parallel imports and market integration – the role of the 'effects doctrine' and the development of the substantive laws. Concurrences 2017(3):185

Chapter 2
Agreements

2.1 Introduction

Unlike EU law, the Cartel Act is not based on the principle of prohibition of agreements that restrict competition. The Cartel Act refers to illegality or unlawfulness. [1] According to the Federal Supreme Court (FSC), agreements that harm competition are not generally prohibited, but are permitted within the limits of the law. [2] The difference was intended to emphasise that only abuses were unlawful, and therefore the 1995 Cartel Act only sanctioned companies if they had violated a previous decision of the COMCO. Much has changed since then, with the enactment in 2003 of a new Article 5(4) CartA on resale price maintenance and absolute territorial protection, together with the powers of the COMCO to sanction unlawful

[1] Article 5 CartA on unlawful agreements affecting competition reads as follows: "1) Agreements that significantly restrict competition in a market for specific goods or services and are not justified on grounds of economic efficiency, and all agreements that eliminate effective competition are unlawful. 2) Agreements affecting competition are deemed to be justified on grounds of economic efficiency if: a. they are necessary in order to reduce production or distribution costs, improve products or production processes, promote research into or dissemination of technical or professional know-how, or exploit resources more rationally; and b. they will under no circumstances enable the parties involved to eliminate effective competition. 3) The following agreements between actual or potential competitors are presumed to lead to the elimination of effective competition: a. agreements to directly or indirectly fix prices; b. agreements to limit the quantities of goods or services to be produced, purchased or supplied; c. agreements to allocate markets geographically or according to trading partners. 4) The elimination of effective competition is also presumed in the case of agreements between undertakings at different levels of the production and distribution chain regarding fixed or minimum prices, and in the case of agreements contained in distribution contracts regarding the allocation of territories to the extent that sales by other distributors into these territories are not permitted."

[2] FSC, judgment of 14 August 2002, 2A.298/2001 and 2A.299/2001, ATF/BGE 129 II 18, *Sammelrevers*, para 3.

P. Këllezi, *Competition Law in Switzerland*,
https://doi.org/10.1007/978-3-031-45117-1_2

agreements directly in the prohibition decision, [3] and not only if the undertakings have infringed a previous decision. At the international level, Article 5(4) CartA has become the flagship intervention of the COMCO, with fines of several millions imposed on foreign companies. BMW, for example, was fined CHF 156 million for restricting parallel and direct imports into Switzerland. [4]

Unlike EU law, not all agreements are subject to fines. This is also one of the consequences of a system of illegality as opposed to the prohibition. Only the most harmful horizontal and vertical agreements between undertakings lead to fines, namely those presumed to eliminate competition under Article 5(3) and (4) CartA, but these are automatic in the sense that the COMCO has no discretion as to whether or not to impose a fine. This means that while in the EU not all undertakings party to an agreement restricting competition by object or effect are actually fined, in Switzerland those who infringe Article 5(3) and (4) CartA are subject to a fine by law, unless they benefit from complete immunity. Conversely, parties to an agreement that restricts competition by object or effect only pursuant to Article 5 (1) CartA, without falling within the scope of Article 5(3) and (4) CartA, cannot be fined in Switzerland, whereas they could be fined in the EU. The ceiling on the amount of the fine is set by the threshold of 10% over the previous 3 years, as opposed to 1 year in the EU. [5]

While 'object' restrictions are interpreted restrictively in the EU, [6] Article 5 (3) and (4) CartA are broadly construed. The broad scope of Article 5(3) and (4) of the Cartel Act, as construed by COMCO, is to some extent designed to compensate for the fact that not all restrictive agreements are subject to fines. The other important difference is that Article 5(3) and (4) CartA creates legal presumptions of elimination of competition, whereas in the EU an agreement falls into the object box only after an assessment of the context surrounding the agreement and the structure of the market, so that even resale price maintenance, for example, cannot be considered or presumed to be restrictive of competition without such an assessment. [7] In contrast to the assessment under Article 101 TFEU, there is no assessment of the economic and legal context of the agreement when classifying such agreements under Article 5(3) and (4) CartA (Sect. 3.2). An assessment in relation to the relevant market is not a requirement under Article 5(3) or (4) CartA, [8] whereas the economic and legal context for finding a restriction by object in the EU is established by taking into consideration the real conditions of the functioning and structure of the relevant market or markets in question. [9] Finally, the context assessment allows the

---

[3] Article 49a CartA.

[4] See Bovet (2013).

[5] Cf. Article 23(2) Regulation 1/2003 and Guidelines on the setting of fines, para 32.

[6] CJEU, judgment of 29 June 2023, *Super Bock*, C-211/22, ECLI:EU:C:2023:529, para 32.

[7] CJEU, judgment of 29 June 2023, *Super Bock*, C-211/22, ECLI:EU:C:2023:529, para 42.

[8] FSC, judgment of 28 June 2016, 2C_180/2014, ATF/BGE 143 II 297 *Gaba*, para 5.5.

[9] CJEU, judgment of 2 April 2020, *Budapest Bank*, C-228/18, ECLI:EU:C:2020:265, para 51. CJEU, judgment of 11 September 2014, *Groupement des cartes bancaires (CB)*, C-67/13 P, ECLI:

pro-competitive effects of an agreement to be taken into account under Article 101 (1) TFEU provided that they are "demonstrable, relevant, intrinsic to the agreement and sufficiently significant", [10] whereas pro-competitive effects can only be taken into account under Article 5(2) CartA, the corresponding provision to Article 101 (3) TFEU.

COMCO has made full use of its sanctioning powers, with deterrence becoming its main means of ensuring that companies comply with the law. As a result, the COMCO Secretariat almost exclusively initiates investigations for agreements covered by Article 5(3) and (4) of the Cartel Act. This explains the importance of knowing what makes an agreement fall under Article 5(3) or (4) CartA and what the consequences are. Practitioners looking for more guidance from the COMCO on Article 5(1) CartA decisions will be disappointed, as there is very little of it.

The principle of illegality does not preclude prohibitions imposed by law, respecting the Constitution. [11] The courts have not only supported COMCO's broad interpretations of Article 5(3) and (4) CartA, but also paved the way for sanctioning all such agreements, further relaxing the standard of proof and making it harder for companies to defend themselves on efficiency grounds.

Perhaps one of the most significant disruptions caused by the courts is the broad interpretation of the 'effects doctrine', which has led to an overly broad extraterritorial scope of the Swiss Cartel Act (see Sect. 1.3.2). [12] This affects all companies that distribute their goods worldwide and rely on standard export prohibition clauses to allocate continents to different distributors. Companies in Asia and America are affected even if they did not consider Switzerland when designing their global distribution strategy, sometimes not even realising that Switzerland is not part of the EU/EEA.

The aim of this chapter is to help practitioners navigate the jargon and presumptions of the Swiss Cartel Act by focusing on the steps of the assessment and the consequences for companies.

EU:C:2014:2204, para 53. CJEU, judgment of 14 March 2013, *Allianz Hungária*, C-32/11, ECLI: EU:C:2013:160, para 36.

[10] CJEU, judgment of 29 June 2023, *Super Bock*, C-211/22, ECLI:EU:C:2023:529, para 36.

[11] FSC, judgment of 28 June 2016, 2C_180/2014, *Gaba*, ATF/BGE 143 II 297, para 5.3.4: "Prohibitions of harmful conduct are perfectly permissible, as the legislator has made explicit in Articles 5(1) and 7(1) of the Cartel Act: Certain agreements and certain conduct are unlawful by virtue of the law. The direct sanctioning under Art. 49a Cartel Act for violations of agreements under Art. 5 paras. 3 and 4 of the Cartel Act and of conduct under Art. 7 of the Cartel Act respects the constitutional requirements". (free translation)

[12] FSC, judgment of 28 June 2016, 2C_180/2014, *Gaba*, ATF/BGE 143 II 297, para 3.

2.2 Agreements Within the Meaning of Article 4(1) CartA

Article 4(1) CartA on agreements reads as follows: "Agreements affecting competition are binding or non-binding conventions and concerted practices between undertakings operating at the same or at different levels of production which have a restraint of competition as their object or effect."

According to the wording of Article 4(1) CartA, two cumulative conditions must be met in order for an agreement to exist: first, there must be an agreement, and second, the agreement must have as its object or effect the restriction of competition.[13]

2.2.1 Agreements Between Independent Undertakings

An agreement has an effect on competition only if it restricts the freedom of action of the parties that existed prior to or in the absence of the agreement, hence the implicit requirement that only agreements between independent undertakings are relevant for the purposes of the Cartel Act. In general, there is a lack of independence when companies belong to the same group and in agency agreements when the agent acts on behalf of the principal, since the parties and the agent are not free to determine their course of action with regard to the parameters that determine effective competition. There is no explicit exception to cover these cases. While COMCO and the courts accept in principle the group privilege or an agency privilege, the scope of such privilege tends to be narrower than what is recognised in EU competition law, particularly with regard to distribution (see Sect. 4.1). This is due to the attempt to cover all conduct that would contribute to higher prices applied in Switzerland. The newly introduced provisions on the abuse of relative market power are worth mentioning, as they aim to capture the unilateral behaviour of foreign companies that apply different, less advantageous conditions in Switzerland (Sects. 5.2.3 and 5.3.3.7).

2.2.1.1 Group Companies

The FSC has confirmed that "agreements between companies belonging to the same group and over which a parent company exercises effective control are not subject to the Cartel Act, since, in the absence of independence, all these companies constitute one and the same undertaking and benefit from the so-called 'group privilege' [. . .] This means in particular that vertical agreements on prices or territorial protection, when concluded between two undertakings belonging to the same group and incapable of acting independently, do not constitute agreements restricting competition

[13] FSC, judgment of 18 May 2018, 2C_101/2016, *Altimum*, ATF/BGE 144 II 246, para 6.4.

within the meaning of Article 4 (1) CartA, nor a fortiori unlawful agreements within the meaning of Article 5 (1) CartA, as long as these agreements do not provide for a foreclosure of the markets by distributors outside the group." [14] (see Sect. 4.1.2).

2.2.1.2 Agency Relationship

Even less clear than the group privilege is the position of COMCO and the courts on agency relationships (see also Sect. 4.1). In a recent case, the FSC left open the question of whether the agency privilege could be incorporated into Swiss law. [15] However, it did not reject it, thus opening up the possibility of relying on it for certain types of restrictions.

However, absolute territorial protection is not the type of restriction that can benefit from the agency privilege. In the case concerning the distribution of French-language books, the FSC found that the risks borne by the Swiss distributor justified the qualification of the agreement as an agency under the CartA, [16] but held that even if an agreement is qualified as an agency agreement, the agency privilege does not cover territorial exclusivity and territorial protection. [17] The presumption of Article 5 (4) CartA remains applicable to such restrictions. [18]

2.2.2 *Form of Agreements*

2.2.2.1 Agreements as a Collective Action

The first condition for agreements is that there must be collective, conscious and deliberate action by the undertakings concerned. [19] The declarations and expressions of intent between the parties to the agreement must be interpreted in such a way as to reveal a deliberate and conscious cooperation between two or more undertakings. [20]

[14] FSC, judgment of 21 December 2021, 2C_43/2020, *Dargaud*, ATF/BGE 148 II 25, paras 7.2 and 7.3.

[15] FSC, judgment of 8 December 2022, 2C_33/2020, *Interforum Suisse SA*.

[16] FSC of 3 March 2020 in the case 2C_44/2020 *Flammarion*, para 6.6. The Court based its assessment on the fact that the Swiss dealer did not become the owner of the books and that it did not bear the risk of unsold books, which was born by the editor.

[17] FSC, judgment of 3 March 2020, 2C_44/2020 *Flammarion*, para 6.7.

[18] FSC, judgment of 8 December 2022, 2C_33/2020, *Interforum Suisse SA*, para 7.6.

[19] FSC, judgment of 18 May 2018, 2C_101/2016, *Altimum*, ATF/BGE 144 II 246 para 6.4.1; cf. FSC, judgment of 14 August 2002, 2A.298/2001 and 2A.299/2001, *Sammelrevers*, ATF/BGE 129 II 18, para 6.3; FSC, judgment of 13 November 1998 ATF/BGE 124 III 495, para 2a.

[20] FSC, judgment of 18 May 2018, 2C_101/2016, *Altimum*, ATF/BGE 144 II 246, para 6.4.1; FSC, judgment of 13 November 1998 ATF/BGE 124 III 495, para 2a.

Unilateral declarations bind the recipient if he or she accepts them expressly or by means of conclusive acts (see Sect. 4.3.1.2). [21]

The forms of agreement referred to in Article 4(1) CartA—agreements and conventions, whether binding or not, and concerted practices—are alternative forms, so that where a convention exists it is not necessary to consider whether there is a concerted practice. [22] The concept of a concerted practice is particularly relevant in cases where there is no convention between the undertakings concerned, whether binding or not.

All types of agreements are covered. Agreements between undertakings operating on the same market are horizontal agreements; agreements between undertakings operating on different market levels are vertical agreements. [23]

The vertical or horizontal relationship between the parties is irrelevant for the establishment of an agreement within the meaning of Article 4(1) CartA. [24] Agreements between undertakings which are not at the same market level or at different market levels, are also covered by Article 4(1) and 5(1) CartA. [25]

The qualification of an agreement as horizontal or vertical is only a condition for the application of paragraphs 3 and 4 of Article 5 CartA, but not for the application of Article 5(1) CartA.

2.2.2.2 Agreements in the Form of Conventions

Contracts and any form of written agreements, binding or non-binding, are considered as conventions. Oral agreements are also considered to be agreements within the meaning of Art. 4(1) CartA; the expression of the intention may be inferred from a written communication or from oral statements made by witnesses. All evidence, both written and oral, will be taken into account in order to determine whether there has been a collective, conscious and deliberate action by the undertakings concerned.

The intention of the parties may be express or implied. The latter includes, in particular, conclusive acts, i.e. acts whose performance implies a certain intention regarding the relationship between the parties. [26] Declarations and expressions of intent between the contracting parties are interpreted in accordance with the general rules of Article 1 ff CO and the principle of trust (18 CO), and the court will take into

---

[21] FSC, judgment of 18 May 2018, 2C_101/2016, *Altimum*, ATF/BGE 144 II 246, para 6.4.1.

[22] FSC, judgment of 18 May 2018, 2C_101/2016, ATF/BGE 144 II 246 *Altimum*, para 6.4.1.

[23] FSC, judgment of 14 August 2002, 2A.298/2001 and 2A.299/2001, *Sammelrevers*, ATF/BGE 129 II 18, para 4; FSC, judgment of 18 May 2018, 2C_101/2016, *Altimum*, ATF/BGE 144 II 246, para 6.4.1.

[24] FSC, judgment of 14 August 2002, 2A.298/2001 and 2A.299/2001, *Sammelrevers*, ATF/BGE 129 II 18, para 4.

[25] FSC, judgment of 12 February 2020, 2C_113/2017, *Hallenstadion*.

[26] Idem, para 6.4.1; FSC, judgment of 19 January 2007, 4C.371/2006, para 5.

account all the circumstances and not only the terms. [27] If the judge is unable to ascertain the real and common will of the parties to a contract, he must have regard to their objective will, [28] after an objective interpretation of the contract or the declarations. [29]

The binding force is not a necessary condition for having an agreement within the meaning of Article 4(1) CartA: the text of the law explicitly mentions agreements without binding force. The binding force is, however, a sufficient condition for concluding that an agreement exists. Moreover, when there is a binding agreement, it is no longer necessary to consider whether this agreement fulfils the conditions of a concerted practice. [30] In the case of price recommendations, on the other hand, their binding force is a necessary condition to qualify them as a convention. [31] For example, sanctions or pressure by one of the parties on the other fulfils the requirements of a binding convention (see Sect. 4.3.1.1). [32]

2.2.2.3 Concerted Practices

The concept of concerted practices has evolved. Two landmark judgments have defined its boundaries, one before the introduction of direct sanctions and the other almost 20 years later. Both cases concerned vertical agreements, one in the form of a bundle of distribution contracts covering the whole book market, the other in the form of price recommendations. A third FAC judgment recently upheld a concerted practice consisting of a horizontal exchange of information on prices.

In the first case, [33] publishers of German-language books had entered into vertical contracts with all downstream distributors up to the retail level to fix the resale price of their own books. There was therefore evidence of vertical agreements. At that time there was only a presumption of elimination of competition for horizontal price-fixing agreements under Article 5(3) of the Cartel Act, and in order to apply the presumption the COMCO built a case for a horizontal agreement in the form of a concerted practice between all participants. The uniform retail price applied by bookshops to each book was not the result of horizontal cooperation but of vertical agreements. These vertical agreements were virtually identical and decided by all publishers and distributors. There was therefore no difficulty in accepting that the

---

[27] FSC, judgment of 18 May 2018, 2C_101/2016, *Altimum*, ATF/BGE 144 II 246 para 6.4.1.

[28] FSC, judgment of 3 March 2022, 2C_44/2020, *Flammarion*, para 9.1; FSC, judgment of 8 December 2022, 2C_52/2020, *Glénat*, para 7.3.2.

[29] FSC, judgment of 8 December 2022, 2C_52/2020, *Glénat*, para 7.3.2.

[30] FSC, judgment of 18 May 2018, 2C_101/2016, *Altimum*, ATF/BGE 144 II 246 para 6.4.1.

[31] Idem, para 6.4.1.

[32] FSC, judgment of 18 May 2018, 2C_101/2016, *Altimum*, ATF/BGE 144 II 246, para 6.4.1.

[33] FSC, judgment of 14 August 2002, 2A.298/2001 and 2A.299/2001, *Sammelrevers*, ATF/BGE 129 II 18.

uniform retail prices for each book were the result of a concerted practice between publishers and distributors. The question of causality was not discussed.

In the second case, [34] COMCO investigated non-binding price recommendations by three pharmaceutical companies for erectile dysfunction drugs (Sects. 4.3.1.1 and 4.3.1.2). The price recommendations were included in the database used by pharmacies to obtain medicines and were visible in their cash registers. There were no contracts and no contact between the pharmaceutical companies and the pharmacists, apart from virtual contact through the database. Retail prices were not uniform, pharmacies were free to set their retail prices and give discounts, and many did so.

The FSC established three conditions for concerted practices under Article 4 (1) CartA: coordination between the market participants, a certain similarity of behaviour in the market and a causal link between the coordination and this market behaviour.

- The *coordination* was maintained because the pharmaceutical companies knew that the retailers would see the price recommendations in the electronic cash register system and the retailers accepted the communication of such price recommendations.
- The *market conduct* relates to the similarity of the retail prices applied by the pharmacies: here it was sufficient that 50–75% of the pharmacies fully complied with the price recommendations in order to maintain this uniform behaviour in the market. This condition was called the follow-up rate, which required most retailers to follow price recommendations in order to demonstrate market behaviour (see Sects. 4.3.1.1 and 4.3.1.2). The fact that about 30% of the pharmacies gave some discounts and that about 10–15% of the pharmacies did not follow the price recommendations at all was not sufficient to disprove the existence of uniform behaviour in the market.
- The third condition on *causality* was also met after applying a number of relaxations of the burden and standard of proof. According to the FSC, a similarity of behaviour such as that observed in this case, in a non-transparent market where there are several hundred retailers operating without advertising and with different cost structures, could only be explained by the existence of a concerted practice based on price recommendations issued by manufacturers.

In the third case, concerning the exchange of information on interest rates and fees between car leasing companies, the FAC confirmed the three conditions for the establishment of a concerted practice, i.e. coordination, market conduct and a causal link between the coordination and the market conduct, but clarified that a specific follow-up rate is not necessary for the establishment of a concerted practice in horizontal relationships. [35] The FAC explains that market conduct exists even if

[34] FSC, judgment of 4 February 2021, 2C_149/2018, *Pfizer*, ATF/BGE 147 II 72. For a detailed analysis of the case, see Sect. 4.3.1.1 about Resale Price Maintenance.

[35] FAC, judgment of 5 June 2023, B-4596/2019 *CA Auto Finance Suisse SA,* para 5.2.3.14.

competitors do not engage in strictly parallel behaviour. [36] What must be shown is the ability of the coordination or contacts, in this case the exchange of information, to influence the behaviour of undertakings in the market. The FAC makes two assumptions about this influence, which also demonstrate the causal link. [37] If there is evidence of regular and long-term coordination, it is presumed that each undertaking participating in the exchange will take this information into account when determining its market conduct. The coordination is therefore considered to influence market behaviour. If, on the other hand, there is parallel behaviour in the market, this parallelism is only one indication of a concerted practice and other evidence must be found to prove a concerted practice. The FAC does not clarify what such other evidence might be, nor does it clarify the standard of proof for using parallel conduct as evidence of a concerted practice.

It follows from the Pfizer case and the more recent FAC judgment that the standard of proof for the three elements of a concerted practice is very much relaxed. It is unclear how these conditions will be applied in other market settings, but the case law opens the door to the use of the concept of concerted practice in situations of quasi-parallel behaviour. This is therefore a risk for companies to consider.

2.2.2.4 Decisions of Association of Undertakings

Unlike Article 101 TFUE, Article 4(1) CartA does not mention explicitly decisions by associations of undertakings. For a long time, it was unclear whether decisions by associations of undertakings constituted agreements and whether the association itself could be a party to an agreement and therefore subject to fines.

In ASCOPA, the TAF considered that the Articles of Association, General Assembly resolutions and Board resolutions were appropriate for expressing the will of the members of the association to enter into agreements. [38] Decisions of associations of undertakings are therefore agreements between the members of such associations. The participation of each member in the agreement is assessed on a case-by-case basis, considering the extent to which the member was represented in the decision-making bodies of the association and whether the member implemented the decisions of the association or distanced itself from such decisions.

---

[36] FAC, judgment of 5 June 2023, B-4596/2019 *CA Auto Finance Suisse SA,* para 5.2.3.13: "It has already been stated above that it is not necessary that the market conduct takes place exactly in parallel. No high requirements are to be placed on the proof of market conduct. The conduct on the market must only have been influenced by the contact. The decisive factor is thus whether the conduct had any effect on the market conduct of the undertakings concerned, without having to be further specified (references omitted). The appellant's objections that an adjustment of its market conduct was not established because an economic analysis showed a heterogeneous distribution of the standard and special interest rates thus miss the point."

[37] FAC, judgment of 5 June 2023, B-4596/2019 *CA Auto Finance Suisse SA,* para 5.2.4.4.

[38] FAC, judgment of 12 December 2022, B-141/2012, *Estée Lauder/ASCOPA*, para 4.4.3.2.2.

It is still open and has not been decided by the courts whether the association itself can be considered a party to an agreement, with the consequence that measures or sanctions can be imposed against the association itself. To date, COMCO has not imposed any fines on associations. In one case, the association agreed in an amicable settlement to ensure that its members would pay the fine. [39]

2.2.2.5 Global or Lasting Agreements

COMCO has developed a concept similar, but not identical, to the EU's single and continuous infringement for hardcore horizontal cartels, namely that of a global or lasting agreement. [40] The FAC has upheld the temporal elements of the concept by confirming that a cartel in the procurement markets can last for more than just a single procurement. [41] The FSC has not yet dealt with the concept.

A recent COMCO decision explains the concept and its main consequence:

> In the case of an overall agreement over a long period of time, the participating undertakings may change over time, making more or less significant contributions or assuming different roles. The diverging interests of the participating undertakings may also lead to a consensus that does not cover all aspects of the agreement. For example, one or more of the parties may have reservations about certain aspects of the agreement, but still adhere to the common plan. In addition, undertakings may apply certain elements of the agreement differently, or there may even be internal conflicts and individual undertakings may temporarily suspend the application of the agreement in order to compete with other participants in the agreement. Finally, the agreement may evolve over time, be strengthened or adapted to new circumstances. None of these factors leads to the exclusion of a global agreement as long as it can be shown that there is a common and lasting purpose. In such a case, the participating undertakings may be held liable for all the actions taken under the global agreement, even if they were directly participating in only some of them. [42]

As explained in this extract, the main consequence is that each participating company can be held liable for the entire duration of the lasting agreement, even if a company only participated for a shorter period. The standard to prove the

[39] COMCO, decision of 25 February 2019, *Fahrlehrertarife Oberwallis*, LPC 2019/2, p. 513. The terms of the amicable settlement read: "The [association] undertakes to ensure that the sanction and the costs of the proceedings are fully covered by its active members." (free translation from German)

[40] In German: *Gesamtabrede* or *Dauerabrede*. In Italian: *accordi globali* or *accordi duraturi*.

[41] FAC, judgment of 1 June 2010, B-420/2008, *Implenia*, LPC 2010/2, p. 368, para 9.1.1; FAC, judgment of 1 June 2010, B-360/2008 *Spalu*, LPC 2010/2, p. 393, para 10.1.1: "Depending on the nature and characteristics of the goods to be procured in the case of public procurement, the markets concerned may exist over various periods of time. It is conceivable that, in addition to markets of short duration, whether they occur at once or recurrently, depending on the specific circumstances and as the following paragraphs show, there may also be a genuine market of unlimited duration and thus a procurement cartel of unlimited duration." (free translation).

[42] COMCO decision of 23 May 2023 *Concessionari Volkswagen*, para 487.

participation of each company in all tenders or markets [43] and for the whole duration is therefore significantly lowered. Contrary to EU law, [44] there is therefore no individualisation of liability in relation to the duration in the case of a global agreement. As the global agreement implies that there is an agreement in a relevant market for a single duration, the fine for each undertaking is calculated in relation to its turnover in that relevant market and for the whole duration of the global agreement, even if that undertaking did not participate in all individual tenders in one relevant market and for the whole duration. This differs from EU case law where duration is determined individually in relation to each undertaking's actual participation and not in relation to the entire duration of the single and continuous infringement.

The individualisation is made in relation to the gravity and nature of the agreement, which takes into account the role and intensity of each undertaking's participation. This in turn serves to determine the percentage of the basic amount of the fine for each participant within the meaning of Article 3 CASO. [45]

In general, therefore, undertakings may have an interest in challenging the notion of a lasting agreement in the case of an agreement of long duration affecting one relevant product or geographic market. In the case of an agreement of short duration affecting several markets, there may be an interest in arguing for a global agreement because there will be one basic amount for the calculation of the fine rather than several. The concept of a global or lasting agreement serves also to extend the limitation period for all undertakings at the end of the global agreement, which allows the COMCO to impose fines for the participation of undertakings that have ceased their cartel activities more than 5 years before the opening of the cartel investigation (Sect. 7.2.8). [46]

2.2.2.6 Rules on Evidence and Standard of Proof

For practitioners, the type of evidence and the standard of proof used to prove an agreement is crucial. Both direct evidence and evidence by indicia are used by the COMCO and the courts to prove an agreement. In the absence of written agreements or direct evidence of the existence of an agreement, the assessment may be based on indications [47] or circumstantial evidence. However, there are no restrictions on the

---

[43] See COMCO decision of 10 December 2012 *Abrede im Speditionsbereich*, LPC 2013/2, p. 142, para 75.

[44] Cf. Castillo de la Torre and Gippini (2017), 3.032 (start of the infringement) and 3.045 (termination).

[45] Ordinance on Sanctions imposed for Unlawful Restraints of Competition (Cartel Act Sanctions Ordinance, CASO; RS 251.5).

[46] Article 49a (3) (b) CartA, which provides that no fine will be imposed if "restraint of competition has not been exercised for more than five years by the time an investigation is opened".

[47] FSC, judgment of 18 May 2018, 2C_101/2016, *Altimum*, ATF/BGE 144 II 246, para 6.4.4.

use of circumstantial evidence. At the same time, the courts have lowered the standard of proof for all types of agreements, including concerted practices.

The FSC assumes that direct evidence of written agreements is in practice very rare and that the facts are by nature difficult to prove, which leads the court not to 'exaggerate' the requirements for evidence and on the standard of proof. [48] According to the court, this does not violate the guarantee of the presumption of innocence.

With regard to the standard of proof, the FSC applies the same threshold developed for the assessment of substitutability in order to define the relevant market and the dominant position. [49] In *Publigroupe*, the Court noted that these relationships are complex, and that the assessment of the degree of substitutability cannot be determined with precision, as it is necessary to rely on certain economic assumptions, which cannot therefore be proved with certainty or required to be strictly proven. [50]

The preponderance of evidence (or 'more likely than not') test established by *Publigroupe* for complex economic assessments is also used to establish an agreement and even to interpret written contracts. In interpreting written distribution agreements, the FSC recalled that "the standard of proof in competition law should not be exaggerated, at least when the facts are, by their very nature, difficult to prove; in particular, it should be borne in mind that direct evidence of the existence of an agreement in competition matters is in practice very rare, so that the assessment of the facts must regularly be made on the basis of indications". [51]

The FSC makes use of the low standard of proof in two notable cases concerning price recommendations. In the first case, the manufacturer put pressure on some of its distributors not to set the retail price 10% lower than recommended. There was very little evidence of the binding nature of the price recommendations, and it is this binding nature that makes them an agreement. The Court begins its analysis by stating that it is inherently difficult to prove that price recommendations are binding, [52] which justifies lowering the standard of proof when assessing indirect or circumstantial evidence. The binding nature of the price recommendations was thus considered to lead to the finding of an agreement on fixed or minimum prices, which is covered by Article 5(4) of CartA and is punishable by fines (Sects. 4.3.1.1 and 4.3.1.2).

The second case also concerns price recommendations. [53] This time, the lower standard of proof is applied to assess the circumstantial evidence of non-binding price recommendations made by three manufacturers of erectile dysfunction drugs

[48] Idem, para 6.4.4; see also ATF 139 I 72, para 8.3.2.

[49] FSC, judgment of 29 June 2012, 2C_484/2010, *Publigroupe*, ATF/BGE 139 I 72, para 8.3.2.

[50] Idem, para 8.3.2.

[51] See for instance FSC, judgment of 8 December 2022, case 2C_52/2020, *Glénat*, para 7.3.3 (free translation).

[52] FSC, judgment of 18 May 2018, 2C_101/2016, *Altimum*, ATF/BGE 144 II 246, para 6.4.4.

[53] FSC, judgment of 4 February 2021, 2C_149/2018, *Pfizer*, ATF/BGE 147 II 72.

through a database used daily by pharmacies and doctors. Thus, in contrast to EU law, which uses a standard of proof close to certainty, a low standard of proof is applied to concerted practices. Communication was presumed, coordination was presumed, homogeneous market behaviour was presumed on the basis of the high rate of pharmacies and doctors who fully or partially followed the price recommendations, and causality was presumed on the basis of the same low standard of proof applied in *Altimum*. The concerted practice thus established using presumptions of facts led to the finding of an agreement on fixed or minimum prices, covered by Article 5(4) CartA, and to fines.

The same standard of proof used in *Publigroupe* for complex market conditions, [54] i.e. the preponderance of the evidence (or more likely than not) test, is used to assess the restriction of competition or the rebuttal of the legal presumption of elimination of competition. [55]

2.2.3 Object or Effect Under Article 4(1) CartA

The condition relating to the restriction of competition distinguishes between agreements that 'aim' to restrict competition and those that 'have the effect' of restricting competition. Agreements that aim to restrict competition, such as agreements that restrict the free formation of prices, are capable of limiting competition and it is therefore not necessary to examine whether the agreement has effects on competition. [56]

The terminology used in Article 4(1) CartA is inspired by the dichotomy of restrictions of competition by object and by effect under Article 101 TFEU. The assessment of whether there is a restriction of competition by object or by effect is different under the Cartel Act and the structure of the Cartel Act takes this into account both in the qualification of the agreement and in the assessment of the restriction of competition. This may give the impression that the conditions for the classification of a restriction of competition by object are more stringent than those set out in Article 101 TFEU, but this is not the case.

The condition in Article 4(1) CartA is assessed rather abstractly, since it is sufficient for an agreement to relate loosely to a parameter of competition in order to fulfil the conditions of an agreement affecting competition within the meaning of Article 4(1) CartA, and the distinction between object and effect has no bearing on the classification of the cooperation as an agreement. [57] The exchange of information

[54] FAC, judgment of 12 December 2022, B-141/2012, *Estée Lauder/ASCOPA*, para 3.2.2.2.8.

[55] Idem, para 6.3.3.3.2.

[56] FSC, judgment of 18 May 2018, 2C_101/2016, *Altimum*, ATF/BGE 144 II 246, paras 6.4.2 and 6.8; FSC, judgment of 14 August 2002, 2A.298/2001 and 2A.299/2001, *Sammelrevers*, ATF/BGE 129 II 18, para 5.1 and 5.2.2.

[57] FAC, judgment of 12 December 2022, B-141/2012, *Estée Lauder/ASCOPA*, para 4.6.4.3.

on prices and sales was considered to threaten the functioning of competition in the market, and it is this threat to competition that is sufficient to qualify an agreement as having the object of restricting competition. [58] If, how and to what extent the agreement on prices or sales affects competition is part of the assessment under Article 5 CartA and not under Article 4(1) of the Cartel Act. The positive effects are considered only under Article 5(2) CartA. [59]

The actual assessment of the restriction of competition takes place under Article 5 CartA, and it is here that the distinction between object and effect becomes relevant, as it defines the limits of the assessment and the extent to which quantitative criteria, such as market shares, need to be examined. The presumption of elimination of competition in Article 5(3) and (4) CartA was designed precisely to provide a simplified framework for the most harmful agreements and to dispense with the assessment of effects. Recent case law of the FAC shows that agreements falling outside the scope of Article 5(3) and (4) CartA may have as their object the restriction of competition. [60] This means that in the context of Article 5(1) CartA, restriction by object means that the agreement significantly restricts competition from a qualitative point of view. In the case of vertical agreements, this would be the case for the qualitatively severe restrictions of competition listed in the COMCO Verticals Notice. Consequently, for these agreements even small quantitative effects are sufficient to reach the threshold of significance under Article 5(1) CartA.

It is important for practitioners to take into account that in both Article 4 and Article 5 of the Cartel Act, only the content of the agreement and the parameter of competition that is the object of the cooperation serve as a basis for qualifying an agreement as having the object, directly or indirectly, of restricting competition. Evidence of communication between the undertakings participating in the agreement on one of the parameters of the competition is the most important type of evidence. Neither Article 4 nor Article 5 of CartA require consideration of the context or the functioning of the market. This is in contrast to the case law of the European Court of Justice, which requires that, in order to determine whether an agreement between undertakings or a decision by an association of undertakings is sufficiently restrictive of competition "by object" within the meaning of Article 101(1) TFEU, "regard must be had to the content of its provisions, its objectives and the economic and legal context of which it forms a part. When determining that context, it is also necessary to take into consideration the nature of the goods or services affected, as well as the real conditions of the functioning and structure of the market or markets in question". [61]

The law qualifies agreements as those that relate to competition, translated in English as "affecting competition"; the text in French, Italian and German says less

[58] Idem, para 4.6.5.2.

[59] Idem, para 4.7.4.2.

[60] FAC, judgment of 12 December 2022, B-141/2012, *Estée Lauder/ASCOPA*, para 4.6.6.

[61] GC, judgment of 11 September 2014, *Groupement des cartes bancaires (CB)*, ECLI:EU:C:2014:2204, C-67/13 P, para 53.

about whether competition is affected or not, since it uses the terms "*accords en matière de concurrence*" in French, "*accordi in materia di concorrenza*" in Italian, and "*Wettbewerbsabreden*" in German. This means that not all agreements are subject to the Cartel Act, but only those agreements that relate to or have an impact on the parameters of competition in the market.

Such qualification will be used to resolve the concerns raised about consortia, which are reflected in the draft law submitted to Parliament in May 2023. [62] Article 4 (1) CartA on the concept of agreements and concerted practices would be supplemented by a new paragraph stating that "agreements and concerted practices on consortia which enable or strengthen effective competition are not considered to be agreements affecting competition". This is in line with COMCO practice on consortia (see Sect. 3.5.2).

2.3 Restriction of Competition Under Article 5(1) CartA

2.3.1 Trivial Restrictions or 'Cas Bagatelle'

The 'bagatelle case' is an insignificant or trivial case which does not appreciably restrict competition within the meaning of Article 5(1) CartA. It concerns the criterion of "substantial" restriction of competition. Until mid-2010, it was not clear what threshold was meant by "significant", whether it was intended to ensure that only significant negative impacts were covered, or whether it was intended to exclude trivial cases from its scope.

The FSC clarified the function of the criterion in 2016: the criterion of the significance of the infringement, referred to in Article 5(1) CartA, is primarily intended to allow the COMCO not to pursue 'trivial cases'. It is therefore intended to be used by the COMCO and its Secretariat to decide whether or not to open an investigation. The second is to make a distinction between insignificant and significant cases. [63] In other words, a significant restriction of competition is something that is not insignificant or trivial. This means that what is not considered to be a trivial case, or what just exceeds the trivial threshold, is where the threshold of significance begins to apply. [64] Where exactly the threshold of significance lies and how it can be demonstrated remains controversial. [65] But the threshold for intervention is low. And there is no qualified trivial threshold in Article 5(1) of CartA, as the

[62] See Federal Council, Press release of 24 May 2023, "Loi sur les cartels: le Conseil fédéral adopte le message concernant la révision partielle", available at https://www.admin.ch/gov/fr/accueil/documentation/communiques/communiques-conseil-federal.msg-id-95384.html. The draft law can be found at: https://www.newsd.admin.ch/newsd/message/attachments/78852.pdf. Accessed 25 May 2023.

[63] FSC, judgment of 12 February 2020, 2C_113/2017, *Hallenstadion*, para 7.3.1.

[64] FAC, judgment of 12 December 2022, B-141/2012, *Estée Lauder/ASCOPA*, para 6.3.2.1.

[65] Idem, para 6.3.2.7.

FAC has recently made clear. [66] There have not been enough cases to consider the case law as settled.

The SME Notice [67] established two safe harbours for undertakings, one relating to market shares and the other applicable to micro-enterprises, both of which are only available for agreements that do not fall under the presumptions of Article 5(3) and (4) CartA.

According to the first safe harbour, agreements have a limited impact on the market if the combined market share of the parties to a horizontal agreement does not exceed 10% on any of the relevant markets affected by the agreement. For vertical agreements, the combined market share threshold is 15% in any of the relevant markets affected by the agreement. [68]

The second safe harbour applies to agreements involving only micro-enterprises. A micro-enterprise is defined as a company with fewer than 10 employees and an annual turnover in Switzerland of less than CHF 2 million. [69]

Trivial restrictions do not correspond to the de minimis concept under EU law, which serves to exclude trivial cases from the analysis and scope of application of Article 101 TFEU, where cases which exceed the de minimis threshold are not presumed to restrict competition. This is not the case under Swiss law. Restrictions that are not trivial or insignificant are likely to be considered a significant restriction of competition. [70]

The second safe harbour for micro-enterprises is very similar to the negative rebuttable presumption of no appreciable effect on trade between Member States. [71] In the EU, this applies to agreements between small and medium-sized enterprises (SMEs) or to agreements where the parties do not have more than a 5% market share and the aggregate annual turnover of the undertakings concerned in the EU does not exceed EUR 40 million, which, unlike the Swiss SME Notice, also applies to hardcore restrictions or restrictions by object.

---

[66] Idem, para 6.3.1.4.1.

[67] Notice on agreements with limited market impact, Decision of the Competition Commission of 19 December 2005 (hereafter 'SME Notice').

[68] SME Notice, para 3.

[69] SME Notice, paras 4 and 5.

[70] This is certainly the case for restrictions under Article 5(3) and (4): if they are not trivial, they are significant.

[71] Known as the NAAT-rule; see Commission Guidelines on the effect on trade concept contained in Articles 81 and 82 of the Treaty, OJ C 101, 27.4.2004, p. 81, paras 50ff. The effect on trade between Member States is a jurisdictional criterion that defines the competence of the EU competition rules. Agreements that do not affect trade between Member States are subject to national competition rules.

2.3.2 *Situations Covered Only by Article 5(1) CartA*

2.3.2.1 Qualitative and Quantitative Criteria to Assess Restrictions of Competition Under Article 5(1) CartA

In this section we will discuss how to assess whether an agreement falling exclusively within the scope of Article 5(1) CartA significantly restricts competition, as opposed to those agreements covered by Article 5(3) and (4) CartA.

The terms qualitative and quantitative aspects refer to the two criteria for assessing the significance of the restriction of competition under Article 5 CartA. The qualitative aspects concern the nature and parameters of the competition to which the agreement or restriction relates, while the quantitative aspects are concerned with the anti-competitive effects of the agreement, with the market share of the parties being the main factor under consideration. It is not necessary to show that a restriction which is severe from a qualitative point of view will also have a negative impact on the market [72] in the sense of an increase in prices or a decrease in quantity, quality or innovation. Neither criterion covers the positive effects of the agreements. These are only taken into account under Article 5 (2) CartA.

For a long time, both qualitative and quantitative criteria had to be met in order to conclude that the infringement was significant. The trend is to use qualitative and quantitative criteria as alternatives when the agreement restricts competition from a qualitative point of view and as complements when the nature of the agreement does not indicate a clear qualitative restriction of competition, but the market position of the parties is such that the agreement may restrict competition from a quantitative point of view. [73] In other words, qualitative criteria are sufficient, but quantitative criteria are not without qualitative criteria. Finally, irrespective of whether qualitative or quantitative criteria are to be assessed in a case, it is not necessary to show actual effects in the sense of an increase in prices or a decrease in quantity, quality or innovation, in order to prove a significant restriction of competition under Section 5 (1) of the Cartel Act. [74]

Broadly speaking, the assessment of the qualitative and quantitative criteria is equivalent with the circumstances considered to distinguish between an agreement by object and an agreement by effect. However, the structure of the Cartel Act is such that the object/effect dichotomy is only part of the assessment of the existence of the agreement under Article 4(1) Cartel Act and not of the significant restriction of competition under Article 5 Cartel Act. A highly conceptual and abstract framework of the relationship between the qualitative and quantitative criteria has emerged, which is rather confusing. Below we present the two cases dealt with by the courts in

[72] See FAC, judgment of 12 December 2022, B-141/2012, *Estée Lauder/ASCOPA*, para 6.3.3.3.5.

[73] Idem, para 6.3.2.

[74] Idem, para 6.3.3.4.

an attempt to extract the actual factual criteria used to assess the restriction of competition. We believe that this is what is most relevant to the practitioner.

As explained above, there are very few cases investigated by COMCO. Even fewer have reached the courts. In the *Hallenstadion* case, the COMCO and courts investigated an agreement that was neither horizontal nor vertical. Hallenstadion Zurich, one of the largest concert halls in Switzerland with a market share of 75%, required event organisers to sell at least 50% of their tickets through Ticketcorner, a company in which one of the Hallenstadion's shareholders had an interest. COMCO found that this clause amounted to de facto exclusivity. In addition to the abuse of a dominant position, the agreement was assessed under Article 5(1) of the Cartel Act. Regarding the relationship between the criteria to be taken into account, the FSC stated that:

> Article 5 (1) CartA requires significance only once. This can be determined either quantitatively or qualitatively, but the overall threshold to be achieved to determine the intervention threshold in a case remains the same. Therefore, if the qualitative element is very important, there is little need for a quantitative element. On the other hand, if there are no qualitative elements, or if the qualitative elements are of little weight, the threshold to reach significance must be determined (primarily) by quantitative elements. Quantitative and qualitative significance thus behave like two communicating vessels [reference omitted]. In [Gaba], the FSC then emphasised that the threshold to reach significance can sometimes be determined on the basis of the object of the agreement. Qualitative criteria therefore have priority [references omitted]. [75]

Due to the lack of interoperability between the systems used by the various ticketing service providers and their complexity, the obligation for organisers to sell at least 50% of their tickets through a partner of the Hallenstadion acted as a de facto exclusivity. Such exclusivity was intended to keep other ticketing service providers out of the market. Although the market context surrounding the exclusivity clause was used to qualify its effects, the exclusionary effects of the agreement was implicitly treated as qualitative. [76]

The court's ruling is more important on the quantitative criterion, where it confirms that the market share is the decisive element to be considered. The FSC uses the same market share threshold of 10% for agreements under Article 5 (1) CartA as for horizontal agreements under Article 5(3) CartA. [77] Once this threshold is exceeded, the restriction is significant.

In this case, starting from a narrow market definition (see Sect. 5.3.3.6), the parties to the agreement had very high market shares: Hallenstadion with around 75% and the partner ticketing company with a 60% share of the ticketing market. The quantitative criterion was undoubtedly met, but the FSC left open the question of whether the quantitative elements alone, as in this case, would be sufficient to confirm a substantial restriction of competition.

---

[75] FSC, judgment of 12 February 2020, 2C_113/2017, *Hallenstadion*, para 7.3.1 (free translation).

[76] Idem, para 7.3.2.

[77] Idem, para 7.3.3.

While the FSC refers to both qualitative and quantitative elements to confirm that the agreement significantly restricted competition under Article 5(1) CartA, the reasoning already indicates the predominance of qualitative criteria in the assessment, and the subordinate role of the quantitative criteria, even for genuine Article 5 (1) CartA cases that do not fall under either of the presumptions of Article 5(3) and (4) CartA.

The second case concerned the exchange of information on gross prices, monthly sales and investments between distributors of luxury cosmetics within the framework of a Swiss trade association, ASCOPA, to which the distributors belonged. The participating companies represented over 80% of the market. The COMCO conducted an extensive investigation, including an economic assessment of the impact of the exchange of information on retail prices, which was inconclusive: the variance in retail prices applied by the distributors was significant and therefore no price or quantity fixing under Article 5(3) CartA could be established. COMCO dropped the Article 5(3) case, finding only a significant restriction of competition under Article 5(1). No fine could be imposed. Only one of the 30 companies that had participated in the information exchange appealed the COMCO decision. Eleven years later, this resulted in a 356-page decision by the Federal Administrative Court (FAC). [78]

As explained above, in this case the FAC clarified that in order to prove a significant restriction of competition under Article 5(1) CartA, the assessment must be based on the sum of quantitative and qualitative criteria. The case is important not only because it is one of the few cases on Article 5(1) CartA, but also because it discusses in detail the facts and circumstances relevant to the qualitative and quantitative elements to be considered in assessing whether a restriction is significant.

The assessment of the *qualitative* elements related to the following factors:

- The parameters of competition that are the subject of the exchange: the list of gross prices, turnover and investment expenditure. In particular, prices are an important and meaningful parameter of competition;
- The nature of the information exchange: whether the exchange was regular, whether it concerned current or historical information, whether the information was confidential, whether it was individualised or aggregated, whether there was an obligation on the members to exchange this information or sanctions, etc. While price lists were exchanged annually, sales figures were exchanged monthly for six product categories and semi-annually or annually for a wider range of products. Investment expenditure was exchanged every 6 months;

[78] See FAC, judgment of 12 December 2022, B-141/2012 *Estée Lauder/ASCOPA*. The time lapse is important because in the meantime the FSC had issued the Gaba decision, which considered the absolute territorial protection covered by Article 5(4) CartA as a significant restriction of competition from a qualitative point of view and ruled that, for this reason, no assessment of the effects or the quantitative elements was necessary, even though the presumption had been reversed.

- The ability of the exchange of this information, in particular gross prices, to reduce uncertainty in the market and thus to influence the behaviour of dealers on the retail market;
- The fact that three types of meaningful information were exchanged (prices, sales and capital expenditure).

The assessment of the *quantitative* elements was also conclusive and related to the following factors:

- Internal competition: the degree of competition between the parties to the information exchange, in particular competition on quality and innovative products, which in this case was weak;
- External, actual competition: the degree of competition exerted on the market by companies not participating in the exchange, parallel imports, duty-free shops and direct imports by consumers from abroad, the maturity of the market. In this case, the pressure from these sources of external competition was considered to be very weak;
- Potential competition: the strength of the brands, some of which are considered luxury products, was an argument against potential competition;
- Countervailing power of retailers, which was also considered as weak.

All these elements were considered as a whole, as the sum of qualitative and quantitative criteria. The assessment showed that the restriction of competition resulting from the exchange of information reached the threshold of what is considered to be 'significant' under Article 5(1) of the Cartel Act. As the conditions for justification on efficiency grounds were not met, the information exchange decided by the members of the trade association infringed Article 5 CartA.

The draft law submitted to Parliament in May 2023 [79] proposes to add to Article 5 (1) CartA an additional paragraph stating that "in assessing the significance of the restraint, both qualitative and quantitative criteria shall be taken into account". This was and is a major concern for the COMCO Secretariat, as it would apply to any agreement, even if the presumption of elimination of competition provided for in Article 5(3) and (4) CartA is reversed (see also Sect. 3.5.2).

2.3.2.2 Justification on Grounds of Economic Efficiency

The absence of justification is a cumulative condition for the unlawfulness of an agreement that substantially restricts competition within the meaning of Article 5

[79] See Federal Council, Press release of 24 May 2023, "Loi sur les cartels: le Conseil fédéral adopte le message concernant la révision partielle", available at https://www.admin.ch/gov/fr/accueil/documentation/communiques/communiques-conseil-federal.msg-id-95384.html. The draft law can be found at: https://www.newsd.admin.ch/newsd/message/attachments/78852.pdf. Accessed 25 May 2023.

(1) CartA. In other words, agreements that substantially restrict competition are unlawful only if they are not justified under Article 5(2) CartA.

The function of Article 5 (2) CartA is to allow the justification of agreements that substantially restrict competition but also have pro-competitive effects. The pro-competitive effects are considered in the context of Article 5(2) CartA and not in the examination of the restriction of competition. [80]

Three cumulative conditions must be fulfilled in order to recognise the existence of an economic efficiency reason capable of justifying an agreement having a significant impact on competition: firstly, the existence of at least one of the economic efficiency reasons mentioned in Article 5(2)(a) CartA. Secondly, the necessity of the agreement in order to achieve the economic efficiency reasons mentioned, and thirdly that the agreement does not eliminate effective competition. [81] The three criteria are discussed in Sect. 2.4.1.2 and in more detail in Sect. 4.2.4.

Article 5(2)(a) CartA provides for a list of justifications. The FSC ruled in the *Sammelrevers*, *Buchpreisbindung* and later in the *Altimum* cases that the list of justifications is exhaustive; the listed justifications are, however, alternative in the sense that it is sufficient for one of the justifications to be fulfilled in order for an economic efficiency justification to be accepted. Moreover, the economic efficiency grounds are open-ended, so that, in principle, any objective efficiency gains can be taken into account. Therefore, the scope and concept of the efficiency grounds must be assessed from a broad and not a restrictive perspective. [82]

In ASCOPA the second criterion relating to the necessity of the agreement to achieve economic efficiency has been interpreted very narrowly even for agreements falling exclusively under Article 5(1) CartA, at least for those that would qualify as restrictions by object under Article 4(1) CartA (see Sect. 4.2.4).

2.3.2.3 Elimination of Competition and No Justification on Grounds of Economic Efficiency

Article 5(2)(b) of the CartA refers to the suppression of competition as a negative condition: an agreement is considered to be justified on the grounds of economic efficiency if the agreement does not in any way enable the undertakings concerned to

[80] The function is thus similar to the US *Leegin* case on minimum prices, i.e. to avoid declaring a vertical price agreement per se illegal (FSC, judgment of 18 May 2018, 2C_101/2016, *Altimum*, ATF/BGE 144 II 246, para 10.2). Cf. CJEU, judgment of 29 June 2023, *Super Bock*, C-211/22, ECLI:EU:C:2023:529, para 36, where the CJEU allows pro-competitive effects to be taken into account under Article 101(1) TFEU.

[81] Article 5 (2)(b) CartA; FSC, judgment of 18 May 2018, 2C_101/2016, *Altimum*, ATF/BGE 144 II 246, para 13; FSC, judgment of 28 June 2016, 2C_180/2014, *Gaba*, ATF/BGE 143 II 297, para 7.1.

[82] FSC, judgment of 14 August 2002, 2A.298/2001 and 2A.299/2001, *Sammelrevers*, ATF/BGE 129 II 18, para 10.3 p. 45; FSC, judgement of 6 February 2007, 2A.430/2006 B*uchpreisbindung*, para 13.2; FSC, judgment of 18 May 2018, 2C_101/2016, *Altimum*, ATF/BGE 144 II 246 para 13.2.

eliminate effective competition. None of these agreements can claim to be justified on economic grounds within the meaning of Article 5(2) CartA.

Agreements that eliminate competition fall into two categories. Firstly, agreements falling under Article 5 (3) and (4) CartA, for which the presumption of suppression of competition could not be rebutted. Secondly, the other agreements which are anti-competitive within the meaning of Article 5 (1) CartA.

2.4 Presumptions of Articles 5 (3) and (4) CartA

The Cartel Act then contains two legal presumptions that competition is eliminated, one for horizontal agreements and one for vertical agreements; the former was included in the original version of the act enacted in 1995 and the latter was introduced by Parliament in 2003. Agreements falling under Article 5 (3) and (4) CartA, such as price agreements, for which the presumption of elimination of competition could be rebutted, may be justified on the grounds of economic efficiency. [83]

According to Article 5(3) CartA on horizontal agreements, "the following agreements between actual or potential competitors are presumed to lead to the elimination of effective competition: a. agreements to directly or indirectly fix prices; b. agreements to limit the quantities of goods or services to be produced, purchased or supplied; c. agreements to allocate markets geographically or according to trading partners."

Article 5(4) of the Cartel Act, which was introduced in 2003, states the following with regard to vertical agreements: "the elimination of effective competition is also presumed in the case of agreements between undertakings at different levels of the production and distribution chain regarding fixed or minimum prices, and in the case of agreements contained in distribution contracts regarding the allocation of territories to the extent that sales by other distributors into these territories are not permitted."

In both Article 5(3) and (4) CartA, the legal presumption of elimination of competition is rebuttable. The consequences are different depending on whether the presumption is reversed (Sect. 2.3.1) or not (Sect. 2.3.2). For the sake of clarity, we therefore distinguish between the two cases, even if this means some repetition.

The presumption mechanism of Article 5 (3) and (4) CartA means that the assessment of the individual case focuses on two questions. [84] First, the question of whether the presumed facts, i.e. the constitutive elements of Article 5 (3) and (4) CartA are covered by the presumption. Second, the rebuttal of the presumption,

[83] FSC, judgment of 14 August 2002, 2A.298/2001 and 2A.299/2001, *Sammelrevers*, ATF/BGE 129 II 18, paras 10.3.2 and 10.3.3 concerning horizontal agreements; FSC, judgment of 18 May 2018, 2C_101/2016, *Altimum*, ATF/BGE 144 II 246, para 13.2 concerning vertical agreements.

[84] FSC, judgment of 28 June 2016, 2C_180/2014, *Gaba*, ATF/BGE 143 II 297, para 4.1.

i.e. the question whether there is still (residual) effective competition in the relevant market, as evidenced by sufficient internal competition (i.e. the fact that the freedom of action of the parties to the agreement is not restricted) or sufficient external competition (i.e. the fact that the freedom of action of a third party affected by the agreement is not restricted).

The answer to the first question boils down to identifying whether an agreement or concerted practice as defined by Article 4(1) CartA is covered by Article 5 (3) CartA were parties are current or potential competitors, and or by Article 5 (4) CartA were parties are in vertical relationship. The FSC has ruled that undertakings participating in an agreement falling under either Article 5(3) or Article 5 (4) CartA fall within the scope of Article 49a CartA and are subject to a fine of up to 10% of their turnover in Switzerland in the preceding three financial years, irrespective of whether the presumption of elimination of competition is rebutted or not. The only difference is that if the presumption is overturned, the companies have the (theoretical) possibility to justify the agreement on the grounds of efficiency. In practice, however, such a justification is virtually impossible, so that agreements falling under either Article 5(3) or Article 5(4) CartA are in almost always unlawful and subject to fines. This is why the qualification of an agreement as one caught by Article 5(3) or (4) CartA is important. Horizontal agreements falling under Article 5(3) of the Cartel Act are discussed in Chap. 3, while vertical agreements falling under Article 5(4) of the Cartel Act are presented in detail in Chap. 4.

Section 2.4.1 examines in detail whether the presumption is reversed, and how the restriction of competition is assessed in this case (Sect. 2.4.1.1). This is also important because not only do the parties have the possibility, albeit theoretical, to raise efficiency grounds (Sect. 2.4.1.2), but also the amount of the fine will be lower if the resumption is reversed (Sect. 2.4.1.3). We will deal with both cases separately below. Cases where the presumption is not reversed, thereby confirming the elimination of competition, are discussed in Sect. 2.4.2.

2.4.1 Reversal of the Presumption

The presumption of elimination of competition is not a fiction, and it can be reversed. This is indeed the case in the majority of cases.

The presumption is reversed if the agreement does not eliminate the autonomy of the parties with respect to all relevant parameters of competition. [85] This means that even if some competition remains in only one of the parameters of competition, the presumption is reversed. This is what is known as the criterion of *residual competition*:

[85] FSC, judgment of 14 August 2002, 2A.298/2001 and 2A.299/2001, *Sammelrevers*, ATF/BGE 129 II 18, para 8.3.2.

> If several of these parameters are relevant, residual competition may exist even if it only functions with regard to individual parameters. The presumption under Article 5 (3) CartA is therefore rebutted not only if it is proven that there is unrestricted competition, but also if it is shown that, despite the agreement giving rise to the presumption, there is still a certain - even if significantly impaired - residual or partial competition. [86]

The elimination of competition, the significance of the individual parameters of competition and the reversal of the presumption are always carried out by considering a relevant market for the products that are the subject matter of the agreement. [87] The relevant market forms the basis of the market assessment, which must also take into account the context of other legal and actual barriers to entry. It is also in relation to this relevant market that residual competition should be assessed. In order to interpret what can constitute residual competition, a terminology has been developed under the Cartel Act. Residual competition can be competition that continues to exist between the parties to the agreement or competition that emanates from undertakings that are not party to the agreement. The former is referred to as internal competition and the latter as external competition:

> The presumption laid down in Article 5 (3) CartA can be rebutted by proving that, despite the agreement, there is effective internal or external competition. Effective external competition exists if there are undertakings which are not party to the agreement and thus create competition to such an extent that effective competition does not appear to have been eliminated. Effective internal competition exists if the agreement is not actually complied with or if, despite the agreement giving rise to the presumption, effective competition continues to exist with respect to individual parameters of competition due to other factors. [88]

In this case, a set of vertical agreements between all publishers, distributors and retailers of German-language books, which therefore had a horizontal effect, had fixed resale prices and eliminated all price competition. However, in the bookselling market, quality is of considerable importance in addition to price, so that the elimination of price competition does not necessarily eliminate all competition. This explains why, despite the elimination of price competition, the FSC found that there was sufficient competition between the parties on quality in the form of service, advice and assortment, another important parameter of competition. Competition on quality was therefore the residual competition that made it possible to rebut the assumption that competition had been eliminated. The conditions of entry and exit from the market were also considered to be a key element in the assessment of the existence of a restriction of competition. Finally, resale price maintenance did not raise barriers to entry. Therefore, potential competition was also a criterion to rebut the presumption. [89]

---

[86] Idem, para 8.3.2.

[87] Idem, para 7.2.

[88] FSC, judgment of 14 August 2002, 2A.298/2001 and 2A.299/2001, *Sammelrevers*, ATF/BGE 129 II 18, para 8.1 (free translation, references omitted).

[89] Idem, para 9.5.5.

Residual competition is also relevant to assess whether vertical agreements are presumed to eliminate competition. In the case of vertical agreements, residual competition takes the form of intra- and inter-brand competition.

Intra-brand competition refers to competition between the distributors of the contractual products. [90] The presumption is rebutted in any event where it is established that there is intra-brand competition. [91] It is therefore sufficient to rebut the presumption. For example, an agreement establishing a price band between resellers does not in principle lead to the elimination of all effective competition, so that the presumption must be regarded as reversed, unless the price band was so small that it could not have any effect on competition. [92] The importer's requirement that resellers' discounts not exceed 10% of the recommended price is considered a sufficient price range to rebut the presumption. [93]

Inter-brand competition in the context of a vertical agreement refers to competition between the different brands on the market that compete with the product that is the subject of the distribution agreement. The SFC has left open the question as to whether inter-brand competition alone would be sufficient to rebut the presumption of the elimination of competition. [94]

2.4.1.1 Significant Restriction of Competition Under Article 5(1) CartA

If the presumption of elimination of competition under Article 5(3) and (4) CartA is rebutted, the assessment continues under Article 5(1) and (2) CartA. This differs from the framework of assessment explained in Sect. 2.2.2.1 above.

The Gaba judgment established the principle that agreements falling under Article 5 (3) and (4) CartA by their very nature (qualitative aspect) significantly impair competition within the meaning of Article 5(1) CartA, without it being necessary to examine the effects of the agreement (quantitative aspect). [95] This implies that agreements covered by Article 5(3) and Article 5(4) of the CartA fulfil the qualitative criterion of significance and that it is in principle not necessary to examine the quantitative criterion or the effects; in other words, the examination of the qualitative and quantitative criteria are not cumulative conditions for these agreements. These agreements are considered to be a significant restriction of competition under Article 5(1) of the Cartel Act.

[90] FSC, judgment of 18 May 2018, 2C_101/2016, *Altimum*, ATF/BGE 144 II 246 para 7.2.

[91] Idem, para 7.2; FSC, judgment of 28 June 2016, 2C_180/2014, *Gaba*, ATF/BGE 143 II 297, para 4.2.

[92] FSC, judgment of 18 May 2018, 2C_101/2016, *Altimum*, ATF/BGE 144 II 246, para 7.2.

[93] FSC, judgment of 18 May 2018, 2C_101/2016, *Altimum*, ATF/BGE 144 II 246, para 7.3.

[94] FSC, judgment of 18 May 2018, 2C_101/2016, *Altimum*, ATF/BGE 144 II 246, para 7.2.

[95] FSC, judgment of 28 June 2016, 2C_180/2014, *Gaba*, ATF/BGE 143 II 297, paras 5.1 and 5.2; judgment of 24 October 2017, 2C_63/2016, para 4.3.1; FSC, judgment of 18 May 2018, 2C_101/2016, *Altimum*, ATF/BGE 144 II 246, para 10.3.

Thus, in the Altimum decision, the FSC considers that a binding price recommendation, qualified as a minimum price, in principle significantly restricts competition within the meaning of Article 5(1) Cartel Act by its very nature (qualitative aspect), without it being necessary to examine the effects of the agreement, nor to search for any evidence of a trivial case. [96] Note the use of the word 'in principle', which announces a general rule subject to exceptions, the scope of which has not been clarified by the FSC beyond minor cases.

The assessment of illegality therefore only concerns whether the agreement would meet the conditions for justification on grounds of economic efficiency under Article 5(2) CartA, which will be explained below.

As explained in Sects. 2.2.2.1 and 3.5.2, the draft law submitted to Parliament in May 2023 [97] proposes to modify Article 5(1) CartA by requiring the COMCO to consider both qualitative and quantitative criteria. A new paragraph would be added to Article 5(1) CartA stating that "in assessing the significance of the restraint, both qualitative and quantitative criteria shall be taken into account". This was and is a major concern for the COMCO Secretariat, as it would apply to any agreement, even if the presumption of elimination of competition provided for in Article 5(3) and (4) CartA is reversed (see also Sect. 3.5.2). If the proposal is adopted by Parliament, the assessment of the restriction of competition in agreements falling under Article 5 (3) and (4) of CartA, for which the presumption is reversed, cannot be based solely on qualitative criteria.

2.4.1.2 Justification on Grounds of Economic Efficiency

In order to be justified on the grounds of economic efficiency, the anticompetitive agreement must be necessary in order to achieve the reasons of economic efficiency invoked by the undertakings (Article 5 (2) (a) Cartel Act). In the case of a minimum price agreement, for example, the imposition of a minimum price must be necessary to combat free riding. [98] The FSC understands this test as an examination of the proportionality of the agreement. [99] In practice, the proportionality test boils down to the question of whether there are less anti-competitive means of achieving the

[96] FSC, judgment of 18 May 2018, 2C_101/2016, ATF/BGE 144 II 246 *Altimum*, para 10.3.

[97] See Federal Council, Press release of 24 May 2023, "Loi sur les cartels: le Conseil fédéral adopte le message concernant la révision partielle", available at https://www.admin.ch/gov/fr/accueil/documentation/communiques/communiques-conseil-federal.msg-id-95384.html. The draft law can be found at: https://www.newsd.admin.ch/newsd/message/attachments/78852.pdf. Accessed 25 May 2023.

[98] FSC, judgment of 18 May 2018, 2C_101/2016, *Altimum*, ATF/BGE 144 II 246, para 13.5.3.

[99] FSC, judgment of 18 May 2018, 2C_101/2016, *Altimum*, ATF/BGE 144 II 246, para 13.5; FSC, judgment of 28 June 2016, 2C_180/2014, ATF/BGE 143 II 297 *Gaba*, para 7.1; FSC, judgment of 14 August 2002, 2A.298/2001 and 2A.299/2001, *Sammelrevers*, ATF/BGE 129 II 18, para 10.4.

objectives of economic efficiency. [100] In the case of agreements which are presumed to be restrictive of competition under Article 5 (4) CartA, the FSC requires proof of the indispensability of the economic efficiency gains, as these agreements are by their very nature likely to significantly harm competition. [101]

The company must prove the necessity of the agreement and the absence of less harmful means by virtue of the parties' duty to cooperate. [102] It is not sufficient to merely assert this fact. For example, the FSC criticised the minimum pricing company for failing to demonstrate that it had developed a strategy based on minimum prices to improve the quality of advice and reduce free riding. [103] The *Altimum* judgment, on the other hand, makes it clear that the COMCO is only required to mention the existence of other means capable of achieving the intended purpose, without having to actually prove them; it is then up to the company to explain why the other means mentioned by the COMCO are not suitable for achieving the intended purpose. [104] The following alternative means are mentioned by COMCO and found convincing by the FSC: the use of a selective distribution system and the obligation for the discounter to have staff in the shop. The FSC adds another means: the imposition of a minimum price agreement limited to certain retailers, such as department stores or those selling via the Internet. [105] The COMCO had also proposed the imposition of minimum contractual obligations to provide advice and the limitation of controls to discounters. [106] Section 4.3.1.1 discusses the case in greater detail.

2.4.1.3 Automatic, but Lower Fines

The reversal of the presumption does not alter the qualification of the agreement as one falling within the scope of Article 5(3) or (4) CartA. This type of agreement therefore also falls within the scope of Article 49a CartA. [107] If the agreement cannot be justified under Article 5(2), it is unlawful. According to Article 49a CartA, the parties to the agreement "shall be charged up to 10 per cent of the turnover that it achieved in Switzerland in the preceding three financial years". As the use of the word "shall" indicates, the COMCO has no discretion not to impose a fine. In other

[100] FSC, judgment of 18 May 2018, 2C_101/2016, *Altimum*, ATF/BGE 144 II 246, para 13.5.1; FSC, judgment of 14 August 2002, 2A.298/2001 and 2A.299/2001, *Sammelrevers*, ATF/BGE 129 II 18, para 10.4.

[101] FSC, judgment of 18 May 2018, 2C_101/2016, *Altimum*, ATF/BGE 144 II 246, paras 13.5.3 and 15.

[102] Idem, para 13.5.3.

[103] Ibid.

[104] FSC, judgment of 18 May 2018, 2C_101/2016, *Altimum*, ATF/BGE 144 II 246, para 13.5.3.

[105] Idem, para 13.5.3.

[106] Idem, para 13.5.2.

[107] FSC, judgment of 28 June 2016, 2C_180/2014, *Gaba*, ATF/BGE 143 II 297, para 9.4.6.

words, the fine is automatically imposed, but the level of the fine is lower than if the presumption had not been reversed.

As explained above, the efficiency defence of Article 5(2) CartA is available to the parties to an agreement for which the presumption of elimination of competition is rebutted. If the parties successfully invoke efficiency grounds and fulfil the other conditions of Article 5(2) CartA, the agreement is lawful and not caught by Article 49a CartA.

2.4.2 *Elimination of Competition*

The presumption implies that the agreement eliminates any autonomy of the parties to determine all the decisive parameters of competition.[108] If the autonomy of the parties is not completely removed, even with respect to one of the relevant parameters of competition, the presumption is reversed (Sect. 2.4.1). As explained above, the presumption of elimination of competition can therefore be rebutted, and this is indeed the case in the majority of cases. In certain cases, it is not possible to rebut the presumption. The consequences in such cases are explained below.

As explained above, for agreements falling under the presumptions of Article 5 (3) and (4) CartA, the two safe harbours set out in the SME Notice are not available.

As the presumption of elimination of competition is not rebutted, the agreement cannot be justified on efficiency grounds under Article 5(2) CartA. The agreement is thus unlawful. According to Article 49a CartA, the parties to the agreement "shall be charged up to 10 per cent of the turnover that it achieved in Switzerland in the preceding three financial years". As the use of the word "shall" indicates, the COMCO has no discretion not to impose a fine. In other words, the fine is imposed automatically (Sect. 7.2). The only issue that is subject to a margin of discretion is the level of the basic amount and the reduction of the fine (see Sect. 7.2.3).

List of Documents

COMCO Notice on agreements with limited market impact, Decision of the Competition Commission of 19 December 2005 ('SME Notice')

Ordinance on Sanctions imposed for Unlawful Restraints of Competition (Cartel Act Sanctions Ordinance, CASO; RS 251.5)

[108] FSC, judgment of 14 August 2002, 2A.298/2001 and 2A.299/2001, *Sammelrevers*, ATF/BGE 129 II 18, para 8.3.2.

References

Bovet C (2013) Parallel imports into Switzerland: the case of motor vehicles. J Eur Competition Law Pract 2013(1):83–86

Castillo de la Torre F, Gippini EF (2017) Evidence, proof and judicial review in the EU competition law. Edward Elgar

Chapter 3
Horizontal Agreements

3.1 Introduction

Horizontal agreements are agreements concluded between undertakings operating at the same level of the production and distribution chain. These companies may be actual or potential competitors. They are assessed under Article 5 of the CartA. [1]

As explained in Chap. 2, the analytical framework differs from the EU system of prohibitions and exemptions. There is no statutory exemption that applies irrespective of whether the agreement restricts competition or not. In addition, the threshold set by the courts for a significant restriction of competition under Article 5 (1) CartA is low, resulting in a broad scope of application of Article 5 CartA.

After a brief reminder of the assessment under Article 5 of the CartA and the available COMCO's notices in this introductory section, we will present the most common types of horizontal cooperation agreements.

[1] Article 5 CartA on unlawful agreements affecting competition reads as follows: "1) Agreements that significantly restrict competition in a market for specific goods or services and are not justified on grounds of economic efficiency, and all agreements that eliminate effective competition are unlawful. 2) Agreements affecting competition are deemed to be justified on grounds of economic efficiency if: a. they are necessary in order to reduce production or distribution costs, improve products or production processes, promote research into or dissemination of technical or professional know-how, or exploit resources more rationally; and b. they will under no circumstances enable the parties involved to eliminate effective competition. 3) The following agreements between actual or potential competitors are presumed to lead to the elimination of effective competition: a. agreements to directly or indirectly fix prices; b. agreements to limit the quantities of goods or services to be produced, purchased or supplied; c. agreements to allocate markets geographically or according to trading partners. 4) The elimination of effective competition is also presumed in the case of agreements between undertakings at different levels of the production and distribution chain regarding fixed or minimum prices, and in the case of agreements contained in distribution contracts regarding the allocation of territories to the extent that sales by other distributors into these territories are not permitted."

P. Këllezi, *Competition Law in Switzerland*,
https://doi.org/10.1007/978-3-031-45117-1_3

The discussions and arguments in the courts focus on the scope of Article 5 (3) CartA, which covers agreements that are subject to fines under Article 49a CartA. Other agreements, which are only covered by Article 5(1) CartA, do not trigger direct sanctions for the parties, unless the parties continue an agreement that has already been declared illegal by a COMCO decision. In other words, the risk of violating Article 5(3) CartA is a high fine and the nullity of the clause or agreement, whereas the risk of violating Article 5(1) CartA is only the nullity of the clause or agreement and damages. Therefore, the distinction between agreements falling under Article 5(3) and other agreements not falling within Article 5(3) is important for practitioners.

The main steps of the risk assessment are as follows:

First, ask whether the agreement falls under the presumption of Article 5(3) of the CartA. If it does, companies risk fines. From a civil law perspective, the clause containing the restriction may be considered null and void and therefore unenforceable and potentially subject to damages.

Second, if the presumption of Article 5(3) CartA is reversed, the agreement will be presumed to significantly restrict competition within the meaning of Article 5 (1) CartA without any further assessment. If the restriction is not justified on efficiency grounds (Article 5(2) CartA), the agreement is unlawful and remains subject to fines pursuant to Article 49a CartA.

Third, if the restriction does not fall within the scope of Article 5(3) CartA, the companies do not risk fines. The question is whether the agreement or clause restricts competition within the meaning of Article 5(1) CartA. In this respect, two questions have to be asked: is there a qualitative or quantitative restriction? (see Sect. 2.2.2.1 above) If the answer to one or both of these questions is in the affirmative, the agreement restricts competition and a third question should be asked: whether the restriction is justified on efficiency grounds (Article 5(2) of the CartA). If this is not the case, the agreement is unlawful. The clause will be unenforceable and the companies may be liable to damages.

Article 6 of the Cartel Act empowers the COMCO to issue notices specifying the conditions under which agreements restricting competition are justified on the grounds of economic efficiency within the meaning of Article 5(2) of the Cartel Act. The provision specifically mentions research and development agreements, specialisation and rationalisation agreements, including agreements on the use of cost accounting systems, agreements granting exclusive rights to purchase or sell certain products or exclusive licences for intellectual property rights, and agreements aimed at improving the competitiveness of small and medium-sized enterprises.

COMCO has issued only a general notice on SMEs and a Notice on calculation schemes specifically applicable to horizontal agreements. [2] The Notice on

[2]Notice on the conditions for the admissibility of agreements on the use of calculation schemes under the Cartel Act, Decision of the Competition Commission of 4 May 1998 (hereafter ‘Notice on calculation schemes’).

calculation schemes is relevant to the assessment of information exchange and other types of horizontal cooperation involving the exchange of data for the purposes of calculating tariffs and is dealt with in the section on information exchange (Sect. 3.6.2 below). The COMCO has adopted a sectoral Notice on homologation and sponsoring of sports articles sports articles, [3] which we will discuss below at Sect. 3.9. There are no notices on R&D, production, specialisation, and other horizontal cooperation agreements. The SME Notice briefly mentions that joint production agreements leading to expansion/diversification of production and quality improvement, as well as joint research and development, can improve competitiveness by increasing efficiency, but does not specify the assessment criteria. [4]

The SME Notice [5] applies to all type of agreements, whether vertical, horizontal, or other. The SME Notice established two safe harbours for undertakings, one relating to market shares and the other applicable to micro-enterprises, both of which are only available for agreements that do not fall under the presumptions of Article 5(3) CartA. According to the first safe harbour, agreements have a limited impact on the market if the combined market share of the parties to a horizontal agreement does not exceed 10% on any of the relevant markets affected by the agreement. The second safe harbour applies to agreements involving only micro-enterprises. Horizontal agreements involving only micro-enterprises within the meaning of the definition of micro-enterprises are as a rule unlikely to have a significant impact on competition within the meaning of Article 5 CartA. A micro-enterprise is defined as a company with fewer than 10 employees and an annual turnover in Switzerland of less than CHF 2 million. [6] The safe harbours are qualified by the use of "in principle" and "as a general rule", which allow for exceptions to the safe harbour. This means that COMCO will not generally open an investigation but does not provide legal certainty in all cases.

3.2 Price Fixing

The first type of horizontal agreement which is presumed to eliminate competition is expressly provided for in Article 5(3)(a) of the CartA, which states that agreements between actual or potential competitors which directly or indirectly fix prices are presumed to lead to the elimination of effective competition.

[3] Notice on the Homologation and Sponsoring of Sports Equipment, Decision of the Competition Commission of 15 December 1997 (hereafter 'Notice on sports equipment').

[4] Notice on agreements with limited market impact, Decision of the Competition Commission of 19 December 2005 (hereafter 'SME Notice').

[5] SME Notice, para 2(2) (a) and (b).

[6] SME Notice, paras 4 and 5.

A price fixing agreement exists when it fixes the final price of a product or when it fixes individual components or elements of the price. [7] A price agreement exists if it directly or indirectly fixes the final price of a product or if it fixes individual components or elements of the price, such as gross prices, price ranges, margins, rebates, discounts, prices of individual components of a final product, prices of shipping or transport or other charges. [8] The method or instrument used is irrelevant, so price lists, the fixing of ratios between the prices of different products, surcharges, discounts, methods of payment such as netting or commission schemes, which are used to determine prices or price elements, also constitute price agreements.

If the final purchase or selling price is fixed, it is covered by the presumption of Article 5(3) CartA. The presumption applies to components or elements of the price if the agreement on those components or elements is relevant when individual undertakings set their market price. [9] The question of whether the fixing of gross prices is covered by Article 5(3) of the Cartel Act depends on whether the undertakings that had fixed the gross prices uses them to determine margins and final market prices and whether the communication of gross prices to customers is a relevant competitive parameter in the market. In other words, the fixing of gross prices falls under the presumption of elimination of competition under Article 5(3) of the Cartel Act if such prices are a relevant piece of information in the market competition between the participating undertakings. An agreement to fix prices may also exist where the parties have the possibility to determine individually part of the price or one of the elements of the price, for example, where they fix a price range, minimum or maximum margins, rebates or gross prices. However, it is not necessary to assess or prove that the agreement has actually led to the same or similar price in the market. In other words, it is not necessary to establish that the agreement has an effect on the market.

The scope of application of Article 5(3)(a) CartA is broad, i.e. as soon as there is evidence that the content of the agreement concerns market prices, elements or components of prices, the agreement is presumed to eliminate competition and is subject to fines. Article 5(3) is broadly interpreted (see also Sect. 3.4). [10] The process of subsuming the facts to the rule of Article 5(3) CartA is hence not the same as the restriction by object under Article 101 TFEU (Sect. 2.1), which is construed restrictively: [11] as stated by the CJEU, "the concept of restriction of competition 'by object' can be applied only to certain types of coordination between undertakings which reveal a sufficient degree of harm to competition for it to be found that there is no need to examine their effects, as otherwise the Commission would be exempted from the obligation to prove the actual effects on the market of agreements

[7] FSC, judgment of 14 August 2002, 2A.298/2001 and 2A.299/2001, *Sammelrevers*, ATF/BGE 129 II 18, para 6.5.

[8] COMCO decision of 10 December 2018 *KTB-Werke*, LPC 2020/1 p. 78, para 844.

[9] COMCO decision of 29 June 2015, *Badezimmer*, LPC 2019/3a p. 606, paras 521 and 522.

[10] COMCO decision of 23 May 2022 *Concessionari Volkswagen*, para 500.

[11] CJEU, judgment of 2 April 2020, *Budapest Bank*, C-228/18, ECLI:EU:C:2020:265, para 54.

which are in no way established to be, by their very nature, harmful to the proper functioning of competition." [12] In contrast to the assessment under Article 101 TFEU, there is no requirement to assess the economic and legal context of which the agreement forms part under Article 5(3) CartA. [13] As a result, while several agreements on multilateral interchange fees in the card payment system were considered to be a restriction by effect under EU law, COMCO and its Secretariat considers these agreements to be price fixing agreements under Article 5(3) CartA. [14]

As explained in Sect. 2.4.1 above, the presumption of elimination can be reversed and the agreement is assessed under Article 5(1) CartA. However, price agreements are presumed to be significant restrictions of competition from a qualitative point of view, without the need for the competition authority to prove that the agreement restricts competition from a quantitative point of view or to prove effects on competition. The reversal of the presumption also opens the way for justification on the grounds of economic efficiency under Article 5(2) CartA, which is difficult, although not impossible, as the payment card cases have shown. [15] If the agreement is not justified on grounds of economic efficiency within the meaning of Article 5 (2) CartA, the participating undertakings are subject to fines under Article 49a CartA.

Although the majority of price-fixing investigations concern domestic cartels, with a high number of investigations into bid rigging in the construction industry, COMCO also pursues international cartels with an impact on domestic markets, such as lately the LIBOR, TIBOR, EURIBOR and Spread derivatives cartels. [16]

---

[12] Idem, paras 37, 54.

[13] Idem, para 51.

[14] See COMCO Secretariat final report of 16 August 2017, *Mastercard Secure Digital Debit Interchange Fee (SDDIF)*, para 51. See also COMCO decision of 1 December 2014 *Kreditkarten Domestische Interchange Fees II (KKDMIF II)*, LPC 2015/2, p. 16, para 81. COMCO Secretariat final report of 31 Mai 2011, *Maestro Fallback Interchange Fee und Debit MasterCard Interchange Fee*, LPC 2012/4, p. 765 para 211.

[15] See COMCO Secretariat final report of 16 August 2017, *Mastercard Secure Digital Debit Interchange Fee (SDDIF)*, LPC 2017/4, p. 542.

[16] Press release of 16 December 2021, 'COMCO fines Swiss franc LIBOR cartel: The Competition Commission has closed its investigation related to the Swiss franc LIBOR benchmark with an amicable settlement and imposes total fines of approximately CHF 33.9 million'. Press release of 21 December 2016, 'COMCO fines banks for participating in Yen LIBOR/Euroyen TIBOR cartels: The Competition Commission has closed its investigation against certain banks related to interest rate derivatives in yen with an amicable settlement and imposes total fines of approximately CHF 14.4 million.' Press release of 21 December 2016, 'COMCO fines Swiss franc Spread cartel: The Competition Commission (COMCO) has closed its investigation related to the bid-ask Spread on Swiss franc interest rate derivatives with an amicable settlement and imposes total fines of approximately CHF 5.4 million.' Press release of 21 December 2016, 'COMCO fines banks for participating in the EURIBOR cartel: The Competition Commission (COMCO) has closed its investigation against certain banks related to interest rate derivatives in euro with an amicable settlement and imposes total fines of approximately CHF 45.3 million.' See the corresponding cartel investigations in the EU, press releases of the European Commission of 4 December 2013 'Antitrust: Commission fines banks Euro 1.49 billion for participating in cartels in the interest

3.3 Quantity Restriction

Agreements between actual or potential competitors to limit the quantities of goods or services to be produced, purchased or supplied are the second type of agreements that are presumed to lead to the elimination of effective competition under Article 5 (3)(b) of the CartA.

The limitation of quantities covers actual production or supply, or agreements aimed at reducing production capacity or commitments not to increase production or supply capacity. Agreements not to supply certain customers, such as boycotts, or to limit the supply of certain goods or services, including the use of infrastructure, are covered by the presumption. The limitation of quantities and capacities may be direct or indirect, and therefore all types of clauses in cooperation or joint venture agreements which risk having a quantity reducing effect are likely to be caught by the presumption of elimination of competition of Article 5(3)(b) of the CartA. This also applies to agreements on joint production, specialisation, or marketing cooperation.

There are relatively few cases of Article 5(3)(b) CartA, but the following case shows that its scope is very broad and covers a wide range of clauses used in cooperation agreements. A clause in a cooperation agreement between Swisscom, the largest telecom operator in Switzerland, and a local electricity company not to include indoor cables in the agreement for the construction of a fibre optic network was considered to be a quantitative restriction under Article 5(3)(b) of the Cartel Act, as this part of the indoor infrastructure could not be rented or used by third parties for the transmission of telecommunications services. [17] In the same agreement, the obligation to supply only customers purchasing a minimum quantity of transmission services excluded other telecommunications operators from access to the optical fibre market and was therefore qualified as a quantity restriction agreement within the meaning of Article 5(3)(b) of the CartA. [18] Finally, a non-compete clause between the parties in the same agreement was also considered to be a quantitative restriction as it limited the ability of the parties to build telecommunications infrastructure with third parties. [19]

The second step in the assessment of such an agreement is to examine whether the presumption of elimination can be rebutted. If this is the case, the agreement will be assessed under Article 5(1) CartA and the main discussion will focus on the justification on the grounds of economic efficiency within the meaning of Article 5 (2) CartA (Sect. 2.4.1.2). If the agreement is not justified on the grounds of economic

---

rate derivatives industry', available at https://ec.europa.eu/commission/presscorner/detail/en/IP_13_1208. Accessed 10 May 2023.

[17] COMCO Secretariat report of 16 February 2012 *FTTH Freiburg*, LPC 2012/2 p. 171, paras 86 and 87. See COMCO Secretariat report of 5 September 2011 in *Glasfaser St. Gallen, Zürich, Bern, Luzern*, LPC 2012/2, p. 209.

[18] COMCO Secretariat report of 16 February 2012 *FTTH Freiburg*, LPC 2012/2 p. 171, paras 108–114.

[19] Idem, paras 88 and 89.

efficiency within the meaning of Article 5(2) CartA, the participating undertakings are subject to fines under Article 49a CartA. This risk may lead undertakings to seek advice from the Secretariat of the COMCO, [20] which is not binding on the COMCO, or to submit a formal notification of the restraint of competition to the COMCO prior to the implementation of the agreement to avoid fines (Chap. 7). In the latter case, the COMCO has 5 months to object to the implementation of the agreement by opening an investigation. However, such advice or notification is not mandatory, and the companies are free to assess and ultimately bear the risks themselves.

3.4 Market Sharing and Customer Allocation

The third type of horizontal agreement that is presumed to eliminate competition under Article 5(3)(c) of the CartA is an agreement between actual or potential competitors to share markets either geographically or according to trading partners.

A market-sharing agreement divides a territory—a geographical area such as a country, region, city or group of cities—between the parties. The parties may be obliged or committed to limit their sales in their allocated territory or not to offer, sell or buy in a territory allocated to the other party.

In a customer allocation agreement, companies agree to allocate customers among themselves by undertaking to sell only to certain customers or not to sell to other groups of customers.

COMCO considers that Article 5(3)(c) of the CartA must be interpreted broadly as it covers the direct or indirect allocation of territories or customers. [21] The means used are irrelevant, what matters is the effect on the market. For instance, market allocation may be direct or indirect, such as the application of a different (higher) price to non-allocated territories. Similarly, customer allocation includes agreements that indirectly lead to customer allocation, such as an agreement to carry out marketing activities only in certain regions or not at other locations, or non-compete clauses in shareholder agreements. [22] Finally, agreements that specify the mechanism, criteria and procedure for allocating counterparties, without necessarily deciding which counterparties or customers will be allocated to which participating undertaking, are also considered to constitute market sharing within the meaning of Article 5(3)(c) CartA. [23] If the undertakings agree among themselves on the criteria for the allocation of territories or customers, this agreement and any

[20] Article 23(2) CartA.

[21] COMCO decision of 23 May 2022 *Concessionari Volkswagen*, para 500.

[22] COMCO decision of 6 December 2021, *Belagswerke Bern,* para 726, see Sect. 3.7 below.

[23] COMCO decision of 19 November 2007 *Strassenbeläge Tessin*, LPC 2008/1, p. 85, para 91.

specific agreement implementing it will be considered as a global agreement on the allocation of territories or customers. [24]

There have been many cases of market allocation, mainly bid rigging (Sect. 3.5.1). [25] Beyond bid-rigging, in a recent case involving a general importer of vehicles in Switzerland and its dealers in the canton of Ticino, [26] the COMCO found a global agreement allocating public tenders to the dealers according to their sales targets. The general importer and its distributors agreed to allocate public tenders in the Canton of Ticino to the general importer and to share the profits between them. In some cases, the general importer and its distributors decided which of them would participate in public tenders in the Canton of Ticino and for which type of vehicles. In addition, the participants divided their territories among themselves by agreeing not to participate in public tenders outside their local territories, not to make more advantageous offers to customers from areas outside their territories and/or not to carry out promotional activities in each other's territories. The presumption of elimination of competition by market allocation under Article 5(3)(c) of the CartA was reversed due to sufficient external competition, but in principle such agreements significantly restricted competition within the meaning of Article 5(1) of the CartA and could not be justified on grounds of economic efficiency under Article 5(2) of the CartA. As a result, the fine imposed on the general importer corresponded to a basic amount of 7%, which in absolute terms amounted to more than CHF 10 million. The basic amount of the other participants varied between 1% and 3%, depending on their level of involvement in the cartel.

As explained in Sect. 2.4.1 above, the presumption of elimination can be reversed and the agreement is then assessed under Article 5(1) of the CartA. Market allocation agreements are presumed to be qualitatively significant restrictions of competition within the meaning of Article 5(1) Cartel Act. The reversal of the presumption opens the way for a justification on the grounds of economic efficiency under Article 5(2) CartA (Sect. 2.4.1.2), but this is unlikely to succeed. If the agreement cannot be justified on the grounds of economic efficiency within the meaning of Article 5(2) CartA, the participating undertakings are subject to fines pursuant to Article 49a CartA (Section 7.2).

[24] COMCO decision of 8 July 2016 *Bauleistungen See-Gaster*, LPC 2020/3a, p. 880, paras 1219–1221.

[25] See for instance COMCO decision of 19 November 2007 *Strassenbeläge Tessin*, LPC 2008/1, p. 85. COMCO decision of 8 July 2016 *Bauleistungen See-Gaster*, LPC 2020/3a, p. 880.

[26] COMCO decision of 23 May 2022 *Concessionari Volkswagen*, paras 498 ff.

3.5 Bid Rigging and Consortia in the Construction Industry

COMCO and its Secretariat have attached great importance to bid-rigging cartels. These are mainly domestic cartels in the construction industry. One of the four divisions of the Secretariat of COMCO is dedicated to investigations in the construction industry, covering building construction, civil engineering, road and motorway construction and specialised construction activities. The Secretariat has investigated a number of cartels and COMCO has imposed several fines in this sector. A number of cases have been appealed to the FAC, but many have not yet reached the FSC. In this area, COMCO has consolidated its practice of global and lasting agreements. This will be covered in Sect. 3.5.1 below.

The broad scope of Article 5(3) CartA, which leads to fines, has raised concerns in the construction sector, where many SMEs operate in local markets. These companies claim that they need to cooperate with each other, sometimes forming consortia, and that the wide scope of Article 5(3) CartA and its extensive interpretation have significantly increased legal uncertainty and therefore their risks. The debate has taken on a political dimension with the introduction in Parliament of a proposal [27] to amend Article 5 CartA, which would oblige the COMCO and its Secretariat to examine both qualitative and quantitative elements of the agreements when deciding whether to prohibit or fine any type of cartel: in particular, the quantitative elements relate to effects on the market, but it is not clear what such elements would be. Obviously, such a proposal is vehemently opposed by the COMCO Secretariat, the investigative arm of COMCO, which fears that it will make its investigations more burdensome. This has led to a rather flexible approach to the assessment of consortia by the COMCO Secretariat in the last few years, at least in appearance, and to a draft law that proposes to amend Article 4(1) CartA. The discussion is relevant to all types of horizontal cooperation and we have therefore chosen to present the broad lines of the COMCO Secretariat's assessment of consortia in Sect. 3.5.2 below.

3.5.1 *Bid Rigging*

The cartels investigated by the COMCO took various forms, ranging from the practice of bid rotation to that of covering bids. In the case of bid rotation, the companies agree to take it in turns to win the contract, which is often the case when

[27] Motion 18.4282, of 13 December 2018: '*La révision de la loi sur les cartels doit prendre en compte des critères tant qualitatifs que quantitatifs pour juger de l'illicéité d'un accord*' (The revision of the Cartel Act should take into account both qualitative and quantitative criteria for judging the illegality of an agreement.), available at https://www.parlament.ch/fr/ratsbetrieb/suche-curia-vista/geschaeft?AffairId=20184282. Accessed 15 May 2023. See the content of the draft law submitted to the Parliament in Sect. 3.5.2.

tenders are organised regularly, albeit for small volumes. This was the case in bid gigging cartels in Ticino and Argau. [28]

In a number of cases, there were cover bids or fictitious bids in which the participating company submitted a slightly higher or much higher offer. Another related practice was the exchange of information during the preparation of bids, whereby companies would send each other the calculation of the bids in order to save time; often companies that were not interested in the construction project would submit a (slightly higher) bid in order to ensure their presence in the market, especially when private companies asked them to submit a bid.

These cartels included elements of market sharing and customer allocation, where companies agreed who would serve certain categories of customers or certain geographic markets. Companies also agreed not to bid, but as far as we know there are no cases of companies withdrawing their bids. All these cases are considered as hardcore cartels within the meaning of Article 5(3)(a) CartA.

In the case of public tenders, there is a particularly high expectation that bidders will act in good faith. The FAC has held that bidders undermine the competitive objective of public procurement law if they arbitrarily manipulate, or even attempt to manipulate, the free will of the bidder by contacting each other. [29] But the private companies are also protected in their expectations, and the same is applicable to the private offers as well. The agreement to rig the award of a public or private contract is presumed to eliminate competition even if it is unsuccessful and the public contract is awarded to another undertaking not participating in the cartel. [30] The companies involved in an unsuccessful cartel will be fined, although the basic amount will be lower.

The total amount of the fines imposed was in several cases in the millions, such as in 2018, when the companies involved in a cartel in the region of Basse-Engadin were fined CHF 7.5 million; [31] in 2016, the companies involved in a cartel in the See-Gaster region were fined CHF 5.5 million; [32] in 2011, the companies involved in a cartel in the canton of Argovie were fined CHF 3.8 million. [33]

---

[28] COMCO, decision of 19 November 2007, *Pavimentazioni stradali in Ticino*, LPC 2008/1, p. 50. COMCO, decision of 16 December 2011, *Wettbewerbsabredenin Strassen- und Tiefbauim Kanton Aargau*, LPC 2012/2, 270.

[29] FAC, judgment of 25 June 2018, B-807/2012 *Wettbewerbsabreden im Strassen- und Tiefbau im Kanton Aargau, ERNE*, para 9.3.2.

[30] FAC, judgment of 25 June 2018, B-807/2012 *Wettbewerbsabreden im Strassen- und Tiefbau im Kanton Aargau, ERNE*, para 9.3.4.2.

[31] COMCO decision of 26 March 2018, *Hoch- und Tiefbauleistungen Engadin I*, LPC 2019/2, p. 322.

[32] COMCO decision of 8 July 2016, *Bauleistungen See-Gaster*, LPC 2020/3a, p. 880.

[33] COMCO decision of 16 December 2011, *Wettbewerbsabreden im Strassen- und Tiefbau im Kanton Aargau*, LPC 2012/2, p. 270.

3.5.2 Consortia

As explained above, the assessment of consortia has raised concerns, particularly among SMEs. The COMCO Secretariat, wishing to reassure industry and avoid amending Article 5 CartA, has used its discretion to narrowly interpret the scope of Article 4(1) CartA on consortium agreements in order to preserve the broad scope of Article 5(3) CartA, which applies to all horizontal cartels. Consortia are not considered unlawful in principle, according to COMCO. [34]

The COMCO Secretariat explained its position in detail in a final report of an investigation into long-term consortia which it had discovered during a cartel investigation, but which it handled separately to distinguish them from price-fixing cartels. [35] The investigation concerned consortia between two undertakings.

The existence of an agreement depends on whether the consortia have as their object or effect a restriction of competition within the meaning of Article 4(1) of the Cartel Act. This depends on whether each company is able to bid on its own and whether the consortium reduces the number of bids compared to not having consortia: [36]

- If neither of the two consortium partners would have submitted a bid, the consortium increases the number of bids in the market. Such a consortium does not restrict competition; on the contrary, it strengthens it. There is therefore no agreement within the meaning of Article 4(1) of the CartA.
- If one of the consortium partners would have submitted a bid but the other would not, the consortium does not lead to more or fewer bids in the market and therefore does not generally restrict competition. There is again no agreement within the meaning of Article 4(1) CartA.
- If each partner in the consortium would have submitted a bid independently, the consortium reduces the number of bids. In this case, there is usually a restriction of competition by object or effect and there is in principle an agreement within the meaning of Article 4(1) CartA.

---

[34] COMCO Annual Report 2013, LPC 2014/1, p. 5, para 3.1.3: "Consortia are and remain in principle unproblematic from the point of view of competition law. Consortia are certainly 'agreements' in the common sense of the term. In most cases, however, they are not competition agreements within the meaning of Article 4 (1) CartA, as this would require that they have the object or effect of restricting competition. On the contrary, consortia often promote competition by giving companies (especially SMEs) the opportunity to submit a bid and carry out a project. Article 5 CartA, which determines which agreements are unlawful and which contain a partial prohibition, applies only to agreements within the meaning of Article 4 (1) CartA. The burden of proof for the existence of such an agreement under current and future law lies with the competition authorities. Only in exceptional cases do consortia restrict competition and are to be qualified as agreements within the meaning of the Cartel Act and examined more closely."

[35] COMCO Secretariat final report of 6 October 2020, *Dauer-ARGE Graubünden*, LPC 2021/1, p. 90.

[36] Idem, para 244.

Consortia that reduce the number of bids compared to the situation without consortia are agreements that fall under the presumption of Article 5(3)(a) and/or (c) CartA and have to be assessed as such. The relevant market must be assessed to determine whether the presumption of elimination of competition is reversed (Sect. 2.4.1), and this is generally the case if there is sufficient external competition from other companies that regularly bid. Since consortia are generally considered to be pro-competitive, as the COMCO itself has stated, the question arises as to whether they can be regarded as a significant restriction of competition from a qualitative point of view under Article 5(1) CartA. The COMCO Secretariat leaves this question open, but answers in the affirmative in the specific case, since the parties submitted individual offers in one third of the cases. [37] The way out of the unlawfulness is the efficiency justification of Article 5(2) CartA, which also examines whether the consortia submitted bids that were 'more advantageous than the individual bids'. In the present case, the COMCO Secretariat does not carry out a full assessment, but proposes some measures and general rules which, if followed and respected by the companies, allowed it to close the investigation. The measures are fact-specific and cannot be applied in all cases, but they can provide an indication of the type of assessment expected from the companies:

- The two companies were allowed to bid together as a consortium for all road projects put out to open or selective tender at cantonal level. If the canton does not put all road projects out to open or selective tender, the companies must assess for each individual tender whether a joint bid as a consortium is appropriate, including an assessment of their cross-project risk.
- The two companies were allowed to bid jointly for municipal and private road projects if: one or both companies do not meet all the eligibility criteria, or it is objectively impossible for one or both companies to carry out the project alone, and this is obvious to an external professional in the sector without having to make further enquiries (i.e. in particular without asking the companies).

In the same report, the COMCO Secretariat provides some information on the exchange of information between companies that are in discussions to form a consortium. The exchange of information that is necessary to assess whether the parties may form a consortium in a specific case is not problematic under the Cartel Act. However, other information that is not necessary for the assessment of whether the parties may form a consortium, such as the parties' intention or interest in other projects or their business strategy, is problematic. [38]

The concerns raised about consortia, especially in the construction industry, are reflected in the draft law submitted to Parliament in May 2023. [39] The main

[37] Idem, LPC 2021/1, p. 90, para 189.

[38] COMCO Secretariat final report of 6 October 2020, *Dauer-ARGE Graubünden*, LPC 2021/1, p. 90, paras 229 ff.

[39] See Federal Council, Press release of 24 May 2023, "Loi sur les cartels: le Conseil fédéral adopte le message concernant la révision partielle", available at https://www.admin.ch/gov/fr/accueil/

amendment concerns Article 5(1) CartA, which is proposed to be supplemented by an additional paragraph stating that "in assessing the significance of the restraint, both qualitative and quantitative criteria shall be taken into account". This was and remains a major concern for the COMCO Secretariat, as it would apply to any agreement, not just consortia. The Federal Council, while expressing concern that the amendment would weaken public enforcement of the Cartel Act, has introduced two other amendments which are believed to be sufficient to address the concerns relating to consortia between SMEs. The first concerns Article 4(1) CartA on the concept of agreements and concerted practices, which is supplemented by a new paragraph stating that "agreements and concerted practices on consortia which enable or strengthen effective competition are not considered to be agreements affecting competition". This is in line with COMCO practice as described in this section. The other amendment concerns in-depth investigations under Article 27 of the CartA, which allows the Secretariat to refrain from opening or continuing an investigation. The proposed amendment reads: "If there are indications of minor infringements, an investigation may not be opened or an investigation that has been opened may be closed". The Federal Council hopes that the latter two amendments will be sufficient to address concerns about consortia and to convince Parliament to reject any amendment to Article 5 CartA.

Under EU competition law, the number of bids and whether each company could have submitted a bid on its own is assessed at the stage of restriction of competition, not at the stage of the existence of an agreement. The new Horizontal Guidelines [40] contain a separate chapter on bidding consortia and their assessment is much clearer than in the previous Guidelines. A consortia agreement is an agreement within the meaning of Article 101 TFEU, but the main question to be asked is whether it restricts competition by object or by effect, depending on the content of the agreement and the specific circumstances of the case. Consortia do not restrict competition within the meaning of Article 101(1) TFEU if the parties could not bid individually. [41] The Horizontal Guidelines distinguish between production consortia and commercialisation consortia, the latter being subject to rules on the limitation of the number of bids: a joint bid by two or more parties capable of bidding individually would in principle amount to a restriction by object; if there is only one party that could bid individually, in principle there is no restriction by object. [42] Regarding Article 101(3) TFEU, the Commission concludes that "the criteria of Article 101(3) can be fulfilled if the joint participation to the tender allows the parties to submit an offer that is more competitive than the offers, they would have submitted alone – in terms of prices and/or quality –

documentation/communiques/communiques-conseil-federal.msg-id-95384.html. The draft law can be found at: https://www.newsd.admin.ch/newsd/message/attachments/78852.pdf. Accessed 25 May 2023.

[40] Guidelines on the applicability of Article 101 of the Treaty on the Functioning of the European Union to horizontal cooperation agreements, OJ 21.7.2023 C 259, p. 1, paras 347–359.

[41] Idem, para 352.

[42] Idem, para 357.

and the benefits in favour of the consumers and the contracting entity outweigh the restrictions to competition." [43]

Against this background, the current practice of the COMCO and the change proposed by the new draft law will result in a further divergence from EU competition law, with the Swiss Cartel Act potentially being more lenient towards consortia.

3.6 Exchange of Information and Calculation Schemes

There have been few cases of information exchange and COMCO has not published any notices on the subject, with the exception of those on calculation schemes, which are discussed below.

3.6.1 Information Exchange

An agreement to exchange information between undertakings, either alone or within a trade association, is considered to be an agreement or a concerted practice within the meaning of Article 4(1) CartA. In ASCOPA, the FAC found that such an agreement, which involved the exchange of gross prices, monthly sales and investments, had as its object the restriction of competition within the meaning of Article 4 (1) CartA. [44] The FAC came to the same conclusion with regard to the regular monthly exchange of information on existing and future credit interest rates and fees between car leasing companies: such an exchange had as its object the restriction of competition within the meaning of Article 4(1) of the Cartel Act. [45] In a recent case, the COMCO examined the market structure, product homogeneity, the nature and scope of the information exchanged, as well as its frequency and duration, in order to confirm that the exchange of information in a cross-directorship situation was capable of restricting competition within the meaning of Article 4(1) of the Cartel Act, without specifying whether the restriction was by object or effect (see also Sect. 3.8). [46]

The central and most debated question is whether the exchange of price information is covered by the presumption of Article 5(3)(a) CartA. The decision practice of the COMCO and the case law has been hesitant, rejecting it in the ASCOPA case

[43] Idem, para 359.

[44] FAC, judgment of 12 December 2022, B-141/2012 *Estée Lauder/ASCOPA*, para 4.6.6. The COMCO had found no price alignment and therefore no evidence of a price-fixing agreement under Article 5(3) CartA, and the FAC was therefore not asked to assess this provision.

[45] FAC, judgment of 5 June 2023, B-4596/2019 *CA Auto Finance Suisse SA*, para 5.3.3.8.

[46] COMCO decision of 6 December 2021, *Belagswerke Bern*, para 751. See Sect. 3.8 below.

and in some bid-rigging cases, but confirming it in the more extensive exchanges of information that took place in the car leasing sector. The trend in case law shows a clear tendency to consider the regular exchange of current and future prices as covered by the presumption of Article 5(3)(a) CartA, as set out below.

ASCOPA concerned distributors of luxury cosmetics who exchanged gross prices, monthly sales and investments within the framework of a Swiss trade association, i.e. ASCOPA. [47] The participating companies represented over 80% of the market. The COMCO conducted an extensive investigation, including an economic assessment of the impact of the exchange of information on retail prices, which was inconclusive: the variance in retail prices applied by the distributors was significant and therefore no price or quantity fixing under Article 5(3) CartA could be established. COMCO Secretariat dropped the Article 5(3) case, finding only a significant restriction of competition under Article 5(1) CartA, which is not subject to fines. The decision in this case was made before the confirmation of the Gaba case by the FSC.

As explained in Sect. 2.3.2.1, the assessment was based on the sum of quantitative and qualitative criteria. The assessment of the *qualitative* elements related to the nature of information exchanged between the parties:

- The parameters of competition that are the subject of the exchange: the list of gross prices, turnover and investment expenditure. In particular, prices are an important and meaningful parameter of competition;
- The nature of the information exchange: whether the exchange was regular, whether it concerned current or historical information, whether the information was confidential, whether it was individualised or aggregated, whether there was an obligation on the members to exchange this information or sanctions, etc. While price lists were exchanged annually, sales figures were exchanged monthly for six product categories and semi-annually or annually for a wider range of products. Investment expenditure was exchanged every 6 months;
- The ability of the exchange of this information, in particular gross prices, to reduce uncertainty in the market and thus to influence the behaviour of dealers on the retail market;
- The fact that three types of meaningful information were exchanged (prices, sales and capital expenditure).

The assessment of the *quantitative* elements was also conclusive and related to the following factors:

- Internal competition: the degree of competition between the parties to the information exchange, in particular competition on quality and innovative products, which in this case was weak;
- External, actual competition: the degree of competition exerted on the market by companies not participating in the exchange, parallel imports, duty-free shops and

[47] See FAC, judgment of 12 December 2022, B-141/2012, *Estée Lauder/ASCOPA*. See also Sect. 2.2.2.1.

direct imports by consumers from abroad, the maturity of the market. In this case, the pressure from these sources of external competition was considered to be very weak;

– Potential competition: the strength of the brands, some of which are considered luxury products, was an argument against potential competition;
– Countervailing power of retailers, which was also considered as weak.

The assessment showed that the restriction of competition resulting from the exchange of information reached the threshold of what is considered to be 'significant' under Article 5(1) of the Cartel Act. As the conditions for justification on efficiency grounds were not met, the information exchange decided by the members of the trade association infringed Article 5 CartA.

In bid rigging case, the FAC considered that participation in an exchange of information—which is usually considered to be business secrets—is different from the cases of protection and submission of a cover offer. Therefore, the application of the presumption of Article 5(3) of the Cartel Act in the case of a genuine exchange of information would not take into account the decisive fact that the companies had not been able to agree on who would receive the work at the time, in contrast to the situation in the case of 'cover offers'. [48] In a recent case, COMCO made an individual assessment and explained in detail why the information exchange in question did not fall within the scope of Article 5(3) CartA. [49] There is therefore no clear and unequivocal exclusion of genuine price exchanges (which do not contain elements of price fixing) from the scope of Article 5(3) CartA. It is therefore conceivable that, depending on the circumstances, an information exchange could be qualified as a price-fixing or market-sharing agreement or concerted practice under Article 5(3) CartA. The exchange of information on essential parameters of competition such as prices, market shares or turnover is a significant restriction of competition within the meaning of Article 5(1) CartA [50] and may or may not be considered justified on the grounds of economic efficiency, depending on the circumstances of the case and the sensitivity of the information. If the exchange of information cannot be justified under Article 5(2) CartA, it is unlawful.

A system for the exchange of information on interest rates developed by car leasing companies was considered by COMCO to be a horizontal agreement under Article 5(3)(a) of CartA. The parties were fined a total of EUR 30 million. [51] Through this system, the companies exchanged information over a number of

[48] FAC, judgment of 25 June 2018, B-807/2012 *Wettbewerbsabreden im Strassen- und Tiefbau im Kanton Aargau, ERNE*, para 10.2.3.

[49] COMCO decision of 6 December 2021, *Belagswerke Bern*, para 758. See for the context of the case Sect. 3.8 below.

[50] See FAC, judgment of 25 June 2018, B-807/2012 *Wettbewerbsabreden im Strassen- und Tiefbau im Kanton Aargau, ERNE*, para 10.2.4.

[51] COMCO, press release of 11 July 2019, La COMCO sanctionne huit entreprises dans l'enquête 'leasing automobile'. Available at https://www.weko.admin.ch/weko/fr/home/medien/communiques-de-presse/nsb-news.msg-id-75781.html. Accessed 21 July 2023.

years on measures taken in the event of incidents and on the elements used to calculate a leasing rate, such as residual value tables and contract fees.

The FAC upheld the finding of a concerted practice and the fine imposed on one of the parties that appealed, [52] and concluded the following:

> In conclusion, the extensive exchange of information and the system for exchanging information on interest rates, residual values, fees and commissions, as well as the full monitoring of interest rates and commissions, were capable of having a price harmonising effect on the leasing rates to be paid by final customers. The agreement therefore had the potential to lead to price fixing. The aim of the complainant and the other captives was to coordinate the pricing of leasing rates through the complex system of information exchange described above. These practices meet the criteria of Article 5(3)(a) of the Cartel Act.

This case concerning a concerted practice on car leasing rates and charges shows that the exchange of price information can fall under Article 5(3)(a) of the CartA and be subject to fines, in particular if the exchange took place on a regular monthly basis, lasted for a long period of time and covered most of the market.

3.6.2 Calculation Schemes

At a very early stage, COMCO had to deal with the use of calculation schemes developed by trade and professional associations and other companies. COMCO saw a risk that competing companies would consciously or unconsciously set their prices in a coordinated manner, and by making calculation schemes available, trade associations or organisations in the same sector could encourage a direct or indirect price agreement between their members. In 1998, the Commission adopted the Notice on calculation schemes, [53] which sets out a framework for the assessment of calculation schemes and a first set of principles for the exchange of information between competitors.

The Notice defines calculation schemes as general guidelines and standardised calculation bases which enable users to calculate or evaluate the costs of their products for the purpose of determining or assessing their selling prices.

The Notice sets out the conditions under which agreements between actual potential undertakings at the same market level or decisions by trade associations on the use of calculation schemes may be justified on grounds of economic efficiency within the meaning of Article 5(2) CartA. To fall within the safe harbour of the Notice, the agreements and actual use of calculation schemes by competing undertakings must fulfil all the following conditions: [54]

[52] FAC, judgment of 5 June 2023, B-4596/2019 *CA Auto Finance Suisse SA*, paras 6.2, 6.2.3.16.

[53] Notice on the conditions for the admissibility of agreements on the use of calculation schemes under the Cartel Act, Decision of the Competition Commission of 4 May 1998 (hereafter 'Notice on calculation schemes').

[54] Notice on calculation schemes, para 3.

- the content of the calculation schemes is limited to data and formulae used to calculate costs or establish prices,
- the schemes serve the purpose of exchanging knowledge and expertise on cost calculation between the parties,
- they leave the parties free to determine the terms and conditions of supply, to fix their purchase prices and to grant rebates and discounts independently,
- they do not involve any exchange of information that could reveal information about the actual behaviour of the parties when making offers or setting final prices and conditions.

If the above conditions are met, the creation and use of calculation schemes as such would not constitute an agreement within the meaning of Article 4(1) CartA. [55] To the extent that they are covered by the Notice on calculation schemes, it is not relevant to assess in detail whether they fulfil the conditions of an agreement under Article 4(1) CartA.

On the other hand, any use of the calculation schemes by a group of undertakings or trade associations to impose or recommend pre-defined costs or price elements in the scheme will be regarded as price agreements under Articles 4(1) and 5(3) CartA. Due to this qualification, the safe harbours of the SME Notice do not apply and, according to the Gaba jurisprudence, [56] the market shares, size or strength of the undertakings using such schemes are not part of the assessment. Even a low market share of the undertakings using the scheme will not reduce the risk of being caught by the sanctions resulting from the application of Article 5(3) CartA.

This is in line with the Notice when it considers that agreements on calculation schemes cannot be considered to be justified on the grounds of economic efficiency if such schemes allow any of the following: [57]

- they impose or suggest lump sums and flat-rate percentages for the settlement of overheads or other additional costs on the undertakings concerned for the purpose of determining their own costs;
- calculating or offering to calculate margins, rebates, other price components or final prices between the undertakings concerned;
- they enable the parties to be informed of the actual behaviour of their competitors, in particular when preparing offers and setting final prices and conditions.

The COMCO Secretariat has issued several consultations on calculation scheme projects submitted under Article 23(2) CartA, particularly in the 2000'. [58] Submissions from trade associations have increased following the introduction of direct sanctions in 2004, as costs schemes are linked to price and tariff calculations and run

[55] See LPC 2008/1, p. 2013, *Bericht über KMU-Bekanntmachung und Bekanntmachung über Kalkulationshilfen: Überprüfung der Auswirkungen und allfälliger Anpassungsbedarf*, para 14.

[56] FSC, judgment of 28 June 2016, 2C_180/2014, *Gaba*, ATF/BGE 143 II 297.

[57] Notice on calculation schemes, para 4.

[58] Advice from the COMCO Secretariat under Article 23(2) CartA is normally published in the LPC.

the risk of falling under Article 5(3) CartA. Article 23(2) CartA proved to be a useful tool to assist companies and their trade associations. COMCO and its Secretariat consulted the main trade associations in 2008 and issued a report on the application of the two notices on calculation schemes and SME. [59] A prior assessment by the COMCO Secretariat is therefore advisable due to the risk involved, if for no other reason than to assess and confirm that the calculation scheme falls within the safe harbours of the Notice.

3.7 Non-competes in a Joint Production Company

In a recent case, a non-compete clause in a shareholders' agreement between the shareholders of an asphalt mix production plant in the Bern region was considered to be a market allocation agreement subject to Article 5(3)(c) CartA. [60]

The non-compete clause prohibited the shareholders from competing with the company operating the production plant through their own asphalt plants or through shareholdings in other plants in a somewhat limited area in Bern. The COMCO based its decision on two main aspects. [61] Firstly, the shareholder base was very broad and included a large proportion of road construction companies and local gravel producers operating in a limited area. The non-compete clause therefore bound a significant number of companies, which could have provided additional competition, from setting up plants in the area. The company had made considerable efforts to integrate other potential competitors into the company as shareholders and to impose the non-compete clause on them, and by integrating new shareholders, the company operating the plant significantly protected itself from competition.

The second aspect was the duration of the non-competition clause in the shareholders' agreement, which was not limited to the initial phase of the company in order to protect investments, but was concluded for an indefinite period and lasted from 1976 to 2016.

COMCO considered that all shareholders of the agreement were at least in a potential competitive relationship with the company operating the asphalt plant, including those companies that did not operate their own asphalt plants during the relevant period. All shareholders were active in either road construction or gravel and concrete production. The probability that these shareholders would build their own plant on their own and in the absence of a non-compete obligation was low, but the COMCO considered that this could not be excluded in principle. In this respect, the fact that the non-compete clause in the shareholders' agreement was in force for

[59] See LPC 2008/1, p. 2013, *Bericht über KMU-Bekanntmachung und Bekanntmachung über Kalkulationshilfen: Überprüfung der Auswirkungen und allfälliger Anpassungsbedarf.*

[60] COMCO decision of 6 December 2021, *Belagswerke Bern*, available at https://www.weko.admin.ch/weko/en/home/praxis/latest-decisions.html. Accessed 15 May 2023.

[61] Idem, paras 715 ff.

40 years have played a role, as the COMCO considers that over a long period of time a company is more likely to enter new businesses, expand existing businesses, establish new production facilities or acquire shares in other companies. From the point of view of potential competition, the COMCO considers it irrelevant that most of the shareholders did not intend to build or take over their own asphalt mix plant or to participate in a competing plant.

The fact that most of the shareholders were not represented on the company's board of directors or on other bodies such as the operating committee was also of no relevance, since the decisive factor was the binding nature of the non-compete clause and not the possibility of influencing the company's activities.

The non-compete clause in the shareholders' agreement qualified as a territorial allocation agreement within the meaning of Article 5(3)(c) of the CartA, [62] even though the clause did not relate to sales and therefore did not directly allocate sales to territories. In the asphalt mix industry, production location and sales market are closely linked due to high transport costs and the supply area of an asphalt plant always covers an area around the plant location. Therefore, an agreement on the location of production also determines the supply areas and can be used to define territories.

The presumption of elimination of competition was reversed on the basis of sufficient internal competition: several shareholders operated their own asphalt plants in other areas and could thus exert a disciplinary effect. [63] The non-compete clause in the shareholders' agreement was then assessed under Article 5(1) CartA.

The COMCO considered that the non-compete clause significantly restricted competition within the meaning of Article 5(1) of the Cartel Act. In the view of the COMCO, the non-compete clause in the shareholders' agreement had the potential to cause substantial harm. As a horizontal territorial agreement (Article 5 (3)(c) Cartel Act), it affected a central parameter of competition. In view of their resources, size and business activities in the building materials sector, several of the shareholders involved in the agreement were significant actual or potential competitors of the company operating the plant. Two of them were important groups that already operated their own asphalt plants in other regions and could have supplied the area. COMCO acknowledges that due to the high barriers to entry and the market conditions, including the existing plants, it would have been difficult for the shareholders to build and economically operate their own plants in the area, so that the likelihood of potential competition was rather low. However, the potential impact of the non-compete clause on competition in the relevant market, namely the prevention of further competing asphalt plants, was considered to be serious. The company operating the plant was found to have a dominant position in the relevant geographic market, which was very narrowly defined. Additional competing plants would have

[62] Idem, para 726.

[63] Idem, para 733.

significantly increased competition. Finally, the anticompetitive agreement lasted for decades until it was abolished in 2016. [64]

The non-compete clause was not justified on the grounds of economic efficiency since neither the significant number of shareholders, nor the long duration of the clause were necessary to ensure the viability of the asphalt plant. COMCO explains the following:

> Uncertainty about the market behaviour of actual and potential competitors is a central element of an economic order based on the concept of competition. By agreeing to protect BERAG from further plant construction by the BERAG shareholders, the parties sought to avoid this uncertainty. This is not a legitimate purpose of a non-compete agreement in a market economy. Rather, the aim should be to secure sales and amortise investments through appropriate market behaviour. Nor is it necessary for sales to include customers in the shareholder structure. The current non-compete clause cannot therefore be justified on the grounds of economic efficiency. It should be emphasised that this conclusion has to be drawn primarily on the basis of the specific circumstances of the case, in particular the nature and the number of parties involved in the non-compete obligation (involvement of a large proportion of actual and potential competitors) and its excessive duration. The same assessment cannot be applied without prejudice and without individual assessment to other non-competition clauses between participants in a joint stock company or other legal form of company. [65]

The COMCO decision prohibits shareholders from entering into non-compete obligations, but the prohibition does not apply if the shareholders have sole or joint control of the asphalt company. The scope of the prohibition and the exception in the case of sole or joint control provide some indication of the possible justification for non-compete clauses for shareholders controlling a joint production company, which needs to be carefully assessed. The COMCO softened the meaning of the exception by adding that this exception "does not say anything about the admissibility of non-competition clauses in the case of joint control in the future. Rather, the legality of a non-compete clause in this situation would have to be determined on the basis of the specific circumstances of each case". [66]

3.8 Interlocking Directorates

The agreement between competing companies to appoint directors to each other's boards was considered to be an agreement having the object or effect of restricting competition through the exchange of information that inevitably arises from joint directorships. [67] There was also evidence that certain information, including pricing

[64] Idem, para 737.

[65] Idem, para 742.

[66] Idem, para 782.

[67] Idem, para 782.

strategy, was exchanged between the companies through their common directors. There was therefore an agreement within the meaning of Article 4(1) CartA.

As there was no evidence of an agreement to fix prices or share markets, nor of a causal link between certain similar market behaviour and the exchange of information on prices, COMCO concluded that there was no agreement or concerted practice to fix prices or share markets within the meaning of Article 5(3) CartA. Therefore, the common directors and the related exchange of information were assessed under Article 5(1) and (2) CartA. Such an agreement could not be justified by the need to benefit from the know-how or experience of other boards or in the industry.

Cross directorships and the related exchange of information were therefore considered unlawful and the companies undertook, firstly, not to appoint or employ any person as a director or officer of a competing company (e.g. a member of the board of directors or management) or as a person who sets prices (e.g. a sales manager or sales director) and, secondly, not to exchange information with competing companies on prices, price components, customers or territories prior to the award of a contract.

3.9 Homologation and Sponsorship Agreements on Sport Products

On several occasions in the 1990', COMCO has had to examine the issue of the financing of competitive sport through sponsorship contracts concluded between sports associations and suppliers of sports equipment (manufacturers, importers, agents), which led it to adopt, very early in 1997, a Notice on the homologation and sponsoring of sports equipment (hereinafter referred to as the 'Notice on sports equipment').

Sports federations, as organisers of sports competitions, carry out quality controls according to predefined criteria for the quality and safety of sports equipment, and homologation refers to the authorisation of sports equipment that has passed such controls to be used in official sports events. Sponsorship, on the other hand, is the financial, material and service support provided by a sponsor to a sports federation and the sport it promotes in exchange for advertising, in particular the mention of its name and brand in public activities. The COMCO considers sponsorship to be completely independent of the quality of the sports equipment. The main requirement of the Notice on sports equipment is to unbundle homologation from sponsorship, thereby opening access to sports products that could be used in sports competitions.

The rules apply to homologation and sponsorship agreements, but although the Notice does not mention it, the idea of unbundling stems more from the power of sports federations in the organisation of their sports events, which, given the pyramidal structure of sports, may have a dominant position in the market for the organisation of their sports competitions. [68] As most sports federations may be in a dominant position on the relevant market in relation to the organisation of their competitions and events, the safe harbours of the SME Notice may not apply to these agreements. For other sports clubs, in particular local clubs, practitioners will need to assess whether the market share safe harbours of the SME Notice, which in our view apply to homologation and sponsorship, are met.

The Notice sets out general conditions and specific criteria for the admissibility of licensing and sponsorship agreements for sports equipment. There are two general conditions: [69]

- The first condition is the decoupling mentioned above: homologation must be completely independent, both formally and materially, from sponsorship and must not be subject to conditions unrelated to the quality of the sports equipment;
- The second condition relates to the absence of agreements on prices or the restriction of sources of supply. Homologation and sponsorship agreements may not contain provisions on prices, distribution or sources of supply; in particular, they may not limit distribution channels or parallel imports.

The Notice then goes on to set out specific criteria for both homologation and sponsorship, setting out clauses that are not permitted and the criteria that must be met for both types of agreement to be considered compliant with the Cartel Act.

According to the Notice, the following are generally unlawful:

- homologation agreements, which limit access to official sporting events to suppliers of sporting equipment with an international reputation or a national distribution network;
- sponsorship agreements that grant exclusivity for the use of sporting equipment of one or more selected sponsors for an entire sporting event for a year, a season or a large part of a season.

The Notice sets out the following criteria for homologation process and agreements [70] to be justified and therefore to be considered lawful:

- *Open access for all suppliers*: the homologation process must be open to all suppliers of sports equipment under the same conditions;
- *Regular and frequent procedure*: the homologation procedure for each sports equipment must be possible and open at any time, with the possibility of combining several procedures into one if this is less costly or if it is necessary from an organisational point of view. The homologation procedures must be carried out at regular intervals so that products which have not yet been homologated can be marketed as such before the start of the sports season;

[68] See for instance COMCO Secretariat, final report of 10 December 1998, *Homologation und Sponsoring von Fussbällen*, LPC 1998/4, p. 56.

[69] Notice on sports equipment, section C.

[70] Notice on sports equipment, section D.

- *Objective quality criteria*: the approval criteria must be established objectively on the basis of the qualitative and technical requirements linked to the use of the specific sports equipment;
- *Impartiality of the persons involved*: the persons establishing the approval criteria, carrying out the procedure and deciding on the approval of a product must be neutral, preferably third parties. Suppliers of sports goods are not involved in these various procedures, except for the presentation of their products;
- *Objective criteria for delegating the process to third parties*: where the approval process is delegated to third parties, the selection of these third parties is based on objective criteria;
- *Acceptance of foreign homologations*: foreign or international type-approvals must be accepted if they comply with the rules laid down in the Notice,
- *Transparency of costs*: the real costs of homologation must be passed on to the suppliers concerned and the calculation of the costs must be transparent;
- *Labelling*: Homologation should be linked to the award of a label.

Sponsorship agreements for the use of sporting goods at official sporting events are generally justified and therefore lawful if they meet the following criteria:

- *Open access:* all suppliers are eligible to become sponsors under the same conditions;
- *Objective selection criteria:* the selection of a limited number of suppliers of sports goods or of an exclusive partner as a sponsor is made on the basis of objectively verifiable criteria, and the duration of the contract and the award procedure are determined in such a way as to ensure effective competition;
- *Exclusivity of limited duration:* the exclusive use of a sponsor's equipment is limited to a single official sports event or to events organised at regular intervals, and the event does not extend over a long period of time;
- *No confusion of logos*: the use and advertising of a sponsor's label does not lead the public to believe that it is a quality label and there is no risk of confusion with homologation labels;
- *No exchange of information on turnover*: if the amount of the sponsorship is calculated on the basis of the number of sports equipment sold or turnover, the communication and monitoring of these figures must not allow sports equipment suppliers to become aware of the sales or turnover of their competitors. Outsourcing the monitoring to a third party is desirable.

The sports equipment Notice was adopted very early, well before the introduction of direct sanctions and Article 5(4) CartA. It is not clear whether there are elements of homologation and sponsorship that would fall under the presumption of Article 5 (3) or (4) CartA and be subject to fines. For example, there could be a risk that Article 5(3)(b) CartA is applied to the boycott and exclusion of equipment suppliers from the homologation process.

Provisions restricting sources of supply or parallel imports in homologation and sponsorship agreements between sports federations and equipment suppliers would normally not fall under Article 5(4) CartA if the federations do not purchase sports equipment for resale. The Notice on sports equipment provides guidance on the criteria that can be met to avoid the risk of fines and potential illegality under Article 5(1) CartA.

List of Documents

COMCO Notice on agreements with limited market impact, Decision of the Competition Commission of 19 December 2005 (SME Notice)

COMCO Notice on the conditions for the admissibility of agreements on the use of calculation schemes under the Cartel Act, Decision of the Competition Commission of 4 May 1998 (Notice on calculation schemes)

COMCO Notice on the Homologation and Sponsoring of Sports Equipment, Decision of the Competition Commission of 15 December 1997 (Notice on sports equipment).

Chapter 4
Distribution Agreements and Vertical Restraints

4.1 Vertical Agreements

Vertical agreements are agreements concluded between undertakings active at different levels of production and distribution chain. [1] They are assessed in accordance with Article 5 CartA. [2] The COMCO has issued a Notice on the treatment of vertical agreements under competition law and an Explanatory note, which explains in detail the current practice of the COMCO and the courts. [3] Both documents provide guidance on how to carry out the assessment of vertical restraints and gives

[1] Articles 4 and 5(4) CartA.

[2] Article 5 CartA on unlawful agreements affecting competition reads as follows: "1) Agreements that significantly restrict competition in a market for specific goods or services and are not justified on grounds of economic efficiency, and all agreements that eliminate effective competition are unlawful. 2) Agreements affecting competition are deemed to be justified on grounds of economic efficiency if: a. they are necessary in order to reduce production or distribution costs, improve products or production processes, promote research into or dissemination of technical or professional know-how, or exploit resources more rationally; and b. they will under no circumstances enable the parties involved to eliminate effective competition. 3) The following agreements between actual or potential competitors are presumed to lead to the elimination of effective competition: a. agreements to directly or indirectly fix prices; b. agreements to limit the quantities of goods or services to be produced, purchased or supplied; c. agreements to allocate markets geographically or according to trading partners. 4) The elimination of effective competition is also presumed in the case of agreements between undertakings at different levels of the production and distribution chain regarding fixed or minimum prices, and in the case of agreements contained in distribution contracts regarding the allocation of territories to the extent that sales by other distributors into these territories are not permitted."

[3] COMCO, Notice on the treatment of vertical agreements under competition law, Decision of the Competition Commission of 12 December 2022 (Verticals Notice). See also Explanatory note of the Competition Commission to the Notice on the assessment of vertical agreements of 12 December 2022 (Explanatory note to the Verticals Notice).

P. Këllezi, *Competition Law in Switzerland*,
https://doi.org/10.1007/978-3-031-45117-1_4

examples of the most common restrictive clauses. Another notice covers distribution in the motor vehicle sector. It is accompanied by an explanatory note. [4]

The vertical relationship between the parties is determined not only by actual activities covered by the contractual relationship (actual competition), but also by potential activities that one of the parties could launch in the near future (potential competition). Potential competition in vertical relationships was read broadly by the COMCO (see Sect. 4.3.7 below). [5] Lack of guidance in that respect increases the risk that the agreement is qualified as a horizontal one, subject to the presumptions of Article 5(3) CartA. In dual distribution scenarios, the Verticals Notice follows the path of the new block exemption Regulation 720/220 which treats agreement concluded in a dual distribution scenario as vertical agreements by exempting them (Sect. 4.3.6.4).

Presumptions of Article 5(4) CartA that relate to absolute territorial protection and resale price maintenance (RPM) apply to all kind of vertical agreements and to contractual clauses in distribution, license, franchise, agency, production or R&D contracts regulating the purchase, sale or resale of contractual products (see also Sect. 4.3.2.1). [6] The reference to "distribution contracts" in Article 5(4) CartA therefore relates to contractual provisions covering the purchase, sale or resale of the products covered by any contract, and not to the nature of such contract. The COMCO has issued guidelines only in relation to distribution agreements; there are no guidelines on IP licence, franchising, R&D or production agreements.

The notion of agreement is defined in Article 4(1) CartA (Sect. 2.2). In the context of vertical agreements, economic incentives and other measures may be based on contract or simply develop within the business relationship. Depending on the bargaining power of each party, one of them may impose obligations on the other or simply implement its own policy, with or without acceptance by the other party. Hence the relevance of the distinction between agreements and unilateral conduct.

Another distinction is inherent in the concept of relevant agreements for competition law, that of the independence between the parties: only agreements among undertakings that are supposed to behave independently on the market have an impact on competition and therefore become relevant (Sect. 2.2.1). [7] This may not be the case for intra-group business relationships and agency agreements. While there is a developed case law on intra-group agreements and the single-entity

[4] Notice concerning the assessment of vertical agreements in the motor vehicle sector, Decision of the Competition Commission of 29 June 2015, and Explanatory note of the Competition Commission on the Notice concerning the assessment of vertical agreements in the motor vehicle sector of 29 June 2015. The Notice expires on 31 December 2023. It will be replaced by an ordinance of the Federal Council, which will be binding on the courts and not only on COMCO, following a motion of the Swiss Parliament. The text of the ordinance had not been published at the time of writing and we have therefore decided not to discuss the COMCO notices and the future Federal Council ordinance on motor vehicle distribution further in this book.

[5] See for instance COMCO decision of 2 December 2019 *AdBlue,* LPC 2020/4, p. 626.

[6] FSC, judgment of 28 June 2016, 2C_180/2014, *Gaba*, ATF/BGE 143 II 297, paras 6.3.1 and 6.4.1.

[7] FAC, judgment of 30 October 2019, B-3975/2013, *Marché du livre écrit en français*, para 6.3.

doctrine, the case law has been rather timid on agency relationships. Below we explain the main factors for assessing risk.

4.1.1 Unilateral Conduct

The issue was discussed by courts for one-side non-compete obligations [8] and price recommendations, [9] and there is a tendency towards a wide interpretation of the concept of agreement encompassing unilateral declarations. The distinction between agreements and unilateral conduct will be the subject of a more detailed discussion in Sect. 4.3.1.2. Combined with the low standard of proof applied by the courts, such a broad interpretation of agreements impinges on the concept of unilateral behaviour. Since it is more difficult to find an abusive conduct in case of unilateral conduct, the extension of the concept of agreement allows the COMCO to act against price recommendations, RPM and non-compete obligations and, consequently, against high prices. In cross-border relations, the new concept of relative market power combined with new abusive behaviour provides another basis for taking action against high prices or unfair terms applied in Switzerland. [10]

4.1.2 Intra-Group Agreements

Agreements concluded among the companies of a group are not relevant to the Cartel Act since the group is considered as a single undertaking and as a consequence the companies of the group are not considered as independent from each-other. [11] Competition restrictions in these agreements are not covered by Articles 4 (1) and 5 CartA. This is called the "group privilege". In 2022, the FSC clarified that this privilege applies to genuinely intra-group companies that are in no way related to agreements concluded with external parties: distribution contracts concluded by a company of a foreign group with third party companies could not benefit from the group privilege on the grounds that their execution on Swiss territory was delegated to another company of the same group (see also Sect. 2.2.1.1). [12]

The strict application of territorial exclusivity and territorial protection restrictions mitigates the group privilege in situations where a company belonging to a group has been appointed by another independent producer to distribute its goods in Europe and this company sub-delegates the distribution in Switzerland to another

[8] FSC, judgment of 13 November 1998, ATF/BGE 124 III 495, pp. 499 and 500, para 2a and 2b.

[9] FSC, judgment of 18 May 2018, 2C_101/2016, *Altimum*, ATF/BGE 144 II 246, para 6.4.1.

[10] Article 4(2) and 7(2)(g) CartA.

[11] FSC, judgment of 21 December 2021, 2C_43/2020, *Dargaud*, ATF/BGE 148 II 25, para 7.2.

[12] Idem, para 7.5.

company of the group (a sister company). The FSC explained that since a distribution contract was concluded between a group company and an external producer, the relationship was subject to the Cartel Act: the internal sub-delegation would not be subject to the Cartel Act as an agreement because of the group privilege, but the group company acting as sub-distributor would be indirectly involved in the execution of the distribution agreement concluded between a group (sister) company and the external producer. [13] This interpretation reduces the scope of the group privilege for distributors who wish to freely structure distribution within the group companies, even if this is done independently of the commitments entered into with the external producer.

A further limitation of the group privilege for distributors seems to result from the distinction that FSC makes between pure producers and producers that also act as distributors with regard to the obligations of these companies not to compete with their distributors in Switzerland. Only pure producers who do not act as distributors can undertake not to sell in Switzerland or to forward enquiries from Swiss consumers and customers to their distributor in Switzerland. No such limitation exists in EU competition law. Producers who also distribute their products through subsidiaries, for example outside Switzerland, cannot undertake not to sell in Switzerland or to forward requests received by their subsidiary to the Swiss distributor. [14] A subsidiary of the "pure manufacturer" based outside Switzerland is treated as if it did not belong to the group.

4.1.3 Agency Agreements

Genuine agency agreements do not fall under the scope of Article 4(1) CartA, since an agent which does not carry out any commercial risk does not act independently (Sect. 2.2.1.2). The COMCO accepts a "agency privilege", however, its practice in the matter is not clearly established and there have been few court cases. The courts and the COMCO refer to the EU law as a guidance tool. [15] Similar to the treatment of unilateral conduct, the tendency is not to readily accept an agency relationship, which enables the COMCO to intervene against pricing and territorial restrictions in vertical agreements. In the case on distribution of books in French, [16] the FAC asks whether the dealer operates as an "auxiliary integrated into the economic

[13] FSC, judgment of 21 December 2021, 2C_43/2020, *Dargaud*, ATF/BGE 148 II 25, para 7.5.

[14] FSC, judgment of 3 March 2022, case 2C_44/2020, *Flammarion*, para 9.1; FSC, judgment of 8 December 2022, 2C_52/2020, *Glénat*, paras 7.4, 7.1.2. et 7.3.6.

[15] Ibidem.

[16] FAC, judgments of 30 October 2019, B-3975/2013, B-4669/2013, B-4019/2013, B-3962/2013, B-3938/2013, B-4111/2013, B-3954/2013, B-1412/2013, B-4014/2013, *Marché du livre écrit en français*.

organization of the supplier taking into account the concrete risks borne by the dealer". [17] The assessment it carried out in the specific case concerned however the risk borne by the dealer, by denying it and consequently the agency relationship, and not whether the dealer was integrated in the economic organization of the supplier. In the same case, the FSC disagreed with the analysis of the FAC by finding that the risks born by the Swiss distributor justified to qualify the agreement as an agency one with respect to the CartA, [18] but denied the agency privilege to territorial exclusivity and territorial protection restrictions. [19] Such restrictions remain subject to the Cartel Act and to the presumption of Article 5(4) CartA. Although the FSC left open the question of whether agency privilege could be adopted in Swiss law, it did not reject it, thus opening the possibility of invoking it for other restrictions.

4.2 Analytical Framework

As explained in Chap. 2, the analytical framework is different from the EU prohibition and exemption system. There is no statutory exemption applying independently of the question whether the agreement restricts or not competition. The Verticals Notice has the status of guidelines. In addition, the threshold of *significant* restriction of competition under Article 5(1) CartA set by courts is low, which results in a broad scope of application of Article 5 CartA. The discussions and arguments in courts focus on the scope of Article 5(4) CartA, which covers agreements that are subject to fines under Article 49a CartA. COMCO's Secretariat investigations focus almost exclusively on Article 5(4) CartA cases. Other agreements that are only covered by Article 5(1) CartA do not trigger direct sanctions for the parties, except in the case where the parties continue an agreement that has already been found illegal by a COMCO decision (Sect. 7.4). In other words, the risk of breaching Article 5(4) CartA is a high fine and the nullity of the clause or agreement and eventually damages, and the risk of breaching Article 5(1) Cart is only the nullity of the clause or agreement. Therefore, the distinction between agreements that are covered by Article 5(4) and other agreements that are not is important for practitioners.

Practically, the main steps of the risk assessment are the following:

First, ask whether the restriction, a clause or an action surrounding vertical relationships falls under the presumption of Article 5(4) CartA. If this is the case, the undertakings risk automatic fines. On the civil law aspect, the clause

[17] FAC, judgment of 30 October 2019, B-3975/2013, *Marché du livre écrit en français*, para 6.4.

[18] FSC, judgment of 3 March 2020 in the case 2C_44/2020 *Flammarion*, para 6.6. The Court based its assessment on the fact that the Swiss dealer did not become the owner of the books and that it did not bear the risk of unsold books, which was born by the editor.

[19] Idem, para 6.7.

incorporating the restriction may be considered null and void, and therefore unenforceable, and potentially subject to damages.

Second, if the presumption of Article 5(4) CartA is reversed, the agreement is deemed to restrict competition significantly within the meaning of Article 5 (1) CartA without having to conduct further assessment of qualitative or quantitative criteria. [20] Where the restriction is not justified on efficiency grounds (Article 5(2) CartA), the agreement is unlawful and remain subject to fines in accordance with Article 49a CartA.

Third, if the restriction is not covered by the scope of Article 5(4) CartA, the undertakings do not risk fines. The issue will be whether the agreement or the clause restricts competition within the meaning of Article 5(1) CartA. In this respect, two questions must be asked: whether the restriction is severe from a qualitative point of view and whether the restriction is severe from a quantitative point of view (Sect. 2.3.2.1). The criteria are alternative, if the response to one of those, or to both, is affirmative, the agreement restrict competition and a third question should be asked: whether the restriction is justified on efficiency grounds (Sect. 2.3.2.2). If this is not the case, the agreement is unlawful. The clause will be unenforceable, and the undertakings will potentially be subject to damages claims.

The Verticals Notice provides guidance on how to carry out the assessment and gives examples of the most common restrictive clauses. [21] It makes a distinction between qualitative and quantitative restrictions, listing what is considered as serious or severe restriction from a qualitative standpoint. [22] The severe restrictions from a qualitative standpoint reflect clauses that restrict competition by their nature: it is the type of restraint that is at issue, irrespective of any quantitative element related to market shares or the actual effect of the agreement on the market. As stated in the Verticals Notice, qualitatively severe agreement listed in Article 15 Verticals Notice may be significant restrictions of competition despite minor effects from a quantitative point of view. [23] On the other hand, an agreement which has significant competitive effects from a quantitative point of view may substantially affect competition even if it is not severe from a qualitative point of view. [24]

For practitioners, it is relevant to know how to use Verticals Notice and for those familiar with the system of EU block exemptions, to what extent it can be used like the EU regulations in this area. Verticals Notice is soft law and provides a simple indication of how the COMCO and its Secretariat will apply the Cartel Act in a

[20] Article 14(a) Verticals Notice.

[21] COMCO, Notice on the treatment of vertical agreements under competition law, Decision of the Competition Commission of 12 December 2022 (Verticals Notice). See also Explanatory note of the Competition Commission to the Notice on the assessment of vertical agreements of 12 December 2022 (Explanatory note to the Verticals Notice).

[22] Article 14 and 15 Verticals Notice.

[23] Article 14 (b) Verticals Notice.

[24] Article 14(b) Verticals Notice.

specific case. It does not establish a statutory exemption that can only be withdrawn by decision, as is the case for Regulation 2022/720. Moreover, the Verticals Notice is not binding on the courts, but it is binding on the COMCO. Although drafted as a regulation, the legal status of the Verticals Notice is similar only to the EU Vertical Guidelines, not to Regulation 2022/720. In Switzerland, there is no statutory exemption or legal instrument equivalent to Regulation 2022/720.

The COMCO has published a document entitled Explanatory note to the Verticals Notice, [25] which aims to summarise COMCO's case law and main decision-making practice on vertical restraints, but also borrows some explanations from the EU Vertical Guidelines. The Verticals Notice and its Explanatory Note do not deal with all types of vertical restraints, but only with those matters that have either been upheld by the courts or decided by COMCO itself. The fact that a type of vertical restraint is not covered by these two documents means that there is no decision-making practice and, more importantly, that COMCO and its Secretariat do not wish to disclose their position on the matter and be bound by it.

The question arises as to whether and to what extent practitioners can refer to the EU Vertical Guidelines for guidance when no guidance is given in the Verticals Notice and its Explanatory note. The answer to this question is "not always" and with caution, as the assessment and outcome prevailing in the EU will be adapted taking into account the legal and economic conditions prevailing in Switzerland. [26] Therefore, where the Verticals Notice and its Explanatory note do not provide guidance on a certain practice, the EU Vertical Guidelines are still relevant to understand how that practice is treated in the EU, but the assessment must always be conducted with reference to the framework and objectives of Article 5 CartA as interpreted by the Swiss courts and the COMCO.

The primary objective of EU compatibility was to open up the Swiss market and integrate it unilaterally into the EU's internal market. For companies based outside the EU and marketing products in the EU and Switzerland, treating Switzerland as an EU country is something they can do with respect to distribution agreements, but it is not sufficient to deal with the broad extraterritorial scope of the Cartel Act (see Sect. 1.3.2 above), especially with respect to territorial restrictions. Export bans do not need to have effect in Switzerland to be caught by Article 5(4) CarA. Basically, trade between Switzerland and other non-EU countries is treated as if the whole world were part of the EU's internal market, this time not because of the (extraterritorial) application of EU competition rules, but because the Cartel Act, after independently incorporating EU competition rules, applies them unconditionally worldwide. In other words, not only Switzerland has to be treated as an EU country, but also the company's home country and any other country where the company markets its products abroad.

[25] Explanatory note to the Verticals Notice.

[26] FSC, judgment of 28 June 2016, 2C_180/2014, *Gaba*, ATF/BGE 143 II 297, para 6.2.3; Verticals Notice, para VII; Explanatory note to the Verticals Notice, para 2. See also Sect. 1.1.

The list of severe restrictions from a qualitative standpoint is larger than the list of hardcore restrictions of Article 4 Regulation 2022/720 since it covers also excluded restrictions of Article 5 Regulation 2022/720, however it has a different function. While in Regulation 2022/720 an agreement that includes a hardcore restriction cannot benefit from the block exemption, the list of qualitative severe restrictions of the Verticals Notice indicates that the market shares safe harbours will not be available to undertakings. The assessment under the Swiss Cartel Act focuses on contractual commitments or restrictive clauses, and it is a particular clause that will be considered justified or not under Article 5(4) CartA, and ultimately lawful or unlawful, and not the whole agreement (Sect. 1.6.6). The notion of excluded restrictions is therefore irrelevant in a system that does not offer a statutory block exemption for agreements.

The Verticals Notice uses two safe harbours related to market shares. The first threshold of 15% [27] concerns the restriction of competition and is the counterpart of the de minimis notice. [28] The second threshold of 30% [29] corresponds to the mechanism of Article 3 Regulation 2022/720. The benefit of both safe harbours announced in the Verticals Notice is weaker compared to the Regulation 2022/720 for the reasons mentioned above. Moreover, the effect of these two safe harbours is tempered by the general nature of the principles set out, which are subject to exceptions: this is announced by the regular use of the expression "as a general rule" in the Verticals Notice, [30] leaving the possibility for the COMCO and its Secretariat not to apply the presumption in certain circumstances. For this reason also, market share safe harbours do not provide the same legal certainty as Article 3 of Regulation 2022/720.

Both safe harbours are nevertheless useful for assessing vertical restrictions and can be used by practitioners in their assessment. Apart from the broader scope of Article 5(4) of the Cartel Act and of qualitatively severe restrictions which may lead to more lenient or stricter results than under EU law, the assessment framework is conceptually similar to that applicable under EU law.

- Agreements covered by Article 5(4) CartA and qualitatively severe restrictions listed in Article 15 (b)–(f) Verticals Notice—that mainly correspond to the hardcore restrictions of Article 4 Regulation 2022/720—do not benefit from any of the market share safe harbours of Articles 16 or 18 of the Verticals Notice. This is similar to the situation in EU law, where the De Minimis Notice does not apply to hardcore and other restrictions by object, [31] and where Regulation 2022/720 does not exempt hardcore restrictions. Vertical restraints that are not covered by the list of severe restrictions of Article 15 Verticals Notice, like certain

[27] Article 16 Verticals Notice.

[28] De Minimis Notice, paras 8 and 10.

[29] Article 18 Verticals Notice.

[30] In German: "in der Regel". In French: "en règle générale". In Italian: "di regola".

[31] De Minimis Notice, para 13.

active sales restrictions, location clauses or restrictions on online advertising that are not aimed at preventing the use of an entire online advertising channel, benefit from both safe harbours.

- Restrictions that correspond to the excluded restrictions under Article 5 Regulation 2022/720—that is non-competes and restrictions related to online intermediation services that qualify as severe restrictions of competition under Article 15 (g)(h)(i) and (j) of the Verticals Notice—benefit from the 15% market share safe harbour of the Verticals Notice. [32] This is like in the EU legislation where the excluded restrictions benefit from the 15% de minimis thresholds, [33] which is particularly useful as these restrictions are not block exempted in Regulation 2022/720. And like in the EU, they cannot benefit from the other safe harbour of 30% [34] related to the justification under Article 5(2) CartA, but they do so if they do not exceed the respective duration limits of the non-compete and other terms related to the know-how or territorial scope of the non-compete (Sect. 4.3.5).

We present below both safe harbours in detail.

The First Safe Harbour Related to 15% Market Share Threshold of Article 16(1)-Verticals Notice As explained above, the first market share safe harbour relates to the appreciability criteria of Article 5(1) CartA and benefits to all non-compete obligations within the meaning of Article 15(g)–(j) Verticals Notice, whether or not they are qualitatively severe, and all other agreements that are not severe from a qualitative point of view and are not covered by Article 5(4) CartA:

> Vertical agreements which do not fall under Article 12 or Article 15 letters b to f Verticals Notice do not normally lead to a significant restriction of competition if no undertaking party to the agreement exceeds a market share of 15% on a relevant market affected by the agreement. [35]

The threshold is lowered to 5% to consider the cumulative effect of parallel vertical agreements used in the market:

> If competition in a relevant market is restricted by the cumulative effect of vertical agreements concluded by different suppliers or distributors for the sale of goods or services (cumulative foreclosure effect of parallel networks of vertical agreements having similar effects on the market), the market share threshold referred to in paragraph 1 shall be reduced to 5%. Individual suppliers or distributors with a market share not exceeding 5 % are normally not considered to contribute significantly to the cumulative foreclosure effect. A cumulative foreclosure effect is unlikely to be present if less than 30 % of the relevant market is covered by parallel (networks of) vertical agreements having similar effects on the market. [36]

---

[32] Article 16(1) Verticals Notice.

[33] De Minimis Notice, para 14.

[34] Article 18(1) Verticals Notice.

[35] Article 16(1) Verticals Notice.

[36] Article 16(2) Verticals Notice.

For selective distribution systems a higher threshold of 50% is applied: a cumulative effect is unlikely if the market share covered by selective distribution is less than 50% or if the combined market share of the five largest suppliers is less than 50%. [37]

Article 16(1) Verticals Notice corresponds to another safe harbour introduced earlier in the SME Notice: "As a general rule, competition agreements have only a limited impact on the market when the market shares held by each of the undertakings party to a vertical agreement (in particular distribution agreements) do not exceed 15% in any of the reference markets concerned by the agreement." [38] The same notice also declares that agreements involving only microenterprises, i.e. those with less than 10 employees and an annual turnover in Switzerland of less than CHF 2 million, do not significantly affect competition, but this rule does not apply to agreements within the meaning of Article 5(4) CartA. [39] This safe harbour for microenterprises is not very useful for cross-border trade involving at least one internationally active enterprise.

The Second Safe Harbour Related to 30% Market Share Threshold of 18(2)-Verticals Notice The second safe harbour concerns the justification on grounds of economic efficiency under Article 5(2) CartA and apply only to agreements that are not covered by Article 5(4) CartA (Article 12 Verticals Notice) and to agreements that are not considered as severe from a qualitative point of view (Article 15 Verticals Notice).

> Vertical agreements shall normally be deemed to be justified without a case-by-case examination if the supplier's share of the relevant market on which it sells the contract goods or services, and the buyer's share of the relevant market on which it acquires the contract goods and services, does not exceed 30 % in each case. This rule does not apply to agreements pursuant to Article 12 and Article 15 of the Verticals Notice as well as agreements which have a cumulative effect on the market. [40]

For the sake of completeness, the list of serious restrictions from a qualitative standpoint contains restraints that are covered by the scope of Article 5(4) CartA (such as restrictions on passive sales) and other restraints that do not fall under its presumption, such as restrictions on active sales or non-compete obligations. Restrictions that are not covered by Article 5(4) CartA but are nevertheless considered as severe restrictions from a qualitative standpoint by Article 15 Verticals Notice are not subject to fines. Finally, the other agreements outside the scope of Article 5(4) CartA that are not considered as severe restrictions from a qualitative standpoint can benefit from all safe harbours related to market shares.

Consequently, having explained how to use the market share safe harbours, it is useful for practitioners to draw three categories of vertical restraints: severe restrictions covered by Article 5(4) CartA (Sect. 4.2.1), severe restrictions from a

[37] Explanatory note to the Verticals Notice, para 20.

[38] SME Notice, Article 3 (b).

[39] SME Notice, paras 4 and 5.

[40] Article 18(2) Verticals Notice.

qualitative point of view not covered by Article 5(4) CartA (Sect. 4.2.2) and other significant restrictions of competition (Sect. 4.2.3).

4.2.1 Severe Restrictions Covered by Article 5(4) CartA

The first category pertains to restrictions of competition that fall under the presumption of Article 5(4) CartA. Two broad categories are covered by Article 5(4). The first is the resale price maintenance (Sect. 4.3.1.1) and the second is the absolute territorial protection covering in particular the restriction of passive sales towards the allocated territories (Sect. 4.3.2.1). These are considered as severe form a qualitative standpoint without further assessment of the position of the parties and their shares on the relevant market. The text of Article 5(4) CartA reads as follows:

> The elimination of effective competition is also presumed in the case of agreements between undertakings at different levels of the production and distribution chain regarding fixed or minimum prices, and in the case of agreements contained in distribution contracts regarding the allocation of territories to the extent that sales by other distributors into these territories are not permitted.

Article 5(4) CartA provides for legal presumptions pertaining to the effects of the agreement and the restriction of competition on the market, with a series of consequences explained in Sect. 2.3. If the suppression of competition is not reversed, and therefore confirmed, the agreement is unlawful and subject to important fines. The argument of justification on efficiency grounds is not available.

The fines imposed for absolute territorial protection are substantial. BMW was fined around CHF 156 million, [41] Nikon with more than CHF 12 million, [42] and Gaba CHF 3.8 million. [43]

The presumption under Article 5(4) CartA relates to the suppression of competition: the COMCO must define a relevant market, assess the market share of the parties, identify competing products in the market and assess whether the presumption could be reversed due to pressure from remaining intra-brand and actual or potential inter-brand competition. The presumption is rebutted in all cases where intra-brand competition continues to exist. [44] An agreement establishing a price range whereby the discounts given by the resellers do not exceed 10% of the recommended price does not lead to the elimination of all effective competition, so that the presumption is reversed, unless the price range was so small that it could

[41] FAC, judgement of 13 November 2015, B-3332/2012, BMW, confirmed in FSC, judgment of 24 October 2017, 2C_63/2016.

[42] FAC, judgement of 16 September 2016, B-581/2012, *Nikon*, LPC 2016/3, p. 831.

[43] FSC, judgment of 28 June 2016, 2C_180/2014, *Gaba*, ATF/BGE 143 II 297, para 9.7.3.

[44] FSC, judgment of 18 May 2018, 2C_101/2016, *Altimum*, ATF/BGE 144 II 246, paras 7.2 and 7.3; FSC, judgment of 28 June 2016, 2C_180/2014, *Gaba*, ATF/BGE 143 II 297, para 4.2.

not affect competition. [45] In the same case, the FSC left open the question whether the maintenance of inter-brand competition alone can also rebut the presumption. [46]

In most cases, the presumption of suppression of competition is reversed. However, the assessment does not stop with the reversal of this presumption. Another presumption comes into play: the restriction is considered as significant under Article 5(1) CartA and it is very difficult for the parties to rebut that presumption or to invoke successfully economic efficiencies. The agreement will undergo an assessment under Article 5(1) Cart and the undertakings remain subject to fines (Sect. 2.4.1.3), and it was this latter point that was confirmed in 2016. [47]

The safe harbour for undertakings having a market share of under 15% is not available: [48] undertakings having very low market shares cannot simply rely on them and conclude that the agreement is not appreciable under Article 5(1) CartA.

In theory, the parties may still demonstrate that the agreement is a "cas bagatelle". There have been no cases yet, but presumably such would be the case if the supplier has a market share of only a few percent (probably around 1–3%).

If market shares of the parties exceed 15%, they have still the possibility to show that the restriction is justified on grounds of economic efficiency under Article 5 (2) CartA, however, as explained above, the safe harbour related to market shares under 30% is not applicable. [49] In all circumstances, the burden of proof is on companies to demonstrate that the restriction is indispensable to achieve economic efficiencies. If the parties prove that the agreement is justified based on economic efficiency grounds of Article 5(2) CartA, the agreement is lawful. To date, there are no cases where the parties to an agreement covered by Article 5(4) of the CartA have been able to successfully invoke economic efficiency arguments. We will explain the narrow interpretation in case law in Sect. 4.2.4. Where no economic efficiency grounds of Article 5(2) CartA are successfully invoked, the agreement is unlawful and the parties subject to fines.

This type of restrictions will be explained in detail at Sects. 4.3.1 and 4.3.2 below.

4.2.2 Severe Restrictions from a Qualitative Standpoint Not Covered by Article 5(4) CartA

Several restrictions not covered by Article 5(4) CartA are considered as severe from a qualitative standpoint. [50] They can be divided in three broad categories: territorial restrictions, such as restriction of active sales (Sect. 4.3.2.2), and customer allocation

---

[45] FSC, judgment of 18 May 2018, 2C_101/2016, *Altimum*, ATF/BGE 144 II 246, para 7.2.

[46] Idem, para 7.2.

[47] FSC, judgment of 28 June 2016, 2C_180/2014, *Gaba*, ATF/BGE 143 II 297.

[48] See Article 16(1) Verticals Notice.

[49] Article 16(2) Verticals Notice.

[50] Article 15 Verticals Notice.

(Sect. 4.3.3), [51] non-compete and single branding type of restrictions (Sect. 4.3.5), [52] and restrictions related to online sales, such as restrictions on the effective use of internet (Sect. 4.3.6.3) and restrictions regarding online intermediation services. [53]

Although such restrictions are qualified as severe, contrary to those covered by Article 5(4) CartA, quantitative criteria related to the situation of the parties are considered as part of the analytical framework. [54] However, there have been no sufficient cases to draw definitive conclusions or soft safe harbours related to market shares.

In theory, the parties can show that their agreement is a "trivial case" (cas bagatelle), either because the market shares of each party are negligible or because the value of the agreement or sales is insignificant to have an appreciable effect on the relevant market. COMCO or the courts have not ruled on the matter. In practice, the COMCO' Secretariat has the discretion to initiate or not a preliminary investigation in such cases, and in practice, very insignificant cases are not pursued by a formal investigation, sometimes also due to a change in company practice. These cases are usually not officially reported and are therefore not public. Nor are there any statistics. Nevertheless, companies wishing to avoid an in-depth investigation are advised to raise the factual elements of a "trivial case" at the outset and support it with evidence of negligible sales in Switzerland and/or low market shares, or to act proactively to eliminate the doubts raised by the Secretariat by changing their business practice.

As in the case of restrictions covered by Article 5(4) CartA, the safe harbour for undertakings having a market share of under 15% is not applicable for a number of severe restrictions from a qualitative standpoint: undertakings having lower market shares cannot simply rely on them and conclude that the agreement is not significant under Article 5(1) CartA. [55] This is the case for the territorial restrictions (if exceptions are not met) and restriction on the delivery of spare parts on final users or non-authorised repairers or maintenance service providers.

By contrast, the safe harbour for undertakings having a market share of under 15% applies to the non-compete obligations and single banding, to restriction to online intermediation services, [56] as well as restrictions on active sales and to customer allocation restrictions.

Lastly, the safe harbour related to the economic efficiency justification for parties having market shares under 30% is not applicable to any severe restrictions from a qualitative standpoint mentioned at Article 15 Verticals Notice. [57] Therefore, the

[51] Article 15(b), (c) and (d) Verticals Notice on active and passive sales restrictions, Article 15 (f) Verticals Notice related to the supply of components and spare parts.

[52] Article 15(g), (h) and (i) Verticals Notice.

[53] Article 15(e) and (j) Verticals Notice.

[54] Article 14(b) Verticals Notice.

[55] Article 16(1) Verticals Notice to be read in conjunction with Article 15(b)–(f) Verticals Notice.

[56] Article 16(1) Verticals Notice to be read in conjunction with Article 15(g)–(j) Verticals Notice.

[57] Article 18(2) Verticals Notice.

restriction of competition and the justification on economic efficiency grounds must follow an assessment of the quantitative criteria taking into account that the qualitative criteria are fulfilled since the clauses are considered to be severe restrictions of competition. The legal consequences of failing to show that the agreement is justified on grounds of economic efficiency are the civil consequences of unlawfulness: nullity and damages.

Finally, restrictions that fall outside the scope of Article 5(4) of CartA do not result in fines, even if they ultimately restrict competition following a thorough assessment of Articles 5(1) and 5(2) of CartA.

4.2.3 Other Significant Restrictions of Competition

The following analytical framework applies to other restrictions that may fall under Article 5(1) of the CartA, provided that they do not fall under Article 5(4) or are not considered to be qualitatively severe restrictions under Article 15 of the Verticals Notice.

First, both qualitative and quantitative elements must be considered to show that the restriction is significant under Article 5(1) CartA.

From a quantitative perspective, all such restrictions benefit from the 15% market share safe harbour: the agreement is not liable to restrict competition if each of the supplier and the buyer do not exceed the threshold of 15% market share in its relevant market. [58] This is valid without having to carry out any additional criteria in the framework of an individual assessment.

If one or both parties exceed the 15% threshold, their agreement may still benefit from the second safe harbour related to justification on grounds of economic efficiency if their market shares do not exceed the threshold of 30%. [59] There is no need for a case-by-case assessment, and any restriction is considered as justified on ground of economic efficiency and therefore as lawful.

In the event one or both parties exceed the threshold of 30% market share, the parties must assess the qualitative and quantitative criteria surrounding their vertical agreement. No vertical agreement within the meaning of Article 5(1) CartA has reached the courts. In *Hallenstadion*, [60] the FSC dealt with an exclusive agreement that was neither horizontal nor vertical, but the assessment is relevant since the agreement was assessed under Article 5(1) CartA (see Sect. 2.2.2.1). It was clarified that the analysis of the qualitative elements has priority, and if the qualitative elements of the restriction of competition are serious, it is not necessary to examine the quantitative elements and, consequently, it is not necessary to define the relevant market. By contrast, if there are no or few qualitative elements pointing to a

[58] Article 16(1) Verticals Notice.

[59] Article 18(2) Verticals Notice.

[60] FSC, judgment of 12 February 2020 2C_113/2017 *Hallenstadion*, p. 7.3.1.

restriction of competition, the assessment will focus on quantitative elements. The decisive element is the market share of the undertakings that are party to the agreement, and this requires the definition of the relevant market. In this case, one of the parties had a market share of 75% and the other approximately 60%, and the agreement therefore constituted a significant restriction of competition under Article 5(1) CartA based solely on quantitative criteria.

4.2.4 *Justification on Grounds of Economic Efficiency*

In this section, we will discuss the analytical framework of Article 5(2) CartA on justification for efficiency grounds. According to Article 5(2) CartA, "agreements affecting competition are deemed to be justified on grounds of economic efficiency if: (a) they are necessary in order to reduce production or distribution costs, improve products or production processes, promote research into or dissemination of technical or professional know-how, or exploit resources more rationally; and (b) they will under no circumstances enable the parties involved to eliminate effective competition." Unlike Article 101(3) TFUE, Article 5(2) CartA does not include a requirement related to "allowing consumers a fair share of the resulting benefit".

All kind of agreements that do not eliminate competition may be justified on grounds of economic efficiency under Article 5(2) CartA. The FSC confirmed that agreements covered by Article 5(4) CartA may also benefit from the justification of Article 5(2) CartA when the presumption of restriction of competition is reversed. [61] In principle, a restraint is justified if the outcome is more efficient than without the restraint and effective competition is not eliminated. [62]

In *Altimum*, the FSC reviewed minimum prices and assessed the arguments raised by the respondent that the agreement on maximum resale prices allowed the general importer to prevent free riding within its network of resellers. The FSC referred to Leegin, by stating that the method used in Leegin is provided into Article 5 (2) CartA:

> the Swiss system deriving from Article 5(1) and (2) CartA [...] and the possibility of justification on grounds of economic efficiency, goes precisely in the same direction as the objective sought by American case law [...]. Thus, in Swiss law, the fact that an agreement is deemed to significantly restrict competition within the meaning of Article 5 (1) CartA will be considered unlawful and therefore subject to sanctions only if it is not justified by reasons of economic efficiency as described in Article 5 (2) LCart, which implies an assessment of the possible procompetitive effects of the agreement [...]. However, it is precisely to consider such positive effects, similar to those mentioned in Article 5 (2) CartA, that the Supreme Court has relaxed its case-law in Leegin [...] in order to avoid declaring a vertical

[61] FSC, judgment of 28 June 2016, 2C_180/2014, *Gaba*, ATF/BGE 143 II 297, para 7.1. FSC, judgment of 4 February 2021, 2C_149/2018, *Pfizer*, ATF/BGE 147 II 72, para 7.2.

[62] FSC, judgment of 4 February 2021, 2C_149/2018, *Pfizer*, ATF/BGE 147 II 72, para 7.2.

> price agreement illegal per se. In the referred case, it indicated [. . .] that vertical price agreements should be examined according to the rule of reason, that is, depending on their effects, as these could be justified by procompetitive effects, such as encouraging resellers to invest in providing services to customers, as well as facilitating access of new producers and new brands to the market [. . .]. [63]

The assessment that followed however did not match the encouraging comments about Leegin. While many arguments can be made on the grounds of economic efficiency, the criterion of necessity or indispensability of the agreement to reach efficiency gains was singled out in *Altimum* as a standalone condition to be fulfilled and construed narrowly. We will examine this judgment in detail, as it sets out not only how COMCO and the judges will apply Article 5(2) CartA in the context of Article 5(4) CartA, but also the tendency to apply the same narrow interpretation for restrictions covered only by Article 5(1) CartA.

Grounds listed in Article 5 (2) CartA are exhaustive, however they are formulated openly, which in principle allows to consider all objective efficiency gains. [64] Most importantly, the FSC held that both the scope of application and the concepts of economic efficiency referred to at Article 5(2) CartA must be construed broadly: the Court calls therefore for a non-restrictive implementation.

Efficiency gains must be of an economic nature, [65] which indicates in our view that non-economic grounds cannot be considered if they are unrelated to economic efficiency. Compelling public interests can be considered by the Federal Council (Sect. 1.7). The FAC gives more weight to the term *Volkswirtschaftlich* as a reference to the national economy, [66] to a kind of total or consumer surplus, when it held in ASCOPA that "the existence of a justification cannot already be affirmed if a conduct relevant under Cartel Act is efficient from the business point of view of an individual undertaking, namely if it mainly serves the cartel rent. It must be efficient from a macroeconomic or national economic perspective." [67] It is not clear what the FAC meant, but in practice it has used this concept to reject efficiencies that would benefit the undertakings involved in an agreement. One result is the introduction of the fair share requirement for consumers which was removed by parliament when the law was passed in 1995.

The Verticals Notice mentions generally a more efficient distribution structure in the sense of an improvement of products or production processes or a reduction of

[63] FSC, judgment of 18 May 2018, 2C_101/2016, *Altimum*, ATF/BGE 144 II 246, para 10.2.

[64] Idem, para 13.2.

[65] FSC, judgment of 28 June 2016, 2C_180/2014, *Gaba*, ATF/BGE 143 II 297, para 7.1. FSC, judgment of 4 February 2021, 2C_149/2018, *Pfizer*, ATF/BGE 147 II 72, para 7.2.

[66] FSC, judgment of 28 June 2016, 2C_180/2014, *Gaba*, ATF/BGE 143 II 297, para 7.1. FSC, judgment of 4 February 2021, 2C_149/2018, *Pfizer*, ATF/BGE 147 II 72, para 7.2: "Der Effizienzbegriff des schweizerischen Kartellgesetzes ist volkswirtschaftlich zu verstehen, und insofern muss die Effizienzsteigerung wirtschaftlicher Natur sein." which can be translated as "The concept of efficiency in the Swiss Cartel Act is to be understood in terms of the national economy, and in this respect the increase in efficiency must be of an economic nature".

[67] FAC, judgment of 12 December 2022, B-141/2012, *Estée Lauder/ASCOPA*, para 6.6.1.2.4.

distribution costs [68] and produces a non-exhaustive list of justification grounds such as the temporary protection of investments for the development of new geographic or product markets, efforts to ensure the uniformity and quality of the contract products, the protection of contract-specific investments that cannot be used outside the business relationship or can only be used at a high loss (hold-up problem), measures that avoid a sub-optimal level of sales promotion measures (e.g. customer advice) which may occur when one producer or distributor is able to divert the promotional efforts of another producer or distributor to their own benefit (free rider problem), measures that avoid double price mark-ups, which can arise if both the producer and the trader have market power (double marginalisation problem), economies of scale in distribution, the transfer of essential know-how and measures that aim at securing financial commitments (e.g. loans) that are not made available by the capital market. [69] The list is long and comprehensive.

In *Altimum*, the FSC discussed in depth the free riding argument brought by the respondent. After defining free riding, it accepted that resale price maintenance ensured a sufficient margin to all resellers encouraging them to compete on the basis of services offered to customers and enables them to encounter free-riding from other resellers. Thus, it can be an adequate means to address the issue of free riding. [70] In the context of minimum prices, the FSC said that such considerations only apply to products objectively requiring pre-sale services and advice: [71]

> In principle, they must be products of a certain complexity, value, or experience or credence products, so that the pre-sale services (advice to customers) are an essential element to the market. [72]

In the case at hand, headlamps, safety harness, ropes, crampons, ice axe and helmets were not considered as complex, they were however considered as technical products. Lack of complexity lead the FSC to consider that the information on the use of such products could be provided online by the manufacturer or the reseller, which finds advice on site unnecessary. The argument related to the possibility to make available information online risk becoming a difficult argument for manufacturers to rebut. However, it was the technical characteristics of the products and their nature (to ensure safety in mountain climbing) that lead the FSC to affirm the usefulness of pre-sales advice to customers.

In *Pfizer*, a case of recommended prices falling under the concept of concerted practices, the FSC considered the double marginalization and the reduction of transaction costs under the heading of the improvement of products or production processes, after confirming the wide interpretation of the concept which is not limited to technical or functional concerns, but also covers, for example, the

[68] Article 18(3) Verticals Notice.

[69] Article 18(4) Verticals Notice.

[70] FSC, judgment of 18 May 2018, 2C_101/2016, *Altimum*, ATF/BGE 144 II 246, para 13.4.4.

[71] Idem, para 13.4.4.

[72] Ibidem.

environmental impact of products. [73] Double marginalisation refers to the situation where both the manufacturer and the retailer have market power and the consumer has to pay the rent of both the manufacturer and the retailer, which leads to a reduction in the quantity sold compared to the scenario of a vertically integrated undertaking. [74] Reduction of the transaction costs was raised in relation to small pharmacies for which it was expensive to calculate the resale prices independently. Health insurance companies would also benefit from the transaction costs reduction.

It is however the indispensability criterion that was construed very narrowly in both cases, resulting at the rejection of all efficiency grounds raised by the respondent, mainly by raising the bar regarding the standard of proof. The FSC found the alternatives mentioned by the COMCO in *Altimum* as less intrusive means to prevent free-riding: minimum pre-sale advice obligations, limiting the application of minimum resale prices to online sales or large retailers as well as the implementation of a selective distribution system. [75] The underlying reason for that was the severe nature of resale price maintenance as such:

> in principle, an agreement imposing a minimum selling price is considered by its very nature capable of significantly restricting competition. Therefore, an exception to this principle can only be accepted if the indispensable nature of the efficiency gains are established. [76]

The same reasoning prevailed in *Pfizer*: the FSC mentioned that price recommendations were considered as a price fixing agreement, and as one of the most harmful vertical agreements, they do not in principle fulfil the conditions of indispensability in relation to double marginalization. [77] The reduction in transaction costs was assessed in the same way, by adding also that price fixing could help inefficient small pharmacies, but that Article 5(2) CartA is not there to protect inefficiency. [78]

Both *Altimum* and *Pfizer* show that the efficiency defence under Article 5 (2) CartA is almost impossible in the case of vertical agreements falling under Article 5(4) CartA, mainly due to the strict interpretation of the indispensability condition.

It is not clear whether the same narrow interpretation would prevail in the case of other vertical agreements that are not covered by Article 5(3) and (4) CartA. Given the limited enforcement of pure Article 5(1) CartA agreements by the COMCO, there are no cases dealt with by the FSC. No efficiency grounds were raised by the companies in the *Hallenstadion* case, and therefore the efficiency grounds were not discussed by the courts. [79]

---

[73] FSC, judgment of 4 February 2021, 2C_149/2018, *Pfizer*, ATF/BGE 147 II 72, para 7.4.1.

[74] Idem, para 7.4.2.

[75] FSC, judgment of 18 May 2018, 2C_101/2016, *Altimum*, ATF/BGE 144 II 246, para 13.5.3.

[76] Ibidem.

[77] FSC, judgment of 4 February 2021, 2C_149/2018, *Pfizer*, ATF/BGE 147 II 72, para 7.4.3.

[78] Idem, para 7.5.2.

[79] See FSC, judgment of 12 February 2020, 2C_113/2017, *Hallenstadion*, para 7.4.

The FAC applied in *ASCOPA* ruling the same strict interpretation to all vertical agreements as is applied to agreements covered by Article 5(4) of the CartA. [80] After referring to Gaba, Altimum and Pfizer, all Article 5(4) CartA cases, the FAC went on to emphasise the overall positive effect that efficiency gains must have on the economy, which must not only benefit companies. The result of the Article 5 (2) CartA assessment for an exchange of gross price lists, sales figures and advertising investments between luxury product manufacturers without any fixing price element was the following:

- The improvement of products and production processes was rejected because the exchange of information did not relate directly to the products. The arguments of benchmarking of luxury products for distributors that had to handle more than hundred products per brand, sometime thousands, did not impressed the COMCO nor the Federal Administrative Court. [81]
- The rational use of resources related to the cost reduction in the information search for all companies, some of them distributors of the size of SMEs, which was less expensive than the purchase of market studies. It was rejected because an increase in the welfare of undertakings is not the same as the consumer or total welfare. [82]
- Lastly, the same fate befell the arguments concerning the reduction of production and distribution costs [83] and the promotion of the research or dissemination of technical or professional know-how· [84]

The main conclusions for practitioners are as follows.

When assessing the risks of a certain practice, focus on the qualification of the restriction of competition on the assumption that the justification on efficiency grounds will be very difficult to prove and to raise successfully for agreements covered by Article 5(4) CartA and for serious restrictions of competition.

When assessing agreements covered only by Article 5(1) of the CartA, the economic efficiency reasons must at least be identified in the risk assessment, and they must be all the more important the higher the parties' market share.

In the event of litigation or proceedings before the COMCO Secretariat, economic efficiency grounds must be raised early and consistently during the proceedings, with supporting evidence. A very common argument in case law is that the parties do not put forward economic efficiency reasons as a justification for their agreements. The task of the parties and their lawyers is to force the authorities and the courts to take these arguments into account by raising them in a coherent way and providing good arguments and evidence for them. The door is not completely closed,

[80] FAC, judgment of 12 December 2022, B-141/2012 *Estée Lauder/ASCOPA*, paras 6.6.1.2 ff.

[81] FAC, judgment of 12 December 2022, B-141/2012, *Estée Lauder/ASCOPA*, para 6.6.3.1.

[82] Idem, para 6.6.3.2.

[83] Idem, para 6.6.3.3.

[84] Idem, para 6.6.3.4.

but the parties must provide substantial evidence that their agreement brings efficiency gains that outweigh the negative effects of agreements.

4.3 Assessment of Most Common Restrictions

4.3.1 Price Restrictions

4.3.1.1 Resale Price Maintenance

Article 5(4) CartA presumes that effective competition is eliminated "in the case of agreements between undertakings at different levels of the production and distribution chain regarding fixed or minimum prices". Therefore, agreements or concerted practices with distributors on minimum or fixed resale prices lead to automatic fines.

The provision covers the obligations or commitments of general importers or distributors who purchase products from the supplier or other wholesale distributor to resell them for resale at a fixed price or at a price not lower than an agreed minimum level. The wholesale or invoice price charged by the supplier to its distributor is not concerned by the regulation of resale price maintenance. [85] The provision covers only obligations or commitments of the distributor to follow a pre-established commercial policy that directly or indirectly leads to fixed or minimum resale prices applied to its sales at the next level of trade (wholesale or retail level).

Reference to minimum and fixed prices leave room for suppliers or distributors to set maximum resale prices. Therefore, setting maximum resale prices is lawful.

The concept of agreement is wide and covers direct or indirect commercial measures leading to the setting of a minimum or fixed resale price. Direct means are contractual clauses setting an obligation on the distributor to respect a fixed price or to set the resale price above a minimum level. Communications between the supplier and the distributor in which they agree on the level of the resale price to be charged to the distributor's customers are also direct means of resale price maintenance. The discussion that leads to setting a resale price can be initiated by the supplier or the distributor itself. In other words, direct means cover any measure and agreement that clearly relate to the level of the resale prices to be applied by the distributor to its customers.

Indirect means cover commercial incentives or actions that would lead the distributor to resell the product at a certain price level, pressure on the distributor if it does not resell the products at the price level requested by the supplier, and any mechanism used to calculate and maintain a certain level of the resale price such as linking the resale price of the distributor to market prices applied by other

[85] Applying different (higher) wholesale prices for resellers or sales in Switzerland may be considered an indirect absolute territorial restriction. See Sect. 4.3.2.

competitors. [86] The examples of indirect means are inspired by the EU Vertical Guidelines and are not exhaustive. Commercial incentives cover the setting or guaranteeing of a fixed or a minimum margin to the distributor, limiting the freedom of the distributor to grant or to set the level of rebates or discounts to its clients, making marketing payments or discounts by the supplier conditional on the implementation by the distributor of a fixed or minimum resale price level or the obligation on the distributor not to advertise or communicate on the market resale prices that are lower than a certain price level (minimum advertised prices or MAPs [87]). Pressure on the distributor that aims at ensuring that the distributor applies a certain level of resale price covers wide range of practices going from threats, intimidation, warnings, sanctions, delays or suspension of deliveries, threat or actual termination of the contract in case the distributor does not apply the price levels requested by the supplier. [88] Under contract law, such pressure or coercion may prevent the conclusion of a contract; [89] however, a different logic prevails in Swiss (and European) competition law, which interprets pressure exerted by one party on another contractual party as a means of reaching and enforcing an agreement within the meaning of Article 4(1) CartA. The last category of indirect means covers measures to ensure that the resale prices charged by the distributor follow the prices set by the supplier's competitors, for example by imposing an obligation on the distributor to calculate its resale price by reference to the price of one or more competing products on the market. This is relevant mainly for distributors active at the retail level.

The FSC has issued two important judgments about resale price maintenance and price recommendations, in the area of sports equipment (*Altimum*) and erectile dysfunction drugs that are not reimbursed by compulsory health insurance (so-called off-list drugs or *Hors-Liste Medikamente, Pfizer* case).

The judgement in *Altimum* [90] is important for at least two aspects: firstly, the distinction between price recommendations and minimum price maintenance and, secondly, the standard of proof for establishing an agreement and its appreciable effect on competition. It is useful for practitioners to briefly describe the facts. Altimum was the general Swiss importer of three of the five brands of sports equipment—headlamps, harnesses, ropes, helmets, ice axes and crampons—and it distributed them through a network of 333 independent sports resellers and retailers. One of the retailers complained to the COMCO that the general importer stopped supplying it because it did not comply with minimum resale prices. The FSC

---

[86] Explanatory note to the Verticals Notice, para 6.

[87] MAPs are lawful in North America and other areas. Companies from those areas that expand their commercial activities in the EU and Switzerland are advised to check their contracts and commercial practices.

[88] Explanatory note to the Verticals Notice, para 6.

[89] See Articles 29 and 30 CO on duress.

[90] FSC, judgment of 18 May 2018, 2C_101/2016, *Altimum*, ATF/BGE 144 II 246.

considered an appeal by the COMCO [91] against the judgment of the FAC which had overturned the COMCO decision on the grounds that it had not proved the existence of an agreement between Altimum and each of its 330 resellers and retailers, but only with 39 of them, which in turn precluded the finding of a significant restriction of competition. The FAC concluded that exchanges between Altimum and the other resellers were only (lawful) price recommendations. It was established that Altimum attempted to prohibit its resellers from setting prices 10% below the recommended price list, and ensured that the recommended prices were applied, by using pressure, threatening them with delay or suspension of deliveries in case of non-compliance. There was evidence that Altimum told the complainant retailer that recommended prices were mandatory and that deliveries would be stopped if the price was 10% below the recommended price. Altimum had also asked some retailers not to apply cash discounts. Written evidence of binding resale prices and pressure was limited to a few retailers.

The case is important because it makes the distinction between binding price recommendations, that are considered agreements, and non-binding unilateral declarations that are allowed. The binding character of a unilateral declaration may manifest itself in threats, refusal to deliver or termination. The FSC held that it is this binding character which leads to the adhesion of the other party to minimum prices, expressly or by conclusive acts, and which is sufficient to retain an agreement within the meaning of Article 4 (1) CartA [92] (see also Sect. 2.2.2.2). Conclusive acts include the retailer following the supplier's price recommendations and other pricing instructions. It was not clear from the case whether the retailer's mere voluntary compliance with the price recommendations, without pressure or threat, would lead to conclusive action and thus to an agreement. This was confirmed in the Pfizer case, where a concerted practice was found.

On the proof to establish an agreement, the FSC considers that the evidence of a binding agreement with 39 resellers is sufficient to establish the existence of a general pricing policy implemented through general conditions applicable to all 333 resellers; [93] the whole constitutes a "bundle of converging and convincing evidence" providing proof of an unlawful agreement on minimum prices that covers all authorised distributors. To reach this conclusion, the FSC lowered the standard of proof for finding an agreement to that required for the establishment of complex economic facts by referring to the *Publigroupe* judgment. [94] In Publigroupe, the FSC had considered the standard of proof required to examine the complex data and economic assumptions related to the definition of the relevant market. The difference is that the agreement to maintain the resale price or the binding nature of price

[91] Technically it is the Department of Economic Affairs (part of the Swiss government) that represents the COMCO in Courts, since the COMCO has no legal personality.

[92] FSC, judgment of 18 May 2018, 2C_101/2016, *Altimum*, ATF/BGE 144 II 246, para 6.4.1.

[93] FSC, judgment of 18 May 2018, 2C_101/2016, *Altimum*, ATF/BGE 144 II 246, para 6.5.

[94] FSC, judgment of 18 May 2018, 2C_101/2016, *Altimum*, ATF/BGE 144 II 246, para 6.4.4. FSC, judgment of 29 June 2012, 2C_484/2010, *Publigroupe*, ATF/BGE 139 I 72, para 8.3.2.

recommendations following pressure or threats is based on facts that cannot be said to be complex or based on economic assumptions. The FSC then goes on to state that circumstantial evidence is sufficient proof in the absence of direct evidence, because in competition law direct evidence of illegal agreements is rare. [95] This means that in the case of circumstantial evidence, the level of proof is no higher than in the presence of direct evidence, and even as low as in the case of evaluating economic assumptions.

For practitioners, the key message is that, first, communications from the supplier or exchanges with the distributor on price recommendations or resale or retail prices risk being interpreted as a binding request or pressure on the distributor to follow the recommended prices, and second, circumstantial or direct evidence of an agreement with only one or a few distributors in the network is sufficient to trigger the application of the presumption of Article 5(4) CartA. The low standard of proof for finding an agreement is important since once an agreement on minimum prices is found, the mechanism of Article 5(4) and (1) CartA does not accept arguments related to the trivial or insignificant impact on the market. Also, the argument that the parties did not implement the agreement is not available. Indeed, on restriction of competition, the FSC considers that agreements on minimum prices are as a general rule not a "trivial matter" (no "cas bagatelle"), so that they generally fall within the scope of Article 5(1) CartA even though the resumption of Article 5(4) is rebutted. [96] The FSC uses the expression "as a general rule" implying the possibility of exceptions, but there is to date no indication of any intention to expand on or give guidance on what such exceptions would be. The analysis of Article 5(1) and (2) CartA applied in this case is relevant in many cases since the presumption of elimination of competition was reversed. The fact that the distributors were free to set a price within the 10% range of the recommended prices was considered sufficient to rebut the presumption of elimination of competition in Article 5 (4) CartA. [97] In view of the above, the only defence to making the agreement lawful remains justification on economic efficiency grounds, but as we will explain below, the threshold for businesses is so high that this justification remains very difficult to achieve.

The judgment is a rare example for the interpretation of justification on efficiency grounds under Article 5(2) CartA by examining concepts such as free riding or pre-sales or after-sales services, very relevant in distribution. As explained before, if the presumption of Article 5(4) CartA is reversed, the resale price maintenance will be deemed to significantly restrict competition under Article 5(1) CartA but can still be justified for grounds of economic efficiency under Article 5(2) CartA. In *Altimum*, the FSC had the opportunity to discuss the efficiency grounds raised by the general importer, ultimately rejecting them because resale price maintenance was not indispensable to achieve them. We will discuss here the efficiency arguments raised in in this case since they were assessed in the context of resale price maintenance.

---

[95] FSC, judgment of 18 May 2018, 2C_101/2016, *Altimum*, ATF/BGE 144 II 246, para 6.4.4.

[96] FSC, judgment of 18 May 2018, 2C_101/2016, *Altimum*, ATF/BGE 144 II 246, para 10.1.

[97] Idem, para 7.3.

The FSC defines a 'free rider' as a competitor who takes advantage of the services of companies that provide additional, decisive sales related services without bearing the costs. [98] This is the case of resellers who take advantage of the promotional efforts and advice given to clients by other resellers. The minimum resale price is one of the adequate means to fight free riding, because it allows to reduce price competition and to shift it to the level of services rendered around or before the purchase, thus increasing the quantity and quality of these services to the benefit of consumers. [99] The FSC thus recognizes the fight against free riding as one of the justifying grounds with positive effects on competition. The positive effects of combating free riding are not, however, recognized in general, but only about products for which pre-sale customer advice is useful: these are products of a certain complexity or value and products of experience or trust. [100] The products themselves must be subject to free riding, in the sense that consumers ask for services prior to purchase and may buy the product from the cheapest dealer after seeking advice from another dealer. Harnesses, ropes, helmets, ice axes and crampons are technical products and therefore of a certain value that can be subject to free riding, which justifies the usefulness of advice before purchase. The FSC uses the criterion of the usefulness of pre-purchase advice for these products, even though it also mentions the fact that these products are also available for sale on the Internet indicates that pre-purchase advice is not essential to the market. [101] Headlamps however do not fall into this category. The benefit of the advice to consumers must be product specific. The risk that consumers will buy an overpriced product in the absence of pre-purchase advice was not relevant, as this risk exists for all products.

However, in order to be justified on grounds of economic efficiency, resale price maintenance must be necessary to achieve these grounds of economic efficiency (Article 5 (2) (a) CartA). It is this condition that is difficult for suppliers or general importers to meet. The supplier must prove that resale price maintenance is necessary and that there are no less harmful means available to it. [102] It is not sufficient to merely allege this fact. For example, the FSC criticized the general importer imposing minimum prices for not having demonstrated that it had developed a strategy based on minimum prices to improve the quality of advice and reduce free riding. It is clear from the FSC's argument that the COMCO, on the other hand, only has to mention the existence of alternative means to achieve the intended objectives without having to show that they are feasible or even available to the distributor concerned; it is then up to the distributor to explain why the alternative means merely alleged by the COMCO are not suitable for achieving the intended goal. [103] The following alternative means were mentioned by the COMCO and considered

---

[98] Idem, para 13.4.3.

[99] Idem, para 13.4.3.

[100] FSC, judgment of 18 May 2018, 2C_101/2016, *Altimum*, ATF/BGE 144 II 246, para 13.4.4.

[101] Idem, para 13.4.5.

[102] Idem, para 13.4.3.

[103] Idem, para 13.4.3.

convincing by the FSC: the use of a selective distribution system and the obligation for the discounter to have staff in the store. The FSC suggests another means: the imposition of a mid-range price agreement limited to certain retailers, such as department stores or those selling via the Internet, in other words only to those distributors who might behave as free riders. The COMCO had also suggested as an alternative that suppliers could impose a contractual obligation on distributors to make pre-sale services available [104] instead of imposing a minimum resale price, but this point was not developed in the judgment.

The second case concerning erectile dysfunction drugs, known also as *Hors-Liste Medikamente*, is important because separates the concept of agreement into two distinctive categories, conventions and concerted practices. We will use here the term *convention* because it fits better the term used in Article 4(1) CartA—*Vereinbarung* in German, *convention* in French and *convenzione* in Italian—and to distinguish from the overall concept of agreement (Sect. 2.2.2.2). It is in the context of concerted practices that the FSC extends the notion of agreement to cover pure price recommendations where there is no evidence of an express or tacit convention. The facts of the case are important for practitioners as they provide the context for FSC findings: Eli Lilly, Bayer and Pfizer had issued non-binding price recommendations for Cialis, Levitra and Viagra to wholesalers, pharmacies and doctors by entering them in a database of drugs used by all of them daily. [105] The database contained other necessary information such as the barcodes. The price recommendations were issued at the request of the retailers, and there was some contact between the manufacturers and some retailers around the issuing of price recommendations. There were about 5000 users of the database—pharmacies, doctors, etc. [106] The database showed the recommended prices in cash registers but there was no further contact between the three drug manufacturers and the pharmacies. The price recommendations were non-binding, and no threats or pressure were applied. A crucial element was the rate of retailers who followed the price recommendations, also called the follow-up rate. The follow-up rates retained by the FSC are as follows: for pharmacies, the overall compliance rate was 89.3%, of which 52% followed the price recommendations strictly and 37.3% followed them partially (with partial discounts of less than 50%); for doctors, the overall compliance rate was 81.7%, of which 75.5% followed the recommendations strictly and 6.2% partially (they applied discounts of less than 50%).

The COMCO could not prove a tacit agreement and therefore went through the concerted practice route. After explaining the constituent elements of a concerted practice—coordination, market behaviour and causality—the FSC applied them to

[104] Idem, para 13.4.2.

[105] The courts have dealt with several appeals from all manufacturers, but we will only refer to the Pfizer judgment here for ease of reference (FSC, judgment of 4 February 2021, 2C_149/2018, *Pfizer*, ATF/BGE 147 II 72).

[106] The case mentions about 1600 pharmacies and 3600 independent doctors.

the price recommendations issued by the three drug manufacturers. The three constituent elements of a concerted practice are explained below.

On the first requirement of *coordination* or *concertation*, the FSC held that when each manufacturer sent the price recommendation to the retailers through the electronic system to cash registers, they knew that by scanning the barcode of the product the retailers would see the price recommendation each time it was scanned. Conversely, retailers accepted the communication of price recommendations. They could also assume that the price displayed in the database represented an optimal retail price, based on the manufacturer's market research and analysis, and that all retailers had the same price information. The retailers were therefore at least partially in tacit agreement with the manufacturer. To this extent, the FSC concluded that a communication took place between each manufacturer and the retailers, which reduced or even eliminated uncertainties about the reactions of other retailers to their own behaviour. [107]

On the second requirement concerning *market behaviour*, the FSC examined the degree of compliance or follow-up rate of price recommendations by retailers. It confirmed the two types of measures of the follow-up rate used by the COMCO which are relevant at two different stages of the legal assessment:

- Firstly, the number of retailers (pharmacies and doctors) who apply the recommended price. This is relevant for the assessment of whether there is a concerted practice under Article 4(1) CartA. The FSC seems to confirm that a threshold of 50% of retailers following price recommendations would be sufficient to reach an agreement, and that in the Pfizer case this threshold was far exceeded. [108]
- Secondly, the number of units sold at the recommended price by the retailers, which is relevant for the assessment of the restriction of competition under Article 5 CartA.

The FSC also answered two questions: what the required or minimum follow-up rate is to achieve a concerted practice, and how to evaluate the discounts granted by retailers. The FSC implicitly accepted as valid the suggestion of the legal doctrine that a market (in this case at the retail level) follow-up rate of 50% is sufficient to hold that there is market behaviour or reaction that could be linked to price recommendations. In applying it to the present case, it considered that the follow-up rate should also include pharmacies and doctors who largely followed the price recommendations, even if they gave small discounts from time to time. This reasoning allowed the FSC to base its judgement on a follow-up rate of 89.3% for retailers and 81.7% for doctors, which were well above the suggested follow-up rate of 50%. The discounts granted by retailers was an argument raised by manufacturers to rebut the existence of a 'market behaviour'. The SCF distinguishes here between *general or systematic discounts* and *selective discounts*. The retailer who grants

[107] FSC, judgment of 4 February 2021, ATF/BGE 147 II 72, *Pfizer*, para 5.2.2.

[108] Idem, para 5.3.7.

general or systematic discounts charges a price other than the recommended price. In this case, the retailer follows an independent pricing policy, and his freedom of action is not limited. Conversely, if retailers only discount selectively from the recommended price, they follow the recommended price. In summary, only those retailers who give general or systematic discounts are considered not to be following the recommended prices.

It is on the third requirement relating to the causal link between coordination *and market behaviour* that the FSC position is most significant. The court relaxes the standard of proof to the point that causation is hardly a requirement. Since coordination took place over several years and prices were also set in accordance with this coordination, the FSC considers that it can be assumed that there is a causal link between coordination and the market behaviour of retailers. [109] The court refers to the relaxed standard of proof used to prove directly or indirectly a price agreement. [110] The first alleviation of the burden of proof is the application of a rebuttable presumption that the undertakings concerned (i.e. pharmacies and physicians) have taken account of the information exchanged when determining their market behaviour (i.e. when fixing their retail prices). The second alleviation of the standard of proof is based on the homogeneity of the retailers' behaviour, which becomes evidence when it leads to conditions of competition that do not correspond to normal market conditions, considering the nature of the products, the importance and number of the undertakings concerned and the size of the relevant market. According to FSC, the fact that 89.3% of all pharmacies and 81.7% of all dispensing doctors sell the drugs in principle at the same prices does not correspond to normal market conditions. Several hundred retailers that operate in a market without advertising, with low transparency, and where all retailers have different cost's structure, cannot explain a similarity of conduct as observed in the case but for a concerted practice based on price recommendations issued by manufacturers. A similarity of behaviour such as that observed in the case in a non-transparent market where there are several hundred retailers operating without advertising and with different cost structures can only be explained by the existence of a concertation based on price recommendations issued by the manufacturers. Causality was the third elements of the concerted practices; price recommendations constituted therefore an agreement within the meaning of Article 4 (1) CartA.

While the treatment of the price recommendations followed by many retailers as an agreement is like what would have prevailed under EU competition law, it is the assessment of the restriction of competition under Article 5(4) of the CartA that differs, in particular regarding its consequences. The EU law considered price recommendations to be restrictions by effect, [111] whereas the Pfizer case subsumed the concerted practice under Article 5(4) CartA, which is similar to a restriction by object. The manufacturers' argument, followed by the FAC, that the price

[109] FSC, judgment of 4 February 2021, 2C_149/2018, *Pfizer*, ATF/BGE 147 II 72, para 5.4.1.

[110] Idem, para 5.4.2.

[111] EU Vertical Guidelines, paras 199 and 200.

recommendations served as a maximum price was rejected as unconvincing. The FSC concludes that the concerted practice was not about a maximum price; since most of pharmacies followed the recommended prices, there was an agreement on fixed prices. [112] Such an agreement is, however, covered by the presumption of Article 5(4) of the Cartel Act, which results in fines for the companies even if the presumption is rebutted. Thus, price recommendations are considered as fixed prices if retailers apply them strictly or with a small discount margin, even if there is no pressure, threat or agreement on the level of the resale price. [113] Explanatory note to the Verticals Notice mentions intensive or regular communication around the price recommendation between the manufacturer and retailers as a risk factor in itself. [114] This shows again that the application of Article 5(4) of the CartA treats price recommendations more severely than in European legislation.

The legal assessment of resale price maintenance has become complex following *Altimum* and *Pfizer* in particular. For practitioners, a few points are useful.

First, the standard of proof for reaching an agreement is low under the Cartel Act and has been further lowered to extend the scope of concerted practices. In practice, this means that advice on RPM and price recommendation should cover communication between suppliers and retailers, which covers direct contact via e-mail or verbal discussions, but also communication that does not involve direct contact between the parties, namely via electronic tools or third parties.

Second, for conventions there is no quantitative element required for the application of Article 5(4) CartA. Implementation is also not required. Once an agreement is established between the supplier and one of its resellers on fixed or minimum prices, Article 5(4) CartA applies with the consequence that fines are imposed.

Third, where there is no direct contact with retailers and therefore no convention, the assessment should not stop there. Following the Pfizer case, practitioners are advised to assess the risk of a concerted practice between the supplier and its distributors.

Fourth, when assessing price recommendations, following the position of EU law is misleading, and the risk assessment should be made exclusively by considering the criteria and jurisprudence of Swiss Cartel Act. Price recommendations are specifically addressed below.

4.3.1.2 Price Recommendations

Price recommendations are a sensitive area of Swiss competition law, which carries a certain risk. They are permitted in principle, but uncertainty about the circumstances in which they may qualify as resale price maintenance means that their issuers are exposed to the risk of fines.

---

[112] Idem, paras 6.4.4. and 6.4.5.

[113] Explanatory note to the Verticals Notice, para 8.

[114] Explanatory note to the Verticals Notice, para 8.

Price recommendations in vertical agreements, which consist of unilateral and non-binding declarations of the supplier, are not, subject to a concerted practice, agreements within the meaning of Article 4(1) CartA, since they are not such as to limit the decision-making autonomy of the parties. [115] In pure unilateral declarations of the supplier, there is no clear and conscious collaboration between two or more undertakings, and therefore there is no agreement within the meaning of Article 4 (1) CartA. [116] This is generally the case for price recommendations, unless these declarations are binding or constitute a concerted practice. [117]

There are three situations in which price recommendations are treated as resale price maintenance.

The first situation is price recommendations that are accompanied by communications between the manufacturer and the distributor that reveal they agreed to consider them as a fixed or minimum resale price. In those circumstances, price recommendation is simply one of the means to communicate the level of the fixed or minimum resale prices, and the parties agree, generally in writing, to set a price by reference to the recommended price. There will usually be direct evidence of such communication, and this would be considered as a convention or agreement. The assessment is similar to EU law.

The second situation is where the price recommendations are binding, either because the manufacturer requires the reseller to comply with them or because it uses pressure, threats or commercial incentives to ensure that the reseller implements them. The recommendation has a binding character for instance if the supplier or general importer determines the resale price to be applied by the distributor, and the latter is exposed to sanctions in case of refusal to apply it. [118] A unilateral declaration may, if it is binding, constitute an agreement within the meaning of Article 4 (1) CartA. [119] A unilateral declaration is binding if the will of the author of the declaration is recognizable for the other party and if the latter accepts it expressly or by a conclusive act. [120] The use of "in particular" by the FSC indicates that the binding character can be inferred from other circumstances. This means that the interpretation of binding character would be wider than in EU law. In this situation, there would be direct evidence on the binding character of the price recommendations or on the use of threats, pressure or commercial incentives. In this case also binding price recommendations would be considered as a convention, a type of an agreement.

The third situation is where there is no direct evidence of an agreement, binding nature or pressure on the distributor, but where resellers follow or respect the

[115] FSC, judgment of 18 May 2018, 2C_101/2016, *Altimum*, ATF/BGE 144 II 246, para 6.4.1.

[116] FSC, judgment of 18 May 2018, 2C_101/2016, *Altimum*, ATF/BGE 144 II 246, para 6.4.1; FSC, judgment of 13 November 1998, ATF/BGE 124 III 495, para 2b.

[117] FSC, judgment of 18 May 2018, 2C_101/2016, *Altimum*, ATF/BGE 144 II 246, para 6.4.1.

[118] Idem, para 6.4.1.

[119] Idem, para 6.4.1.

[120] Idem, para 6.4.1.

recommended prices. In this case, the issuance of price recommendations that are widely followed by dealers may, in certain circumstances, amount to a concerted practice aimed at maintaining resale prices. Whether the criteria for a concerted practice can be met is the most difficult aspect to assess.

Following the SFC judgment in Pfizer case, the follow-up rate is a criterion used to establish a concerted practice on resale price maintenance. The criterion relating to the follow-up rate of price recommendations by retailers or distributors was therefore used to distinguish price recommendations that had an impact on the market, probably as a focal point, from those that didn't. Although in this case the SFC relied on a follow-up rate of more than 50% of their drug retailers (pharmacies) which could correspond to the market itself (i.e. almost all pharmacies and doctors sold all three brands of drugs), the judgment did not establish clear criteria on when compliance with (i.e. the follow up of) the price recommendations by (only some) distributors could be qualified as resale price maintenance. The SFC's evasive response can be found here:

> It is therefore not the case that compliance alone is not sufficient for the assumption of a concerted practice or that pressure or other elements are necessarily required in addition to compliance. Conversely, it is also not the case that compliance alone is sufficient in every case. In this respect, an overall assessment is necessary [references omitted]. The interaction between coordination and success of such coordination must therefore be of a certain qualitative magnitude so that a concerted practice can be assumed. The price recommendation to be assessed must therefore present itself as a form of conduct which either meets the requirements of the statutory definition or does not. [121]

The "global assessment" technique therefore leaves the way open for a case-by-case assessment. The consequence is that once a price recommendation is qualified as a price related agreement under Article 4(1) Cartel Act, it falls under Article 5 (4) CartA in the framework of which market shares, or any other criterion related to the effects on the market, is irrelevant to assess whether that practice is unlawful. In other words, there is no market share safe harbour for the price recommendations. The 30% safe harbour used in Regulation 2022/720 cannot serve as guidance. The outcome of the assessment of price recommendations in the third situation differs from EU law in that the application of Article 5(4) CartA results in automatic fines. In the EU, price recommendations are exempted if the parties' market shares are below 30% and this exemption can only be withdrawn by decision in the case of cumulative effects. If such market share thresholds are exceeded, they may be restrictive of competition by effect but do not necessarily result in fines.

The previous Article 15(3) of the Verticals Notice presented the criteria that would lead COMCO's Secretariat to open an investigation. [122] It is worth

[121] FSC, judgment of 4 February 2021, ATF/BGE 147 II 72, *Pfizer*, para 4.5.1 (free translation).

[122] We reproduce the old version here because it gives an indication of the COMCO mindset on price recommendations, which also led to the investigation of the Pfizer case*: Article 15 Price recommendations "(1) In the case of price recommendations from suppliers to their resellers or their distributors, it is necessary to examine on a case-by-case basis whether there is an unlawful competition agreement within the meaning of Article 5 (4) and (1) CartA. (2) Price*

mentioning that those criteria are now found in the Explanatory note to the Verticals Notice.[123]

In particular, the following circumstances may give rise to the use of recommended prices and shall be used in the risk assessment:

- the fact that manufacturers or suppliers exert pressure on retailers and traders to comply with the recommended prices;
- the fact that manufacturers or suppliers grant incentives to resellers and distributors to comply with the recommended prices;
- the fact that the price recommendations are actually followed by a significant proportion of the resellers or traders;
- the fact that price recommendations are not made generally available, but only to resellers or dealers;
- the fact that recommended prices expressed in Swiss francs by manufacturers or suppliers on products, packaging or in catalogues etc. are not expressly designated as non-binding;
- the fact that the price level of the products affected by the price recommendations is significantly higher than in the neighbouring country for a comparable consideration.

4.3.1.3 Maximum Resale Prices

Setting or recommending maximum resale prices is lawful. The same applies to indirect measures such as an agreement on the maximum margin level of the reseller. The setting of the maximum resale price must be clearly indicated as such and must leave the reseller free to set his resale price below the maximum level. The reseller is not free if the manufacturer or importer exerts pressure or gives negative incentives when the reseller sets his resale price below the maximum level. Maximum resale prices are covered by Article 5(4) CartA if, as a result of pressure or incentives, they effectively have the effect of fixed or minimum selling prices.[124]

The setting of maximum prices may be included in an agreement with the reseller or communicated unilaterally by the manufacturer or importer to its downstream

recommendations are in principle considered to be significant restrictions to competition if they have the same effect as agreements imposing fixed or minimum prices, due to pressure or incentives from an undertaking party to the agreement (see Article 10(1)(a)). (3) The circumstances that may give rise to the investigation of price recommendations include:(a) the fact that price recommendations are not generally available, but issued to resellers or distributors only; (b) the fact that the price recommendations in Swiss francs indicated by producers or suppliers on products, packaging or in catalogues etc., are not expressly designated as non-binding; (c) the fact that the price level of the products concerned by the recommendations is - for comparable services - significantly higher than in neighbouring countries; (d) the fact that price recommendations are actually followed by a significant proportion of resellers or distributors."

[123] Explanatory note to the Verticals Notice, para 9.

[124] Explanatory note to the Verticals Notice, para 8.

distributors. In practice, it is important to communicate and record explicitly that the agreed resale price level is a maximum and that the reseller remains free to set the price below this level. Unclear communication of maximum resale prices could lead to a risk of misunderstanding and reclassification of the maximum price as a fixed (or minimum) resale price if resellers understand and treat it as such.

Price recommendations that recommend a maximum price level shall also be clearly communicated as such. A recommendation on a predetermined price level will not be considered as a maximum price where no indication was made to the resellers that the recommended level was a maximum cap. In the *Pfizer* case, the FSC disagreed with the FAC's view that price recommendations acted in practice as a maximum price level, [125] which implies that a maximum price recommendation must be clear and that, where the argument is based on how the recommendation was understood and applied by retailers, it must be demonstrated that it was applied as a maximum price level. This case shows that maximum prices cannot be assumed from the circumstances but must be clearly communicated as such.

Finally, there is no indication in the case law that genuine agreements or recommendations on maximum prices could qualify as resale price maintenance if some or most resellers apply exactly the maximum level of the agreed or recommended price. Therefore, in our view, the *Pfizer* case law [126] would not be applicable to the setting of genuine maximum prices.

4.3.2 Territorial Allocation and Restrictions

4.3.2.1 Absolute Territorial Protection Against Other Distributors

Absolute territorial protection is covered by the presumption of Article 5(4) CartA which refers to "agreements contained in distribution contracts regarding the allocation of territories to the extent that sales by other external distributors into these territories are not permitted". [127] Undertakings party to agreements that include absolute territorial protection provisions risk automatic fines, in addition to the risk of nullity and damages. We will deal first with the constituent elements of absolute territorial protection, but practitioners should be aware that the same result can be

---

[125] FSC, judgment of 4 February 2021, 2C_149/2018, *Pfizer*, ATF/BGE 147 II 72, paras 6.4.2 and 6.4.3.

[126] Idem.

[127] In German: "Die Beseitigung wirksamen Wettbewerbs wird auch vermutet [...] in Vertriebsverträgen über die Zuweisung von Gebieten, soweit Verkäufe in diese durch gebietsfremde Vertriebspartner ausgeschlossen werden". In French: "Sont également présumés entraîner la suppression d'une concurrence efficace [...] les contrats de distribution attribuant des territoires, lorsque les ventes par d'autres fournisseurs agréés sont exclues." In Italian: "La soppressione di una concorrenza efficace è pure presunta in caso di [...] di accordi relativi all'assegnazione di zone nell'ambito di contratti di distribuzione, per quanto vi si escludano vendite da parte di distributori esterni."

achieved by indirect means, which are also covered by Article 5(4) of the CartA and which we will deal with later in this section.

There are three conditions for finding an absolute territorial protection: [128] a distribution agreement, territorial allocation and exclusion of sales from one territory to another. The last two conditions—territorial allocation and exclusion of sales—can be achieved by indirect means, which are also covered by Article 5(4) of the CartA, [129] and which are addressed in the discussion of the three conditions below.

First, parties must have concluded a distribution agreement. The concept of distribution agreement covers all kind of vertical agreements and individual contractual clauses in distribution, license, franchise, agency, [130] production or R&D contracts regulating the purchase, sale or resale of contractual products (see Sect. 4.1 above). The absolute territorial restrictions may be included in one or more distribution agreements concluded between the supplier and the dealer in Switzerland or abroad. Only agreements between suppliers or distributors that exclude sales into a territory in Switzerland are covered, and not unilateral decisions of distributors not to sell or provide services to Swiss customers and consumers. A distributor or retailer may well decide of its own accord not to sell to Swiss customers or consumers. In other words, the prohibition of absolute territorial protection of Article 5(4) CartA does not directly or indirectly imply an obligation for distributors to deliver goods or services in Switzerland.

Second, the agreement should assign or allocate a territory to one of the parties, usually the dealer or the distributor in Switzerland. Article 5(4) CartA covers territorial allocation, not contractual appointment of particular distributors which is only a way to allocate territories. The Supreme Court explains this requirement in this way:

> A vertical distribution agreement allocates territory when it contains a clause allocating a territory which refers to an identified or identifiable area (e.g. Switzerland, which constitutes a potentially closed market, which justified the introduction of Art. 5 (4) CartelA). [131]

Consequently, it is not necessary that the supplier also "allocates" other territories outside Switzerland. The Supreme Courts further explains that:

> In order for the presumption of suppression of competition laid down in Art. 5 (4) CartA to come into play in connection with a distribution contract relating to Switzerland, it is not necessary to establish the existence of other allocations of territories made by the undertaking acting as supplier, i.e. to show that the latter has at the same time allocated territories other than Switzerland to undertakings other than the Swiss distributor (e.g. the allocation of France to a French distributor). The allocation of the Swiss market on an exclusive basis to an official distributor, as is the case here, is sufficient. [132]

---

[128] FSC, judgment of 28 June 2016, 2C_180/2014, *Gaba*, ATF/BGE 143 II 297, para 6.3.

[129] FAC, judgment of 16 September 2016, B-581/2012, *Nikon*, LPC 2016/3, p. 831, para 7.3.2.

[130] FSC, judgment of 3 March 2022, case 2C_44/2020, *Flammarion*.

[131] FSC, judgment of 21 December 2021, case 2C.43/2020, *Dargaud*, para 8.2; FSC, judgment of 28 June 2016, 2C_180/2014, *Gaba*, ATF/BGE 143 II 297, para 6.3.2.

[132] BGer 2C_39/2020 of 3.08.2022, *Diffulivre*, para 7.5.

The type of contractual assignment is not relevant: the distributor may be appointed as the sole distributor for a territory, as one of a limited number of exclusive distributors (shared distributors) or one of the selective distributors or simply non-exclusively. The type of selective distribution—qualitative or quantitative—is also irrelevant. Even territories covered by non-exclusive distribution agreements—the so-called open or free distribution—may be de facto allocated by excluding sales from distributors appointed in other territories. [133] In other words, it is not the form of contractual appointment or the form of the distribution system that counts, but the fact that (part of) the Swiss territory may be contractually or factually allocated to one or more distributors by excluding sales from one or more distributors appointed in other territories. The assigned area can be a country, part of a country or supranational territorial areas such as EMEA. [134]

It is wrong to assume that if no distributor is appointed (inside or outside Switzerland) to supply Switzerland or part of the Swiss territory, and the supplier does not reserve (part of) Switzerland for himself, there would not be territorial allocation within the meaning of Article 5(4) CartA. Suppliers take a risk when they include broad export bans with distributors outside Switzerland, even if they do not intend to market the goods in Switzerland or have neglected the Swiss market for various reasons. [135]

The Swiss territory can be allocated also indirectly, for example by introducing exclusive sourcing obligations for the purchase or supply of products, or an obligation to source after-sales or warranty services in Switzerland. [136] Therefore, exclusive purchase obligations or clauses under which the buyer must purchase the goods from a source within the allocated territory are covered by the prohibition of absolute territorial protection provision of Article 5(4) of the CartA. Such exclusive purchasing obligations may be found in the distribution agreements between the Swiss subsidiary or the general importer on the one hand and the independent (sub)-distributors in Switzerland on the other.

Third, the agreements should exclude sales from one territory to another. While the first two conditions are rather straightforward, the third is decisive for the qualification of absolute territorial protection under Article 5(4) and the most difficult to assess. The third condition covers undertakings of the supplier or obligations on the supplier or on distributors outside the allocated territory ensuring that sales from other territories are excluded. The undertakings or obligations could be found either in the contract entered between the supplier and the distributor to whom a territory in Switzerland is allocated, or in the agreements among the supplier and other distributors based outside the allocated territory (outside Switzerland). It is the exclusion of those sales that negatively affect Swiss customers and consumers.

---

[133] FAC, judgment of 16 September 2016, B-581/2012 *Nikon*, LPC 2016/3, p. 831, para 7.3.3.

[134] COMCO, decision of 9 April 2018 *RIMOWA*, LPC 2018/2 p. 363, para 39; FSC, judgment of 21 December 2021, 2C.43/2020, *Dargaud*, pt. 8.2.

[135] See Explanatory note to the Verticals Notice, para 11.

[136] FAC, judgment of 16 September 2016, B-581/2012, *Nikon*, LPC 2016/3, p. 831, para 7.3.2.

For example, the FSC considers that the third condition is fulfilled when the supplier undertakes in a distribution contract with the Swiss importer not to sell or allow its products to be sold on Swiss territory by companies other than the Swiss importer, to refrain from any direct or parallel distribution in Switzerland, or to make its best efforts to avoid any circumvention of the Swiss importer's exclusivity. [137] By entering into such commitments, the supplier undertakes not only not to supply its products to Swiss distributors themselves, but also to ensure that no other distributor of its products outside Switzerland competes with the importer by selling the same products as the latter to Swiss retailers. Such undertakings by the supplier towards the Swiss importer is sufficient to establish an absolute territorial protection. It is therefore not necessary to prove in addition that the supplier has included prohibitions on passive sales to Switzerland in its contract with distributors outside Switzerland or that these clauses have been implemented. [138] On the other hand, mere contractual clauses which designate an exclusive distributor in a territory, and which do not expressly undertake to use all means to ensure the distributor's exclusivity are not considered to grant absolute territorial protection and therefore fall outside the scope of Article 5(4) CartA. [139]

In the view of the FAC, the exclusion may target the sales to appointed distributors or to any distributor or retailer in the allocated territory even though they have no contractual relationship with the supplier or the general importer. [140] This clearly covers distributors and retailers active in all levels in an open distributor system. In addition, the presumption covers exclusion of passive sales to professional customers or consumers based in Switzerland. [141] The location of the buyer at the time of ordering the goods or services is irrelevant: the final customers or consumers may either cross the Swiss border and be denied goods or services outside Switzerland, like the case in BMW, or attempt to acquire goods or services from Switzerland, such as in case of online sales. [142]

Finally, any single case of exclusion falls under the presumption: consequently, protection against all or significant sales from external distributors is not a requirement. Parallel imports, online sales or the possibility for Swiss consumers and retailers to buy from online platforms such as Amazon do not rule out the finding of an absolute territorial protection. [143] Proof on exclusion of only a few sales is

[137] FSC, judgment of 3 August 2022, 2C_39/2020, *Diffulivre*, para 7.6.5.

[138] FSC, judgment of 3 August 2022, 2C_39/2020 *Diffulivre*, para 7.6.6.

[139] FSC of 21 December 2021, 2C_43/2020, *Dargaud.* FSC of 14 June 2022, cause 2C_37/2020, *Albert le Grand.*

[140] FAC, judgment of 16 September 2016, B-581/2012, *Nikon*, LPC 2016/3, p. 831, para 7.3.

[141] Explanatory note to the Verticals Notice, para 11. FSC, judgment of 24 October 2017, 2C_63/2016, *BMW*, ATF/BGE 144 II 194, para 6.4.

[142] COMCO, decision of 9 April 2018 *RIMOWA*, LPC 2018/2, p. 363.

[143] FSC, judgment of 21 December 2021, 2C.43/2020, *Dargaud,* ATF 148 II 25. FSC, judgment of 3 August 2022, 2C_39/2020, *Diffulivre*, para 7.6.6.

sufficient, although the parties may raise the argument of de minimis or *cas bagatelle*.

The third condition on exclusion of sales within the meaning of Article 5 (4) CartA covers the restriction of passive sales, not the restriction of active sales. According to FSC, the presumption of Article 5(4) CartA covers only absolute territorial protection that is implemented by restricting passive sales. Restriction of active sales is only a "relative" territorial protection, it does not fall under the presumption and therefore there is no risk of fines. Restriction of active sales is however considered as a severe restriction from a qualitative standpoint, [144] and could also to be unlawful under certain conditions (Sect. 4.3.2.2).

The Verticals Notice defines passive sales as "sales made in response to unsolicited requests from individual customers, including the supply of goods to or provision of services for such customers, which have not been initiated by targeting the relevant customers, customer groups or customers in the relevant territories and which include sales made as a result of participation in public procurement procedures or private call for tenders". [145] The definition is consistent with the EU.

The key criterion related to the definition of passive sales is "unsolicited request from individual customers", which can be all type of resellers (wholesale, intermediate distributors or retail), end customers or consumers. Therefore, the restriction of so-called direct imports by Swiss consumers who order online, cross the border or travel to another foreign country to buy products are also covered by Article 5 (4) CartA, not only parallel imports or sales to resellers. [146] Sales can be passive in relation to the allocated territory or in relation to allocated customers: only territorial passive sales fall under the presumption of Article 5(4) CartA, not passive sales related to customer allocation. The distinction is important for instance to understand the restriction on online sales, which are considered as sales to a particular group of customers. Restrictions of online sales are not covered by the presumption of Article 5(4) CartA if such restriction does not target (only or mainly) customers from the allocated territory. These are called special or qualified circumstances and will be discussed in Sect. 4.3.6 below.

Sales can be excluded by indirect means. This is the case if the supplier refuses to provide warranty services to resellers or end users who have not purchased the products through resellers in Switzerland. [147] Another situation where sales are excluded indirectly is where the supplier charges higher purchase or invoice prices to Swiss resellers, or charges higher prices to resellers based abroad (e.g. in the EU)

[144] Explanatory note to the Verticals Notice, para 13; Article 15(b), (c) and (d) Verticals Notice.

[145] Article 3 Verticals Notice.

[146] Explanatory note to the Verticals Notice, para 12, footnote 37, which clarifies the terminology used.

[147] FAC, judgment of 16 September 2016, B-581/2012, *Nikon*, LPC 2016/3, p. 831, para 7.3.2.

for products intended for resale to resellers or end users based in Switzerland. [148] Explanatory note to the Verticals Notice also add measures that generally induce distributors not to serve requests from end users or resellers based in Switzerland or to limit products intended for resale to resellers or end users based in Switzerland, such as refusing or reducing bonuses or rebates, discontinuing supply, limiting or reducing supply quantities, threatening to terminate or not to renew the agreement in place. [149]

To date, the COMCO and the Courts have found that the following contractual clauses amount to an absolute territorial restriction which we consider useful to reproduce.

In a production licence agreement between the licensor Gaba and the licensee Gebro:

> GABI [Gaba International AG] undertakes to prevent the export of the contract products [Elmex Toothpaste, Elmex Gelée, Elmex Fluid and Aronal Forte Toothpaste] to Austria with all means at its disposal and to distribute itself neither directly nor indirectly in Austria. For its part, Gebro undertakes to manufacture and sell the contractual products exclusively in the territory [Austria] which is its contractual right, and not to export goods directly or indirectly to other countries. [150]

In a distribution agreement between the manufacturer and dealers based in the EEA:

> Export The dealer is not permitted to deliver new BMW vehicles and Genuine BMW parts directly or through third parties to customers in countries outside the EEA nor to convert/modify vehicles for such purposes. [151]

> The Customer is prohibited from marketing the supplied goods beyond the Territory or to deliver them to third parties for the purpose of marketing outside the Territory. [152]

---

[148] COMCO Secretariat *Rabattdifferenzierung bei Lieferungen in die Schweiz*, LPC 2012/3, p. 524; see also COMCO Secretariat *Beratung betreffend Preisdifferenzierung bei Importen in die Schweiz*, LPC 2016/2, p. 373, where the COMCO Secretariat considers higher wholesale prices for exports of books to Switzerland as indirect absolute territorial protection. Both were advice provided by the COMCO Secretariat to undertakings under Article 23(2) CartA.

[149] Explanatory note to the Verticals Notice, para 12. Cf. EU Vertical Guidelines, para 204.

[150] Free translation, in German: "GABI [Gaba International AG] verpflichtet sich, die Ausfuhr der Vertragsprodukte [Elmex Zahnpaste, Elmex Gelée, Elmex Fluid und Aronal forte Zahnpaste] nach Österreich mit allen ihr zu Gebote stehenden Mitteln zu verhindern und auch selbst weder direkt noch indirekt in Österreich zu vertreiben. Gebro verpflichtet sich ihrerseits, die Vertragsprodukte ausschliesslich in dem ihr vertraglich zustehenden Gebiet [Österreich] herzustellen und zu vertreiben und weder direkt noch indirekt Exporte in andere Länder vorzunehmen." FSC, judgment of 28 June 2016, 2C_180/2014, ATF/BGE 143 II 297 *Gaba*.

[151] Free translation, in German: "Export Dem Händler ist es weder gestattet, unmittelbar oder über Dritte neue BMW Fahrzeuge und Original BMW Teile an Abnehmer in Länder ausserhalb des EWR zu liefern noch Fahrzeuge für solche Zwecke umzurüsten." FSC, judgment of 24 October 2017, 2C_63/2016, *BMW*, ATF/BGE 144 II 194.

[152] LPC 2021/4, p. 837 *Pöschl Tabakprodukte*, para 7.

> The Customer is prohibited from distributing the delivered goods outside the contractual Territory or from delivering them to third parties for distribution outside the contractual Territory. [153]

> The Customer shall refrain from marketing or selling the Products to third parties outside the Territory and from supplying the Products to third parties for the purpose of marketing or selling them outside the Territory. [154]

In a selective distribution agreement between the Swiss subsidiary of a manufacturer and the Swiss dealers:

> The Distributor and its affiliates may obtain the contract products only from Nikon or another Nikon Authorized Distributor in the Territory. [155]

In selective distribution agreements between supplier and wholesalers/general importers in the EU (Germany, Austria, Slovenia, Hungary and Greece):

> The Distributor and its subsidiaries and affiliates may purchase the Contractual Products only from Nikon or another Nikon authorised distributor in the Contract Territory. [156]

> However, the [D]istrib[u]tor [Greece] may sell the products direc[tl]y or indirectly within any country of the European Community (EC), and[,] after its entry into force[,] [of] the European Economic Area (EEA), but the Distributor shall refrain, out-side the territory and in [the] relation to the Products, from seeking customers, from establishing any branch and from maintaining any distribution depot.

In an agreement between the manufacturer subsidiary in the USA and its online retailers in the USA:

> In no event shall customer [dealer] directly or indirectly, transmit, send, or export any product outside the territory [USA]. [157]

In agreements where a publisher appoints an exclusive distributor for the Swiss territory and where the publisher undertakes to protect the exclusivity of the reseller:

> [the publisher] entrusts [the distributor], who accepts it, with the exclusive dissemination and distribution for all channels of the work entitled [. . .] on Swiss, French, Belgian and Canadian territory, under the following general conditions. [the publisher] will take all necessary measures to ensure that [the distributor's] exclusivity is respected. [158]

---

[153] LPC 2021/4, p. 837 *Pöschl Tabakprodukte*, para 7. Free translation, in German: "Dem Abnehmer ist es untersagt, die gelieferte Ware außerhalb des Vertragsgebiets zu vertreiben oder diese an Dritte zum Vertrieb außerhalb des Vertragsgebiets zu liefern."

[154] LPC 2021/4, p. 837 *Pöschl Tabakprodukte*, para 7.

[155] Free translation, in German: "Der Distributor und dessen Tochter- und Schwestergesellschaften dürfen die Vertragserzeugnisse nur von Nikon oder einem anderen von Nikon autorisierten Distributor im Vertragsgebiet beziehen." FAC, judgment of 16 September 2016, B-581/2012, *Nikon*, LPC 2016/3, p. 831.

[156] Free translation, in German: "Im Übrigen verpflichtet sich der Grosshändler bzw. der Vertragshändler, die Nikon[-]Produkte ausserhalb des EWR nicht zu verkaufen." FAC, judgment of 16 September 2016, B-581/2012, *Nikon*, LPC 2016/3, p. 831.

[157] FAC, judgment of 16 September 2016, B-581/2012 *Nikon*, LPC 2016/3, p. 831.

[158] Free translation, in French: "[l'éditeur] confie [au distributeur] qui l'accepte la diffusion et la distribution exclusives pour tous les réseaux de l'ouvrage intitulé [. . .] sur territoires suisse,

4.3.2.2 Relative Territorial Protection Against Other Distributors

Relative territorial protection mainly designates restrictions to active sales. Relative territorial protection falls outside Article 5(4) CartA. [159] Undertakings entering into agreements limiting active sales are not subject to Article 5(4) CartA and to fines. However, they may result in a significant restriction of competition under Article 5 (1) CartA and be unlawful. Practitioners are advised to carefully draft their contractual clauses or communications to distributors to ensure that only active sales are covered by restrictive covenants, and to avoid passive sales restrictions that leads to the application of Article 5(4) CartA.

Active sales are defined as "the targeting of customers through visits, writings, emails, phone calls or other forms of direct communication or through targeted advertising and promotion, offline or online, for example through print or digital media, including online media, price comparison services or search engine advertising, by targeting customers in specific territories or from specific customer groups, by operating a website with a top-level domain corresponding to specific territories or by offering language options on a website that are customary in specific territories, provided that these languages differ from those that are customarily used in the territory in which the customer is established." [160] The definition is consistent with the EU.

Restriction of active sales are considered as severe restrictions of competition in general, [161] however the same exceptions as those of Article 4 Regulation 2022/720 apply. As a result, the following four group of active sales restrictions are not considered as severe restrictions of competition.

First, the obligation on the buyer to limit active sales by the buyer and its direct customers into a territory or to a customer group reserved to the supplier or allocated by the supplier exclusively to a maximum of five exclusive distributors. [162] Note the limitation to the buyer's direct customers: the supplier cannot oblige the distributor to limit or pass on active sales restrictions to other downstream customers. The definition of the exclusive distribution system gives an additional condition for the exception to operate: the supplier must restricts all its other buyers from actively selling into the exclusive territory or to the exclusive customer group reserved to the supplier or allocated by the supplier exclusively to a maximum of five exclusive distributors. [163] Therefore, the restriction of active sales imposed on one of its buyers is not a qualitatively severe restriction only if the supplier imposes the same

---

français, belge et canadien, aux conditions générales qui font suite. [l'éditeur] prendra toutes mesures utiles afin que l'exclusivité [du distributeur] soit respectée". FSC, judgment of 21 December 2021, 2C_43/2020, *Dargaud*, ATF/BGE 148 II 25, para 10.1.

[159] FSC, judgment of 28 June 2016, 2C_180/2014, *Gaba,* ATF/BGE 143 II 297, para 6.3.5.

[160] Article 2 Verticals Notice. Cf. Article 1(l) Regulation 2022/720.

[161] Article 15 Verticals Notice.

[162] Article 15(b)(i) Verticals Notice. Cf. Article 4(b)(i) Regulation 2022/720.

[163] Article 4 Verticals Notice. Cf. Article 1(h) Regulation 2022/720.

restrictions on all its distributors, i.e. worldwide. This condition related to the parallel protection of the exclusive territory in Switzerland was introduced in 2022 as a result of the adaptation of the Verticals Notice following the new Regulation 2022/720 which requires parallel protection only within the EU. The scope of the clause in the Verticals Notice makes it almost impossible to fulfil a condition which was already difficult to implement in the EU/EEA. Such restrictions of active sales are not considered as qualitatively severe restrictions regardless of the distribution system operated by the supplier, such as an exclusive, [164] selective [165] or open [166] (neither exclusive nor selective) system.

Second, the obligation on the buyer to limit active (or passive) sales by the buyer and its customers to unauthorised distributors located in a territory where the supplier operates a selective distribution system for the contract goods or services. Such restrictions of active sales are not considered as qualitatively severe regardless of the distribution system in which operates the buyer and its customers outside the territory where the supplier operates a selective distribution system, such as an exclusive, [167] selective [168] or open [169] (neither exclusive nor selective) system.

Third, the restriction of active or passive sales to final consumers by an exclusive distributor, [170] by members of the selective distribution system, [171] or by a buyer in an open distribution system, [172] operating at the wholesale level.

Fourth, the restriction of the buyer's ability to sell components actively (or passively), supplied for the purposes of incorporation, to customers who would use them to manufacture the same type of goods as those produced by the supplier. The buyer here can be an exclusive distributor, [173] a member of a selective distribution system [174] or a distributor operating in an open distribution system (neither exclusive nor selective). [175]

In the four above-mentioned groups, restriction of active sales are not a severe restriction of competition within the meaning of Article 15 Verticals Notice, and therefore the agreements benefit from both safe harbours related to market shares. First, it is presumed that there is no restriction of competition within the meaning of Article 5(1) CartA where no undertaking party to the agreement exceeds a market

[164] Article 15(b)(i) Verticals Notice. Cf. Article 4(b)(i) Regulation 2022/720.

[165] Article 15(c)(i)(1) Verticals Notice. Cf. Article 4(c)(i)(1) Regulation 2022/720.

[166] Article 15(d)(i) Verticals Notice. Cf. Article 4(d)(i) Regulation 2022/720.

[167] Article 15(b)(ii) Verticals Notice. Cf. Article 4(b)(ii) Regulation 2022/720.

[168] Article 15(c)(i)(2) Verticals Notice. Cf. Article 4(c)(i)(2) Regulation 2022/720.

[169] Article 15(d)(ii) Verticals Notice. Cf. Article 4(d)(ii) Regulation 2022/720.

[170] Article 15(b)(iv) Verticals Notice. Cf. Article 4(b)(iv) Regulation 2022/720.

[171] Article 15(c)(i)(4) Verticals Notice. Cf. Article 4(c)(i)(4) Regulation 2022/720.

[172] Article 15(d)(iv) Verticals Notice. Cf. Article 4(d)(iv) Regulation 2022/720.

[173] Article 15(b)(v) Verticals Notice. Cf. Article 4(b)(v) Regulation 2022/720.

[174] Article 15(c)(i)(5) Verticals Notice. Cf. Article 4(c)(i)(5) Regulation 2022/720.

[175] Article 15(d)(v) Verticals Notice. Cf. Article 4(d)(v) Regulation 2022/720.

share of 15% on a relevant market affected by the agreement.[176] Second, if the share of the supplier and the share of the buyer on the relevant market on which each of them offers or purchases the contract goods or services does not exceed 30%, the agreement is deemed to be justified within the meaning of Article 5(2) CartA without examination of other elements or whether a restriction of competition is significant.[177] Where the market share of the supplier or buyer exceeds 30% of the relevant market on which each of them is active as a supplier or buyer, restrictions on active sales must be subject to a full assessment of the quantitative elements of the restriction of competition and any grounds for justification,[178] which corresponds to the individual assessment provided for under Article 101 TFUE. The four groups of exceptions correspond to those of Regulation 2022/720, except that parallel protection of the exclusive territory must be worldwide and is therefore more difficult to achieve under the Swiss Verticals Notice than it is under Regulation 2022/720.

The following two group of active sales restrictions are considered as severe restrictions of competition from a qualitative standpoint and do not benefit from any of the market share safe harbours mentioned above.

First, the restriction, agreed between a supplier of components and a buyer who reuses those components, of the supplier's ability to sell the components as spare parts to end users, repairers, wholesalers or other service providers whom the buyer has not entrusted with the repair or servicing of its goods.[179]

Second, the restrictions of actives sales within a selective distribution system, the first sub-group concerning the restriction of active sales when such restrictions aim at limiting the cross-supplies between such members operating at the same or at different levels of trade,[180] and the second sub-group the restriction of active (or passive) sales to final consumers by members of the selective distribution system operating at the retail level.[181]

The assessment of active sales restrictions in such circumstances must be subject to a full assessment of the significance of the restriction of competition and any grounds for justification: since those two groups of active sales restrictions qualify as severe restrictions, they satisfy the qualitative criterion of significance, and even a low level of quantitative elements[182] would be sufficient for the clause to be considered as a significant restriction of competition under Article 5(1) CartA. Such agreements can still be justified on grounds of economic efficiency within the meaning of Article 5(2) CartA,[183] however the recent FAC case law makes a

[176] Article 15(1) Verticals Notice.

[177] Article 18(2) Verticals Notice.

[178] Article 18(3) and (4) Verticals Notice.

[179] Article 15(f) Verticals Notice. Cf. Article 4(f) Regulation 2022/720.

[180] Article 15(c)(ii) Verticals Notice. Cf. Article 4(c)(ii) Regulation 2022/720.

[181] Article 15(c)(iii) Verticals Notice. Cf. Article 4(c)(iii) Regulation 2022/720.

[182] Article 14(b) Verticals Notice.

[183] Cf. Article 18(3) and (4) CartA.

narrow application of the criteria in case of restrictions that would have as object of affecting competition, [184] which would be the case for all those restrictions qualified as severe in the Verticals Notice.

4.3.2.3 Territorial Protection Against the Supplier

In addition to protection against other distributors, the supplier may commit in the distribution agreements not to sell into the distributor's allocated territory or customer group, or to refer enquiries from customers in the allocated territory to its general importer in the territory. In other words, suppliers undertake not to compete directly with the general importer or distributor. Under EU competition law, territorial or customer protection against the supplier is unconditionally lawful without time limits, irrespective of whether the supplier is a manufacturer or an independent reseller, and the nature of the sales in question—active or passive, offline or online. [185] Only spare parts cannot be subject to such protection against the supplier. [186]

The situation is different in Swiss competition law, which not only differentiates between passive and active sales, but also treats suppliers in their role as resellers differently from manufacturers who directly supply importers or general distributors in Switzerland: while manufacturers may undertake to limit their sales to protect the general importer or distributors, a reseller outside Switzerland who appoints a general importer or sub-distributor in Switzerland may not. [187] The reason given is that the text of Article 5(4) CartA applies to restrictions on sales by independent distributors, and not by manufacturers. In other words, the obligations imposed on the latter do not fall within the scope of Article 5(4) of the CartA, but those imposed on independent dealers do.

The following questions need to be asked to assess whether suppliers are committed to resellers.

First, is the supplier the company or one of the companies in the group that produces the contracted goods or services? If this is the case, commitments by the supplier not to sell, actively or passively, in the territory of the general importer or distributor in Switzerland, are not presumed to eliminate competition under Article 5 (4) CartA and are not subject to fines. These commitments are to be assessed under Article 5(1) CartA, based on qualitative and quantitative criteria. [188] Furthermore, the restrictions are not qualified as severe restriction of competition from the

---

[184] FAC, judgment of 12 December 2022, B-141/2012, *Estée Lauder/ASCOPA*.

[185] Cf. EU Vertical Guidelines, para 222: "Article 4, point (b) of Regulation 2022/720 applies only to restrictions imposed on the buyer. The supplier may therefore accept restrictions on sales by itself, both online and offline, into the exclusive territory or to some or all of the customers belonging to an exclusive customer group."

[186] Cf Article 4 (f) Regulation 2022/720; EU Vertical Guidelines, para 245.

[187] FSC, judgment of 3 March 2022, case 2C_44/2020, *Flammarion*, para 9.1.

[188] Idem, para 9.1: "It is possible that these agreements are nevertheless illegal under Article 5 (1) CartA, insofar as they are likely to significantly restrict competition on the market in question,

qualitative point of view by the Verticals Notice, [189] which refers only to obligations and restrictions imposed on or assumed by distributors or buyers, and not to obligations on suppliers. These commitments are deemed not to restrict competition significantly when neither the producer nor the distributor concerned has more than 15% of the market share in the territory. [190] The producer's or manufacturer's commitments may be justified under Article 5(2) CartA, and this is presumed when neither the producer nor the distributor concerned has more than 30% of the market share in the territory. [191]

Second, is the supplier an independent general importer or a distributor who does not belong to the company producing the contract goods or services? If this is the case, a distinction must be made according to whether the commitment entered by the supplier cover passive or active sales and whether it concerns territorial or customer protection:

- Commitments by the supplier not to sell *passively* in the territory (i.e. a commitment not to respond to unsolicited requests from customers or consumers in Switzerland) are presumed to eliminate competition under Article 5(4) CartA and are subject to fines (absolute territorial protection, see also Sect. 4.3.2.1).
- Commitments by the supplier not to *actively* sell in the territory of the general importer or distributor in Switzerland are not presumed to eliminate competition under Article 5(4) CartA and are not subject to fines (relative territorial protection, see also Sect. 4.3.2.2). These commitments are to be assessed under Article 5 (1) and (2) CartA. The restrictions are not qualified as a severe restriction of competition from the qualitative point of view by the Verticals Notice, [192] which refers only to obligations and restrictions imposed on or assumed by distributors or buyers, and not to obligations on suppliers. Undertakings given by the supplier not to sell actively in the territory of the general importer or distributor in Switzerland are deemed not to restrict competition significantly where neither the supplier nor the distributor concerned has more than 15% of the market share in the territory, [193] and to be justified under Article 5(2) CartA where neither the supplier nor the distributor concerned has more than 30% of the market share in the territory. [194]

---

or that they result from an abuse of a dominant position within the meaning of Article 7 CartA by the protected distributor." (free translation)

[189] See Article 15(b)(i), (c)(i)(1) and (d)(i) Verticals Notice.

[190] Article 16(1) Verticals Notice.

[191] Article 18(2) Verticals Notice.

[192] See Article 15(b)(i), (c)(i)(1) and (d)(i) Verticals Notice.

[193] Article 16(1) Verticals Notice.

[194] Article 18(2) Verticals Notice.

4.3.2.4 Restriction of the Distributor's Place of Establishment

Location clauses are obligations on the distributor to operate or refrain from operating in a certain area or territory. The place of its establishment is therefore defined or limited in the contract. In EU vertical restraints law, restriction on the buyer to have its distribution outlets and warehouses to a particular address, place, or territory, or at a specific area for mobile distribution outlets, are exempted [195] and lawful without restriction or conditions. The supplier is therefore free to work with location clauses. [196]

Restriction of location is an element of active selling, and where the choice of location serves a group of customers, it amounts to a relative territorial protection or customer protection under the Cartel Act. Location clauses are therefore not covered by the presumption of Article 5(4) CartA. Undertakings by the supplier who is also a producer of the contract goods or services not to open shops or showrooms in the area or to impose location clauses on other distributors are also not covered by the presumption of Article 5(4) CartA. [197]

Restrictions of the distributor's place of establishment are to be assessed under Article 5(1) CartA, based on qualitative and quantitative criteria. This is the case regardless of whether the supplier is a producer or a reseller. Location clauses are not considered as severe restrictions from a qualitative point of view under Article 5 (1) CartA. [198] This applies to all distribution systems. Consequently, location clauses are deemed not to restrict competition significantly where neither the supplier nor the distributor concerned has more than 15% of the market share in the territory. [199] Moreover, location clauses are deemed to be justified under Article 5(2) CartA where neither the supplier nor the distributor concerned has more than 30% of the market share in the territory. [200] Due to the lack of practice, it is impossible to predict what the outcome of the assessment would be when the 30% market share threshold is exceeded by one of the parties. The assessment will focus on how location clauses are used by a supplier in view of the nature of the business, in particular activities where distance is an important factor, and the impact on intra-brand competition. In addition, it will also depend on whether it is a common practice of other suppliers marketing competing products that could reduce inter-brand competition. Even then, in our view, location clauses can be justified to protect ongoing investments.

The restriction of online sales is not considered a location clause and therefore cannot be assessed as such. [201]

---

[195] EU Vertical Guidelines, paras 224, 231 and 242.

[196] Wijckmans and Tuytschaever (2018), paras 6.129 ff.

[197] FSC, judgment of 3 March 2022, 2C_44/2020, *Flammarion*, paras 9.1 ff; see explanations in Sect. 4.3.2.3.

[198] See Article 15(b)(iii), (c)(i)(3) and (d)(iii) Verticals Notice.

[199] Article 16(1) Verticals Notice.

[200] Article 18(2) Verticals Notice.

[201] On online sales, see Sect. 4.3.6.

4.3.3 Customer Allocation and Restrictions

Customer allocation, protection or restrictions refer to the obligations of the supplier or buyer in relation to groups of customers which can be defined by reference to a common characteristic, for example:

- the level of trade such as wholesale or retail,
- by reference to specialisation such as professionals versus consumers, specialised versus non-specialised users or retailers, customers of a sector of the economy such as wine growing, the watch industry or financial services,
- by reference to the size and turnover of customers, such as large accounts versus small buyers, supermarkets versus small shops,
- by reference to the type of products manufactured or marketed by the customer, such as products in competition with the contract products.

Three basic questions need to be asked when assessing the legality of customer allocation and protection under Article 5 CartA: which customers need to be protected or excluded, from whom, and for what type of sales (passive or active)? In other words, which group of customers may be protected from a particular type of distributor? From whom should this group be protected, from sales by other distributors or by the supplier? Which customer groups can be excluded from protection? Where a class of customers can benefit from protection by all distributors or by a particular type of distributors, that class of customers may be allocated to a distributor on an exclusive basis or to distributors in a selective distribution network and sales by other distributors may be excluded.

Allocation and restrictions regarding the clientele or customer groups are not covered by Article 5(4) CartA, which only concerns territorial allocation. Neither passive nor active customer sales restrictions are covered by Article 5(4) CartA. This is regularly confirmed by the courts, here is an extract from a recent FSC judgment:

> It should be pointed out in this respect that the clear text of Article 5 (4) CartA refers only to market allocations based on 'territories'. The presumption of elimination of effective competition provided for in this provision does not therefore apply to distribution agreements that allocate the market according to a 'customer base' [*reference omitted*]. A customer exclusive agreement whereby a supplier undertakes to sell its products only to one distributor for the purpose of resale to a specific customer group (e.g. to customers in a specific profession or on a list drawn up on the basis of a specific criterion [*reference omitted*]) does not in principle fall within the scope of Article 5 (4) CartA, unless of course the customer group in question is defined on the basis of a geographical criterion only. [202]

There are two caveats that need to be borne in mind. The first is the risk of defining customer groups by reference to (an area in) Switzerland. Particular attention must therefore be paid to the territorial aspects of customer restrictions if they restrict passive sales to resellers or end users in Switzerland, which poses a particular risk

---

[202] FSC, judgment of 3 March 2020 in the case 2C_44/2020, *Flammarion*, para 7.2 (free translation).

when applying the Cartel Act to trade with Switzerland. Restrictions on resellers to respond to unsolicited requests (i.e. passive sales restrictions) from a group of resellers or end users in an area in Switzerland allocated to a reseller are covered by Article 5(4) CartA on absolute territorial protection (See Sect. 4.3.2.1). An obligation on a group of customers in Switzerland to purchase from suppliers established in Switzerland also constitutes indirect absolute protection under Article 5(4) CartA (See Sect. 4.3.4 on exclusive purchase obligations and Sect. 4.3.2.1 on absolute territorial protection). Only territorial restrictions on active sales in the territory (e.g. the whole of Switzerland) or a customer group in Switzerland exclusively allocated to no more than five distributors are not qualitatively severe, provided that these distributors are protected by active sales from all other distributors, i.e. worldwide (see Sect. 4.3.2.2).

The second risk relates to the way in which COMCO may classify the competitive relationship between the allocated customer groups as horizontal or vertical and apply Article 5(3)(c) of the Cartel Act, which refers to horizontal market sharing agreements or by trading partner. This is particularly the case where the supplier allocates certain customer groups to different distributors or between itself and distributors in Switzerland, and the distributors may be potential competitors of each other. This risk was highlighted in the *AdBlue* case, where the customer allocation clauses in the distribution agreement between the supplier and its resellers were considered to be horizontal agreements and therefore were not assessed under the Verticals Notice (see also Sect. 4.3.7).[203] In this case, COMCO found that there was no agreement within the meaning of Article 5(3) of the Cartel Act, but that the customer allocation constituted a significant restriction of competition in both qualitative and quantitative terms, which, in the absence of any justification, was unlawful under Article 5(1) of the Cartel Act.

With these two general caveats in mind, we will now discuss the two main protection needs in practice, namely protection against sales by other distributors (Sect. 4.3.3.1) and protection against sales by the supplier (Sect. 4.3.3.2).

4.3.3.1 Customer Protection Against Other Distributors

Customer protection against different distributors may arise in a number of situations, including different distribution formulas, different levels of trade and specific products such as components or spare parts. As explained above, customer restrictions are considered to be active sales restrictions and this section only deals with active sales restrictions; this section only discusses certain cases that are considered to be absolute territorial protection in order to illustrate the distinction between passive and active sales restrictions, general caveats on absolute territorial protection having been set out in Sect. 4.3.3 above.

[203] COMCO decision of 2 December 2019, *AdBlue,* LPC 2020/2, p. 626, paras 50ff, in particular para 56.

A group of customers (resellers, retailers or end users) defined by specialisation, industry, or purchase volume which is allocated exclusively to a maximum of five other exclusive distributors can be protected against active sales from other distributors and their direct customers regardless of the level of trade where are active the exclusive distributors to be protected. [204] Note the limitation to the direct customers of the distributors: the supplier cannot oblige the other distributors to limit active sales restrictions or to pass them on to the customers of the distributors' downstream customers. The definition of the exclusive distribution system gives an additional condition for the exception to operate: the supplier must restricts all its other buyers from actively selling to the exclusive customer group allocated by the supplier exclusively to a maximum of five exclusive distributors. [205] Therefore, the restriction of active sales imposed on one of its buyers is not a qualitatively severe restriction only if the supplier imposes the same customer restrictions on all its distributors, i.e. worldwide. This condition related to the parallel protection of the exclusive group of customers was introduced in 2022 as a result of the adaptation of the Verticals Notice following the new Regulation 2022/720.

Authorised members of a selective distribution system can be defined as a group of customers and protected from sales by other unauthorised distributors. The members of a selective distribution system in a territory may be protected against active or passive sales by all other distributors of the supplier and their customers to unauthorised distributors located in the selective distribution territory. [206] This means that sales to unauthorised distributors can be excluded. Warranty and after-sales services may also be restricted and reserved for the members of the selective distribution system only. [207] Such restrictions are not considered to be qualitatively severe restrictions of competition. The ban on selling to unauthorised distributors protects authorised members from having unauthorised distributors selling contract products in their territory.

This is valid for sales in the territory where operates a selective distribution system, and not in territories where no such system is in place. Only active sales can be restricted under certain condition to protect an exclusive distribution system elsewhere, for example in Switzerland. And if the products are distributed in Switzerland under a free or open distribution system, the restriction imposed on members of a selective distribution system in an EU/EEA territory to respond to unsolicited requests (passive sales restrictions) from resellers established or intending to sell in Switzerland amounts to an absolute territorial protection under

[204] Article 15(b)(i), (c)(i)(1) and (d)(i) Verticals Notice. Cf. Article 4(b)(i), (c)(i)(1) and (d)(i) Regulation 2022/720.

[205] Article 4 Verticals Notice. Cf. Article 1(h) Regulation 2022/720.

[206] Article 15(b)(ii), (c)(i)(2) and (d)(ii) Verticals Notice. Cf. Article 4(b)(ii), (c)(i)(2) and (d)(ii) Regulation 2022/720. Explanatory note to the Verticals Notice, para 17.

[207] Explanatory note to the Verticals Notice, para 17.

Article 5(4) CartA, [208] and restrictions on active sales in such a territory would amount to a qualitatively severe restriction of competition. [209]

By contrast, authorised members of a selective distribution system at any level of trade cannot be protected against sales from other authorised members of the selection distribution system. The restriction of cross-supplies between members of the selective distribution system operating at the same level of trade or at different levels of trade is a qualitatively severe restriction of competition, [210] whereas the restriction of passive sales (as a form of cross-supplies) in response to unsolicited requests from members of the selective distribution system in Switzerland constitutes an absolute territorial protection under Article 5(4) CartA. The same applies to the restriction on passives sales in response to unsolicited requests from end users established in Switzerland, which is also considered to be absolute territorial protection and is covered by Article 5(4) CartA. [211]

With regard to retailers as a customer group, the question arises as to the extent to which such a customer group can be protected against sales by other distributors. If such retailers as a group of customers is exclusively allocated to no more than five distributors, the same protection against active sales by other distributors can be provided irrespective of the distribution system used by the supplier and irrespective of the level of trade at which the exclusive distributors to be protected are active (wholesale or other level of distribution). [212] The conditions for such protection are explained above.

End-users can also be defined as a group of customers allocated to retailers. The question arises to what extent retailers can be protected from sales to their final customers by other distributors of the supplier.

- If the other distributors against whom protection is being sought are wholesalers, the prohibition on these distributors to sell directly, to end users, either passively or actively, is not considered a severe restriction of competition from a qualitative point of view. This applies irrespective of the distribution system used by the supplier. [213] The same position applies under Regulation 2022/720. [214] Since online sales are usually sales to end users, this would mean that the retailer would normally also be protected against online sales by the wholesaler and that the supplier could prohibit the wholesaler from selling the products online. [215] Such contractual protection is deemed not to restrict competition significantly where neither the supplier nor the distributor concerned has more than 15% of the

[208] Explanatory note to the Verticals Notice, para 11.

[209] Article 15(b)(c) and (d) Verticals Notice.

[210] Article 15 (c)(ii) Verticals Notice. Cf. Article 4(c)(ii) Regulation 2022/720.

[211] Explanatory note to the Verticals Notice, para 18.

[212] Article 15(b)(i), (c)(i)(1) and (d)(i) Verticals Notice. Cf. Article 4(b)(i), (c)(i)(1) and (d)(i) Regulation 2022/720.

[213] Article 15(b)(iv), (c)(i)(4) and (d)(iv) Verticals Notice.

[214] Cf. Article 4(b)(iv), (c)(i)(4) and (d)(iv) Regulation 2022/720.

[215] We haven't found this confirmed in the Verticals Notice or EU Vertical Guidelines.

market share in the territory, [216] And are deemed to be justified under Article 5 (2) CartA where neither the supplier nor the distributor concerned has more than 30% of the market share in the territory. [217] In our view, this protection can be justified under Article 5(2) CartA even if the 30% market share threshold is exceeded by one or both of the parties.
- If the other distributors against which protection is being sought are members of a selective distribution system operating at the retail level of trade, restrictions imposed on these retailers not to sell, either passively or actively, to end users are considered to be a severe restriction of competition from a qualitative point of view. [218] Restrictions on active or passive sales to end users imposed on members of a selective distribution system are subject to a full assessment under Article 5 (1) and (2) CartA: as these restrictions qualify as severe restrictions, they fulfil the qualitative criterion of significance and even a low level of quantitative elements [219] would be sufficient for the clause to be considered as a significant restriction of competition under Article 5(1) CartA. Neither of the safe harbours relating to market shares of 15% or 30% is available. Such agreements can still be justified on the basis of economic efficiency pursuant to Article 5(2) CartA, [220] but recent FAC case law has applied the criteria narrowly. [221]

A final question arises to what extent the supplier can restrict sales by other distributors to end users that buy components for incorporation. The restriction of active or passive sales to end users who purchase components for incorporation into products competing with those produced by the supplier is not considered to be a severe restriction of competition from a qualitative point of view. [222] This applies irrespective of the distribution system used by the supplier.

4.3.3.2 Customer Protection Against the Supplier

The question to be addressed in this respect is whether the supplier can undertake in the distribution agreements not to sell to the distributor's customer group or to refer enquiries from customers allocated to the distributor. Under EU competition law, customer protection against the supplier is unconditionally lawful without time

[216] Article 16(1) Verticals Notice.

[217] Article 18(2) Verticals Notice.

[218] Article 15 (c)(iii) Verticals Notice. Cf. Article 4(c)(iii) Regulation 2022/720.

[219] Article 14(b) Verticals Notice.

[220] Cf. Article 18(3) and (4) CartA.

[221] FAC, judgment of 12 December 2022, B-141/2012, *Estée Lauder/ASCOPA*.

[222] Article 15(b)(v), (c)(i)(5) and (d)(v) Verticals Notice. Cf. Article 4(b)(v), (c)(i)(5) and (d)(v) Regulation 2022/720.

limits and irrespective of the market shares of the supplier or the distributor, [223] and the nature of the sales in question—active or passive, offline or online.

The assessment framework is different in Swiss competition law.

Commitments by the supplier not to sell passively or actively to customers allocated to the distributor are not presumed to eliminate competition under Article 5 (4) CartA and are not subject to fines. This is the case regardless of whether the supplier is a producer or a reseller. [224]

Commitments entered by the supplier not to sell actively or passively to customers groups allocated to the distributor are not qualified as a severe restriction of competition from the qualitative point of view by the Verticals Notice, [225] which refers only to obligations and restrictions imposed on or assumed by distributors or buyers and does not limit obligations on suppliers.

There is no practice and no cases regarding commitments entered by the supplier not to sell actively or passively to customers groups allocated to the distributor. Therefore, it cannot be assumed that these clauses are not covered by Article 5 Cartel Act. In our view, these commitments are to be assessed under Article 5(1) and (2) CartA, based on qualitative and quantitative criteria. As mentioned above, the restrictions do not qualify as a severe restriction of competition from a qualitative point of view under the Verticals Notice, which allows the use of safe harbours under the Verticals Notice. Undertakings given by the supplier not to sell passively or actively to customers allocated to the distributor are deemed not to restrict competition significantly where neither the supplier nor the distributor concerned has more than 15% of the market share in the territory, [226] and to be justified under Article 5 (2) CartA where neither the supplier nor the distributor concerned has more than 30% of the market share in the territory. [227]

Finally, spare parts cannot be subject to customer protection against the supplier both according to Regulation 2022/720 [228] and the Verticals Notice, whose Article 15(f) considers as a severe restriction from a qualitative point of view the restriction of the supplier's ability to sell the components as spare parts to end users, repairers, wholesalers or other service providers whom the buyer has not entrusted with the repair or servicing of its goods. This means that the market share safe harbours of Articles 16 and 18 of the Verticals Notice do not apply and that such restrictions are deemed to fulfil the conditions of Article 5(1) of the CartA. In the absence of efficiency grounds, such restrictions are unlawful.

---

[223] Cf. EU Vertical Guidelines, para 222: "Article 4, point (b) of Regulation (EU) 2022/720 applies only to restrictions imposed on the buyer. The supplier may therefore accept restrictions on sales by itself, both online and offline, into the exclusive territory or to some or all of the customers belonging to an exclusive customer group."

[224] Cf. Sect. 4.3.2.3 above. Territorial restrictions are treated differently depending on whether the supplier is a producer or an independent reseller.

[225] See Article 15(b)(i), (c)(i)(1) and (d)(i) Verticals Notice.

[226] Article 16(1) Verticals Notice.

[227] Article 18(2) Verticals Notice.

[228] Cf. Article 4 (f) Regulation 2022/720; EU Vertical Guidelines, para 245.

4.3.4 Exclusive Purchase Obligations

Exclusive purchasing or the designation of the source where the buyer may purchase the contract products is treated differently in Switzerland due to the emphasis on territorial protection of the Swiss market. Whereas in the EU, exclusive purchasing is a hardcore restriction only in the context of a selective distribution system, certain exclusive purchasing obligations are covered by the prohibition of absolute territorial protection of Article 5(4) CartA, irrespective of the distribution formula used. The test used is whether exclusive purchasing obligations amount to territorial protection of the Swiss market in the specific case. What is prohibited is rather the geographical scope of the purchase obligation or the overall effect of such contractual obligations on distributors, which would aim to oblige buyers to purchase from a source in Switzerland. Such obligations are considered as indirect allocation of the Swiss territory which may lead to an absolute territorial protection covered by Article 5(4) CartA.

NIKON was the first case where an obligation on the distributors to purchase all their contract goods from the general importer in Switzerland was considered as an indirect absolute territorial restriction covered by Article 5(4) CartA. [229] This was a particular case in that NIKON challenged the COMCO's finding that it had set up a selective distribution system. As a result, the FAC did not differentiate between selective and exclusive distribution, and the ban on the obligation to purchase exclusively in Switzerland applies to both systems. The following contractual provisions constituted an indirect allocation of Swiss territory, even though the contract did not contain a prohibition of passive sales from abroad:

> The contract territory is Switzerland and the Principality of Liechtenstein. [. . .] The distributor and its subsidiaries and affiliated companies may only purchase the contractual products from Nikon or from another distributor authorised by Nikon in the contractual territory. [230]

Bucher Landtechnik was another case where an obligation on distributors in Switzerland to purchase tractors and spare parts for tractors exclusively from the Swiss general importer was considered as an indirect absolute territorial protection. [231] The exclusive purchase obligations were applied in a purely internal context in Switzerland, in contractual provisions between a Swiss general importer and its distributors in Switzerland. Foreign tractor manufacturer did not restrict passive sales or unsolicited requests from Switzerland. Exclusive purchasing obligations indirectly reduced the sales of another Swiss distributor of spare parts, which used to source from abroad: the less sales the spare parts distributor made in Switzerland due to the existence of exclusive purchasing obligations in the market, the less it would have asked to purchase abroad (which leads to fewer passive sales and potentially a higher

---

[229] FAC, judgment of 16 September 2016, B-581/2012, *Nikon*, LPC 2016/3, p. 831.

[230] Idem, para 7.3.2.

[231] COMCO, decision of 1 July 2019, *Bucher Landtechnik/Ersatzteilhandel Traktoren*, LPC 2019/4, p. 1155.

price for spare parts in Switzerland). It was therefore considered that the exclusive purchasing obligation indirectly led to the exclusion of passive sales by other spare parts distributors in Switzerland and to the application of the legal presumption that effective competition within the meaning of Article 5(4) CartA had been eliminated. [232]

These cases show that if a supplier considers Switzerland as part of its EU-wide exclusive distribution network, it cannot rely on similar rules to those applied in the EU to exempt exclusive purchasing obligations when the supplier and its distributors do not each exceed the 30% market share threshold.

One case that has been treated similarly to the EU situation is where the supplier is a manufacturer based in the European Union and imposes an exclusive purchasing obligation (only) on its Swiss general importer. [233] In gym80, an exclusive distribution agreement between a German fitness equipment manufacturer and its general importer in Switzerland obliged the latter to buy exclusively from the manufacturer. [234] COMCO held that an obligation on the Swiss general importer to acquire all its contract products from the manufacturer based abroad is not covered by the presumption of Article 5(4) CartA, [235] by referring to the EU vertical block exemption regulation.

However, the COMCO immediately adds a caveat to cover the case where the general importer sets up a selective distribution system in Switzerland and obliges its resellers to buy exclusively from itself:

> The situation would be different if, among other things, a general importer (who has concluded an exclusive distribution agreement with its supplier containing an exclusive purchasing obligation) has implemented a selective distribution system in Switzerland and, within this framework, imposes on its authorised resellers the obligation to purchase products exclusively from the Swiss general importer. [236]

In our view, only the exclusive purchase obligations included in the distribution contracts between this general importer and its authorised distributors in Switzerland would be covered by Article 5(4) CartA, and not the exclusive obligation in the contract between the manufacturer abroad and its general importer. If the general importer is free to choose the distribution system that suits him and to decide independently, unconstrained by any obligation towards the manufacturer, the general importer risks infringing Article 5(4) CartA, but not the manufacturer who would not be part of that selective distribution system.

Another question related to exclusive purchase obligations is the referral by the manufacturer abroad of requests from Swiss customers to its general importer in Switzerland. Are those passive sales covered by Article 5(4) CartA? The COMCO

---

[232] Idem, para 69.

[233] COMCO, decision of 27 November 2017, *Gym80*, LPC 2018/2, p. 237.

[234] Idem. See also COMCO, decision of 1 July 2019, *Bucher Landtechnik/Ersatzteilhandel Traktoren*, LPC 2019/4, p. 1155 ff, para 67.

[235] COMCO, decision of 27 November 2017, *Gym80*, LPC 2018/2, p. 237, para 42.

[236] Idem, para 43.

confirmed its practice that those referrals by the manufacturer are not considered as passive sales restrictions covered by Article 5(4) CartA. Furthermore, it pointed out that in this case downstream distributors and end customers in Switzerland were free to buy the contract products abroad, and that the manufacturer's market share in Switzerland was below 10%. [237]

Later, the FSC clarified that the rule applies only to manufacturers, and not to wholesale distributors based abroad, based on a kind of presumption that an obligation imposed on the manufacturer applies only to the manufacturer, and not to other distributors, whereas an obligation imposed on an EU wholesale distributor would also apply to other distributors. [238]

From the above cases, the following exclusive purchasing obligation are covered by Article 5(4) LCart:

- An obligation to purchase exclusively from one or more sources based solely in Switzerland included in selective distribution contracts concluded between a supplier (manufacturer or distributor) and the general importer in Switzerland.
- An obligation to purchase exclusively from one or more sources based solely in Switzerland included in distribution contracts concluded in the downstream tier of import by a distributor or subsidiary acting as general importer in Switzerland, irrespective of the distribution system in place in Switzerland or the EU. These purchase obligations, especially when they cover most distributors or levels of trade downstream of the import into Switzerland and down to the retail level, constitute an indirect absolute protection of the Swiss market against passive sales from abroad.

As explained in Sect. 4.2 above, once the application of Article 5(4) CartA has been ruled out, the practitioner must consider whether the restraint is severe from a qualitative point of view. As exclusive purchasing obligations are not listed in Article 15 of the Verticals Notice, the COMCO decided in the *Gym80* case that an obligation on the Swiss general importer to purchase exclusively from the foreign manufacturer did not constitute a severe restriction of competition from a qualitative point of view and could therefore be considered not to be a significant restriction of competition under Article 5(1) of the Cartel Act, or that it fulfilled the conditions of Article 5(2) of the Cartel Act because the market shares of each of the parties were below 10%. [239]

The COMCO has not dealt with cases where the buyer has to purchase less than 80% of its requirements from the supplier, where exclusive purchase obligations are concluded for a period not exceeding 5 years or both (i.e. less than 80% for a period not exceeding 5 years). It cannot therefore be assumed that such situations are excluded from the scope of Article 5(4) CartA.

---

[237] COMCO, decision of 27 November 2017, *Gym80*, LPC 2018/2, p. 237, paras 54–55.

[238] FSC, judgment of 3 March 2022, 2C_44/2020, *Flammarion*, para 9.

[239] Article 16 Verticals Notice. The COMCO decision refers to the previous numbering of the Verticals Notice, that is Article 12 and 13.

4.3.5 Non-Compete Obligations

The Verticals Notice defines non-compete obligations as:

1. any direct or indirect obligation causing the buyer not to manufacture, purchase, sell or resell goods or services which compete with the contract goods or services; or
2. any direct or indirect obligation on the buyer to purchase from the supplier or from another undertaking designated by the supplier more than 80% of the buyer's total purchases of the contract goods or services and their substitutes on the relevant market, calculated on the basis of the value or, where such is standard industry practice, the volume of its purchases in the preceding calendar year. [240]

The definition is borrowed from Regulation 2022/720 and covers both non-compete obligations in respect of competing brands and obligations to source products from the supplier or another undertaking designated by the supplier. The purchase of all or a majority of the buyer's total purchases of the contract goods or services from the supplier or a source designated by the supplier is covered by the definition of non-compete obligation under Article 7(b) of the Verticals Notice, but where the source of purchase is in Switzerland, this may result in an indirect restriction on passive sales covered by Article 5(4) of the CartA. [241] Sourcing obligations must therefore be assessed as exclusive purchasing obligations and not as non-compete obligations (see Sect. 4.3.4 above).

Non-compete obligations are listed at Article 15 of the Verticals Notice dealing with severe restrictions of competition and with conditions under which such obligations are not considered as severe. Severe restriction within the meaning of Article 15 (g)–(j) of the Verticals Notice corresponds to the notion of excluded restrictions of Article 5 Regulation 2022/720. Since the Verticals Notice does not establish a statutory block exemption for entire agreements, the difference between hardcore restrictions and excluded restrictions is not relevant, and the Verticals Notice treats both categories as severe restrictions. As explained in Sect. 4.2, the Verticals Notice has a similar status to the EU Vertical Guidelines.

The list of Article 15 (g)–(j) of the Verticals Notice sets the conditions for four types of non-compete obligations.

The first type covers non-compete obligations *during the term of agreement* (Article 15(g) Verticals Notice).

Non-competition obligations on the distributor during the term of the agreement are considered as severe restrictions of competition if they exceed a duration of 5 years or are concluded for an indefinite period. [242] These obligations must be fully assessed under Article 5(1) and (2) CartA, assuming that they restrict competition in qualitative terms. From a quantitative point of view, non-compete obligations benefit

---

[240] Article 7 Verticals Notice.

[241] Explanatory note to the Verticals Notice, para 36.

[242] Article 15(g) Verticals Notice. Cf. Article 5(1)(a) Regulation 2022/720.

from the 15% market share safe harbour of the Verticals notice; this means that the non-compete clause will not restrict competition significantly within the meaning of Article 5(1) CartA if neither party exceeds a market share of 15% on the relevant market. If one or both parties exceed that threshold, the non-compete clause entered for more than 5 years or for an indefinite period restricts competition and is unlawful unless it is justified on efficiency grounds under Article 5(2) CartA. However, they do not benefit from the 30% market share safe harbours of the Verticals Notice [243] and the other justification criteria under Article 5(2) CartA will be applied restrictively.

Tacit extension beyond the period of 5 years is not considered as indefinite or as a duration exceeding 5 years, and therefore the non-compete does not qualify as a severe restriction of competition if the buyer can effectively renegotiate or terminate the agreement containing the obligation with a reasonable period of notice and at a reasonable cost, so that it could effectively change its supplier after the expiry of the 5-year period. [244] Where neither the supplier nor the distributor exceeds the 30% market share threshold, the non-compete obligation is deemed to be justified under Article 5(2) CartA without the need to assess its anti-competitive effects. If one or both parties exceed this threshold, a full assessment under Article 5(1) and (2) CartA is required, focusing on whether the clause restricts competition in quantitative terms and on the efficiency grounds.

A non-compete obligation entered into for more than 5 years is not considered as severe restrictions of competition if on the one hand, the contract goods or services are sold by the buyer in premises and on land owned by the supplier or rented or leased by the supplier from third parties not connected with the buyer and, on the other hand, the non-compete obligation does not extend beyond the period during which the buyer uses such premises and land. [245] This means that where neither the supplier nor the distributor exceeds the 30% market share threshold, the non-compete obligation is deemed to be justified under Article 5(2) CartA without the need to assess its anti-competitive effects; on the contrary, if one or both parties exceed this threshold, a full assessment under Article 5(1) and (2) CartA is required, focusing on whether the clause restricts competition in quantitative terms and on efficiency grounds.

The second type of the non-compete obligations covers obligations that extend *after the terms of the agreement* (Article 15(h) Verticals Notice).

Post-term non-compete obligations are considered as severe restrictions of competition from a qualitative standpoint if their duration exceeds 1 year or is unrelated to contractual products or concerns premises other that those operated during the terms of the agreement or is not essential to protect a know-how transferred by the

[243] The 15% market share safe harbour of Article 16(1) and the 30% market share safe harbour.

[244] Explanatory note to the Verticals Notice, para 36. Cf. EU Vertical Guidelines, para 248.

[245] Article 15(g) Verticals Notice. Cf. Article 5(2) Regulation 2022/720; EU Vertical Guidelines, para 249.

supplier to the buyer. [246] These non-compete obligations must be fully assessed under Article 5(1) and (2) CartA, assuming that they restrict competition in qualitative terms. From a quantitative point of view, post-term non-compete obligations benefit from the 15% market share safe harbour of the Verticals notice; this means that the non-compete clause will not significantly restrict competition within the meaning of Article 5(1) CartA if neither party exceeds a market share of 15% on the relevant market. If one or both parties exceed that threshold, the non-compete clauses restrict competition and would be unlawful unless it is justified on efficiency grounds under Article 5(2) CartA. However, they do not benefit from the 30% market share safe harbours of the Verticals Notice [247] and the other justification criteria under Article 5(2) CartA will be applied restrictively.

Conversely, a post-term non-compete obligation on the distributor are not severe restrictions from a qualitative standpoint if all the following are met: (1) the obligation relates to goods or services in competition with the contract goods or services, (2) it is limited to the premises and land from which the buyer has operated during the term of the contract, (3) it is essential for the protection of know-how [248] transferred by the supplier to the buyer, and (4) it is limited to 1 year from the expiry of the agreement. [249] Where neither the supplier nor the distributor exceeds the 30% market share threshold, the non-compete obligation is deemed to be justified under Article 5(2) CartA without the need to assess its anti-competitive effects. If one or both parties exceed this threshold, a full assessment under Article 5 (1) and (2) CartA is required, focusing on whether the clause restricts competition in quantitative terms and on whether it is justified on efficiency grounds.

The third type of *non-compete obligations concerns single branding in selective distribution system* (Article 15(i) Verticals Notice).

Direct or indirect obligations causing the members of a selective distribution system not to sell the brands of competing suppliers are considered as severe restrictions of competition from a qualitative standpoint. [250] Therefore, the restriction of multi-branding in a selective distribution system by targeting specific brands of competing suppliers is also considered as severe restriction of competition, like in the EU law.

By contrast, a non-compete clause covering all other competing brands is not considered as severe restriction of competition from a qualitative standpoint. Such clauses would benefit from the safe harbour related to 30% market share threshold

---

[246] Cf. Article 5(1)(b) Regulation 2022/720.

[247] The 15% market share safe harbour of Article 16(1) and the 30% market share safe.

[248] Know how is defined at Article 8 Verticals Notice as 'a package of non-patented practical information, resulting from experience and testing by the supplier and which is (i) secret, i.e. not generally known or not easily accessible, (ii) substantial, i.e. significant and useful to the buyer for the use, sale or resale of the contract goods or services, and (iii) identified, i.e. described in a sufficiently comprehensive manner so as to make it possible to verify that it fulfils the criteria of "secrecy" and "substantiality"'. Cf. Article 1(1)(j) Regulation 2022/720.

[249] Verticals Notice Article 15(h). Cf. Article 5(3) Regulation 2022/720.

[250] Cf. Article 5(1)(c) Regulation 2022/720.

without the need to assess its anti-competitive effects. Where thresholds are exceeded, a full assessment under Article 5(1) and (2) CartA is required, focusing on whether the clause restricts competition in quantitative terms and on justification on efficiency grounds.

The fourth type covers non-compete obligations in *online intermediation services* (Article 15(j) Verticals Notice), such as parity obligations, most-favoured clauses or cross-platform parity obligations. Any direct or indirect obligations causing a purchaser of online intermediation services not to offer, sell or resell goods or services to end consumers under more favourable conditions via competing online intermediation services constitute a severe restriction of competition from a qualitative point of view. [251]

Online intermediation services are defined as services that allow undertakings to offer goods or services, (1) to other undertakings, with a view to facilitating the initiating of direct transactions between those undertakings, or (2) to final consumers, with a view to facilitating the initiating of direct transactions between those undertakings and final consumers, irrespective of whether and where the transactions are ultimately concluded. The definition does not refer to information society services, which is not relevant in Swiss law. [252] Reference to competing services is to be understood as covering wide parity obligations. The conditions relate to prices, inventory, availability or other terms of offer or sale. [253]

The Explanatory note to the Verticals Notice refers to the EU Vertical Guidelines, by distinguishing between wide and narrow parity clauses: while wide parity obligations at the retail level are severe restriction of competition from a qualitative standpoint, narrow parity clauses are not. Wide parity clauses must be subject to full assessment under Article 5(1) and (2) CartA, assuming that they restrict severely competition in qualitative terms. From a quantitative point of view, wide parity clauses benefit from the 15% market share safe harbour of the Verticals notice; this means that the clause will not significantly restrict competition within the meaning of Article 5(1) CartA if the online intermediation platform has less than 15% of market share on the relevant market. If the online intermediation platform exceeds that threshold, the wide parity clause is unlawful unless it is justified on efficiency grounds under Article 5(2) CartA. However, they do not benefit from the 30% market share safe harbours of the Verticals Notice [254] and the other justification criteria under Article 5(2) CartA would be applied restrictively.

The position is consistent with previous COMCO practice. Wide parity clauses applied by *Booking.com, HRS* and *Expedia* were the object of a COMCO

[251] Cf. Article 5(1)(d) Regulation 2022/720.

[252] Cf. Article 1(1)(e) Regulation 2022/720, referring to information society services within the meaning of Article 1(1), point (b), of Directive 2015/1535 of the European Parliament and of the Council of 9 September 2015 laying down a procedure for the provision of information in the field of technical regulations and of rules on Information Society services, OJ L 241, 17.9.2015, p. 1. Directive 2015/1535 does not apply in Switzerland.

[253] Cf. EU Vertical Guidelines, para 356.

[254] The 15% market share safe harbour of Article 16(1) and the 30% market share safe.

decision. [255] The COMCO excluded in this case the application of Article 5(4) CartA but found that wide parity clauses constituted severe restrictions of competition between online booking platforms under Article 5(1) CartA which could not be justified by efficiency grounds and were, consequently, unlawful. The reasons mentioned were the elimination of price signals to the end customers regarding the level of the parties' commissions and inability of hotels to react to a more expensive online booking platform, which lead to the elimination of competition with regard to commissions between the online booking platforms. [256] From a quantitative standpoint, the decision highlights the horizontal effects go beyond the relevant market. [257]

Narrow parity clauses were excluded from the COMCO investigation and therefore not prohibited. [258] This led to numerous complaints from businesses in the hotel sector, prompting the adoption of a specific provision in the Unfair Competition Act which declared narrow parity clauses illegal, effective from 1 December 2022:

> **Article 8a Use of parity clauses restricting the freedom of accommodation establishments**
> Anyone who, as the operator of an online platform for booking accommodation services, uses general terms and conditions which directly or indirectly restrict the pricing and supply of accommodation by means of parity clauses, in particular with regard to rates, availability or conditions, is acting unfairly. [259]

4.3.6 *On-line Sales*

COMCO's position on online sales has been hesitant, unsure whether to use its preferred intervention tool, Article 5(4) CartA, to regulate restrictions on Internet sales. Internet sales are indeed a way to reduce prices in Switzerland by giving consumers the possibility to buy abroad. It would have preferred to do so, and the previous versions of the Verticals Notice clearly stated that Internet sales were considered as passive sales, which indicated a readiness to handle online sales restrictions as absolute territorial restrictions. [260] But the text of Article 5(4) CartA was not so wide and Internet sales were also considered as sales to a particular group of customers, namely online customers, and therefore could not automatically fall under the presumption of Article 5(4) CartA. The same applies to the RPM rules

---

[255] COMCO decision of 19 October 2015, *Online booking platforms for hotels*, LPC 2016/1, 77.

[256] Idem, para 312.

[257] Idem, para 364.

[258] Idem, para 411.

[259] Article 8a UCA.

[260] See the definition of passive sales in Article 3 of the previous version of Verticals Notice adopted in 2010 and amended in 2017.

which would not capture restrictions on the distributor's use of the Internet. All previous COMCO cases have therefore been assessed under Article 5(1) CartA, but the reasoning of the decisions has already announced qualified circumstances that would make restrictions on Internet sales fall under the presumptions of Article 5 (4) CartA and subject to fines. The new Verticals Notice retains this warning on qualified circumstances in relation to Article 5(4) of CartA and borrows heavily from Regulation 2022/720 and the EU Vertical Guidelines.

The main categories of online restrictions are discussed in the following sections.

4.3.6.1 Absolute Territorial Protection

Restrictions on online sales in vertical agreements may constitute an agreement on absolute territorial protection if the specific circumstances of the case reveal the existence of qualified circumstances. The Explanatory note to the Verticals Notice gives a few examples of qualified circumstances: [261]

- Obligations on the online seller to prevent customers from another territory from viewing its website or to redirect views on its website to the online shop of the manufacturer or another buyer; the mere use of links to the online shops of the supplier or other sellers without preventing or automatically redirecting the visitors is not a qualifying circumstance.
- Obligations on the online seller to terminate online transactions of end customers as soon as their credit card data shows an address that is not in the seller's territory.

Both examples of qualified circumstances were announced in previous online restrictions cases handled by the COMCO. [262] They correspond to the first two types of geo-blocking measures treated as hardcore territorial protection in the EU Vertical Guidelines, [263] linked to the restriction of effective use of the Internet as a hardcore restriction listed in Article 4(e) Regulation 2022/720.

The other examples of hardcore restrictions on online sales mentioned in paragraph 206 of the EU Vertical Guidelines are not considered qualified circumstances for the application of Article 5(4) of the CartA, but examples of qualitatively severe restrictions in the form of a limitation on the effective use of the Internet announced in Article 15(e) of the Verticals Notice, explained here in the Sect. 4.3.6.3.

[261] Explanatory note to the Verticals Notice, para 26.

[262] See LPC 2011/3, p. 381, *Behinderung des Online-Handels*, para 74; LPC 2014/1, p. 198, *Kosmetikprodukte*, para 142; LPC 2014/2, p. 413, *Jura*, para 62.

[263] EU Vertical Guidelines, para 206, sub-paragraphs (a) and (b).

4.3.6.2 Resale Price Maintenance

Restrictions on the buyer's freedom to set his resale price in the context of online sales are covered by Article 5(4) of the Cartel Act if the circumstances of the case demonstrate the existence of an agreement in the form of a convention or concerted practice and the classic conditions for price fixing in vertical agreements are met. The reader is referred to Sect. 4.3.1.1 on resale price maintenance and Sect. 4.3.1.2 on price recommendations.

A mere obligation on distributors not to sell online does not in itself constitute price fixing within the meaning of Article 5(4) of the CartA. As with the absolute territorial restrictions explained in Sect. 4.3.6.1, a ban or other restrictions on online sales may constitute price fixing within the meaning of Article 5(4) CartA if the specific circumstances of the case reveal the existence of qualified circumstances. The concern is mainly about the circumstances in which the ban on online sales is used as an indirect means to force a certain price level in online sales.

To understand COMCO's concerns, it is most useful for practitioners to refer to the reasoning of the latest decisions on online sales, which we believe is still relevant:

> [T]he introduction of a ban on online sales can be seen as a remedy for the (undesired) price-fixing behaviour of some retailers. Thus, as far as the prohibition or restriction of online sales is concerned, as long as it is not accompanied by other qualifying circumstances, it cannot be considered as resale price maintenance. However, a resale price maintenance may exist, for example, when:
> - in addition to a ban on online sales, there is a link to price recommendations or agreements that influence the discount policy of the resellers, or
> - measures such as threats, intimidation, warnings, penalties, delays or suspension of deliveries and termination of the contract in case of non-compliance with a certain price level are imposed or implemented in the context of an online sales ban. [264]

4.3.6.3 Restrictions on the Effective Use of the Internet

Restrictions on the effective use of the Internet is a new type of agreement falling under Article 5(1) CartA. The Vertical Notice considers such restrictions to be qualitatively severe restrictions of competition which are not covered by Article 5 (4) of the CartA. The assessment of such agreements shall cover qualitative and quantitative criteria, and that of Article 5(2) CartA the criteria related to efficiency grounds.

Article 15(e) of the Verticals Notice borrows from the list of hardcore restrictions of Article 4 Regulation 2022/720 by treating as a qualitatively severe restriction of competition "the prevention of the effective use of the Internet for the sale of the contract goods or services by the buyer or its customers, as this constitutes a

[264] LPC 2011/3, p. 381, *Behinderung des Online-Handels*, para 71; the latest confirmation is to be found in LPC 2014/2, p. 413, *Jura*, para 61.

restriction of the territory into which or of the customers to whom the contract goods or services may be sold within the meaning of points (b), (c) or (d) [of Article 15 Verticals Notice], without prejudice to the possibility of imposing on the buyer the following: (i) other restrictions on online sales or (ii) restrictions on online advertising that are not aimed at preventing the use of an entire online advertising channel."

The Explanatory note to the Verticals Notice mentions some examples [265] of what might prevent the effective use of the Internet but does not borrow the full list of examples from paragraph 206 of the EU Vertical Guidelines. In our view, the practices mentioned in this paragraph are relevant for the interpretation of Article 15 (e) of the Verticals Notice and would be considered qualitatively severe restrictions of competition within the meaning of Article 5(1) of the CartA. We will present here both set of examples for practitioners Both sets of examples are presented here for the sake of completeness.

The Explanatory note to the Verticals Notice mentions restrictions on online sales or online advertising that de facto prohibit the buyer from using the internet to sell the contract goods or services, or restrictions that prevent the use of one or more online advertising channels (e.g. search engines or price comparison services) or the establishment or operation of an online shop. Consequently, the prohibition of the distributor to sell contractual products online clearly constitute a severe restriction of competition under Article 5(1) CartA. The prohibition of the distributor from using online advertising channels is also a severe restriction of competition. Since such restrictions of online sales qualify as severe restrictions, they satisfy the qualitative criterion of significance, and even a low level of quantitative elements [266] would be sufficient for the clause to be considered as a significant restriction of competition under Article 5(1) CartA.

In 2014, the COMCO found that the quantitative test was not fulfilled, with the result that the prohibition on the distributor to sell cosmetic products online was not a significant restriction within the meaning of Article 5(1) CartA, mainly due to a market share of less than 10% on the market and sufficient competition from competing brands (inter-brand competition). [267] The case was decided before the FSC judgment in Gaba [268] and the FAC judgement in ASCOPA, [269] which seems to indicate that qualitatively severe restrictions of competition tend to meet the significance test under Article 5(1) CartA. However, in our view, the assessment made in 2014 would still be valid today and the undertakings can still submit arguments showing that market shares are low and therefore the restrictive effects are not significant due to sufficient inter-brand competition in the market. Finally, restrictions of online sales that are considered as qualitatively severe can be justified on

[265] Explanatory note to the Verticals Notice, para 27.

[266] Article 14(b) Verticals Notice.

[267] LPC 2014/1, p. 198, *Kosmetikprodukte*, paras 226 ff.

[268] FSC, judgment of 28 June 2016, 2C_180/2014, *Gaba*, ATF/BGE 143 II 297.

[269] FAC, judgment of 12 December 2022, B-141/2012, *Estée Lauder/ASCOPA*.

grounds of economic efficiency within the meaning of Article 5(2) CartA, [270] subject to the recent FAC case law narrowly applying the criteria in the case of restrictions which would have the object of affecting competition. [271]

As explained above, in our view other indirect measures mentioned in paragraph 206 of the EU Vertical Guidelines satisfy the qualitative restriction of competition criterion of Article 5(1) CartA. This is the case of obligations on the distributor to sell the contract goods or services only in a physical space or in the physical presence of specialised personnel, [272] obligations on the distributor to seek the supplier's prior authorisation before making individual online sales transactions, [273] or prohibiting the distributor from using the supplier's trademarks or brand names on its website or in its online store. [274]

The Explanatory note to the Verticals Notice lists on the other hand restrictions that are not considered as qualitatively severe, [275] borrowing mainly from paragraph 208 of EU Vertical Guidelines. This applies regardless of the distribution system used by the supplier. These online sales restrictions are deemed not to restrict competition significantly where neither the supplier nor the distributor concerned has more than 15% of the market share in the territory, [276] and to be justified under Article 5(2) CartA where neither the supplier nor the distributor concerned has more than 30% of the market share in the territory. [277] We will list the examples for the sake of completeness:

- requirements intended to ensure the quality or a certain appearance of a buyer's online shop.
- requirements regarding the presentation of the contractual goods or services in the online shop (for example, the minimum number of items displayed, the way in which the supplier's trademarks are presented);
- a direct or indirect ban on the use of online marketplaces;
- a requirement that the buyer operates one or more physical sales outlets or showrooms, for example as a condition for becoming a member of the supplier's selective distribution system;
- a requirement that the buyer sells the contract goods or services off-line in an absolute minimum volume by value or quantity, but not as a proportion of its total turnover, in order to ensure the efficient operation of its physical sales outlet; this requirement may be identical for all buyers or may be set differently on the basis

[270] Cf. Article 18(3) and (4) CartA.

[271] FAC, judgment of 12 December 2022, B-141/2012 *Estée Lauder/ASCOPA*.

[272] EU Vertical Guidelines, para 206 (c).

[273] EU Vertical Guidelines, para 206 (d).

[274] EU Vertical Guidelines, para 206 (e).

[275] Explanatory note to the Verticals Notice, paras 28 and 29.

[276] Article 16(1) Verticals Notice.

[277] Article 18(2) Verticals Notice.

of objective criteria, such as the size of the buyer compared to other buyers or its geographical location.

Such obligations and restrictions must not have as an indirect purpose of preventing the effective use of the internet for the sale of the contract goods or services by the buyer or its customers, and this will not be the case if the buyer is free to operate its own online shop and to advertise online.

4.3.6.4 Dual Pricing

Dual pricing refers to a higher wholesale or invoice price applied by the supplier to the distributor depending on whether the products will be sold online, compared to products that will be sold offline (in physical shops) by the same distributor, called also hybrid distributor. It is well known that physical selling points require more investments in infrastructure and personnel, and therefore imply higher distribution costs. Higher wholesale prices aim at protecting the network of physical selling points from the competition coming from low online sales.

Dual pricing for one and the same (hybrid) retailer was considered a hardcore restriction under the previous block exemption Regulation 330/2010. Investments in the physical infrastructure could be only funded with fixed payments. With the new Regulation 2022/720, applying higher wholesale prices to hybrid retailers for their online sales is not a hardcore restriction and consequently benefits from the block exemption where each party market share remains below the 30% threshold. The dual pricing schemes do not benefit from the exemption if they fall under two other type of hardcore restrictions: [278] first, if they have the object of restricting sales to particular territories or customers under Article 4(b)(c) and (d) Regulation 2022/720, and second, if the pricing difference of the schemes has the object of preventing the effective use of the internet by the buyer to sell the contract goods or services to particular territories or customers under Article 4(e) Regulation 2022/720. Dual pricing would prevent effective use of the internet where the difference in the wholesale price makes selling online unprofitable or financially unsustainable, or where dual pricing is used to limit the quantity of products made available to the buyer for sale online. Conversely, dual pricing can benefit from the block exemption where the difference in the wholesale price is reasonably related to differences in the investments and costs incurred by the buyer to make sales in each channel.

Explanatory note to the Verticals Notice goes in the same direction, by stating that the "requirement that the buyer pays a different wholesale price for products sold online than for products sold offline (dual pricing system) does not normally constitute a qualitatively serious vertical restraint of competition where the difference in the wholesale price is reasonably related to differences in the investments

[278] EU Vertical Guideline, para 209.

and costs incurred by the buyer to make sales in each channel." [279] If the difference in prices for online and offline sales are reasonably related to differences in the investments and costs incurred by the buyer to make sales in each channel, such dual pricing is deemed not to restrict competition significantly where neither the supplier nor the distributor concerned has more than 15% of the market share in the territory, [280] and to be justified under Article 5(2) CartA where neither the supplier nor the distributor concerned has more than 30% of the market share in the territory. [281] In our view, this price difference fulfils the conditions of Article 5(2) CartA, even if one or both parties have more than 30% market share in their respective markets, because it is justified by a different level of investment.

Like in the EU law, dual pricing may be considered as territorial or a customer restriction. Firstly, a different (higher) price charged to a hybrid retailer for online sales may constitute indirect absolute territorial protection covered by Article 5 (4) CartA. [282] This is the case if a higher wholesale price is applied to products to be sold online in Switzerland. [283] Secondly, a different (higher) price charged to a hybrid retailer for online sales to a particular type of customer may constitute an indirect allocation of customers, which is considered a severe restriction of competition within the meaning of Article 5(1) CartA, [284] even if the allocation of customers is not covered by Article 5(4) CartA.

Applying a higher wholesale or invoice price to a pure online retailer or to different retailers has always been allowed under EU competition law. [285] The supplier was and still is free to define its pricing policy regarding wholesale prices and the incentives it applies to its distributors, including applying different price or incentive levels. In this case, the supplier does not have to show that the difference with the prices charged to its other retailers is related to investments or cost differences. A cautionary note is made for cases where the purpose of a different wholesale price to online retailers is to restrict exports or partition markets. [286] In our view, the same reasoning applies to Article 5 CartA. The supplier should remain free

[279] Explanatory note to the Verticals Notice, para 30.

[280] Article 16(1) Verticals Notice.

[281] Article 18(2) Verticals Notice.

[282] Explanatory note to the Verticals Notice, para 12.

[283] See also COMCO Secretariat, *Beratung betreffend Preisdifferenzierung bei Importen in die Schweiz*, LPC 2016/2, p. 373, where the COMCO Secretariat considers higher wholesale prices for book exports to Switzerland as indirect absolute territorial protection. See also COMCO Secretariat *Rabattdifferenzierung bei Lieferungen in die Schweiz*, LPC 2012/3, p. 524, where the distributor in the EU should pay a higher purchase price at the wholesale level through a corresponding discount differentiation depending on whether the products are to be offered at retail in Switzerland or at retail in the EU. In both cases, the difference in wholesale prices for products to be sold in Switzerland was considered as indirect territorial protection covered by Article 5(4) CartA.

[284] See Article 15 Verticals Notice.

[285] See EU Commission Staff Working Document, Report from the Commission to the Council and the European Parliament, Final report on the E-commerce Sector Inquiry of 10 May 2017, para 597.

[286] Ibidem, footnote 322.

to set its wholesale prices to purely online retailers, even if this price is significantly higher than the wholesale price charged to other types of retailers (hybrid or offline). The same caveat applies to dual pricing applied to hybrid retailers: higher wholesale prices for online sales in Switzerland may constitute indirect absolute territorial protection covered by Article 5(4) CartA or indirect customer allocation which is a sever restriction of competition under Article 5(1) CartA.

4.3.6.5 Differentiated Conditions for Online and Offline Sales

For selective distribution system, the criteria for online and offline had to be equivalent, this is not the case anymore, and the Explanatory note to the Verticals Notice explains that considering that online and offline channels have different characteristics, a supplier operating a selective distribution system does not restrict competition severely from a qualitative point of view when it imposes on its authorised distributors criteria for online sales that are not equivalent to those imposed for sales in physical shops, provided that the requirements imposed for online sales do not indirectly have the object of preventing the effective use of the internet by the buyer to sell the contract goods or services to particular territories or customers. [287]

4.3.7 Dual Distribution

Dual distribution occurs where a supplier of goods or services is also active at the downstream level, thereby competing with its independent distributors. [288] The question arises whether agreements between the supplier and its distributors are still vertical even though the supplier is also a competitor of the distributor. The COMCO Verticals Notice follows the EU Regulation 2022/720 and the EU Vertical Guidelines which confirm that such agreements will be treated as vertical and not as horizontal agreements. Under EU law, this means that the agreements will be exempted under the conditions of Regulation 2022/720. In Swiss law, this implies that the COMCO will follow the Verticals Notice principles when assessing these agreements.

According to Article 2 defining its scope, the Verticals Notice applies where "competitors enter into non-reciprocal vertical agreements and a) the supplier is active at an upstream level as a manufacturer, importer, or wholesaler and at a downstream level as an importer, wholesaler, or retailer of goods, while the buyer is an importer, wholesaler, or retailer at the downstream level and not a competing undertaking at the upstream level where it buys the contract goods, or b) the supplier

[287] Explanatory note to the Verticals Notice, para 31. Cf. EU Vertical Guidelines, para 235.

[288] EU Vertical Guidelines, para 94.

is a provider of services at several levels of trade, while the buyer provides its services at the retail level and is not a competing undertaking at the level of trade where it purchases the contract services." [289] Non-reciprocal means in particular that the buyer of the contract goods or services does not supply competing goods or services to the supplier. [290]

Distribution at the wholesale or retail level can take place offline or online at both levels. Dual distribution scenarios have become common due to the digitalisation of business and the entry of manufacturers into the online consumer business. Digitisation has increased efficiency in distribution and consumer experience. The lower costs of digitalisation now allow middle-sized brands to expand their distribution and reach customers outside their physical distribution systems, making them less dependent on large distributors or retailers. The COVID crisis has further accelerated the trend. However, the treatment of dual distribution as defined under paragraph 2 letters a and b of the Verticals Notice as vertical agreement does not apply to the provision of online intermediation services where the provider of the online intermediation services is a competing undertaking on the relevant market for the sale of the intermediated goods or services. [291]

In December 2019, COMCO had treated an agreement whereby an importer had kept for itself big accounts, and the distributor was specialised in retail and small clients in Switzerland. The parties were therefore not direct competitors, but potential competitors. Such a customer allocation between an importer and its downstream distributor was assessed as a horizontal agreement since the importer was not a producer and therefore the agreement could not qualify as a dual distribution covered by the old Vertical Notice. [292] The agreement did not meet the conditions of Article 5 (3)(c) CartA, and therefore there were no fines. But the agreement was considered as a severe restriction of competition under Article 5(1) CartA. As for the quantitative criterion, it was fulfilled given the market shares between 20% and 30% of the importer, even though the distributor had less then 10%. The parties did not invoke any efficiencies to justify the agreement and therefore it was considered as unlawful. The rather short assessment is explained because of the amicable agreement reached with the parties.

The treatment of dual distribution of *AdBlue* [293] is due to the situation under the old Vertical Communication, which reflected the block exemption of Regulation 330/2010. The situation of suppliers that were not manufacturers or service providers was not clear in the old EU Vertical Guidelines, which defined as dual distribution covered by the block exemption only the case of producers entering the downstream market of wholesale or retail distribution, and not that of general

[289] Cf. the same definition in Article 2(4) Regulation 2022/720.

[290] EU Vertical guidelines, para 93.

[291] Article 10(4) Verticals Notice.

[292] COMCO decision of 2 December 2019, LPC 2020/4, p. 626, *AdBlue*, para 55.

[293] COMCO decision of 2 December 2019, LPC 2020/4, p. 626, *AdBlue*.

importers. This has been clarified in the new Regulation 2022/720, which applies the dual distribution exception to general importers.

Practitioners should nevertheless pay attention to Article 10(5) Verticals Notice, which reminds companies that a situation can always be qualified, in whole or in part, as a horizontal restriction of competition under Article 5(3) CartA or be covered by Article 7 CartA on abuse of dominance, irrespective of whether the agreement benefit from the exception on dual distribution.

Another question is how to assess the exchange of information between the supplier and its distributor in a dual distribution scenario. The rise of dual distribution and the introduction of multi-channel and omnichannel strategies by brands requires cooperation with all distributors down to the retail level. Cooperation also requires an exchange of information between the supplier and the distributors, and as usual, competition law treats the exchange of information suspiciously. Like the EU regulations, [294] the Verticals Notice excludes from the dual distribution exception "the exchange of information between the supplier and the buyer that is either not directly related to the implementation of the vertical agreement or is not necessary to improve the production or distribution of the contract goods or services, or which fulfils neither of those two conditions." [295] This type of information exchange must be assessed separately as an exchange of information among competitors. The COMCO has not issued guidelines on horizontal cooperation, [296] the assessment of the exchange of information should be subject to Articles 4 and 5 CartA.

The Verticals Notice and the accompanying Explanatory note do not provide further guidance similar the EU Vertical Guidelines. Paragraph 100 of EU Vertical Guidelines lists for instance as not directly related to the implementation of the agreement or not necessary to realise efficiencies exchange of information on future resale prices or information on private label brands of the distributor. While the EU Vertical Guidelines provides valuable information, there is a tendency to interpret agreements and concerted practices broadly under Article 4(1) and Article 5(3) of the CartA on horizontal agreements, and practitioners should therefore carefully assess information exchanged in a dual distribution context.

A contrario, the exchange of information between the supplier and the buyer which is directly related to the implementation of the vertical agreement in dual distribution settings, or which is necessary to improve the production or distribution of the contract goods or services, will follow the outcome of the assessment of the agreements under the Verticals Notice. Again, the Verticals Notice and the accompanying Explanatory note do not provide further guidance similar the EU Vertical Guidelines.

In order to be allowed, the information to be exchanged should be directly related to the implementation of the vertical agreement and the exchange should be relevant

---

[294] Article 2(5) Regulation 2022/720.

[295] Article 10(3) Verticals Notice.

[296] Cf. Guidelines on the applicability of Article 101 of the Treaty on the Functioning of the European Union to horizontal cooperation agreements, OJ 21.7.2023 C 259, p. 1.

to the type of distribution formula used: for example, exchange of information on sales in relation to the exclusive territory or customer groups, information relevant to a uniform franchise model or information on selection criteria in a selective distribution system. [297]

Information which is necessary to improve the production or distribution of the contract goods or services can relate to different type of situations and services, [298] and is related to the extent of cooperation. The most relevant in dual distribution and multi- and omnichannel strategies are in our view logistical information such as inventory, stocks and returns, sales volumes, repair and pre- or after-sales services. The exchange of such information is necessary to increase services to end-customers and consumers and should be considered necessary for the distribution agreement and therefore allowed.

4.3.8 Restrictions on Spare Parts, Repair and Maintenance Services

Restrictions on the supply of spare parts or repair and warranty services arise when the producer or supplier does not supply spare parts or warranty services to customers or final consumers who have acquired the products through a channel other than the authorised or exclusive distributor in the territory. Such restrictions make more difficult passive sales into the territory, parallel imports or direct imports from Swiss consumers in other territories.

Restrictions on the supply of spare parts or repair and warranty services may qualify as an indirect absolute territorial protection covered by Article 5(4) CartA and subject to fines. [299]

Article 15(f) of the Vertical Notice target specifically the delivery of spare parts to independent repairers, by qualifying as a severe restriction of competition from a qualitative point of view "the restriction, agreed between a supplier of components and a buyer who reuses those components, of the supplier's ability to sell the components as spare parts to end users, repairers, wholesalers or other service providers whom the buyer has not entrusted with the repair or servicing of its goods". [300]

---

[297] EU Vertical Guidelines, para 98.

[298] EU Vertical Guidelines, para 99.

[299] Explanatory note to the Verticals Notice, para 12. For a recent case, see COMCO Secretariat, Final Report of 10 May 2022, *Vertriebssystem von Yamaha - Produkten*, para 214. The Secretariat closed the investigation following commitments from Yamaha importer in Switzerland to adjusts its contracts with the Yamaha partners and with the manufacturer to clarify that the manufacturer's warranty for vehicles and original spare parts is granted regardless of whether the vehicle has been imported by the general importer or not.

[300] Cf. Article 4(f) Regulation 2022/720.

List of Documents

COMCO Explanatory note of the Competition Commission to the Notice on the assessment of vertical agreements of 12 December 2022 (Explanatory note to the Verticals Notice).

COMCO Notice on the treatment of vertical agreements under competition law, Decision of the Competition Commission of 12 December 2022 (Verticals No-tice).

Commission Guidelines on vertical restraints, OJ C 248, 30.6.2022, p. 1

Commission Notice on agreements of minor importance which do not appreciably restrict competition under Article 101(1) of the Treaty on the Functioning of the European Union (de minimis), OJ 2014 C 291, p. 1

Commission Regulation 2022/720 of 10 May 2022 on the application of Article 101 (3) of the Treaty on the Functioning of the European Union to categories of vertical agreements and concerted practices, OJ L 134, 11.5.2022, p. 4

Notice on agreements with limited market impact, Decision of the Competition Commission of 19 December 2005 (SME Notice)

Reference

Wijckmans F, Tuytschaever F (2018) Vertical agreements in EU competition law. Oxford University Press

Chapter 5
Abusive Conduct by Dominant Undertakings and Undertakings with Relative Market Power

5.1 Introduction

The Swiss Cartel Act does not prohibit a dominant position or a position of relative market power, but only its abuse. [1] The FSC has stated that a dominant position "is not in itself abusive, since the purpose of competition is precisely to achieve a dominant position through market success and internal growth". [2]

The conduct of a company in a dominant position becomes unlawful when its conduct is qualified as an abuse, which is why the dominant company bears a special responsibility for its market conduct. The first consequence of the special responsibility is that dominant companies must protect what is left of competition in the market. [3] The second consequence is more specific: the special responsibility means that undertakings in a dominant position should act carefully and clarify whether their conduct is in compliance with the Cartel Act. [4] This second element has been

[1] Article 7 of the CartA on unlawful practices by dominant undertakings and undertakings with relative market power reads as follows: "1) Dominant undertakings and undertakings with relative market power behave unlawfully if, by abusing their position in the market, they hinder other undertakings from starting or continuing to compete, or disadvantage trading partners. 2) The following behaviour is in particular considered unlawful: a. any refusal to deal (e.g. refusal to supply or to purchase goods); b. any discrimination between trading partners in relation to prices or other conditions of trade; c. any imposition of unfair prices or other unfair conditions of trade; d. any under-cutting of prices or other conditions directed against a specific competitor; e. any limitation of production, supply or technical development; f. any conclusion of contracts on the condition that the other contracting party agrees to accept or deliver additional goods or services; g. the restriction of the opportunity for buyers to purchase goods or services offered both in Switzerland and abroad at the market prices and conditions customary in the industry in the foreign country concerned."

[2] FSC, judgment of 29 June 2012, case 2C_484/2010, *Publigroupe*, ATF/BGE 139 I 72, para 10.1.1; FSC, judgment of 2 November 2022, 2C_596/2019, *SIX DCC*, para 8.2.1.

[3] FSC, judgment of 9 December 2019, case 2C_985/2015, ATF/BGE 146 II 217, para 6.3.3.

[4] FSC, judgment of 2 November 2022, case 2C_596/2019, *SIX DCC*, para 9.3.3; FSC, judgment of 9 December 2019, case 2C_985/2015, ATF/BGE 146 II 217, para 8.3.6.

P. Këllezi, *Competition Law in Switzerland*,
https://doi.org/10.1007/978-3-031-45117-1_5

discussed in a recent case in the context of determining whether the wrongful conduct was attributable to the company, and on this point the decisive factor is an objective lack of care in the sense of an organisational fault. [5] Therefore, dominant companies should be doing more in terms of compliance efforts than non-dominant companies.

No special responsibility for companies with relative market power has yet been established by courts.

Dominance may trigger the obligation to notify a concentration. According to Article 9(4) CartA, notification of concentration is mandatory if one of the undertakings concerned has in a final and non-appealable decision been held to be dominant in a market in Switzerland, and if the concentration concerns either that market or an adjacent market or a market upstream or downstream thereof (see Sect. 6.5.2). The dominant position may be established in the statement of reasons of a final and non-appealable decision following an in-depth procedure under the Competition Act; a statement in the operative part of the decision is not required. [6] Relative market power is not a trigger for a notification requirement.

Abuse of a dominant position is punishable by a fine of up to 10% of the turnover achieved in Switzerland in the previous three financial years. [7] Abuse of relative market power is not subject to direct sanctions. The sanction increases with the duration and gravity of the unlawful conduct. Although the law considers the likely profit made from the illegal conduct, in practice profits play only a minor role in determining the amount of the fine.

Zurich Airport was one of the first companies to be fined for abuse of a dominant position, with a fine of around CHF 100,000. [8] Publigroupe was the first company to be fined in the millions, CHF 2.5 million, for discrimination against business partners. [9] The Publigroupe case was also an opportunity to test the robustness of the legal basis before the courts, which is why we'll be discussing it further below. Swisscom was hit with the largest fine of around CHF 333 million for excessive pricing, [10] but the fine was annulled by the FAC. Swisscom was not so lucky with another fine of CHF 220 million for price squeeze, [11] although it was reduced to CHF 186 million by the FAC. Swisscom was further sanctioned with a fine of around CHF 72 million for refusal to deal and tying in the sports rights market, [12]

---

[5] FSC, judgment of 2 November 2022, case 2C_596/2019, *SIX DCC*, para 9.3.3.

[6] FAC, judgment of 19 January 2022, case B-2597/2017, *Kommerzialisierung von elektronischen Medikamenteninformationen*, para 10.6.

[7] Article 49a CartA. See also Chap. 7.

[8] COMCO decision of 18 September 2006, *Valet Parking*, LPC 2006/4, p. 625.

[9] COMCO decision of 5 March 2007, *Richtlinien des Verbandes Schweizerischer Werbegesellschaften VSW über die Kommissionierung von Berufsvermittlern (Publigroupe)*, LPC 2007/2, p. 190.

[10] COMCO decision of 5 February 2007, *Terminierung Mobilfunk*, LPC 2007/2, p. 241.

[11] COMCO decision of 19 October 2009, *Preispolitik Swisscom ADSL*, LPC 2010/1, p. 116.

[12] COMCO decision of 9 May 2016, *Sport im Pay-TV*, LPC 2016/4, p. 920.

followed by a fine of CHF 30 million to its competitor and complainant UPC for the same practices. [13] SIX/DCC was fined approximately CHF 7 million for tying and refusal to deal. [14] Galenica was fined CHF 4.5 million for exclusive dealing practices, [15] followed by Naxoo, a local cable operator which was fined around CHF 3.6 million [16] also for exclusive dealing. Swiss Post was fined CHF 22 million for discriminatory and exclusionary practices. [17]

5.2 Dominant Position and Relative Market Power

5.2.1 The Relevant Market

The relevant market is defined in Article 11(3)(a) and (b) of the Merger Control Ordinance. [18] This definition is used as the starting point in all cases: the assessment of dominance must always be made by reference to the relevant product and geographic market. [19] According to the definition, "the product market comprises all those goods or services that are regarded as interchangeable by consumers on the one hand and by suppliers on the other hand with regard to their characteristics with regard to their characteristics and intended use. The geographic market comprises the area in which on the one hand consumers purchase and on the other hand suppliers sell the goods or services that constitute the product market." Besides, the COMCO refers regularly to the Commission Notice on the definition of relevant market for the purposes of Community competition law. [20]

5.2.2 Dominant Position

Article 4(2) CartA defines the dominant undertakings as "one or more undertakings in a specific market that are able, as suppliers or consumers, to behave to an

[13] COMCO decision of 7 September 2020, *Eishockey im Pay-TV*, LPC 2021/1, p. 160.

[14] COMCO decision of 29 November 2010, *SIX/DCC*, LPC 2011/1, p. 96.

[15] COMCO decision of 19 December 2016, *Kommercializierung von Elektronischen Medikamenteninformationen*, LPC 2020/3a, p. 1144.

[16] COMCO decision of 11 December 2017, *Supermédia (Naxoo)*, LPC 2018/3, p. 508. The abuse was confirmed but the fine was reduced by FSC to around CHF 3.1 million, see FSC, judgment of 9 May 2023, 2C_395/2021, *Naxoo*.

[17] COMCO decision of 30 October 2017, *Geschäftskunden Preissysteme für adressierte Briefsendungen*, LPC 2020/2, p. 433.

[18] Ordinance on the Control of Concentrations of Undertakings (Merger Control Ordinance, MCO; RS 251.4).

[19] FSC, judgment of 17 June 2003, 2A.520/2002, *EEF*, ATF/BGE 129 II 497, para 6.3.1.

[20] OJ 1997 C 372, p. 5.

appreciable extent independently of the other participants (competitors, suppliers or consumers) in the market." Both single and collective dominance is considered as a dominant position triggering the duty not to abuse this position.

The criteria to determine dominance are market shares of the undertaking and its closest competitors, the number of competitors in the market, barriers to entry and potential competition, countervailing market power and other circumstances of the market.

According to the FSC, a high market share is not in itself evidence of a dominant position. However, there is a strong indication of dominance once the market share exceeds 50%. [21] High and stable market shares of the undertaking under investigation are generally indicative of a dominant position, while volatile and declining market shares tend to argue against it, although declining market shares do not preclude a finding of dominance as long as the market share remains high.

Specifically, an overall market share of over 90% is a very strong indication of a dominant position, and even factual ambiguities do not alter the fact that the 'critical threshold' of 50% would in any case be far exceeded. [22] The same reasoning was applied to the Hallenstadion with a market share of 75%: the 'critical threshold' of 50% was exceeded by a wide margin. [23] A market share of 63% was sufficient to demonstrate that Publigroupe had a dominant position.

Potential competition examines the extent to which the company is directly exposed to competitive pressure from the possibility that other companies not currently active in the relevant market may enter the market as new competitors. Entry must be reasonably likely to occur within a foreseeable period of 2–3 years and must have a sufficient impact on competition. Entry is reasonably likely if it can be expected based on concrete economic, technical or other evidence. A mere theoretical possibility is not sufficient. [24]

Countervailing power examines whether the buyers of the product in question have special bargaining power that enables them to exert sufficient competitive pressure on the company under investigation to prevent it from acting independently. The absence of bargaining power on the part of customers confirms that the undertaking under investigation is behaving independently and that countervailing market power cannot offset or neutralise high market shares and weak actual or potential competition. [25]

[21] FSC, judgment of 29 June 2012, case 2C_484/2010, *Publigroupe,* ATF/BGE 139 I 72, para 9.3.3.2.

[22] FAC, judgment of 19 January 2022, B-2597/2017, *Kommerzialisierung von elektronischen Medikamenteninformationen*, para 9.2.1.19.

[23] FSC, judgment of 12 February 2020, 2C_113/2017, *Hallenstadion*, para 5.5.2.

[24] FAC, judgment of 19 January 2022, B-2597/2017, *Kommerzialisierung von elektronischen Medikamenteninformationen*, paras 9.2.2.5 ff.

[25] FSC, judgment of 12 February 2020, 2C_113/2017, *Hallenstadion*, para 5.5.2. FAC, judgment of 19 January 2022, B-2597/2017, *Kommerzialisierung von elektronischen Medikamenteninformationen*, paras 9.3.3.5 ff.

5.2.3 Relative Market Power and Economic Dependence

The text of Article 4(2bis) CartA in force since 1 January 2022 defines an undertaking with relative market power as "an undertaking on which other undertakings are dependent for the supply of or demand for goods or services in such a way that there are no adequate and reasonable opportunities for switching to other undertakings." There is no such provision or case law at EU level, but Member States are free to introduce such rules at national level. [26]

The law adopted in 1995 covered only the dominant position of an undertaking with the power to behave independently in the market. That definition referred to the paramount market position of one or more undertakings.

The movement to encompass market power short of dominance started in 2003, where the Parliament slightly amended the definition of the dominant position by indicating that a dominant undertaking could behave independently to an appreciable extent towards suppliers, without having to act independently of its competitors in the market. This was achieved by changing an "and" to an "or", so that the undertaking could behave independently towards either "competitors, suppliers *or* consumers", and not towards all of them ("competitors, suppliers *and* consumers"). This amendment introduced the concept of "economic dependence" into the Cartel Act. By amending the Cartel Act in 2003, the legislator also made it clear that the assessment should not be limited to market structure but also focus on concrete interdependencies. [27] The new provision was criticised and construed narrowly by most scholars. The COMCO applied the new provision to COOP, through an amicable settlement. [28]

A few scholars found this unsatisfactory and continually called for more intervention, in particular starting from 2010' following an exchange rate shock during which the price differences in Switzerland and neighbouring countries were made visible for consumers. The image of the Switzerland as an "island of high prices" (*îlot de cherté* ou *Hochpreisinsel*) was predominant in the media, with consumer associations once again calling the prices charged in Switzerland by foreign brands a rip-off. It is against this background that a group of small undertakings, backed by a couple of scholars, launched in 2016 a federal popular initiative against the high prices applied in Switzerland, [29] using the German concept of relative market power.

Considering the initiative as highly likely to be accepted by the people, the Federal Council presented an amended proposal of the initiative to the Parliament, which adopted an amendment the Cartel Act in March 2021. The amendment revised three provisions of the Cartel Act: Article 4(2bis) CartA defining the relative market power as distinct from the dominant position; Article 7(g) CartA introducing a new

[26] Article 3(2) of Regulation 1/2003.

[27] FSC, judgment of 12 February 2020, 2C_113/2017, *Hallenstadion*, para 5.5.1.

[28] See Këllezi (2008), pp. 55–88.

[29] See the historic of the initiative "Stop the island of high prices - for fair prices (Fair Prices Initiative)," at https://www.bk.admin.ch/ch/f/pore/vi/vis469.html.

abusive behaviour targeting foreign suppliers (Sect. 5.3.3.7); and Article 49a CartA on fines making sure that abuse of relative market power does not trigger direct sanctions (Sects. 5.3.1 and 7.2.1).

Article 4(2bis) CartA defines the situation where one or more undertakings are dependent for the supply of or demand for goods or services on another undertaking having relative market power. Only undertakings can be in a situation of dependency on another undertaking with relative market power and benefit from the protection of the Cartel Act, not consumers.

Article 4(2bis) CartA goes on to explain the dependency relationship by the fact that "there are no adequate and reasonable opportunities for switching to other undertakings". The existence of adequate and reasonable switching opportunities becomes therefore one of the main criteria to establish relative market power. If customers have adequate and reasonable alternatives to buy or sell their products, they are not dependent on undertakings selling or buying from them, and such undertakings are not considered to have relative market power vis-à-vis these customers.

The criterion requires first that no alternatives must exist in the market for the affected undertaking. It is up to the undertaking alleging a dependency to show that no reasonable alternatives exist, and for that to happen the undertaking that wants to rely on the new rules on relative market power must have tried first to find reasonable alternatives, without success. [30]

If there are no alternatives at all in the market to satisfy the need of the affected undertaking, this means that the criterion of "no adequate and reasonable alternatives" is satisfied without having to enquire the adequateness and reasonableness. No alternative means no substitutes in the market, which hints to a dominant or a monopoly position in the relevant market, and therefore the relative market power concept becomes redundant with the dominant position. Theoretically, both scenarios could apply.

Once alternatives are identified, the assessment must qualify them both as adequate and reasonable to rule out a situation of relative market power. In an explanatory note, the Secretariat of the COMCO [31] states that the question whether alternatives are adequate and reasonable must always be assessed on a case-by-case basis. The explanatory note gives however some general guidance on criteria to consider when assessing whether alternatives are adequate and reasonable. [32]

An alternative is *adequate* if available offers can meet adequately the needs of the undertaking that alleges to be in a dependency situation. Although the adequate quality of the offer will be assessed in relation to the dependent undertaking, it will be done considering objective criteria and cannot rely on the subjective assessment of that undertaking alone. The following criteria can play a role in assessing whether

---

[30] COMCO Secretariat, Explanatory note of the of 6 December 2021 regarding relative market power (Explanatory note on relative market power), para 10.

[31] Explanatory note on relative market power.

[32] Idem, para 8.

there are adequate alternatives: the characteristics of the product, the purchasing conditions, the reputation of the brand and brand loyalty of consumers as well as the market share of the undertaking presumed to possess relative market power.

Whether an alternative is *reasonable* is explained negatively in the explanatory note, by stating that an alternative can be unreasonable for the dependent undertaking if that alternative is not an option given the individual characteristics of that dependent undertaking. Individual characteristics of the dependent undertaking may relate for instance to specific investments made by that undertaking in relation to a business relationship, the costs of changing suppliers or buyers, the specific contractual relationship, the turnover affected compared to the total turnover and the circumstances surrounding the alleged dependence at hand, including what caused the dependency considering also the decisions made by the affected undertaking.

The explanatory note further explains that dependency may have different causes. [33] A retailer may be dependent on certain producers' products in its assortment. A supplier may find itself dependent on certain buyers because there are no other reasonable alternatives. A dependency relationship may also arise when an undertaking focuses its activities on a long-term business relationship.

5.3 Abusive Conduct

5.3.1 Definition and Criteria

According to Article 7(1) CartA, "dominant undertakings and undertakings with relative market power behave unlawfully if, by abusing their position in the market, they hinder other undertakings from starting or continuing to compete, or disadvantage trading partners." Article 7(2) CartA supplements the first paragraph with specific examples of conduct considered abusive and therefore unlawful: "a. any refusal to deal (e.g. refusal to supply or to purchase goods); b. any discrimination between trading partners in relation to prices or other conditions of trade; c. any imposition of unfair prices or other unfair conditions of trade; d. any under-cutting of prices or other conditions directed against a specific competitor; e. any limitation of production, supply or technical development; f. any conclusion of contracts on the condition that the other contracting party agrees to accept or deliver additional goods or services; g. the restriction of the opportunity for buyers to purchase goods or services offered both in Switzerland and abroad at the market prices and conditions customary in the industry in the foreign country concerned."

The provision was extended to undertakings with relative market power in March 2021 which is in force since 1 January 2022. As with any type of conduct that meets the criteria of Article 7(1) CartA, the commercial conduct of an undertaking with relative market power may be considered an abuse, those listed in Article 7(2) CartA

[33] Idem, para 9.

being examples. [34] The amendment of March 2021 introduced an obligation to supply on foreign terms and was intended to apply mainly to companies with relative market power based abroad, but it applies also to dominant companies and covers Swiss-based companies that sell abroad. Abuse of relative market power however does not trigger direct sanctions; companies with relative market power risk fines only if they do not comply with a COMCO decision. However, the COMCO can order the companies to deal with other companies or to waive certain conditions. [35]

It has taken the courts several years to establish the relationship between the two paragraphs of Article 7 of CartA and to define criteria that set the limits of abuse. The concept of abuse is still vague and fluctuating and has not yet been defined in relation to all types of abuse. The discussion on the boundaries of abuse has been guided by Article 7 of the ECHR on the principle of legality, as all abusive practices are subject to a fine under Article 49a of the CartA. In the following paragraphs, we will outline how the criteria for establishing an abuse have evolved over the last 10 years.

In the *Publigroupe* case concerning the discrimination of business partners, the federal Administrative Court (FAC) decided in 2010 that Article 7 (1) CartA on its own did not satisfy the requirements of the principle of legality enshrined in Article 7 ECHR (*nulla peine sine lega certa*). [36]

While reviewing the same case, the FSC left this question open and focused on the joint reading of Article 7 (1) CartA with Article 7 (2) CartA. It held that Article 7 (2)(b) CartA prohibiting discrimination against business partners, taken together with Article 7 (1) CartA, constitutes a sufficient legal basis under Article 7 ECHR. In other words, the question of whether a discriminatory practice is abusive must be considered in the light of the general clause of Article 7 (1) of the Cartel Act, which highlights the principle that there can only be an abuse of a dominant position if the practice in question has anticompetitive effects on the market. Furthermore, in reaching its conclusion, the FSC indicated that the content of Article 7 CartA can be clarified on the basis of the criteria developed by case law and doctrine, including the practice relating to Article 102 TFEU, even though Switzerland is not a member of the EU or the EEA. [37] This means that it was the combination of the abusive conduct and its effect that is relevant for the question whether a situation falls under Art. 7 Cartel Act and not a list of rules of conduct. [38] The FSC continues to require that Articles 7(1) and 7(2) CartA be applied jointly. [39]

In 2019, the FSC answered the question left open in 2012 by stating that Article 7 (1) CartA alone, as clarified by the relevant EU case law and the practice of the

---

[34] Article 7(2)(g) CartA. Explanatory note on relative market power, paras 11ff.

[35] FSC, judgment of 9 May 2023, 2C_395/2021, *Naxoo*, para 5.3.

[36] FAC, judgment of 27 April 2010, case B-2977/2007, *Publigroupe*, LPC 2010/2, p. 239, para 8.1.5.1.

[37] FSC, judgment of 29 June 2012, case 2C_484/2010, *Publigroupe*, ATF/BGE 139 I 72.

[38] FSC, judgment of 9 December 2019, case 2C_985/2015, *Preispolitik Swisscom ADSL*, ATF/BGE 146 II 217, para 8.3.3.

[39] FSC, judgment of 9 May 2023, 2C_395/2021, *Naxoo*, para 10.1.3.

COMCO and its Secretariat, meets the requirements of Article 7 ECHR. [40] A practice of a dominant undertaking which is not covered by the list in Article 7 (2) CartA could therefore constitute an abuse of a dominant position if this practice impedes the access to or the exercise of competition by other undertakings or causes a disadvantage to trading partners within the meaning of Article 7(1) CartA. Moreover, the examples given in paragraph 2 of Article 7 CartA are merely illustrative and do not say anything about the illegality of the practices mentioned or, where applicable, about the seriousness of the infringement. It follows that, on the one hand, the practices listed in Article 7(2) CartA do not constitute abusive practices *per se*, but they must hinder competitors or disadvantage partners within the meaning of Article 7(1) CartA in order to be considered unlawful, and that, on the other hand, practices which are not listed in Article 7(2) CartA but which nevertheless hinder competitors or disadvantage partners within the meaning of Article 7(1) CartA are abusive and therefore unlawful, and there is nothing to prevent such practices from being considered serious and subject to heavy fines. The central element of the abuse is therefore to hinder or disadvantage competitors or partners in the sense of restricting or harming competition, as required by the wording of Article 7 (1) CartA. The FSC refers for the first time to the EU Commission's Guidance on Article 102 TFEU to highlight the seriousness of the abusive conduct listed there.

In SIX DCC, [41] 3 years later, the FSC no longer discusses Article 7 CEDH, but at the same time downplays the requirements of Article 7(1) CartA, not only by referring to *potential* effects on competition, but also by carrying out an abstract assessment of the conduct and of the effects on the competitor, while refusing to identify any criteria related to market circumstances that would explain why the tying in the specific case had potential negative effects on the market (and not only on the complainant in the abstract). It also points out that tying, which is listed in Article 7(2) of the Cartel Act, is a type of conduct which poses a risk to competition, irrespective of its actual effects on the market. The FSC again refers to the EU Commission's guidance on Article 102 TFEU to show that the conduct listed therein constitutes a potential threat to competition and that the threat alone is sufficient to establish an abuse: in addition to tying and bundling, this conclusion would apply to exclusive dealing, predation, refusal to supply and margin squeeze. [42]

FSC ruling in SIX DCC confirmed the trend initiated by the FAC [43] in 2018 to water down the assessment of why certain conduct is likely to have exclusionary effects on the market, but also on a particular competitor, given the context, the relevant facts of the case and the market circumstances. It is unclear whether the

---

[40] FSC, judgment of 9 December 2019, case 2C_985/2015, *Preispolitik Swisscom ADSL*, ATF/BGE 146 II 217.

[41] FSC, judgment of 2 November 2022, case 2C_596/2019, *SIX DCC*.

[42] See the conduct listed in EU Commission, Guidance on the Commission's enforcement priorities in applying Article 82 of the EC Treaty to abusive exclusionary conduct by dominant undertakings, OJ C 45, 24.2.2009, p. 7.

[43] FAC, judgment of 18 December 2018, B-831/2011, *SIX DCC*; FAC, judgment of 19 January 2022, B-2597/2017, *Kommerzialisierung von elektronischen Medikamenteninformationen*.

trend will focus only on the extent to which the COMCO must prove potential or actual harm to competition, or whether it will also limit the ability of dominant undertakings to show that their conduct is not capable of foreclosing competitors or having any significant effect on the market. The most striking element is that while the EU Commission's guidance on Article 102 TFEU has been the flagship of the more economic approach to competition law, the EU guidance is being used to justify a formal legal assessment and to dispense with a proper examination of the relevant facts of the case.

The FSC has established a two-step test to determine whether conduct by a dominant undertaking constitutes an unlawful abuse.[44] The first step of the test examines the distortions of competition (i.e. the hindrance or disadvantage to market participants). The second step examines possible justifications, also known as 'legitimate business reasons'. The conduct is considered unlawful if there is no objective reason for the discrimination, exploitation or hindrance.[45] The distortion of competition and the lack of objective justification are therefore constitutive elements of the abusive conduct, and this has remained unchanged even after SIX DCC.

The FSC adds that the general yardstick for the question of whether conduct is legal or illegal is, on the one hand, institutional protection and, on the other, individual protection or, in other words, the guarantee of effective competition.[46] Therefore, both effective competition as an institution in itself and the individual undertakings that could suffer from a distortion of effective competition are worthy of protection under Article 7 CartA.[47]

Having clarified that the main conditions of an abusive practice are that it hinders competitors or disadvantages trading partners, as set out in Article 7(1) CartA, the main question is what are the practices that hinder competitors and discriminate against trading partners. In the classic terminology of EU competition law, the former covers exclusionary conduct, and the latter covers exploitative abuses.

The FSC uses a broad language to describe abusive conduct.[48] Exclusionary conduct prevents actual or potential competitors and other market participants from entering the market, for example by erecting barriers to entry, or from competing in the market. Exclusionary conduct includes all measures taken by dominant undertakings which do not constitute fair competition on the merits, which are directed against actual and potential competitors, whether rivals or trading partners, and which restrict their scope of action in the dominant market or in neighbouring

---

[44] FSC, judgment of 9 May 2023, 2C_395/2021, Naxoo, para 10.1.3.

[45] FSC, judgment of 29 June 2012, case 2C_484/2010, *Publigroupe*, ATF/BGE 139 I 72, para 10.1.2.

[46] Idem, para 10.1.2.

[47] Cf. Sect. 1.4 on the choice between public and private enforcement.

[48] FSC, judgment of 9 December 2019, case 2C_985/2015, *Preispolitik Swisscom ADSL*, ATF/BGE 146 II 217, para 4.1.

markets. Exclusionary conduct may take place in the dominant undertaking's market or in an upstream or downstream market.

In exploitative conduct it is the other side of the market, such as the suppliers or customers of the exclusionary undertaking, that is disadvantaged by the imposition of exploitative conditions or prices. The dominant undertaking gains an economic advantage by exploiting its dominant position to the detriment of the interests of trading partners and consumers.

Certain types of conduct by dominant undertakings may be both exclusionary and exploitative. The classification of conduct as exclusionary or exploitative is therefore irrelevant. These categories are therefore only of heuristic value, in FSC's view. However, it is always important, according to the FSC ruling in *Preispolitik Swisscom ADSL*, to establish the abusive nature of the disputed conduct, including the harm to competition, the distortion of competition or the anti-competitive effects, [49] on the basis of a case-by-case analysis. [50] The manner in which and the criteria by which the existence of harm or distortion of competition is to be established are specific to each type of abuse. In the casuistic approach, there is a tendency to disregard factual elements linked to the way the market and competitors compete in favour of presumptions or abstract formal criteria.

5.3.2 Abusive Conduct Covered by Article 7 (1) CartA

Article 7(1) CartA covers any type of conduct that satisfies its conditions and does not fall within one of the examples in Article 7(2) CartA. This is the case, for example, with price squeezes.

In *Preispolitik Swisscom ADSL*, [51] the FSC confirmed that the practice of price squeeze (*Kosten-Preis-Schere*) by a vertically integrated dominant undertaking can be qualified as an abuse of a dominant position on the basis of Article 7 (1) CartA alone, and is punishable as such. The amount of the fine of CHF 186,036,840 was also confirmed. It therefore answers the question left open in 2012 in the *Publigroupe* case [52] by stating that Article 7 (1) CartA, clarified with the help of the relevant EU case law and the practice of the COMCO and its Secretariat, meets the requirements of Article 7 ECHR (*nulla peine sine lega certa*).

---

[49] In German, *Wettbewerbsschädigung*, *Wettbewerbsverfälschungen* or *wettbewerbswidrige Auswirkungen*. See respectively FSC, judgment of 9 December 2019, case 2C_985/2015, *Preispolitik Swisscom ADSL*, ATF/BGE 146 II 217, para 4.1; FSC, judgment of 29 June 2012, case 2C_484/2010, *Publigroupe*, ATF/BGE 139 I 72, para 10.1.2; FSC, judgment of 12 February 2020, 2C_113/2017 *Hallenstadion*, para 6.1.

[50] FSC, judgment of 9 December 2019, 2C_985/2015, *Preispolitik Swisscom ADSL*, ATF/BGE 146 II 217, para 4.1.

[51] Idem.

[52] FSC, judgment of 29 June 2012, 2C_484/2010, *Publigroupe*, ATF/BGE 139 I 72.

A price squeeze constitutes an abusive conduct under the following conditions: (1) the dominant undertaking is vertically integrated, i.e. it is present on both the upstream and downstream markets; (2) the undertaking is dominant in the upstream market; (3) its customers in the downstream market are at the same time its competitors in the downstream market; (4) insufficient price margin of those who compete with the dominant undertaking at the retail level. There are mainly two ways to achieve this last condition:

- the wholesale prices charged by the dominant undertaking to its customers in the downstream market are higher than the prices charged by the dominant undertaking to its own final customers, or
- the margin resulting from the difference between the wholesale prices charged by the dominant undertaking to its downstream customers and the prices charged by the dominant undertaking to its own retail customers does not allow the dominant undertaking's downstream customers to cover their costs.

The FSC held that, as in EU law, whether the margin available to competitors is sufficient (or insufficient) must be determined by reference to the costs of the dominant undertaking itself. Only in exceptional cases should the price and cost data of actual competitors be used. [53] This is essentially an application of the 'as efficient competitor' test.

In *Preispolitik Swisscom ADSL*, COMCO had carried out both tests and calculated the actual margin of the dominant undertaking and that of the injured competitors. A margin squeeze was confirmed after concluding that the two margins were insufficient. [54] First, the analysis focused on whether the dominant undertaking's retail activities are profitable, taking into account the prices charged at the wholesale level. If the dominant undertaking's retail activities are not profitable, it is unlikely that competitors will be profitable on the retail market. Secondly, the test examines the margins of the competitors: if these are found to be insufficient, the dominant undertaking is committing an abuse in the form of a margin squeeze. [55] The COMCO did not differentiate between negative and insufficient margins, as both tests had shown that the costs of competitors and those of Swisscom (consisting of the wholesale price and other operating costs in the retail market) exceeded the price in the retail market, resulting in a loss for the operators of broadband Internet services. Three elements were considered relevant for calculating the profitability of operators: the wholesale price charged by the dominant undertaking, the retail price charged on the market and the retail costs incurred by all operators. In this case, a difference of 19.45% between the wholesale and retail price was considered insufficient, and the expertise of the telecom regulator (Ofcom) had concluded that

---

[53] FSC, judgment of 9 December 2019, case 2C_985/2015, *Preispolitik Swisscom ADSL*, ATF/BGE 146 II 217, *para* 5.4.

[54] COMCO, decision of 19 October 2009, *Preispolitik Swisscom ADSL*, LPC 2010/1, p. 116.

[55] Idem, paras 223 ff.

a margin of between 23% and 30% between the wholesale and retail price would have been appropriate. [56]

The criteria set by FSC in this case are in line with those developed by the EU courts under Article 102 TFEU. [57] The FSC confirms the independent abuse approach followed by EU case law, according to which the abuse of the margin squeeze does not depend on a pricing abuse of the wholesale or retail price charged by the dominant undertaking.

As regards the seriousness of the abuse, the FSC makes no distinction between the abuses covered by Article 7(1) and those explicitly mentioned as examples in Article 7(2) CartA. [58] This means that the list of abuses contained in Article 7 (2) CartA is not more serious than those covered (only) by Article 7(1) CartA, and vice versa: the price squeeze or other abuses that may be covered in the future by Article 7(1) CartA are not less serious, and may also result in heavy fines.

5.3.3 Specific Examples of Abuse Covered by Article 7 (2) CartA

Paragraph 2 of Article 7 CartA provides examples of abusive behaviour. We will discuss each of these examples in a separate section below.

5.3.3.1 Refusal to Deal

Unlike Article 102 TFUE, Article 7(2)(a) CartA considers as unlawful "any refusal to deal (e.g. refusal to supply or to purchase goods)". The provision covers all types of refusal to deal. [59] The case law is still developing, but so far we can say that the refusal to deal is perhaps the area where the Swiss law and the EU law differ the most.

Refusal to deal was used by COMCO at a very early stage to open up the electricity transmission network, and hence electricity generation, to competition at a time when the legislator had not yet liberalised the market (Sect. 1.3.3). The case concerned the refusal by the operator of an electricity transmission system (EEF), vertically integrated in the markets for the generation, transport and distribution of electricity, to grant access to its transmission network to a competing electricity

---

[56] COMCO, decision of 19 October 2009 *Preispolitik Swisscom ADSL*, LPC 2010/1, p. 116, paras 277, 281.

[57] CJEU, judgment of 14 October 2010, *Deutsche Telekom*, C-280/08 P, ECLI:EU:C:2010:603, paras 155ff; CJEU, judgment of 17 February 2011, C-52/09, *TeliaSonera*, ECLI:EU:C:2011:83.

[58] FSC, judgment of 9 December 2019, 2C_985/2015, *Preispolitik Swisscom ADSL*, ATF/BGE 146 II 217, *para* 9.2.3.3.

[59] FAC, judgment of 18 December 2018, B-831/2011, *SIX DCC*, para 791.

supplier (Watt), thereby preventing the latter to transmit its electricity to its client, one the biggest supermarket chain in Switzerland (Migros). In its decision, the COMCO took the view that EEF's refusal to allow its competitor Watt to transmit electricity over its network was an abuse of a dominant position within the meaning of Article 7 CartA, without specifying whether EEF infringed Article 7(1) CartA or Article 7(2)(a) CartA. [60] The decision was based on the essential facility doctrine. The FSC confirmed the decision. By preventing its competitor (Watt) from using its electricity network, EEF excluded its competitor from entering the electricity supply market because for legal and economic reasons it is practically impossible for Watt to build a parallel transmission network itself. EEF's refusal therefore excluded any competition between energy suppliers. According to the FSC, EEF had used its dominant position resulting from its transmission network to avoid opening to competition. [61]

Twenty years later, using Article 7(2)(a) of CartA, COMCO opened up the gas market. [62] The practice of a local gas company controlled by the City of Lucerne and a regional gas company to supply natural gas only to final customers in the local network area of the local gas company led to a de facto supply monopoly of the public local gas company. As a result, third-party suppliers were prevented from entering the market for the supply of natural gas to final customers in the network area of Lucerne. [63] This time, the opening of the gas market resulted in a fine of CHF 2,610,480 for regional gas pipeline operators.

We will continue below with two cases that were upheld by the Federal Administrative Court and some specific cases that were dealt with by the civil courts.

SIX DCC is a case in the card payments and terminals, mainly based on the duty to deal. [64] SIX provides stock exchange services, financial information and banking services in Switzerland. One of its subsidiaries holds a dominant position with more than 70% share in the market for acquiring Visa and Mastercard credit cards and in the market for acquiring the Maestro debit card and offered a currency exchange functionality called DCC, which allowed customers to pay in CHF or in foreign currency at the merchant's terminal. Another SIX' subsidiary offered terminal payments to merchants and could offer the currency exchange DCC function provided by its sister subsidiary.

A competing manufacturer of terminal payments wanted to install the SIX DCC functionality in its own terminal offered to merchants. After the SIX subsidiaries refused to allow the manufacturer to install the currency exchange DCC in its payment terminals, the manufacturer requested the interface information so that its

[60] COMCO, decision of 5 March 2001, LPC 2001/2, p. 255, *Watt/Migros—EEF*, paras 165 ff.

[61] FSC, judgment of 17 June 2003, 2A.520/2002, *EEF,* ATF/BGE 129 II 497, para 6.5.3.

[62] See Andreas Heinemann: Keeping competition policy up to date, Interview conducted by Pranvera Këllezi and David Mamane, Concurrences N° 2-2022 p. 13.

[63] COMCO, decision of 25 Mai 2020, *Netzzugang EGZ und ewl*, para 166.

[64] COMCO, decision of 29 November 2010, *SIX/Terminals mit Dynamic Currency Conversion (DCC)*, LPC 2011/1 p. 96.

own terminal could communicate with the SIX DCC currency conversion function. After SIX refused, it complained to the COMCO. This manufacturer that complained did not intend to develop its own currency conversion function. It had a market share of between 20% and 30%. There were eight manufacturers in the market offering payment terminals. Three other terminal manufacturers integrated other DCC solutions used internationally in cooperation with acquirers, while the others continued to operate payment terminals without currency conversion functionality. The inability to work with the DCC function provided by SIX Group meant that the complainant potentially lost approximately 20% of its turnover, but it confirmed that the SIX DCC function was not indispensable for its business.

The COMCO found that the SIX Group, through its subsidiaries, had unlawfully refused to disclose the necessary interface information to payment terminal manufacturers other than its subsidiaries (Article 7(2)(a) CartA). The same conduct was considered to constitute, on the one hand, discrimination because the group company only dealt with its sister company and not with companies outside the group (Article 7(2)(b) CartA) and, on the other hand, restriction of technical development (Article 7(2)(e) CartA). Finally, the conduct also constituted a technical coupling of the purchase of services with the DCC function and of terminal equipment with the DCC function, and thus an unlawful tying within the meaning of Article 7(2)(f) CartA. [65]

The Federal Administrative Court (FAC) confirmed the refusal to deal and the tying, which was sufficient to confirm the fine of CHF 7 million and stated that it was not necessary to discuss discrimination and restriction of technical development. [66] The Swiss Federal Court (SFC) confirmed tying and the fine but found it unnecessary to discuss the refusal to deal. [67] In total, the proceedings lasted 16 years. After the COMCO decision, it took SIX Group 11 years to obtain a final judgement. This case shows that appeals do not focus on whether each abuse finding was factually and legally justified, but on the fine. The full amount of the fine is upheld even if only one type of abuse is found. The other abuses and the resulting remedies are not discussed.

The FAC ruling in this case is the most recent and relevant case law addressing the duty to deal under Article 7(2)(a) CartA. The FAC defines the general, necessary criteria that must be present in all cases of refusal to deal: (1) a dominant position in a relevant market, (2) a potential or existing business relationship, (3) a request to deal, followed by (4) a refusal to deal, taking into account (5) the particularities of the case and (6) the distortion of competition, and finally (7) the lack of justification. On the other hand, the criteria relating to (8) intellectual property rights, (9) the indispensability of the input, (10) the introduction of a new product and (11) a remuneration

[65] COMCO, decision of 29 November 2010, *SIX/Terminals mit Dynamic Currency Conversion (DCC)*, LPC 2011/1 p. 96.

[66] FAC, judgment of 18 December 2018, B-831/2011, *SIX DCC*.

[67] FSC, judgment of 2 November 2022, 2C_596/2019, *SIX DCC*.

scheme constitute specific elements of the offence which must be present only, or to varying degrees, in certain types of refusal to deal. [68]

The FAC limited the facts of the case to the refusal to disclose interface or interoperability information and set the criteria only in relation to this type of abuse. Having denied copyright protection for lack of individuality (or originality), [69] the FAC held that it was not necessary to prove that the competitor was about to introduce a new product. As the subject matter of the refusal was the interoperability information, which was not protected by copyright, and not the product itself (the DCC function), the condition of indispensability did not apply. [70] Similarly, the existence of substitutes on the market should not be assessed in the context of indispensability, but in the context of the criteria relating to the restriction of competition. In its assessment of the criteria relating to the restriction of competition, the FAC held that Article 7 of Cartel Act does not require the restriction of competition to be significant and therefore there is no de minimis threshold for abusive conduct. [71] The FAC also held that the elimination of competition was not a necessary criterion for refusal to supply interoperability information. [72] Nor is the exclusion or elimination of the company that requested the interoperability information a necessary condition. [73] It is sufficient that refusal of interoperability information adversely or negatively affects the economic activity of the undertaking requesting the information. [74]

Although the FAC does not define the criteria for each type of refusal to deal, it sets a precedent that neither the elimination of all competition in the market nor the elimination of a competitor or customer is required to find an abusive refusal to deal. The FAC does not rule out that the elimination of competition, indispensability and the use of the IP for a new product may be required in certain types of refusals to deal, such as the refusal to licence intellectual property. In general, however, the threshold for establishing a restriction of competition is set at a very low level for all types of abusive conduct.

The case has been compared to the Microsoft case in the EU. However, the facts and the reasoning are very different:

- While the companies requiring interoperability with the Microsoft Windows operating system offered their own product—servers for business customers—the company requesting interoperability information from SIX Group did not develop its own DCC functionality but wanted this information to have direct

[68] Idem, paras 800–801.

[69] See FAC, judgment of 18 December 2018, case B-831/2011 *SIX DCC*, paras 578 and 625.

[70] Idem, paras 997 ff.

[71] Idem, paras 1132, 1144, 1146.

[72] Idem, para 1173.

[73] Idem, para 1192.

[74] Idem, para 1192.

access to SIX Group's DCC functionality.[75] In other words, the SIX DCC case is not just about interoperability information, but about access to a separate functionality or product of the dominant company.

- With 90% of the operating system market and by refusing to supply essential information to allow competing products in the server market to interface with its operating system, Microsoft was able to significantly restrict competition in the server market and, by denying access to 90% of customers using its own operating system, to significantly impede the development of such competing products and innovation. In the case of SIX DCC, there was no evidence of such negative effects, neither on competitors nor on the market for terminal payments or for the DCC function.
- In the Microsoft case, the EU Commission assumed that the interface code was protected by copyright and argued that Microsoft's rights would be better protected if the strict conditions for a compulsory licence were met. In the SIX DCC case, the COMCO and the FAC assume that the interface code is not protected by copyright, ignoring the fact that the provision of interoperability information under relaxed conditions is an order for access to the copyrighted SIX DCC function itself.
- The FAC held that interoperability refusals need not meet the indispensability requirement. The FAC adds that, in general, interface code is almost always essential anyway. In the Microsoft case, indispensability was a condition for interoperability information, but because interoperability was of significant competitive importance in that market, this condition was satisfied even if the lack of availability of interoperability information would lead to the elimination of competition only gradually and not immediately.
- In Microsoft, the elimination of competition was a clear requirement, but the court accepted that the EU Commission cannot wait until competitors have been eliminated from the market or until their elimination is sufficiently imminent, hence the reference to the *risk* of elimination of competition. In SIX DCC, the FAC dispensed with any requirement of elimination of competition and did not even require a significant reduction of competition for all or the majority of operators in the secondary market. An economic disadvantage for the complainant was sufficient.

The intervention of COMCO made interoperability information available to all operators in the market, even though the interface information or the DCC product of the dominant company was not indispensable to operate in the secondary terminal market and even though competition was not significantly reduced, as shown by the presence of other operators who did not use such interface information or the DCC product of the dominant company. The FAC ruling was limited to the obligation to provide interoperability information, paving the way for regulatory intervention in markets where interoperability would enhance competition. In this case, competition

[75] See for instance COMCO, decision of 29 November 2010 *SIX/Terminals mit Dynamic Currency Conversion (DCC)*, LPC 2011/1, p. 96ff, para 470.

law was used as a tool to regulate the market for card payments and payment terminals, and the conditions for access to interoperability information are set in such a way that the same intervention can be made in other markets that would function better if interoperability information were made available to all operators.

The second group of cases concerns access to media rights for national football and ice hockey competitions. The aim of the cases was to limit the competitive advantage derived from the use of an exclusive input by making such a resource available to all telecom operators in the IPTV market. Swisscom, the incumbent telecoms operator, was the first to show interest in the sports rights as it sought to expand its IPTV and fibre broadband businesses. Swisscom bought the sport media rights in open tenders from the Swiss national associations that organise national football and ice hockey competitions in Switzerland. The other IPTV operators either did not win the rights or did not bid for them. Some of the matches were given to the public broadcaster for free-to-air transmission and Swisscom acquired the exclusive rights for IPTV and other media rights for 5 years. After an initial period of exclusivity, Swisscom offered its sports channels to some telecom operators and broadcasters, but not to all. The cable operator, which lost the rights in an open tender, and other small broadcasters also complained to the COMCO.

The COMCO found that the exclusive sports rights for football and ice hockey competitions gave Swisscom a competitive advantage in the IPTV and fibre broadband markets and, conversely, hindered the development of its competitors UPC and Sunrise in the same markets. Both football and ice hockey media rights were considered indispensable to operate in the secondary IPTV market and Swisscom was ordered to license all its sports rights to national football and ice hockey competitions or its main sports channels to its competitors in the IPTV market. [76] Swisscom was ordered to pay a fine of CHF 71,818,517. The FAC confirmed the refusal to supply. [77]

A few years later, in an open tender, UPC acquired the hockey rights for the next 5 years. Swisscom in turn requested access to the hockey media rights, which UPC refused, in an attempt to gain market share in the IPTV market. In the meantime, Swisscom had acquired the exclusivity of the media rights for football and had licensed sports channels to the other telecom operators. COMCO again intervened and found that the hockey rights were indispensable to operate in the IPTV market and ordered UPC to grant a licence to Swisscom and other operators, [78] even though Swisscom continued to gain market share in the IPTV and broadband markets, while UPC had continued to lose market share in both IPTV and cable. The elimination of all competition was not a condition for granting a licence for sports media rights, but

[76] COMCO, decision of 9 May 2016, *Sport im Pay-TV*, LPC 2016/4, p. 920.

[77] FAC, judgment of 10 May 2022, B-4003/2016, *Sport im Pay-TV*.

[78] COMCO, decision of 7 September 2020, *Eishockey im Pay-TV*, LPC 2020/4b, p. 1858. An appeal against this decision is lodged with the FAC. Swisscom's request for interim measures was previously rejected by the COMCO. See LPC 2017/3, p. 410.

a restriction of competition was considered sufficient to find an abuse against UPC. UPC was ordered to pay a fine of CHF 29,995,979.

A couple of cases have been presented before the civil courts in relation to protected designation of origin (PDO). In *L'Etivaz*, the FSC [79] confirmed the abuse of a dominant position by a cooperative managing the protected designation of origin (PDO) of a cheese, L'Etivaz. The cooperative had refused access to its maturing cellar to a farmer based in the geographical area of the PDO and who wished to produce cheese under the L'Etivaz PDO.

Starting from a narrow definition of the market covering only the PDO cheese in question, the cooperative found itself in a dominant position on this market and on the operation of its cellar. The lower court and the FSC did not follow the opinion of the COMCO which had defined a wider market covering the maturing of all substitute hard cheeses (Sect. 1.6.4). While the parties and the lower civil court had discussed the objective and subjective qualities of a PDO cheese such as L'Etivaz to argue for or against substitutability between different kinds of cheese, the FSC did not discuss the substitutability at all and considered only the legal context of the PDO to define one market for one PDO. Given that, on the basis of the law on agriculture, [80] everyone in the geographical area of the PDO has the right to compete in the market by using an PDO if they believe they have an interest in it and if they comply with the PDO's specifications, the FSC deduces "[w]here a competitor claims to be unlawfully prevented from gaining access to a PDO, the determining market is necessarily restricted to that, real or supposed, of the PDO in question." As for the abuse, since the cooperative was the only one operating a cellar that complied with the PDO requirements, the refusal to grant access to the cellar prevented the applicant from marketing its cheese under the L'Etivaz PDO, which, in the absence of objective justification in the specific case, constitutes an unlawful abuse. The cooperative had invoked the limited capacity of its maturing cellar as an objective justification for its refusal, but the limited capacity was not confirmed as a matter of fact. The cooperative was ordered to accept the applicant as a member, [81] with the result that he was granted access to the cooperative's cellar to mature his cheeses and, finally, to the L'Etivaz PDO.

Another application concerning Gruyère PDO/AOC, one of Switzerland's most famous cheeses, was rejected by the FSC. [82] The claimant produced and sold cheese under the Gruyère PDO. An inspection by the certification body found that this producer had used milk from neighbouring areas, which were not part of the PDO area, to produce the cheese. The producer was prohibited from selling his cheese as Gruyère PDO. In the appeal proceedings against the prohibition of the use of the

---

[79] ATF 139 II 316 of 23 May 2013, 4A_449/2012, *L'Etivaz*.

[80] Federal act on agriculture; RS 910.1.

[81] The order to offer membership to the cooperative is the result of the procedural steps taken by the cooperative in response to the formal claims raised, and not necessarily a remedy based on competition law for the refusal to grant access to the maturing cellar.

[82] FSC, judgment of 5 October 2015, 2C_1004/2014, *Interprofession du Gruyère*.

Gruyère PDO, the producer tried to use the L'Etivaz judgment to argue that the prohibition of the use of milk from other areas constituted a refusal to deal and infringed the Cartel Act. The FSC held that the exclusion of the use of milk from geographical areas other than that of the PDO was a measure inherent in the PDO regulations and therefore excluded from the scope of the Cartel Act in accordance with Article 3(1) CartA (Sect. 1.3.3). A PDO had to define a territory and therefore the implementation of the provisions relating to the protected area of the PDO did not fall within the scope of the Cartel Act and therefore did not infringe it.

Once a refusal to deal is established, the dominant undertaking has an obligation to deal, which raises the question of the price to be charged by the dominant undertaking. The FSC has held that the price can be negotiated between the parties and that the fixing of a price is a matter of civil law. In any event, if a dominant company were to charge an unfair price under the duty to deal, a new procedure under Article 7(2)(c) CartA could be initiated before the COMCO. [83]

5.3.3.2 Discrimination

Article 7(2)(b) CartA considers as unlawful "any discrimination between trading partners in relation to prices or other conditions of trade". The object of discrimination is price or other terms and conditions of trade, and the term "other terms and conditions of trade" is to be understood broadly. Trading partners are companies that operate upstream or downstream of the market in which the company holds a dominant position. [84] The FSC defines discrimination as treating similar situations differently or treating different situations the same. A first level of justification for unequal treatment is therefore different situations or factors that could explain unequal conditions: the FSC explains that unequal treatment does not constitute discrimination or abuse if it can be justified by objective reasons, such as different transport or distribution costs. [85] Such conduct is an abuse if the discrimination of trading partners hinders competitors or disadvantages the customers within the meaning of Article 7 (1) CartA and there are no objective reasons to justify it.

In *Publigroupe*, [86] the first case to apply a fine to discrimination of business partners, the FSC stated that the company had abused its dominant position by refusing to commission certain professional intermediaries on the basis of unjustified criteria contained in the guidelines applied by the group. In particular, the FSC confirmed the discriminatory nature of the following terms used by the dominant company: obligation to act for several independent advertisers, obligation to carry

[83] FSC, judgment of 17 June 2003, 2A.520/2002, *EEF*, ATF/BGE 129 II 497, para 6.5.9.

[84] FSC, judgment of 29 June 2012, case 2C_484/2010, *Publigroupe*, ATF/BGE 139 I 72, para 10.2.2.

[85] Idem, para 10.2.3.

[86] Idem.

out this activity on a principal basis and for all advertising sections (universal intermediary), and obligation to generate a minimum annual turnover.

The case was the occasion for the FSC to provide important guidance on the concept of discrimination as an abuse.[87] Discrimination involves the regular application of unfavourable conditions to the trading partner, which distorts the competitive structure of the market at various levels. The abusive nature of discrimination results from either exploitation or exclusionary effects on competition, or both.

Discrimination is first and foremost an undue disadvantage for trading partners who, due to the dominant position of their trading partner, do not have adequate alternatives. This affects their competitive position in upstream or downstream markets. The main purpose of Article 7 (2) (b) of the Cartel Act is to protect competition in the market in which the traders are active. If an undertaking in a dominant position applies discriminatory conditions, this has the effect of favouring another group of trading partners in addition to disadvantaging one group of partners. If the dominant company offers favourable conditions to its customers, it makes it more difficult for its competitors to operate in the market and may even deliberately exclude them. Such behaviour excludes competition in the dominant undertaking's own market, i.e. the market level at which the dominant undertaking operates. The FSC therefore clarified that it is not necessary to prove that "second-level competition" or competition between trading partners is affected, but that distortion or discrimination at the primary level—in the market where the company is dominant—is also covered by the provision. Finally, the FSC confirmed that exclusionary conduct may also be directed against potential competitors.

Publigroupe was a case of discrimination of business partners having an effect only on the downstream market where business partners were active. In fact, Publigroupe refused to accept and remunerate professional intermediaries who worked with only one advertiser, did not cover all types of advertising or did not reach a certain turnover, and discriminated between them and professional intermediaries who covered all advertising media, had several advertisers as clients and reached a certain turnover. This policy discriminated between different groups of intermediaries by not allowing them to operate in the market under the same conditions as others. It also increased the barriers to entry for new professional intermediaries wishing to enter the market. Publigroupe was fined with an amount of CHF 2.5 million.

In a case concerning rebates granted form the Swiss Post to its clients,[88] the rebates covered around 70% of the volume of mail sent by the Swiss Post. The complainant offered addressed bulk mailings for catalogues and mailings, flyers as well as newspapers and magazines, and was competing with the Swiss Post in this sector. Its complaint focused on the cross-subsidization of the competitive service by

---

[87] FSC, judgment of 29 June 2012, 2C_484/2010, *Publigroupe*, ATF/BGE 139 I 72 para 10.2.2.

[88] COMCO, decision of 30 October 2017, *Geschäftskunden Preissysteme für adressierte Briefsendungen*.

the monopoly activities of Swiss Post, on which the monthly target volume discount system was based. The most negative impact on the complainant was the monthly additional rebate of between 0% and 3%, which was determined based on the forecasted turnover of the client. During investigations, the Swiss Post's rebate system was also considered to be non-transparent in that it was difficult for the Swiss Post's customers to calculate what part of the rebate they would lose if they switched part of their business to the complainant. In addition, around 20–30% of the discounts actually granted by Swiss Post to its customers could not be explained by the discount scheme communicated to its customers. The COMCO confirmed that the negative effects of the discrimination on competition in both the primary and secondary lines were covered by Article 7(2)(b) of the Cartel Act. The COMCO pointed to the large volume and number of customers who were subject to unclear and discriminatory rebates and the importance of the resulting marginal discounts for some of them to demonstrate the competitive disadvantages of trading partners. [89] The freedom to negotiate with its customers and to grant additional discounts not provided for in the general rebate scheme was not considered an objective justification to offset its negative effects on competition. Consequently, the whole of the rebate scheme was unlawful and not just the additional rebate which had a negative impact on the complainant. The rebate scheme was also considered abusive under Article 7(2)(c) CartA on limitation of production, supply or technical development.

In the case of vertically integrated companies, there were cases of discrimination and the negative effects were felt in the secondary market where the dominant company's subsidiaries operated, despite the fact that the dominant company applied the same rebate scheme to all its downstream customers. For example, Swisscom was found to have abused its dominant position on the market for wholesale broadband services by discriminating against ADSL service providers in favour of one of its subsidiaries. Swisscom had set up a linear rebate system based on turnover, but the last tranche de facto benefited only its subsidiary. Swisscom's subsidiary received a rebate of around 20%, while its competitors could only obtain a rebate of up to 7% under this scheme. [90]

In 2021, [91] COMCO dealt with preferential rebates of around 15% granted by an asphalt producer to its shareholders. Non-shareholders did not receive such discounts and therefore there was a discrimination against them. After defining the relevant market narrowly, as all asphalt mixes produced within a 32-minute drive of an asphalt mixing plant, the COMCO found that the company operating that plant was dominant. As regards the disadvantage to the partners and the restriction of competition in the market, the COMCO considered the fact that price is the most

[89] COMCO, decision of 30 October 2017, *Geschäftskunden Preissysteme für adressierte Briefsendungen*, paras 912 ff, 970 ff, 981 ff.

[90] COMCO, decision of 15 December 20023, LPC 2004/2, p. 407, *Swisscom ADSL*. The conclusion on discounts was confirmed by ACCI, LPC 2005/3, p. 505, but annulled on other points and referred to COMCO for a new decision. The investigation was closed following Swisscom's abandonment of the discount system, LPC 2007/3, p. 420.

[91] COMCO, decision of 6 December 2021, *Belagswerke Bern*.

important competitive parameter in the road construction market and that the cost of asphalt mix is a significant part of the cost. Therefore, discriminatory treatment regarding the price of asphalt mix was likely to distort competition in the road construction market, since a contractor paying significantly more for asphalt mix would be forced to charge higher prices or accept a lower margin than its competitors. Thus, non-shareholders were prevented from entering and competing in the road construction market by the higher price of asphalt mix compared to shareholders. [92]

5.3.3.3 Unfair Prices or Conditions of Trade

Article 7(2)(b) CartA considers as unlawful "any imposition of unfair prices or other unfair conditions of trade". The provision requires that prices or other trading conditions must be imposed by the dominant undertaking, that these prices or other trading conditions must be unfair and, finally, that such unfair prices or other trading conditions cannot be justified by legitimate business reasons. [93] Article 7(2)(c) CartA explicitly cover not only prices but also all other trading conditions. Prices can also refer to rebates, bonuses, discounts or other methods of calculating the price. Commercial terms are all other terms agreed between the dominant undertaking and its trading partner in the context of a transaction. Exclusive supply and exclusive dealing may also be considered as unfair terms.

A notable case was that of the mobile termination fees charged by Swisscom. [94] The COMCO found that Swisscom charged excessive, unfair termination fees pursuant to Article 7(2)(c) CartA to its business partners—the other two mobile network operators in Switzerland—and imposed a sanction of CHF 300 million on Swisscom. [95] The FAC and FSC disagreed and cancelled the fine. According to the FSC, the criterion of 'imposition' has a specific meaning and does not follow from the mere existence of a dominant position. [96] In order to understand the FSC's reasoning, it is necessary to place the Swisscom case in its context. The other two mobile network operators refused to refer the matter to the telecom regulator, although they were legally entitled to request that Swisscom's tariffs be regulated. Since the telecom regulator could not act on its own, the COMCO decided to take up the case and ordered Swisscom to reduce its termination charges. The FSC found that the other two operators had the choice of paying the termination fees or referring

[92] COMCO, decision of 6 December 2021, *Belagswerke Bern*, paras 670 ff.

[93] FAC, judgment of 16 February 2021, B-2798/2018, *Naxoo/Supermédia*, para 11.3.

[94] SFC, judgment of 11 April 2011, 2C_343/2010 and 2C_344/2010, *Swisscom/Mobile termination fees*, ATF/BGE 137 II 199.

[95] COMCO, decision of 5 February 2007, *Terminierung Mobilfunk*, LPC 2007/2, p. 241; FAC, judgment of 24 February 2010, B-2050/2007, LPC 2010/2, p. 242.

[96] SFC, judgment of 11 April 2011, 2C_343/2010 and 2C_344/2010, *Swisscom/Mobile termination fees*, ATF/BGE 137 II 199, para 4.3.4.

the matter to the telecom regulator, so that there was no 'imposition' by Swisscom.[97] In doing so, the FSC rejected the argument that the element of 'imposition' merely reflects a causal link between the dominant position and an unfair price level: the term 'imposition' is a distinct behavioural element of this abusive practice.[98] The FSC assumes that unfair terms may be voluntarily accepted by business partners, for example for economic reasons, and that these terms are not necessarily contrary to their economic interests. It clarifies that for the requirement of 'imposition' to be met, the trading partners must not be able to find alternative solutions or have any say in the economic pressure exerted by the dominant undertaking in the form of unfair trading conditions.[99]

The Swisscom mobile termination case cannot be generalised to apply the condition of 'imposition' narrowly in all circumstances. In subsequent cases, the FAC has held that the threshold for the application of the 'imposition' condition must not be too high; it is sufficient that the dominant undertaking exerts pressure, even implicit pressure, on the counterparty to accept its prices or conditions.[100] We will briefly discuss the reasoning of the FAC, since the FSC judgment in the same case[101] did not consider it necessary to examine this type of abuse.

Whether business partners are obliged to accept unfair commercial or contractual terms depends on the circumstances of the case. In the *Naxoo/Supermédia* case,[102] the FAC found that the operator of TV-cable network could impose its general terms and conditions on building owners because the latter had to offer the TV-cable connection with the rental contract. The general conditions required exclusivity in the sense that building owners could not offer or enable the transmission of other TV connections, including satellite TV signals, on their internal TV cable network. However, the owners were not obliged to accept any condition relating to the modernisation of the cable network of the buildings because such modernisation was not strictly necessary. Consequently, the condition of 'imposition' was fulfilled in relation to the general terms and conditions, but not in relation to the modernisation contract, which imposed a 5-year exclusivity period.[103]

In *Naxoo/Supermédia*, the FAC recognised the need to achieve economies of scale of the operator of the local TV-cable network.[104] However, the terms included the right of the operator to terminate the TV cable contract with the building owner if the latter used the indoor cable in the building to transmit other TV signals. This was

---

[97] SFC, judgment of 11 April 2011, 2C_343/2010 and 2C_344/2010, *Swisscom/Mobile termination fees*, ATF/BGE 137 II 199, para 5.5.

[98] Idem, paras 4.3.3 and 4.3.4.

[99] Idem, para 4.3.4.

[100] FAC, judgment of 16 February 2021, B-2798/2018, *Naxoo/Supermédia*, para 11.3.3.1.

[101] FSC, judgment of 9 May 2023, 2C_395/2021, *Naxoo*. The FSC considered Article 7(2)(e) CartA, see Sect. 5.3.3.5.

[102] Idem.

[103] Idem, para 11.3.3.6.

[104] Idem, paras 11.3.4.3 ff.

an obstacle for a technology box operator who wanted to use the same indoor cable to allow tenants to receive a broadcast satellite signal. However, the satellite TV channels were in competition with the local TV cable network.

The question of whether the terms are unfair requires a balancing of the interests of the dominant undertaking against the commercial freedom of the trading partners.[105] In this context, the FAC also applies the principle of proportionality. There must be a reasonable relationship between the interests of the dominant undertaking and the extent to which the terms infringe the commercial freedom of the trading partners. This is the case if the conditions applied by the dominant undertaking are primarily favourable to the dominant undertaking and particularly unfavourable to the trading partner, thereby severely restricting the latter's ability to compete. The assessment must also consider whether the conditions applied by the dominant undertaking to its trading partners create barriers to third parties, in particular to competitors of the dominant undertaking. The conditions are even more unfair if they significantly impede the ability of third parties to compete in the market. In this respect, the FAC points out that the dominant undertaking has a particular responsibility not to undermine the already weakened residual competition in the market by its behaviour.

The FAC also discussed the "as efficient competitor test" raised by the local TV cable network operator, recalling that the test is used in particular in cases of price abuses such as predation and margin squeeze. In the FAC's view, the structure of the market and the nature of the dominant undertaking's exclusivity abuse were such that the as efficient competitor test could not be applied:

> In any event, in a situation such as the present one, characterised by the fact that the appellant enjoys a very strong dominant position, as well as structural advantages, in particular the fact that it is the only undertaking to provide access to the TV-cable network in the city of Geneva and the fact that connection to the TV-cable network is indispensable for building owners, the application of the criterion of the equally efficient competitor would be irrelevant in so far as the structure of the market renders the emergence of such an effective competitor practically impossible.[106]

The FAC concluded that the balance between the interests of the appellant, the infringement of the freedom of property owners and the significant impairment of the ability of third parties to compete on the market for telecommunications services was no longer reasonable in this case. Consequently, the commercial conditions—according to which the appellant assumes exclusive use of the indoor cable installations or which imply that the appellant will not connect the building to the cable TV network if the indoor installation is not used exclusively for access to its

[105] Idem, para 11.3.4.1.

[106] Idem, para 11.3.4.5.

services—were considered unfair within the meaning of Article 7(2)(c) CartA. [107] A fine of CHF 3,571,936 was imposed on the local TV-cable network operator. [108]

In the Sport im Pay-TV case, the media rights licence agreements between the Swisscom subsidiary and the other telecom companies as licensees contained a prohibition to acquire and operate other similar sports media rights, which acted as a non-compete clause. This clause was used by the Swisscom subsidiary as leverage in negotiations and in the event that these telecom companies made a bid for the next season of the same football and ice hockey media rights. The FAC upheld the COMCO's classification of this clause as an unfair term under Article 7(2)(b) CartA and therefore unlawful. [109]

5.3.3.4 Under-Cutting of Prices or Other Conditions

Article 7(2)(d) CartA considers as unlawful "any under-cutting of prices or other conditions directed against a specific competitor". The scope of this provision is unclear, as no cases have been brought before the courts, and so far it has not been a favoured type of abuse by the COMCO. In this respect the case-law of the EU Commission and the EU courts is of importance, and the also the fact that the practice is listed in the EU Guidance on Article 102 TFUE. [110] According to recent FSC case law, [111] undercutting of prices or other conditions could be considered as 'risk-based conduct' and therefore lead to abuse without further assessment of adverse effects on the market or competitors.

The legislative intent presents the undercutting of prices as "a classic form of conduct consisting in excluding a competitor from the market by means unrelated to its performance. If a dominant undertaking systematically undercuts a weaker competitor without any prospect of a rapid improvement in its profitability, it can be presumed that the dominant undertaking is attempting to eliminate its competitor from the market. Once the competitor has given up, the dominant firm can raise its prices above the initial level to recoup its losses. This behaviour harms both the foreclosed competitor and consumers, who end up paying more for less choice." [112] It also explains that the price does not have to be below cost to be undercutting. Excessively high purchase prices are also a way to exclude a competitor from the market, for instance in the case of a shortage of raw materials, where the dominant

[107] Idem, para 11.3.4.6.

[108] FSC, judgment of 9 May 2023, 2C_395/2021, *Naxoo*. The FSC considered Article 7(2)(e) CartA sufficient to impose a fine, which was reduced to around CHF 5.1 million. See also Sect. 5.3.3.5.

[109] FAC, judgment of 10 May 2022, B-4003/2016, *Sport im Pay-TV*, para 9.4.7.

[110] Guidance on the Commission's enforcement priorities in applying Article 82 of the EC Treaty to abusive exclusionary conduct by dominant undertakings, OJ C 45, 24.2.2009, p. 7, in particular paras 63 ff on predation.

[111] FSC, judgment of 2 November 2022, 2C_596/2019, *SIX DCC*. See also Sect. 5.2.1.

[112] See Message on the Federal Act on Cartels and other restrictions of competition (Cartel Act, LCart) of 23 November 1994, FF 1995 p. 472ff, p. 568.

undertaking can use such a pricing policy to gain access to large quantities of a particular product and thus prevent competitors from acquiring this necessary input.

In one of the decisions of the COMCO, while abandoning the undercutting of prices, it stated the following:

> The Competition Commission and the Secretariat have already examined these practices. In particular, they have examined whether there is a systematic approach, who the strategy is directed against, whether there is a possibility of maximising profits in the short term and whether there is a possibility of raising prices again once competitors have been driven out of the market. In each of the cases, particular attention was paid to the pricing during the low-price strategy. In the previous cases, it was examined whether prices were below average variable costs. It was also examined whether a possible low-price strategy was common in the industry. [113]

Given the current state of enforcement of the provision, we will not discuss this practice further and recommend that practitioners refer to EU case law and the EU Guidance on Article 102 TFEU, taking into account the recent development and the fact that evidence of foreclosure or recovery may not be a meaningful requirement under Article 7(2)(e) CartA, either in law or in fact.

5.3.3.5 Limitation of Production, Supply or Technical Development

Article 7(2)(e) CartA considers as unlawful "any limitation of production, supply or technical development". The FSC first ruled on the provision in 2023. [114] Article 7 (2) (e) CartA covers in principle all forms of exclusionary and predatory conduct of a dominant undertaking towards its competitors and thus constitutes a catch-all offence in comparison with the other forms of conduct mentioned in Article 7 (2) CartA. [115] FSC confirmed that Article 7(2)(e) is broader than Article 7(2) (c) CartA. [116]

The FSC acknowledged that the provision incorporates Article 102 TFUE and should therefore be interpreted in the same way, [117] by using the following example to illustrate: [118]

> By way of example, based on European practice, Art. 7 al. 2 let. e CartA covers situations in which a dominant undertaking makes an expensive infrastructure available free of charge to its commercial partners, on condition that the latter use it exclusively to resell its products to consumers. This approach may encourage the resellers concerned to obtain supplies only from that undertaking for the type of products concerned, which makes it very difficult for

[113] COMCO, decision 19 December 2016, *Kommerzialisierung von elektronischen Medikamenteninformationen*, para 459.

[114] FSC, judgment of 9 May 2023, 2C_395/2021, *Naxoo*, para 10.3.3.

[115] FAC, judgment of 19 January 2022, B-2597/2017, *Kommerzialisierung von elektronischen Medikamenteninformationen*, para 12.2.1.

[116] FSC, judgment of 9 May 2023, 2C_395/2021, *Naxoo*, para 10.3.

[117] FSC, judgment of 9 May 2023, 2C_395/2021, *Naxoo*, para 10.3.3.

[118] Idem.

> potential competitors to enter the market or expand, even though there is demand for their products (see judgment of the Court of First Instance of the European Communities [now the Court of the European Union], Van den Bergh Foods Ltd v Commission of the European Communities of 23 October 2003, T-65/98, nos. 154 ff).

EU case law was used by the FSC to support a finding of abuse in the *Supérmedia (Naxoo)* case, [119] where the FAC had confirmed the finding of an abuse in the form of restriction of market opportunities and technological development of third parties under Article 7(2)(e) CartA. The local cable operator obliged building owners not to use the coaxial cable inside the building to transmit signals from other operators or TV channels received by satellite, and therefore required the installation of a second coaxial, indoor cable in the presence of a third-party system. In addition, it was difficult for building owners and third parties to easily obtain the technical specifications of the cable operator. Third parties and owners were thus caught in a contractual system set up and controlled solely by the cable operator. [120] Therefore, the local cable operator had hindered the ability of third parties active in the market for telecommunications services, in particular satellite television, to compete, and this was not the result of normal market conditions. The FSC upheld the FAC's decision, finding that: [121]

> From this point of view, it must be admitted that certain clauses contained in the modernisation and connection contracts restrict the markets and technological development of other undertakings within the meaning of Art. 7(2)(e) CartA. It has to be borne in mind that this provision is specifically intended to cover situations in which a dominant undertaking, such as the appellant, takes steps to ensure the exclusive use of a facility essential for access to a market, in this case coaxial IDIs, by exerting pressure on its commercial partners *[references omitted]*. Article 7(2)(e) CartA also typically covers cases where a dominant undertaking - such as the appellant - makes available to its partners, free of charge, an infrastructure or a service necessary for the distribution of its products - in this case the provision of an enhanced coaxial IDI - on condition that the said partners use it exclusively for that purpose, thereby inducing them to forgo commercial relations with other undertakings which may also need it *[references omitted]*.

In a 2022 ruling, the FAC defines the following cumulative conditions for Article 7 (2)(e) CartA: (1) a dominant undertaking, (2) conduct by that undertaking that restricts production, sales or technical development, (3) the conduct creates an artificial shortage, and (4) the restriction of production, sales or technical development resulting from the conduct is not justified by objective reasons. [122] One of the conditions of abuse is that the dominant undertaking's restriction of production, sales or technical development results in an artificial shortage in the market, which the FSC endorses. [123] This condition appears to replace the requirement that the

[119] FSC, judgment of 9 May 2023, 2C_395/2021, *Naxoo*, para 10.3.7.

[120] FAC, judgment of 16 February 2021, B-2798/2018, *Naxoo/Supermédia*, paras 11.4ff.

[121] FSC, judgment of 9 May 2023, 2C_395/2021, *Naxoo*, para 10.3.7.

[122] FAC, judgment of 19 January 2022, B-2597/2017, *Kommerzialisierung von elektronischen Medikamenteninformationen*, para 12.2.3.

[123] FSC, judgment of 9 May 2023, 2C_395/2021, *Naxoo*, para 10.3.1.

conduct of dominant undertakings must restrict competition within the meaning of Article 7(1) CarA (hindering competitors or disadvantaging trading partners).

A dominant undertaking restricts production, supply and technical development when its conduct makes the products or services of its competitors less attractive or less marketable. On the other hand, conduct by a dominant undertaking which improves the availability or quality of its products or services does not fall within the scope of the provision. [124]

In this case, the FAC [125] confirmed the decision of the COMCO, [126] which in 2016 had found that a health care provider had abused its dominant position by using exclusivity clauses and tying practices. The initial fine of CHF 4,546,123 was reduced to CHF 3,778,794. HCI Solutions Ltd, a subsidiary of Galenica, a fully integrated healthcare provider, held a dominant position on the market for processed, machine-readable data relating to medicinal product information and on the market for access to electronic data sets relating to medicinal product information in Switzerland. The drug information was used by software vendors who provided drug information and other services to pharmacies, doctors, hospitals and other healthcare providers in their software databases. It had tied software houses to an exclusive purchase obligation and prohibited them from using data from other sources or their won data in their software. Exclusive purchasing obligations were present in 47% of contracts concluded by the dominant undertaking, [127] and claimed that competitors were free to deal with the majority of software companies in the market. According to FAC, if a potential competitor has to incur high fixed costs to enter a new market, a company already active in the market can prevent its entry without having concluded exclusive contracts with all buyers. In the present case, this was the case in the relevant markets for data, data indexing and software. Exclusive contracts with only a few customers can prevent a competitor from reaching the minimum efficient scale necessary to survive. [128] This view is based on what the FAC calls the post-Chicago economic literature, [129] which the COMCO had not used.

The FAC goes on to discuss the requirement of the artificial shortage, which is the expression of the distortion of competition or of the exclusionary effect. In this regard, it adopts the theory of the *Gefährdungstatbestand* or of the 'risk-based conduct' by stating that this approach is compatible with the EU case law:

---

[124] FAC, judgment of 19 January 2022, B-2597/2017, *Kommerzialisierung von elektronischen Medikamenteninformationen*, para 12.4.2.

[125] FAC, judgment of 19 January 2022, B-2597/2017, *Kommerzialisierung von elektronischen Medikamenteninformationen*.

[126] COMCO, decision 19 December 2016, *Kommerzialisierung von elektronischen Medikamenteninformationen.*

[127] FAC, judgment of 19 January 2022, B-2597/2017, *Kommerzialisierung von elektronischen Medikamenteninformationen*, para 12.4.24.

[128] Idem, para 12.4.25.

[129] Idem, para 12.4.5.

> The Federal Administrative Court concluded that the classification of Article 7 of the Cartel Act in terms of risk-based conduct is appropriate and in line with EU competition practice. This is because the competition authority must be able to intervene to protect competition as soon as it becomes aware that an economic behaviour has a negative effect on the market. Otherwise, the negative effects on competition would be prolonged and both the restriction on other competitors and the position of the dominant undertaking would be strengthened. Moreover, an adverse effect on competition does not necessarily translate into a clearly quantifiable harm to other competitors that can be verified by the competition authorities. This is because other competitors do not usually react to unreasonable conduct by the dominant undertaking by withdrawing from the market immediately but try to circumvent or at least mitigate the restrictions resulting from the unreasonable conduct and the resulting business pressure by other economic measures (decision B-831/2011, SIX, paragraphs 1209 ff). [...] These general principles also apply in the present case. The conduct in question must therefore be capable of affecting competition. [130]

The FAC presented the facts found by the COMCO, such as the fact that the exclusivity clauses raised barriers to entry for others and that two companies were prevented from entering and developing their activities in the market but held that it was not necessary to prove that competition was ultimately actually affected. The mere possibility of an adverse effect on competitors is sufficient to establish that the conduct in question poses a risk to competition. It is not necessary to show that there is an actual adverse effect on competition. [131] In other words, the factual assessment of the adverse effects on the market carried out by COMCO is replaced by the FAC's own formal assessment.

Rebates are another area where Article 7(2) (e) CartA can be applied, in particular those rebate schemes that have loyalty or exclusivity effects. A rebate scheme of the Swiss Post to its clients was considered to limit supply in the market in addition to discrimination of trading partners. [132] In its assessment of the restrictive effect on competitors, the COMCO pointed out that Swiss Post has a monopoly for addressed letters weighing up to 50 g. Separate relevant markets were defined for mailings below and above 50 g, but the monopoly for mailings below 50 g prevented competitors from meeting the demand for bulk mailings in other markets. The complainant for instance specialized in bulk mailings over 50 g with long delivery times, targeting mainly customers who wanted significantly lower prices. In markets with strong economies of scale and scope, such as the addressed letter market, it was difficult to challenge the position of the Swiss Post as a former monopolist with a partial monopoly addressed letters weighing up to 50 g and strong logistics which competitors could not match, as demonstrated by the complainant's difficulty in establishing a nationwide service. In terms of volume and market coverage, bulk mail accounted for 60–70% of the total volume and 50–60% of the turnover of the

[130] FAC, judgment of 19 January 2022, B-2597/2017, *Kommerzialisierung von elektronischen Medikamenteninformationen*, paras 12.5.7 and 12.5.9.

[131] Idem, paras 12.5.1ff, 12.5.16.

[132] COMCO, decision of 30 October 2017, *Geschäftskunden Preissysteme für adressierte Briefsendungen.* On the application of Article 7(2)(b) on discrimination of trading partners, see Sect. 5.3.3.2 above.

contract customers of the Swiss Post, while contract customers accounted for 80–100% of the volume and turnover of the complainant (which was also Swiss Post competitor). A large proportion of the complainant's customers were therefore affected by the Swiss Post rebate system. Consequently, the rebate scheme had the effect of restricting access to the market segment of bulk mail and therefore had a strong hindering effect on the complainant and on competition in the market. [133] It was also relevant that the discount system had been introduced by Swiss Post with a view to the full opening up of the market and the entry of new competitors. The segmentation of customers in the rebate scheme made it possible for the Swiss Post to adjust prices more quickly and in a more targeted manner and thus to adapt to future competition. Swiss Post was fined with CHF 22,622,641.

In another recent case, [134] one dominant firm introduced a loyalty rebate by removing all or part of the customer's loyalty bonus for past purchases if the customer's annual purchase fell by more than 2/3 of the average purchase over the previous 10 years. The COMCO considered that it was not obliged to demonstrate that competition was actually restricted, but only that the rebate scheme is capable of hindering competition, in other words that it has potential effects. [135] The COMCO highlighted the loyalty effects of the scheme, based on the fact that the discount also affected future purchases, and that purchases in subsequent years in turn trigger a loyalty bonus for the next 10 years. Such a bonus system thus creates an incentive for its customers to continue purchasing the product from the dominant undertaking. [136] By tying customers to itself through the specific design of its rebate system, the dominant undertaking reduced the sales of its competitors. Such rebate systems therefore constituted a restriction of production, markets or technical development within the meaning of Art. 7 (1) CartA in conjunction with Art. 7 (2) (e) CarA. [137]

5.3.3.6 Tying and Bundling

Article 7(2)(f) CartA considers as unlawful "any conclusion of contracts on the condition that the other contracting party agrees to accept or deliver additional goods or services". There have been few cases of tying and bundling in the practice of the COMCO, and the most prominent cases have been found in recent years. Tying and bundling practices have become the focus of the debate as to whether a finding of abuse requires that the conduct has an anti-competitive effect on the market and, if so, to what extent such an effect needs to be demonstrated. We will discuss two cases, *Hallenstadion* and *SIX/DCC*, the later marking a shift in the case law on abuse

[133] COMCO, decision of 30 October 2017, *Geschäftskunden Preissysteme für adressierte Briefsendungen*, para 137 ff.

[134] COMCO, decision of 6 December 2021, *Belagswerke Bern*, paras 411 ff.

[135] Idem, para 698.

[136] Idem, para 700.

[137] Idem, para 713.

of a dominant position with consequences for the application of all cases of abuse of a dominant position. Both cases have been debated at various levels of the judiciary for over a decade and have kept practitioners in suspense as to the outcome. However, the final outcome is far from clear and leaves many questions unanswered.

The investigation into the practices of the Hallenstadion, one of the largest concert halls in Zurich, began in 2010 after a ticketing company complained to the COMCO about an agreement between the Hallenstadion and Ticketcorner, a ticketing provider and competitor of the complainant. Hallenstadion required its customers, event organisers, to sell at least 50% of their tickets via Ticketcorner. COMCO considered that this clause resulted in de facto 100% exclusivity, but that Hallenstadion did not hold a dominant position and could therefore not be accused of abusing it. The FAC annulled the decision and referred the case back to the COMCO. It found that the exclusivity clause concluded between Hallenstadion and Ticketcorner constituted an unlawful agreement within the meaning of Article 5 (1) CartA (Sect. 2.3.2.1). Ticketcorner also abused its dominant position by imposing an exclusivity obligation on event organisers, which constituted an abuse of a dominant position by Hallenstadion. It is this FAC judgment that is the subject of the appeal by Hallenstadion and Ticketcorner to the Federal Supreme Court, which discussed among other the tying practices. [138]

The FSC confirms the FAC's definition of the relevant market, which was much narrower definition than that adopted by COMCO. The relevant market is limited to the rental of halls for large one-off events [139] with an audience of between 6500 and 17,000 in German-speaking Switzerland. [140] On the basis of such a narrow definition of the relevant market, Hallenstadion had a market share of around 75% and was therefore in a dominant position. Ticketing was a separate market and Ticketcorner's market share was estimated at around 60%.

The FSC held that Hallenstadion had committed an abuse of a dominant position in the form of tying within the meaning of Article 7 (2) (f) CartA. This abuse consists of four conditions: [141] (1) the existence of two separate products, (2) a 'coupling' of the two products, (3) a restriction of competition, and (4) the absence of objective justification. Concert hall rental is a separate service from ticket sales, so the second condition is met, which was obvious in this case given that the services were provided by two different companies. The particularity of the case is that the two tied services—hall rental and ticketing—are offered by two different undertakings, which are independent from a competition law point of view, and not by a single dominant undertaking which is supposed to combine the two services to its advantage. The abuse approach of transferring power from the dominant market to another

[138] FSC, judgment of 12 February 2020, 2C_113/2017 *Hallenstadion*.

[139] *Mega-Einzel-Bühnenshows*, the relevant product market.

[140] Geographical market, which includes in the market the large concert halls in Berne and Basel in addition to the one in Zurich, Arena PostFinanz in Berne, Hallenstadion in Zurich and St. Jakobshalle in Basel.

[141] FSC, judgment of 12 February 2020, 2C_113/2017, *Hallenstadion, para* 6.2.1.

market through tying is therefore not common, as the dominant undertaking is not present in the tied market. [142] With regard to the restriction of competition, the FSC requires a demonstration of such an effect, contrary to the FAC, which assumed that such an effect is presumed when two separate products are tied together. The FSC then moved on to an abstract argumentation of the effects of the practice: firstly, the coupling of the services of two independent companies constitutes an exploitative practice in that it restricts the autonomy of the organisers; secondly, the coupling restricts competition on the market for the tied product (tickets) and strengthens Hallenstadion's dominant position on its market for the rental of concert halls by raising barriers to entry on this market.

The FSC judgment in Hallenstadion was consistent with the FSC's previous case law since Publigroupe, according to which a practice constitutes an abuse if it objectively leads to anti-competitive effects, such as the hindering, exploitation or suppression of competition within the meaning of Article 7(1) CartA. Only 2 years later, in the SIX DCC case which will be discussed below, the FSC further diluted the meaning and the criteria of hindering, exploiting or suppressing competition within the meaning of Article 7(1) Cartel Act.

The SIX DCC case [143] began in 2006 when a payment terminal manufacturer filed a complaint against the SIX Group, which held a dominant position with more than 70% of the market for acquiring Visa and Mastercard credit cards and the market for acquiring the Maestro debit card. The SIX Group also offered payment terminal services and one of its subsidiaries offered a currency conversion function called DCC, which allowed customers to pay in CHF or in foreign currency at the merchant's terminal (Sect. 5.3.3.1). In 2010, COMCO found that SIX tied the acquiring services for credit and debit cards, the purchase of services with the DCC function and of terminal equipment with the DCC function, and that this constituted an unlawful tying within the meaning of Article 7(2)(f) CartA. [144] The COMCO's decision on tying was confirmed by the FAC in 2018 [145] and by the SFC in 2022. [146]

The FSC confirmed that an illegal tying can take place in several steps: a twofold tying, as in this case, was therefore possible. Otherwise, a dominant undertaking could circumvent the prohibition of tying by structuring the link between the main product and the tied product not directly but indirectly through the inclusion of

[142] It should be noted that Ticketcorner Holding holds a 5% stake in Hallenstadion and that the other shareholder of Ticketcorner Holding's parent company (Ringier) holds 48% of Good News, a shareholder of Hallenstadion. These shareholdings do not, however, confer control over Hallenstadion, but may justify an alignment of commercial and financial interests between the two companies.

[143] For the facts of the case, see also Sect. 5.3.3.1 on refusal to deal.

[144] COMCO, decision of 29 November 2010, *SIX/Terminals mit Dynamic Currency Conversion (DCC)*, LPC 2011/1 p. 96.

[145] FAC, judgment of 18 December 2018, B-831/2011, *SIX DCC*.

[146] FSC, judgment of 2 November 2022, 2C_596/2019, *SIX DCC*.

another tied product.[147] However, the most important development of the case was in the area of restrictions of competition. The FSC judgment significantly watered down the requirements for finding a restriction of competition and unlawful tying. FSC's reasoning starts with the four conditions for finding a tying by changing the third condition: the 'restriction of competition' criterion becomes 'potentially adverse competitive effects'.[148] The FSC states:

> In the context of Article 7 (2) (f) of the Cartel Act, it is not necessary to prove that competition has been harmed or distorted in a specific way. Rather, it is the inevitable consequence of a combination of separate products without any justification. Accordingly, the prohibition of tying is fulfilled if the unlawful tying, which is not justified by commercial practice, objective connection or other objective reasons, is as such incompatible with Article 7 (2) (f) Cartel Act; an analysis of the effects is not required. In the [*Hallenstadion*] decision, the Federal Supreme Court also assumed that an impact-related analysis was not necessary because the tying at issue led to detrimental effects on competition (exploitation of the other side of the market by restricting freedom of choice; crowding-out effect on the market for the tied product). The situation is no different here; the risk of the unwanted effect occurring is sufficient, as the lower court [FAC] rightly pointed out. On the one hand, the dealers' freedom of choice is restricted by the double tying and, on the other hand, the tying strengthens the position of J._'s[149] sister company in the market for terminals and, at the same time, eliminates competition there, as the Federal Administrative Court rightly found. In their appeal, the appellants focus on the proof of an impact-related analysis, which, as explained above, is not necessary.[150]

It is not clear what the FSC meant in this paragraph, namely whether there is no need to prove any restriction of competition, or whether there is no need to prove actual exclusionary effects, as opposed to potential exclusionary effects as announced in the four conditions of abusive tying. The judgment is even more ambiguous when the degree of restriction of competition is used as a criterion to determine the gravity of the abuse in order to determine the basic amount of the fine (Sect. 7.2.3.1). In this context, gravity means the objective seriousness of the infringement, irrespective of fault. The decisive factor is the abstract potential danger; other factors to be considered include the degree of harm to competition, the effectiveness of the infringement and the number of persons involved.[151] The FSC explains:

> In that regard, the subjective elements put forward by the appellants are irrelevant. The starting point for the calculation of the basic amount is the infringement, i.e. in this case the tying of two products which are not objectively related. As mentioned above, this has two adverse effects on competition: First, merchants in the dominant company's market are restricted in their freedom of choice; if they conclude an acquiring agreement without the DCC function, they can expect less favourable conditions. On the other hand, tying

[147] Idem, para 8.5.3.

[148] Idem, para 8.3: "Damit der Tatbestand des Art. 7 Abs. 2 lit. f KG erfüllt ist, müssen neben der marktbeherrschenden Stellung die folgenden vier Tatbestandsmerkmale erfüllt sein: Getrennte Güter, Koppelung, *potentiell nachteilige Wettbewerbseffekte*, fehlende sachliche Rechtfertigung." (*references omitted, we emphasise*)

[149] J. was a SIX subsidiary active in the credit and debit card acquiring market.

[150] FSC, judgment of 2 November 2022, 2C_596/2019, *SIX DCC*, para 8.6.

[151] FSC, judgment of 2 November 2022, 2C_596/2019, *SIX DCC*, para 10.2.3.

> strengthens the position of its sister company in the market for terminals, at the same time eliminating competition there and forcing its potential competitors out of the market. This already shows that tying is particularly problematic. Moreover, as already explained, Article 7(2)(f) of the Cartel Act is a risk-based conduct, which is why the appellants' objections that the adverse effects on the relevant market would be minor are unfounded, as the Federal Administrative Court also correctly found. The considerable risk potential of tying is also indicated by the fact that the European Commission included tying as one of its enforcement priorities in applying Article 82 of the EC Treaty to abusive exclusionary conduct by dominant undertakings (hereinafter 'Communication on Enforcement Priorities; OJ C 45 of 24 February 2009, p. 7 ff) and dealt with it in detail (para. 2 in conjunction with para. 47 ff). In the Communication on Enforcement Priorities, the Commission announced its priorities with regard to what constitutes harm to competition. [152]

The criteria applied by the FSC are not related to the market position or market shares of SIX in the tying or tied market but consider the potential of the tying to raise barriers to entry and foreclose competitors. As a result, the mere tying of two or more separate products became unlawful without an assessment of the potential of the tying to restrict competition in the light of the market circumstances of the case. This reasoning can be applied to all abusive practices under Article 7(1) CartA.

5.3.3.7 Refusal to Supply on Foreign Terms

Article 7(2)(g) CartA considers as unlawful "the restriction of the opportunity for buyers to purchase goods or services offered both in Switzerland and abroad at the market prices and conditions customary in the industry in the foreign country concerned".

The provision applies to undertakings with a dominant position or with relative market power vis-à-vis a company established in Switzerland which claims to be dependent on it. What is considered to be relative market power has been explained in Sect. 5.2.3 above.

The other criterion concerns the products concerned. The provision only applies to "goods or services offered both in Switzerland and abroad". [153] This raises the question of what it means to "offer" and who is supposed to offer the products in Switzerland or abroad. In practice, the two most relevant situations are direct distribution (by one of the group companies) and distribution by independent distributors.

A group of companies selling directly or through subsidiaries in Switzerland and abroad fulfils this condition. It does not matter whether the head of such a group is based in Switzerland or elsewhere. The provision therefore covers intra-group arrangements aimed at redirecting Swiss customer enquiries to the Swiss subsidiary

---

[152] Idem, para 10.2.3. Free translation, we have translated '*Gefährdungstatbestand*' as 'risk-based conduct'.

[153] In French: "des biens ou des services proposés en Suisse et à l'étranger"; in German: "Waren oder Leistungen, die in der Schweiz und im Ausland angeboten werden"; in Italian: "di beni e servizi offerti in Svizzera e all'estero".

of the group—in order to generally buy at a higher price in Switzerland—arrangements which fall outside the scope of the agreements under Articles 4 and 5 of the Cartel Act (Sects. 2.2.1.1 and 4.1.2). As a consequence, intra-group agreements of non-dominant companies which allocate and redirect Swiss customers to the Swiss subsidiary must be assessed under the new provisions on the abuse of relative market power. In a ruling confirming the existence of a group privilege for distribution agreements, the SFC referred for the first time to the new provisions on relative market power.:

> This does not mean, however, that the law does not prohibit such an approach. [...] the legislator revised the Cartel Act with the intention of offering better protection to Swiss companies wishing to acquire goods and services abroad. From 1 January 2022, Article 7 of the Cartel Act will be extended to provide that companies with a dominant position or relative market power in Switzerland are prohibited from preventing Swiss buyers from purchasing goods or services abroad at market prices and under conditions customary in the industry (*references omitted*). The new provision [...] is intended to facilitate the fight against price discrimination by making it easier for the competition authorities, as well as purchasing companies, to initiate proceedings against certain large commercial groups, which can partition the Swiss market by evading the rules of Article 5 Cartel Act due to group privilege (*references omitted*). Before this revision, it was already accepted that a foreign company's refusal to supply a Swiss customer at the prices and conditions prevailing abroad could constitute abusive commercial behaviour and therefore inadmissible within the meaning of Article 7 (1) and (2) of the Cartel Act: it had to be shown, however, that the undertaking had a dominant position on the relevant market, which was not easy. [154]

The COMCO Secretariat has already received a first set of complaints. One of them concerned the foreign subsidiaries of a German manufacturer that refused to sell directly to a Swiss wholesaler and transferred the wholesaler's demands to its Swiss subsidiary. [155] It concerns food supplements and a decision would have to define the conditions under which a manufacturer would be considered to have relative market power and could be forced to sell to a Swiss wholesaler. Another one is the complaint lodged by Payot, a Swiss bookshop chain. Payot wants to be supplied with books directly by a French publisher on French market terms, rather than by the independent distributor based in Switzerland. [156] The COMCO Secretariat has intended that the decisions in these two cases will clarify the scope of the provision and serve as guidance for COMCO practice in this area. Both cases are therefore to be followed.

A company based abroad that sells in Switzerland through independent distributors is also covered. The independent distributor may be based in Switzerland or abroad, e.g. an Austrian distributor to whom the supplier has allocated (part of) the

---

[154] FSC, judgment of 21 December 2021, 2C_43/2020, *Dargaud*, ATF/BGE 148 II *25* para 7.4. Free translation from French, references omitted.

[155] See "L'allemand Fresenius visé par une plainte de la Comco" of 2 September 2022, available at https://www.zonebourse.com/cours/action/GALENICA-AG-34532681/actualite/L-allemand-Fresenius-vise-par-une-plainte-de-la-Comco-41682990/.

[156] See Le Temps of 21 September 2022, "Payot attaque Gallimard auprès de la Commission de la concurrence".

Swiss territory. Conversely, a Swiss company that also sells abroad through independent distributors or directly through subsidiaries is also covered by the provision. Only domestic sales are excluded, e.g. for example a Swiss company that sells only in Switzerland, and does not sell the products on foreign markets.

It is not clear whether Article 7(2)(g) CartA applies where the products are available in Switzerland or abroad as a result of parallel imports or sales by the supplier's customers. This would be the case, for example, where a foreign supplier does not sell directly to Swiss customers and has not assigned Switzerland to a distributor or, conversely, where a Swiss company does not market its products abroad but its Swiss customers sell them in other markets. In our view, "offer" implies that the company is targeting Switzerland by selling directly, allocating the territory or knowingly serving the Swiss market indirectly. If the situation is not covered by Art. 7(2)(g) Cartel Act, refusals to deal and discriminatory conditions by companies with relative market power could be covered by Art. 7(2)(a), (b) or (e) Cartel Act. Therefore, not selling or even prohibiting resale in Switzerland would not shield foreign companies from the relative market power regime.

The provision applies when the foreign undertaking in a dominant position or with relative market power restricts the opportunity for buyers to purchase such products, either by refusing to sell or provide services at the foreign market price or by referring the Swiss buyer to another distributor or subsidiary in Switzerland or abroad which applies a different (higher) price or different conditions. This implies that the undertaking in a dominant position or enjoying relative market power applies prices that are higher than the market prices prevailing in the foreign country or wishes to apply conditions that are not customary in the industry in the foreign country.

5.4 Justification on Objective Grounds

Article 7 of CartA does not explicitly mention justifications, the practice of the authorities and the courts has confirmed them at a very early stage, following also the legislative intent. [157] A conduct will only be abusive if the undertaking does not have any objective reasons or, in other words, any 'legitimate business reasons' for the conduct in question. The absence of legitimate business reasons is thus a constitutive element of abuse (Sect. 5.3.1). [158]

Unlawful conduct occurs when there is no objective justification for conduct that hinders competitors or disadvantages business partners. An example of such reasons

[157] Legitimate business reasons have been mentioned in the explanatory memorandum that accompanies the draft law submitted to the Parliament. See Message on the Federal Act on Cartels and other restrictions of competition (Cartel Act, LCart) of 23 November 1994, FF 1995 p. 472ff, p. 564.

[158] See Sect. 5.2.1. FSC, judgment of 29 June 2012, 2C_484/2010, ATF/BGE 139 I 72, *Publigroupe*, para 10.1.2.

is when the conduct is justified by the other party's bad debt credit. Creditworthiness is one of the so-called business reasons or 'commercial principles' that can be used to justify a certain type of conduct. Dominant undertakings or those with related market power can therefore pursue their business objectives. Other objective reasons include changes in demand, cost savings, administrative simplification, transport and distribution costs or technical reasons. [159] This means that efficiency matters and can be invoked by dominant companies to defend their conduct. Also, the dominant undertaking will have no obligation to provide services if it will no longer be able to fully meet the needs of its own customers, or to provide access to its facilities if their capacity is insufficient. [160] In other words, companies are free to put forward all kinds of economic arguments to justify their conduct.

Only behaviour that can be considered as competition on the merit is taken into account. [161] Competition by means that do not reflect competition on the merits cannot be invoked as objective reasons, otherwise the efforts of the Cartel Act to protect competitive behaviour would be undermined. Arguments relating to the business model of the undertakings in a dominant position or to freedom of contract have not proved to be very successful. In the EEF case for instance, the electricity transmission network company, invoked its public service mission by claiming that the electricity it sold to the customer who wanted to buy electricity from EEF's competitor accounted for about 4% of the total energy it supplied, a significant proportion, and that the loss of this business would have jeopardised its public service mission. FSC rejected this argument, arguing that the mere fact that a dominant company loses market share because of the arrival of new competitors cannot justify the exclusion of competition. On the contrary, it was precisely the purpose of the Cartel Act to challenge the market shares of different suppliers through competition. [162] In the case concerning discriminatory rebates granted by the Swiss Post, the freedom to negotiate with its customers and to grant additional discounts not provided for in the general rebate scheme was not considered sufficient as an objective justification, reminding also the special responsibility of undertakings in a dominant position. [163] In another case concerning rebates, [164] the fact that the companies receiving preferential and lower rebates were shareholders and therefore took a risk in operating the plant was not considered an objective reason to justify rebates of around 15% of the price of the product supplied by the plant compared to non-shareholders.

---

[159] FSC, judgment of 29 June 2012, case 2C_484/2010, *Publigroupe*, ATF/BGE 139 I 72, para 10.1.2.

[160] FSC, judgment of 23 May 2013, case 4A_449/2012, *L'Etivaz*, ATF/BGE 139 II 316, para 8; FSC, judgment of 17 June 2003, 2A.520/2002, *EEF*, ATF/BGE 129 II 497, para 6.5.4.

[161] FSC, judgment of 9 December 2019, case 2C_985/2015, *Preispolitik Swisscom ADSL*, ATF/BGE 146 II 217, para 5.9.

[162] FSC, judgment of 17 June 2003, 2A.520/2002, *EEF*, ATF/BGE 129 II 497, para 6.5.5.

[163] COMCO, decision of 30 October 2017, *Geschäftskunden Preissysteme für adressierte Briefsendungen*, para 933.

[164] COMCO, decision of 6 December 2021, *Belagswerke Bern.*

The requirements for companies with a dominant position or relative market power are substantial. The burden of proof that such reasons exist and are relevant to the conduct in question is on those undertakings. Objective reasons justifying exclusionary or exploitative abuses must be set out in sufficient detail by the dominant undertaking. It is not enough to make a general claim. [165] The COMCO is obliged to examine only those reasons which are manifestly obvious in the case in question; other reasons must be invoked and substantiated by the dominant undertaking. [166] This means that it is up to the dominant undertakings to explicitly invoke business reasons at an early stage of the investigation, and not to COMCO or the court. If companies do not invoke business reasons to defend their conduct, the second step of the abuse test would be fulfilled, and the conduct would be declared unlawful.

Requiring reasons to be objective is another way of checking the business reasons that companies use to justify their behaviour. The first meaning follows from the need for the company's reasoning to be detailed and based on real facts. The second meaning adds an external perspective to the assessment of the legitimacy of business reasons: it is not only the company's view that matters, but also whether, having regard to its own objectives, COMCO considers that the reasons given are objectively justified. As regards efficiency grounds, the requirement of objectivity means that efficiency would be related to the economy as a whole and not only to the economic efficiency of the dominant undertaking. For example, to the argument that refusal to grant access to a product (software) and interoperability or interface information would reduce the dominant undertaking's incentive to innovate, COMCO responds as follows:

> In conclusion, in the present case it is not evident why the incentives to invest and innovate in multipay/card solutions would be lost by the disclosure of the interface information. On the contrary, it can be assumed that the positive effects of the disclosure of the interface information on competition in terms of innovation outweigh the disadvantages. Multipay's refusal cannot therefore be justified on objective grounds. [167]

The FSC mentions necessity as a criterion, stating that the conduct is only necessary if the object of the conduct cannot be achieved by other, less anti-competitive means. [168] This is in line with COMCO's additional criterion of proportionality of the conduct to the business objective in question:

[165] FSC, judgment of 9 December 2019, 2C_985/2015, *Preispolitik Swisscom ADSL,* ATF/BGE 146 II 217, para 4.2.

[166] FAC, judgment of 16 February 2021, B-2798/2018, *Naxoo/Supermédia,* para 11.3.5.2.

[167] COMCO, decision of 29 November 2010 *SIX/Terminals mit Dynamic Currency Conversion (DCC)*, LPC 2011/1, p. 96ff, para 469.

[168] FSC, judgment of 9 December 2019, 2C_985/2015, *Preispolitik Swisscom ADSL*, ATF/BGE 146 II 217 para 5.9.

> An objective justification can only be considered if the principle of proportionality is respected. This means, in particular, that no alternative behaviour was available which would have had a less distortive effect on competition (indispensability requirement). [169]

The requirement that there is no other less anti-competitive way of behaving also makes it difficult for the dominant undertaking to behave like other undertakings in the market. While the FAC accepts that, in general, a dominant undertaking that behaves in the same way as other undertakings without influence on the market is behaving in a way that is objectively necessary, it also states that this is not always the case and that, even if the conduct is customary in the market, dominant undertakings must choose other means to achieve the same objective that do not restrict competition in the market. [170]

Proportionality means that any business conduct must not go beyond what is necessary to achieve the business reason behind it. Examining whether other alternatives would allow the same objective sought by the dominant company to be achieved paves the way for the COMCO and the courts to take control of the business conduct available to companies.

The objectivity and proportionality tests make it difficult for companies to use arguments such as product safety or technical considerations. In relation to product safety, for example, the FAC maintains the classic, restrictive view that:

> It is, however, for the public authorities to define the health and safety standards of a product or service in specific laws or by reference to customs or professional standards. It is not for the dominant undertaking to take initiatives to eliminate a product or service which it considers, rightly or wrongly, to be dangerous or inferior in quality or safety to its own product or service. [171]

The objective justification mechanism under Article 7 CartA is similar to the objective justifications used by EU courts to justify abusive behaviour under Article 102 TFEU. [172] The same type of business or efficiency reasons can be invoked under Article 7 CartA, with the exception of public interest reasons, which can only be invoked before the Federal Council on the basis of Article 8 CartA (Sect. 1.7). Article 7 CartA's objective justification mechanism is also inspired by Article 5 (2) CartA's criteria. [173] This is similar to the parallelism with Article 101(3) TFUE used by the EU Commission. [174] The main difference lies in the fact that the relaxed

---

[169] COMCO, decision of 29 November 2010, *SIX/Terminals mit Dynamic Currency Conversion (DCC)*, LPC 2011/1, p. 96ff, para 409.

[170] FAC, judgment of 16 February 2021, B-2798/2018, *Naxoo/Supermédia*, para 11.3.5.2.

[171] Idem, para 11.3.5.2.

[172] See for instance the CFI, judgment of 17 September 2007, *Microsoft*, T-201/04, ECLI:EU:T:2007:289, paras 668 ff; ECJ, judgement of 15 March 2007, *British Airways*, C-95/04 P, ECLI:EU:C:2007:166, paras 84ff.

[173] See COMCO, decision of 30 October 2017 *Geschäftskunden Preissysteme für adressierte Briefsendungen*, LPC 2020/2 p. 433, para 850.

[174] Cf. Guidance on the Commission's enforcement priorities in applying Article 82 of the EC Treaty to abusive exclusionary conduct by dominant undertakings, JO 2009 C 45 p. 2, paras 28ff, para 30.

conditions for finding a restriction of competition under Article 7 CartA allow for a wider range of conduct to be considered abusive than in the EU, making it more difficult to justify such conduct by using the same business strategy argument or business model that was considered to be hindering competitors or disadvantaging business partners in the first place.

List of Documents

Commission Notice on the definition of relevant market for the purposes of Community competition law, OJ 1997 C 372, p. 5

Explanatory note of the COMCO Secretariat of 6 December 2021 regarding relative market power

Guidance on the Commission's enforcement priorities in applying Article 82 of the EC Treaty to abusive exclusionary conduct by dominant undertakings, JO 2009 C 45 p. 2

Ordinance on the Control of Concentrations of Undertakings (MCO; RS 251.4)

Reference

Këllezi P (2008) Abuse below the threshold of dominance? Market power, market dominance, and abuse of economic dependence. In: Art. 82 EC: new interpretation, new enforcement mechanism?, MPI Studies on Intellectual Property, Competition and Tax Law, Springer

Chapter 6
Merger Control

6.1 Introduction

Switzerland introduced a merger control in 1996 with the adoption of the Cartel Act. Mergers must be notified to the Secretariat of the COMCO in Bern. The Secretariat confirms that the notification is complete, which triggers the 1 month', respectively 4 months', deadlines. The decision to open an in-depth investigation is taken by a chamber of the COMCO, currently composed by the three members of its presidency. The decision to prohibit, to conditionally authorise or not to oppose the concentration is taken by the COMCO in corpore.

Notification thresholds are high compared to other similar European countries. In 2004, specific lower thresholds for media were abolished by the Parliament. Currently, there are no plans to modify the thresholds.

The substantial test is conditioned on the creation or reinforcement of a dominant position. In 2010, the attempt to introduce the substantial lessening of competition (SLC) test failed before the Parliament in a package that included other controversial amendments. The current dominant position test is perceived to be one of the reasons for the timid intervention of the COMCO in the 2000', particularly in the consumer goods sector. In the last decade, the COMCO has however blocked two mergers: one in the mobile telecommunication (2010) and the other in the online ticketing (2017).[1]

In May 2023, the Federal Council submitted a draft law to Parliament. The draft law amends the Cartel Act to introduce a clear SLC test. The proposed amendment to Article 10(1) and (2) CartA reads as follows: [2]

[1] A first prohibition ordered in 2004 was quashed by ACCI, which authorised the transaction with obligations. See COMCO, decision of 19 January 2004, *Berner Zeitung AG/20 Minuten (Schweiz) AG*, LPC 2004/2, p. 529; FSC, judgment of 22 February 2007, 2A.327/2006, *Berner Zeitung AG/Tamedia AG*.

[2] See Federal Council, Press release of 24 May 2023, "Loi sur les cartels: le Conseil fédéral adopte le message concernant la révision partielle", available at https://www.admin.ch/gov/fr/accueil/documentation/communiques/communiques-conseil-federal.msg-id-95384.html. The draft law can

P. Këllezi, *Competition Law in Switzerland*,
https://doi.org/10.1007/978-3-031-45117-1_6

(1) Concentrations subject to notification are examined by the Competition Commission if a preliminary examination (Art. 32 para. 1) reveals indications that they may substantially impede effective competition, in particular by creating or strengthening a dominant position.
(2) The Competition Commission may prohibit the concentration or authorise it subject to conditions and obligations if the examination reveals that the concentration

   a. substantially impedes effective competition, in particular by creating or strengthening a dominant position; and
   b. does not lead to efficiencies for customers which are justified and verifiable by the notifying undertakings, which result specifically from the concentration and which outweigh the disadvantages of the substantial impediment to competition.

The draft law proposes to simplify and abolish the notification requirement for concentrations with an EU dimension for which each of the product markets affected by the transaction can be defined geographically in such a way that it includes Switzerland and at least the European Economic Area. Such concentrations are examined by the European Commission. The undertakings notifying such transactions to the European Commission are required to submit a complete copy of the notification to the COMCO within 10 days of the notification. The COMCO Secretariat will promptly inform the participating companies if it considers that such notification is nevertheless necessary. [3]

The COMCO makes a classical competitive assessment based on the impact of the transaction on the market; it takes into account the position of the concerned undertakings, including any risk for insolvency of one of the undertakings, but its assessment does not include public interest's arguments. The Federal Council has a residual competence to authorise transactions on grounds of public interest. Upon request of the undertakings concerned, the Federal Council may, in exceptional cases, authorise a probated transaction if it is necessary for compelling public interest reasons (Sect. 1.7).[4]

The Swiss Financial Market Supervisory Authority, FINMA, has a competence to assess and decide on concentrations between banks for reasons related to creditor protection. In such cases, FINMA takes the place of the COMCO with regard to the assessment of competition law and takes all decisions pursuant to the Cartel Act. [5] The latter is invited by FINMA to submit an opinion. The Cartel Act gives therefore priority to the interests of creditors over the protection of competition. Banks must always notify their concentrations to COMCO, which informs FINMA, [6] but

---

be found at: https://www.newsd.admin.ch/newsd/message/attachments/78852.pdf. Accessed 25 May 2023.

[3] Message concernant la révision partielle de la loi sur les cartels, p. 36. Available at https://www.newsd.admin.ch/newsd/message/attachments/78850.pdf. Accessed 29 May 2023.

[4] Article 11 CartA.

[5] Article 10(3) CartA.

[6] Article 10 MCO.

FINMA may assert its competence and provisionally authorise a concentration even before it has been notified to the COMCO. [7]

6.2 Mandatory Notification System

6.2.1 Mandatory Notification

Certain transactions must be notified to the Competition Commission for approval before their completion.[8] The Cartel Act provides for two types of triggering elements: the turnover thresholds and the existence of a dominant position (see Sect. 6.5). The notification is compulsory if one of these notification triggers is fulfilled. There is no possibility to make a voluntary notification, but if there is any doubt as to whether the conditions of Article 9(4) CartA are fulfilled, the parties may submit a notification (see Sect. 6.5.2). In addition, the Secretariat may, upon request, give an opinion on whether or not a transaction is a concentration subject to mandatory notification.[9]

If one of these notification triggers is met, the concentration is deemed to have effects in Switzerland within the meaning of Article 2(2) of the Cartel Act, irrespective of the location of the undertakings concerned (see Sects. 1.3.2 and 6.5.2).

Pursuant to Article 11(1) of the Swiss-EU Air Transport Agreement, the EU Commission has "exceptionally full jurisdiction to assess potential competition concerns in Switzerland and, in particular, any concerns on routes between Switzerland and third countries" under Regulation 4064/89 if the notification thresholds at EU level are met. [10] Mergers with a Community dimension are therefore only notified to the EU Commission. Those which do not reach the Community dimension, but only the thresholds of Article 9 Cartel Act, are notified and assessed by the COMCO for effects in Switzerland.

There is no obligation in terms of timing of the notification, except that the notification must be filed before completion and that the transaction cannot be completed before obtaining the clearance from the COMCO. The envisaged transaction may be notified as soon as the parties have concluded a binding term sheet covering the main terms of the transaction or another document testifying their

---

[7] Article 17 MCO reads: "If the Swiss Financial Market Supervisory Authority deems a concentration of banks necessary for reasons related to creditor protection, it may, at the request of the banks involved or ex officio, allow implementation at any stage of the proceedings and, if necessary, prior to the receipt of the notification of the planned concentration in accordance with Articles 32 paragraph 2 and 33 paragraph 2 in conjunction with Article 10 paragraph 3 Cartel Act. Prior to its decision, it shall invite the Competition Commission to comment."

[8] Articles 9, 32 CartA.

[9] Article 23 (2) CartA.

[10] See for instance EU Commission, decision of 4 July 2005, COMP/M.3770—*Lufthansa/Swiss*.

intention to merge or acquire control. In the case of public bids, the transaction must be notified after the publication of the offer, however contrary to the EU regime, parties must file a request for provisional implementation.[11] Concerned undertakings may contact the Secretariat before the notification for guidance.

In exceptional circumstances, the parties may request and convene an early investigation by the COMCO. This was the case of the Basel Canton's intention to merge its public hospitals, which project was subject to the vote of the cantonal parliaments and possibly subject to a referendum. The COMCO accepted the notification 3 years before its planned implementation and authorised it subject to an obligation for the parties to notify any changes to the transaction and to the possibility of a new notification in the event one of the parties acquired another (private) hospital before implementation.[12]

6.2.2 *Failure to Notify*

In the event a transaction in the scope of merger control is not notified, the COMCO may start an investigation *ex officio*.[13] Undertakings concerned have a duty to provide all information and documents to the COMCO.[14] If the concerned parties have implemented the concentration and the COMCO prohibits or conditionally authorises it, the undertakings concerned may be required to restore effective competition.[15] The undertakings concerned must submit proposals to restore effective competition. If undertakings do not submit proposals or their proposals are insufficient, the COMCO may order any measure to restore effective competition, such as the separation of any combined undertakings or assets or the divestment of participations.

Undertakings that implement a notifiable concentration without filing a notification or fail to observe the suspension obligation are subject to administrative fines up to one million Swiss francs.[16] In addition, individuals that implement such a concentration risk a fine up to CHF 20,000.[17] There have been a few fines on companies that breached the duty to notify. In 1998, the COMCO opened an investigation *ex officio* on a transaction reported in the media.[18] The transaction concerned a change from joint to exclusive control. The COMCO developed in the

---

[11] See Sect. 6.4 below.

[12] COMCO, Communication of 18 September 2017, *Universitätsspital Basel/Kantonsspital Baselland.*

[13] Article 35 CartA.

[14] Article 40 CartA.

[15] Article 37 CartA.

[16] Article 51 CartA. See Sect. 7.4.1.

[17] Article 55 CartA. See Sect. 7.4.2

[18] COMCO, *Curti & Co. AG*, LPC 1998/4, p. 613.

Curti decision three criteria for fixing the amount of fines:[19] (1) the basis of the fine is fixed according to the turnover that was notified, (2) the potential effects on the market, particularly in case of overlap and whether the market shares exceeded the thresholds of 20% (the new entity) or 30% (each company), and (3) the risk that the transaction eliminates effective competition. To calculate the basis of the fine, the COMCO applies a basis of 0.1 per thousand to the notified turnover in Switzerland but capped the base at CHF 300,000 as a matter of principle. This basis was increased by 50% following the assessment of criteria (1) and (2). The resulting amount was decreased by 50% due to lack of elimination of competition (criteria iii). In *Curti*, the company was fined with an amount of CHF 68,400.

In 2000, the COMCO fined a company for failure to notify before the completion of a public offer,[20] which was launched in March 1999 in a foreign stock exchange. The takeover of 65.2% of the shares was completed and confirmed by the Financial Supervisory Authorities of the foreign country in August 1999. The successive offers and withdrawals were completed successfully in January 2000, which resulted in the acquisition of 98% of the target company shares. The transaction was notified in Switzerland end of March 2000 and was cleared following a Phase I assessment. The following grounds were not accepted to justify the late notification: the fact that the parties had no knowledge of the thresholds in Switzerland and that the transaction was not notifiable in the headquarters' country and in the European Union, the fact that the suspension period according to the applicable law of the takeover lasts until the completion of the whole offers and, lastly, the fact that the transaction was notified late in other countries and none of them had issued fines. The basis of the fine was set according to the criteria developed in *Curti*,[21] and reduced twice by 50%: the company was fined with an amount of CHF 30,000.

In 2012, the COMCO fined a company for failure to notify a share acquisition that was linked[22] with another transaction, but only the later was notified.[23] The shares of two companies were acquired from a single seller by two separate companies which were part of two separate groups only in appearance, but were in fact run by identical board members and had consolidated accounts. The parties had considered that each transaction was a separate one, and according to their view, the first transaction did not reach the notification thresholds. The COMCO took the opposite line considering that the two buyers were part of a single economic entity and that the two transactions were therefore considered as a single transaction. Consequently, the notification threshold was reached for both share transfers. The decision is important

[19] Idem, paras 30 ff.

[20] COMCO, decision of 18 December 2000, *Banque Nationale de Paris (BNP)/Paribas*, LPC 2001/1, p. 144.

[21] See above, COMCO, Curti & Co. AG, LPC 1998/4, p. 613.

[22] Each share transferred was a condition precedent for the other, and therefore constituted a unique transaction. See COMCO, decision of 10 December 2012, *SWICA/ProVAG/PROVITA*, LPC 2013/2, paras 50–51.

[23] COMCO, decision of 10 December 2012, *SWICA/ProVAG/PROVITA*, LPC 2013/2.

for setting the boundaries of the corporate group according to Article 5 MCO. The fine was calculated in accordance with criteria set in Curti:[24] the basis was set at 0.1 per thousand of the notified turnover of the whole group, reduced by 50% because of lack of potential negative effects, the result of which was reduced by another 50% because there was no risk of elimination of effective competition. The COMCO reduced further the amount by 50%, after recognising the good faith of the parties, which is a new criterion compared to previous cases. The company was fined with a final amount of CHF 35,000.

6.3 Suspension Obligation

6.3.1 Suspension Period

The aim of the prior (*ex ante*) control is to preserve effectively the structure of the market, that's why the suspension or *stand still* obligation. The contracting parties cannot implement the transaction before the expiry of the 1-month period from the notification, unless the COMCO announces before expiry of the 1-month period that it will not carry out an in-depth investigation.[25] The stand-still obligation during the first 1-month period is statutory and therefore automatic. The parties may file a request to the COMCO for provisional implementation on important grounds before the 1-month period.[26] The COMCO gives notice to companies within 1-month whether it will conduct an in-depth investigation. The decision states the preliminary assessment of the transaction and decides whether to extend the suspension period during a period of 4 months.

6.3.2 Legal Effects of Transactional Arrangements

The legal effects of a notifiable concentration are suspended during the preliminary and in-depth assessment.[27] The effect of contractual arrangements entered into between the parties are governed by condition precedents provisions under Article 151 CO.[28] This means that transactional arrangements are not null and void, but provisionally ineffective. The arrangements take effect with the decision or communication of non-opposition by the COMCO, or the laps of the respective deadlines of

[24] See above COMCO, Curti & Co. AG, LPC 1998/4, p. 613 and COMCO, decision of 18 December 2000, *Banque Nationale de Paris (BNP)/Paribas*, LPC 2001/1, p. 144.

[25] Article 32 (1) and (2) CartA.

[26] Article 32 (2) CartA.

[27] Article 34 CartA.

[28] FAC, judgment of 3 Mai 2018, B-3871/2017, *Ticketcorner Holding AG v COMCO*, para 15.

Phase I and II investigation in case of non-opposition. The contractual arrangements may foresee specific mechanisms that regulate the rights and obligations of parties until the COMCO's decision. Additional conditions are possible provided they do not conflict with the statutory suspension of legal effects and the stand still obligation provided for under the Cartel Act. The standstill obligation means that the parties have a duty not to close the transaction during Phase I or Phase II assessment periods, and therefore should arrange their relationship by using for instance conditions precedent or organise a simultaneous signing and closing after the COMCO's approval. If the parties close the transaction without complying with the standstill obligation, they cannot rely on the statutory suspension of legal effects of Article 34 CartA to argue that the closing had no legal effect. Consequently, the contractual arrangements must at least provide condition precedents on the COMCO approval.

A prohibition establishes definitely the ineffectiveness of arrangements, subject to an appeal.[29] In the event of an appeal raised by all concerned parties, the statutory suspension of legal effects will be prolonged until the entry into effect of the COMCO decision.[30] The suspensive effect of an appeal to the FAC is not applicable for refusals of an authorisation (for negative decisions) and therefore has no bearing on the legal effect of contractual arrangements of the transaction.[31]

6.3.3 Completion in Breach of the Suspension Period (Gun-Jumping)

Undertakings that do not observe the suspension obligation are subject to administrative fines up to CHF 1 million.[32]

Constitute completion all legal acts that confer lasting control or perfect a merger under the applicable laws to contractual arrangements. Under Swiss law, such acts include for instance the actual transfer of shares and if applicable the holding of a general assembly approving such transfer, modification of the board of directors, the payment of the consideration, the holding of a general assembly approving a merger and the resulting inscriptions to the register of companies.

Intermediate acts that do not confer actual and lasting control are not considered as completion, such as: signing of a share purchase agreement, signing of shareholders' agreements, approval of the content of the share purchase agreements or of the merger agreements by the general assemblies of the companies, negotiations as

[29] FAC, judgment of 3 Mai 2018, B-3871/2017, *Ticketcorner Holding AG v COMCO*, paras 15–17.

[30] Idem, para 18. In the same judgment, the FAC found inadmissible the appeal of one of the parties in the concentration, holding that the appeal against a prohibition decision must be raised by all concerned undertakings. See Sect. 6.8.6 below.

[31] FAC, judgment of 3 Mai 2018, B-3871/2017, *Ticketcorner Holding AG v COMCO*, para 16.

[32] Article 51 CartA. See Sect. 7.4.1.

well as execution of due diligence. There have been no cases on the exchange of information or other contractual provisions included in the share purchase or shareholders' agreements that confer rights to the purchaser between signing and closing, for instance on the investments or material arrangements that can be concluded by the target. Article 5 CartA applies however during such period and notifying parties should refrain from coordinating their business activities before the COMCO's approval.

In 1998, the COMCO fined two foreign companies for closing a notified transaction before authorisation.[33] The ACCI upheld the fine.[34] The notifying undertakings notified the transaction in Switzerland after having received clearance from the EU Commission, stating that they planned to proceed to closing within 3 weeks from the filing of the notification—that was before the 1-month suspension period provided by the CartA—but that they would suspend sales in Switzerland until the COMCO authorisation. The COMCO authorised the concentration within 1 month from the date that the notification was declared complete, but after the actual closing of the transaction. It simultaneously opened a procedure for breach of the suspension obligation. The ACCI held that the COMCO should base its fine on objective criteria and on fault, but that the risk taken by the parties constituted a wrongful act. Articles 9 (1) and 32 (2) CartA were clear on the obligation on the parties not to close the transaction, and that was applicable to all companies, even foreign ones. The fine provided for under Article 51 CartA was automatic, meaning that the COMCO has no discretion whether to order a fine; the COMCO enjoys nevertheless a discretion on the amount of the fine. The ACCI approved the three criteria used by the COMCO to determine the fine: (1) the turnover of the company in Switzerland, by taking a rate of 0.1 per thousand, (2) which will be increased or decreased according to the potential effect of the concentration, (3) which amount will be further increased or decreased according to the degree of danger of elimination of effective competition. The basic amount was reduced by 50% in application of the first two limbs. Suspension of sales in Switzerland was not considered a criterion that could be taken into account, nor the short period between the closing and the reception of the authorisation (18 days). Each notifying party was fined CHF 60,000.

[33] COMCO, decision of 21 December 1998, *Rhône-Poulenc SA/Merck & Co Inc.*, LPC 1998/1, p. 96.

[34] ACCI, decision of 7 march 2002, *Rhône-Poulenc SA/Merck & Co Inc.*, LPC 2002/2, p. 386, confirmed by the FSC, judgment of 24 April 2001, *Rhône-Poulenc SA et Merck & Co. Inc (Merial)*, ATF/BGE 127 III 219.

6.4 Provisional Implementation

The COMCO gives notice to companies within 1-month whether it will conduct an in-depth investigation. The decision states the preliminary assessment of the transaction and decides whether to extend the suspension period or authorise its implementation provisionally. There is no need to file a separate request for provisional implementation,[35] although the undertakings may file a request for provisional implementation at any time after the notification by stating important grounds. The request for provisional derogation before notification is possible[36] but should remain an exception and subject to certain conditions: the request must include essential information on the transaction, the parties must submit valid reasons explaining why they cannot provide a complete filing, and the transaction must be reversable.[37]

The authorisation to implement the concentration before Phase I or Phase II clearance is provisional and granted only on exceptional circumstances. The parties must demonstrate that there are important grounds to implement the transaction provisionally, such as the fact that the suspension obligation would jeopardize the transaction, that the concerned undertakings or other parties risk important damages and that the transaction does not threaten competition.[38]

The authorisation to provisionally implement the transaction may be subject to conditions and obligations.[39] In the event of a public offer, the COMCO may restrict the voting rights acquired by the offeror to the preservation of the value of its investment.[40] Contrary to Regulation 139/2004,[41] neither the Cartel Act nor MOC include a statutory derogation from the suspension obligation. The parties must therefore file a request for provisional implementation and cannot rely on the fact that the acquirer does not exercise its voting rights except to preserve the value of its investment.[42] As in the example presented in this section above, the offeror risks an administrative fine if the public bid is completed before notification or the approval by the COMCO.[43] The request may be filed before the notification, provided that the request includes the essential information allowing the COMCO's Secretariat to assess the case, the parties submit valid reasons explaining why they cannot provide a complete filing, and it would be always possible to reverse the transfer of shares.[44]

---

[35] Article 33 (2) CartA.

[36] Cf. Article 7(3) Regulation 139/2004, where as a general rule the derogation may be granted at any time, be it before the notification or after the transaction.

[37] COMCO, decision of 17 September 2008, *Schaeffler/Continental*, LPC 2009/1, p. 85, para 18.

[38] Idem, para 21. Cf. Article 7(3) Regulation 139/2004.

[39] Article 16 (2) MCO.

[40] Article 16 (2) MCO.

[41] See Article 7(2) Regulation 139/2004.

[42] COMCO, decision of 17 September 2008, *Schaeffler/Continental*, LPC 2009/1, p. 85, para 14.

[43] See COMCO, decision of 18 December 2000, *Banque Nationale de Paris (BNP)/Paribas*, LPC 2001/1, p. 144.

[44] COMCO, decision of 17 September 2008, *Schaeffler/Continental*, LPC 2009/1, p. 85, para 18.

FINMA enjoys a competence to authorise prior implementation of transactions involving banks on grounds of creditors protection. FINMA may authorise a concentration between banks at any stage of the procedure and even before notification to the COMCO.[45] This was the case when UBS took over Credit Suisse in March 2023 following the latter's liquidity crisis, which would have triggered a global financial stability crisis. [46] The COMCO gives its opinion to FINMA before the latter's final decision.

6.5 Notification Triggers

The Cartel Act provides for two types of notification triggers: one is the classic criteria related to the turnover of the concerned undertakings, and the other relates to the dominant position of one of the concerned undertakings.

In general, the two type of notification triggers justify jurisdiction of Swiss Authorities. The criteria of effects in Switzerland is not relevant for establishing jurisdiction in the field of merger control:[47] the Federal Supreme Court has confirmed that the turnover thresholds in Article 9 (1) CartA embody the effects principle,[48] and therefore no separate assessment of effects is necessary. This position is also reinforced by the judgment of the FSC in a case concerning parallel imports, in which the Court held that a mere possible effect in Switzerland is sufficient to assert jurisdiction; intensity of the effect is neither relevant, nor can it be assessed in individual case (Sect. 1.3.2).[49]

One notable exception are full function joint ventures which business activity has no connection with Switzerland. This is also valid for joint ventures of Swiss parent companies. There is no duty to notify when the joint venture does not carry out any activity, does not have any sales in Switzerland and such activities or turnover in Switzerland are neither planned nor expected in the future.[50] Another exception would be the case of un undertaking achieving the turnover thresholds in the financial year preceding the concentration, but which sells the Swiss business at the beginning of the following year. The undertaking has probably no duty to notify a subsequent transaction not related to Switzerland based on the turnover realised in

[45] Articles 10 (3) CartA and 17 MCO.

[46] FINMA decision of 19 March 2023 based on Article 32 (2) CartA (unpublished).

[47] Article 2 CartA. See Notice of the Secretariat of the COMCO, Practice regarding the notification and assessment of concentrations of 25 March 2009, para 7 (Notice on concentrations from the Secretariat).

[48] FSC, judgment of 24 April 2001, *Rhône-Poulenc SA et Merck & Co. Inc (Merial),* ATF/BGE 127 III 219, para 4.b.

[49] FSC, judgment of 28 June 2016, case 2C_180/2014, *Gaba*, ATF/BGE 143 II 297, para 3.7.

[50] Notice on concentrations, para 4.

Switzerland in the previous financial year.[51] However, there is no clear rule on the above and parties might be well advised to carefully assess that there is no duty to notify.

6.5.1 *Turnover of Concerned Undertakings*

According to Article 9 (1) CartA, a concentration of undertakings must be notified to the Competition Commission before its implementation if in the financial year preceding the concentration:

(a) the undertakings concerned together reported a turnover of at least 2 billion Swiss francs, or a turnover in Switzerland of at least CHF 500 million, and
(b) at least two of the undertakings concerned each reported a turnover in Switzerland of at least CHF 100 million.

The second limb of the notification threshold sets a high bar, as the turnover of at least two of the undertakings concerned must have exceeded CHF 100 million each in the previous year.

The concentration is deemed to take place at the time of signing, or if the parties have not signed an agreement, at the time of the signing of any letter of intent. [52] The financial year for the calculation of the turnover precedes therefore the signing of the transaction, and not the closing date.

All sales in Switzerland are relevant for the calculation of the turnover: it is not necessary for the participating companies to have subsidiaries, branches or other branches in Switzerland.[53] For the allocation of the turnover in Switzerland it is relevant the location of the customer of the products and services: the turnover is allocated in Switzerland if the product is delivered to a customer in Switzerland. The place of the billing is not relevant for the allocation of the turnover: if the invoicing is made in Switzerland but the products are delivered to customers outside Switzerland, then the turnover is not considered to be related to Switzerland and is not taken into account in the calculation of the turnover. Conversely, if the invoicing is made outside Switzerland but the delivery of products or services is made to customers in Switzerland, then the turnover is relevant for the notification in Switzerland. The rule does not necessarily apply to services, which require a case by case assessment.

---

[51] See COMCO, communication of 16 October 2017, *Tamedia/Tradono Switzerland*, LPC 2017/4, p. 579, paras 12–17.

[52] See Advice from the COMCO Secretariat, *Meldeflicht Worldline/Ingenico*, LPC 2020/2, p. 422, para 10.

[53] Notice on concentrations from the Secretariat, para 8.

6.5.1.1 Undertakings Concerned and Turnover Calculation

The undertakings concerned are the merging undertakings or the controlling and controlled undertakings.[54] Only the divested part of the undertaking constitutes the undertaking concerned, not the whole group. This means that only the target undertaking will be considered as undertaking concerned in the event the target is divested and does not remain under the (joint) control of the selling party. The selling company or group of companies is not a concerned undertaking and therefore their turnover is not relevant for the calculation of the turnover.

The turnover from the sale of products and the provision of services within the ordinary business activities of the undertakings concerned in the preceding financial year is meant net. All discounts, rebates, value added tax and other consumption taxes as well as other taxes directly related to turnover are deducted from the gross turnover.[55] From the turnover must be deducted also taxes and royalties collected to be paid to collective societies.

If, within a period of 2 years, two or more transactions take place between the same undertakings resulting in the acquisition of control over parts of these undertakings, those transactions shall be treated as a single concentration for the purposes of calculating the turnover.[56] The decisive date is the date of the last transaction. This situation is to be distinguished from that where two or more transactions take place between different undertakings, even though the successive transactions are separate steps aiming at transferring a target from the seller to a final buyer. In this later case, the notifying parties or the COMCO cannot rely on Article 4 (3) MCO but has to assess the various transactions in accordance with the newest practice of the COMCO Secretariat.

6.5.1.2 Identification of Corporate Group

The turnover of an undertaking concerned includes the turnover from its own business activities and the turnover of the companies that are part of the same group.[57] Those include subsidiaries, parent companies, sister companies and companies own jointly by two of the group companies.

Subsidiaries are companies in which the concerned undertaking owns more than a half of the capital, more than a half of the voting rights, in which it is entitled to appoint more than half of the members of the bodies legally representing the undertaking or in which it otherwise has the right to manage the undertaking's affairs. The right to manage the affairs of another company may result from contracts or organisational regulations that govern who has decisive influence: a group

[54] Article 3 MCO.

[55] Article 4 MCO.

[56] Article 4 (3) MCO.

[57] Article 5 MCO.

holding company may have the right to manage another group holding company and therefore both holdings form part of the same economy entity within the meaning of Articles 2 and 5 MCO.[58] The turnover of both holdings shall be taken into account for the purpose of the notification.

Parent companies are companies which alone or jointly own more than half of the capital or have more than a half of the voting rights of the concerned undertaking, which are entitled to appoint more than half of the members of the bodies legally representing the concerned undertaking or otherwise have the right to manage the concerned undertaking's affairs. Sister companies are undertakings in which a parent company has the above-mentioned rights or powers. Joint venture companies are group companies over which two or more group companies jointly have the above-mentioned rights or powers.

In calculating the total turnover of an undertaking concerned, the turnover from business activities among the undertakings of the same group shall not be considered,[59] to avoid taking such turnover into account twice. The rule of Article 5 (2) MCO is therefore applicable only to group turnover calculated in accordance with Article 5 (1) MCO. Conversely, there is no deduction for the turnover of a branch with another group unit if the turnover of that unit was not included in the turnover of the branch. [60] The turnover of a joint venture that is jointly controlled by the undertakings concerned of different groups is allocated among those undertakings in equal parts.[61]

6.5.2 Dominant Position of One of the Concerned Undertakings

Notification is mandatory if, first, one of the undertakings concerned is found to be in a dominant position in a market in Switzerland, and second, if the concentration concerns either that market or an adjacent market or a market upstream or downstream thereof.[62] The duty to notify is irrespective of the turnover of concerned undertakings in Switzerland and also irrespective of the effects that the transaction might have in Switzerland.[63]

Undertaking refers to a group of companies, therefore companies that are part of a group of companies are subject to a duty to notify if a company in the group was held to be in a dominant position and the transaction concerns that market, or an adjacent,

[58] See COMCO, decision of 10 December 2012, *SWICA/ProVAG/PROVITA*, LPC 2013/2, p. 222, para 60.

[59] Article 5 (2) MCO.

[60] See Advice from the COMCO Secretariat, LPC 2020/4a, p. 1656, paras 12ff.

[61] Article 5 (3) MCO.

[62] Article 9 (4) CartA.

[63] See also FSC, judgment of 28 June 2016, 2C_180/2014, *Gaba*, ATF/BGE 143 II 297, para 3.7.

downstream or upstream one.[64] A notification obligation exists in the following cases: one of the merging parties was found to be in a dominant position, an undertaking within the group of the undertaking acquiring exclusive or joint control was found to be in a dominant position, or the target undertaking was found to be in a dominant position. On the other hand, there is no obligation to notify if the seller of a controlling stake is in a dominant position.

The dominant position is understood as a position that enables an undertaking to behave to an appreciable extent independently of the other participants (competitors, suppliers or consumers) in the market (Sect. 5.2.2). The dominant position may concern an individual or a joint dominance. The position of economic dependence or of relative market power without the existence of a dominant position is not relevant for the duty to notify. There is a duty to notify even if the target is active in a foreign geographic market and has no activities in Switzerland. [65]

The dominant position must have been established in the statement of reasons of a final and non-appealable decision following a procedure under the Cartel Act, and not necessarily in the operative part of the decision. [66] The FAC has recently confirmed that, in order to trigger the obligation to notify, it is sufficient for the COMCO decisions, following phase II of the control of concentration or abuse of a dominant position, to establish in their statement of reasons a dominant position in a specific relevant market. The COMCO decision establishing the dominant position must be final at the time of signing the agreement, [67] meaning that if the COMCO decision is challenged before a court at the time of signing, there will be no obligation to notify under Article 9 (4) CartA. A dominant position can be established also by the FAC or the FSC.

The concentration at stake must concern either the market on which one of the concerned undertakings is found to be in a dominant position or an adjacent product or geographic market, or a market upstream or downstream thereof. The concept of "adjacent" on the one hand and "downstream or upstream" on the other, may give rise to legal uncertainty for undertakings, as a consequence they must be construed narrowly in the context of administrative sanctions under Article 51 of the Cartel Act (see Sect. 7.4.1),[68] but the obligation to notify is of a purely administrative nature. [69] For the purpose of assessing a notification obligation under Article 9(4) CartA, the provision must be interpreted broadly to cover all situations where a risk to

[64] See the facts of the FAC, judgment of 29 April 2014, B-6180/2013 *The Swatch Group AG*. The Swatch Group AG was an undertaking subject to a duty to notify because one of its subsidiaries, ETA, was found to be in a dominant position.

[65] See for instance COMCO, final report of 12 April 2007 *Swisscom AG/Fastweb S.p.A.*, LPC 2007/2, p. 312, paras 15ff.

[66] FAC, judgment of 19 January 2022, B-2597/2017, *Kommerzialisierung von elektronischen Medikamenteninformationen*, para 10.6.

[67] Advice from the COMCO Secretariat, *Meldeflicht Worldline/Ingenico*, LPC 2020/2, p. 422, paras 6 et 9.

[68] FAC, judgment of 29 April 2014, B-6180/2013, *The Swatch Group AG,* para 2.1.

[69] FAC, judgment of 6 October 202, B-1471/2016, *TX Group AG*, paras 2.43–2.46.

competition in adjacent or neighbouring markets cannot be ruled out from the outset. [70] Any actual assessment of the effects of the concentration must be left to the substantive assessment under Article 10 CartA and must not be carried out at the stage of notification. [71]

In the context of an administrative sanction for failure to notify under Article 9 (4) CartA, the FAC has identified two types of adjacent product markets, according to a strict interpretation of the provision:

- Products that show a certain degree of demand or supply substitution with the dominant position market. The aim would be here to capture transactions that would allow an undertaking to acquire potential competitors.[72] The Courts have not yet considered the scope and degree of substitutability that might be covered.
- Products that show complementarity with the products of the dominant market. This second type of adjacent market was discussed at length by the Federal Administrative Court, by narrowing the scope of Article 9(4) CartA. Only goods and services that can be offered or bought together in bundle are considered as complementary.[73] The market should be "adjacent" to the dominant market, and the COMCO cannot extend the scope of Article 9(4) CartA to any input that is used for a final product: the decision established that ETA had a dominant position in the *ebauche* market, and that the adjacent market was the market for *movements*. The market for *case* watches (boîtiers) could not be considered as adjacent to *ebauche*'s market simply because case watches are a product which assembles *ebauches* and *movements*. Watch *cases* may be considered as adjacent to *ebauches* if customers buy both components together, which was not the case.

The above interpretation must be distinguished from the interpretation of the FAC in a notification context outside the sanctions of Article 51 CartA. In the aforementioned TX Group/Tamedia case, the FAC refused to discuss the criteria that would define the adjacent market, stating that it was neither possible nor desirable to establish any such criteria for establishing a duty to notify: "Rather, the only question to be examined is whether competitive effects on the markets affected by the merger proceedings [. . .] can be excluded from the outset." [74]

Therefore, only transactions aimed at expanding activities in a market which is in no way related to the relevant market in which the undertaking concerned holds a dominant position do not have to be notified.

The scope of Article 9(4) CartA is important for the assessment of the obligation to notify and also for the administrative and criminal sanctions in case of failure to notify (see Sect. 7.4). As the FAC has held that Article 9(4) CartA is to be interpreted

[70] Idem, paras 2.43–2.41.

[71] Idem, paras 2.43–2.46.

[72] FAC, judgment of 29 April 2014, B-6180/2013, *The Swatch Group AG,* para 2.3.

[73] Idem, para 2.3.1.

[74] FAC, judgment of 6 October 202, B-1471/2016, *TX Group AG*, para 2.41.

broadly for the purpose of identifying a duty to notify, [75] there is a certain degree of uncertainty in assessing the situations covered by Article 9(4) CartA. In order to reduce this uncertainty, undertakings may request an opinion from the Secretariat pursuant to Article 23 (2) CartA. Alternatively, they may request the COMCO to issue a declaratory decision on the duty to notify pursuant to Article 25 APA, a decision which may be challenged before the FAC. To obtain a challengeable declaratory decision, the parties will have to show they have an interest that is worthy of protection. These two options are subject to a fee calculated on an hourly basis. Finally, the notifying parties may submit a (simplified) notification, in which case the Secretariat will determine whether a duty to notify exists. In this case, the parties must pay a forfeit of CHF 5,000. [76]

If an undertaking has failed to notify and is subject to sanction proceedings, it may argue for a strict interpretation of Article 9(4) CartA with regard to the sanction provided for in Article 51 CartA. This means that it would have to notify, but that the COMCO would probably waive a fine for distant adjacent, upstream or downstream, markets.

6.5.3 Undertaking Having a Duty to Notify

Undertakings concerned are the merging companies, the acquiring and selling companies as well as the target company or companies. Not all concerned companies have a duty to notify. In the case of an acquisition of an exclusive control, only the company acquiring exclusive control has a duty to notify, not the seller.

In the case of joint control, all companies acquiring joint control have a duty to notify. The target and the seller have no such a duty. In the case of a merger, both merging parties have jointly a duty to notify.[77] The merging companies and companies acquiring joint control form a community of interest with respect to the duty to notify and are therefore jointly and severally liable.[78] The companies having a duty to notify must appoint at least one joint representative to communicate with the COMCO Secretariat, and those having their seat abroad must provide an address in Switzerland. [79]

---

[75] FAC, judgment of 6 October 202, B-1471/2016, *TX Group AG*, paras 2.43–2.41.

[76] These three options were discussed in FSC, judgement of 23 September 2021, 2C_934/2020, paras 5.3 and 5.4.

[77] Article 9 MCO.

[78] FAC, judgment of 3 Mai 2018, B-3871/2017, *Ticketcorner Holding AG v COMCO*, para 54.

[79] Article 9 (3) MCO.

6.6 Meaning of Concentration

The definition of concentrations is quasi-identical with the definition given in the EU regulations and covers mergers of two or more previously independent undertakings and acquisition of control by which one or more undertakings acquire direct or indirect control of one or more previously independent undertakings or parts thereof.[80]

6.6.1 Mergers

Concentration covers the merger of two or more previously independent undertakings. The concept of merger is larger than that of mergers as regulated by company or merger regulations under the applicable laws and includes de facto mergers[81] that bring under a common direction a set of undertakings.

By contrast to acquisition of control, one or all companies cease to exist without going to liquidation as a result of the merger process. The previously independent companies become one single entity, either by the act of absorption of one company by the other one, or by creation of a new entity into which are amalgamated all previously independent companies. In the case of absorption, the absorbed entity ceases to exist but the absorbing company retains its legal personality. Because of the amalgamation of the previously independent companies to the new one, all previous companies cease to exist after being merged into the newly created legal entity.

6.6.2 Acquisition of Control

Acquisition of control is relevant for the control of concentration if the transaction leads to the acquisition of an independent undertaking or a part of an undertaking. An independent undertaking is a company or a group of companies. A part of an undertaking is qualified as an undertaking within the meaning of Article 4 (3) CartA if first, the business has its own market presence and, second, market turnover can be

[80] Article 4 (3) CartA who reads as following: "Concentration of undertakings are: a. the merger of two or more previously independent undertakings; b. any transaction, in particular the acquisition of an equity interest or the conclusion of an agreement, by which one or more undertakings acquire direct or indirect control of one or more previously independent undertakings or parts thereof."

[81] The case of Price Waterhouse and Coopers&Lybrand was considered as a de facto merger by both EU Commission and the COMCO. See Case IV/M.1016, *Price Waterhouse/Coopers&Lybrand,* which refers to the concept of "single economic entity" at para 17; COMCO, communication of 20 April 1998, *Revisuisse Price Waterhouse/STG-Coopers & Lybrand*, LPC 1998/2, p. 214, paras 18–20. See also Consolidated Jurisdictional Notice, para 10.

attributed to the business. A branch office [82] or a business unit [83] are examples of a part of undertaking that can be acquired by another undertaking, usually through an asset deal.

The concept of control is given a wide definition. Control is defined as the ability to exercise a decisive influence over the activities of another undertaking.[84] All undertakings involved preserve their legal personality, but the link between them is modified into a relationship of control.

The means of obtaining control may in particular involve the acquisition of shares or rights to use all or parts of the assets of an undertaking, or conclusion of agreements which confer a decisive influence on the composition, deliberations, or decisions of the organs of an undertaking. Control may be exercised by a majority shareholder. Acquisition of minority shareholdings that give decisive control over one undertaking or part thereof is also covered.[85]

The control may be acquired either by a single undertaking or a number of undertaking acting jointly.

6.6.2.1 Exclusive Control

The undertaking acquiring control may be a new shareholder or an existing shareholder of the target undertaking acquiring a majority shareholding or a minority shareholding conferring de facto control of the target undertaking. Exclusive control may also arise through contracts or other circumstances that confer decisive influence on the target, such as loans or other financial arrangements. The concept is essentially the same as in the EU Merger Regulation.

6.6.2.2 Joint Control over a Full Function Entity

Swiss competition law distinguishes between the acquisition of joint control in an existing company and creation of a joint company by two or more companies.[86] The

[82] Advice from the COMCO Secretariat, LPC 2020/4a, p. 1656, para 8.

[83] COMCO, communication of 29 July 2014, *LGT Bank (Switzerland) Ltd./Unternehmensteil HSBC Private Bank (Suisse) SA*, LPC 2014/3, p. 512, where the private banking unit of a bank covering customer relationships, employees and certain assets was considered a part of undertaking.

[84] Article 1 MCO.

[85] See for instance COMCO, communication of 15 March 2004, *RTL Group S.A./Métropole Télévision S.A.*, LPC 2004/2, p. 525 (factual control resulting from a capital ownership of 34%).

[86] Article 2 MCO on joint ventures reads as follows: "(1) A situation whereby two or more undertakings acquire joint control over an undertaking which they previously did not jointly control shall be deemed a concentration of undertakings within the meaning of Article 4 paragraph 3 letter b Cartel Act if the joint venture performs all the functions of an autonomous economic entity on a lasting basis. (2) If two or more undertakings found an undertaking that they intend to control jointly, this constitutes a concentration of undertakings if the joint venture performs the functions

company jointly controlled must "perform all the functions of an autonomous economic entity on a lasting basis"[87] in both cases. The COMCO has never applied the distinction according to which the full function criteria applies only to creations of new companies controlled jointly by its parent. Following *Austria Asphalt*,[88] it is therefore EU law which comes closer to the Swiss law.

Full Function Joint Venture The joint entity performs all the functions of an autonomous economic entity on a lasting basis if the following conditions are met:

- The joint entity is present in a market as provider or purchaser of goods and services. When the joint entity is a provider of goods and services, it is deemed to fulfil the full function criteria.[89] By contrast, if the joint entity is only a purchaser of goods or services from the parent company, it should be assessed whether the joint entity fulfils only a purchasing function for parent companies and therefore is not a full function entity. Also, the creation of a holding company for the management of shareholding interests which has no other business activities does not fulfil the requirement of the market presence. [90]
- The joint entity acts as an independent entity on the market, by following its own commercial strategy. The joint entity must act independently from an operational and functional standpoint, but this does not mean that it must take all decisions independently from its parent companies.
- The joint entity should perform its activities on a lasting basis, which means that the joint venture entity should be set for a long term or indefinitely. If no term is provided contractually, the long-lasting criteria should be assessed on a case by case basis.[91]
- The joint entity must have its own management and resources such as staff, capital and financial resources and assets.

Creation of a New Joint Venture The same criteria apply to the creation of a new joint venture. In order to fulfil the full function criteria, at least one of the parent companies must transfer part of its business to the newly created joint entity.[92]

In principle, the mere contribution of capital to the joint entity is not sufficient to create a notifiable full function joint-venture to the joint entity. The only exception is the contribution in capital (1) in the financial services sector (2) where the capital is

set out in paragraph 1 and if business activities from at least one of the controlling undertakings are transferred to the joint venture."

[87] Article 2 (1) MCO.

[88] CJEU, judgment of 7 September 2017, *Austria Asphalt GmbH & Co OG v Bundeskartellanwalt*, C-248/16, ECLI:EU:C:2017:643.

[89] See for instance COMCO, communication of 24 Mai 2017, *BSL AG/Transport Ferroviaire Holding SAS*, PLC 2017/3, p. 469, para 37.

[90] See Advice from the COMCO Secretariat, PLC 2019/4, p. 1140.

[91] See for instance COMCO, communication of 24 Mai 2017, *BSL AG/Transport Ferroviaire Holding SAS*, PLC 2017/3, p. 469, para 42.

[92] Art. 2 (2) MCO.

used by the joint venture for its business activity (for instance loans to customers).[93] The exception was not applied to a joint venture in the fintech sector that received capital from its parent companies to enable the provision of blockchain technologies to SMEs, but which capital was not intended to fund the provision of financial services; in addition, the parent companies did not transfer any of its business activities, know-how or staff to the joint venture.[94] As a consequence, the joint venture was not considered as full function and there was no duty to notify.

6.6.2.3 Change of Control

Change of control is covered by the concept of concentration. The COMCO and its Secretariat follow in principle the EU Consolidated Jurisdictional Notice. The determining factor is change in the quality of control.

The first scenario is the change from exclusive to common control, and vice-versa. Entry of a new shareholder may result in a change from exclusive to common control. By contrast, exit of a shareholder may change a common control to exclusive.

The second scenario is the modification in the number of shareholders having joint control over one undertaking, by an increase or reduction in the number of shareholders or a replacement of a shareholder. Such modification of the shareholding will be considered as a change of control if it results in a change of the quality of the control. The entry of an additional shareholder and the replacement of an existing one will be usually considered as a change in the quality of the common control. By contrast, the exit of a shareholder does not necessarily modify the quality of the common control exercised by the remaining shareholders. This is the case when the same arrangements continue to apply to the positive and negative powers of the remaining shareholders.

6.6.3 Interdependent Transactions as a Single Economic Unit

There is no express provision in the Cartel Act that regulates to what extent two or more related transactions are notifiable as a single transaction. MCO provides for a rule that prevent companies slicing the transaction in different parts in order to avoid

[93] Advice from the COMCO Secretariat on the notification of a French joint venture, PLC 2017/2, p. 277, paras 6 and 7; see also PLC 2006/4, p. 677 *GE/CSFBPE/GIMP*, para 19; PLC 2008/1, p. 124, *Joint Venture: General Electric Company/Credit Suisse Private Equity/Mubadala Development Company PJSC*; PLC 2006/4, p. 677, *GE/CSFBPE/GIMP*, para 19; PLC 2005/2, p. 360 *Cashgate/Zürcher Kantonalbank, Schwyzer Kantonalbank und Valiant Holding*.

[94] Advice from the COMCO Secretariat on the notification of a French joint venture, PLC 2017/2, p. 277, paras 6 and 7.

reaching notification thresholds.[95] The COMCO refers regularly to the European Commission Consolidated Jurisdictional Notice[96] and therefore a situation covered by the Consolidated Jurisdictional Notice would be handled similarly in Switzerland.

Understanding whether interdependent transactions would be considered as one transaction is important because mergers and acquisition of control often involve various transitional transactions between the same or different undertakings, which as a whole aim to transfer common or exclusive lasting control from one set of undertakings to another. From the perspective of the scope of merger control, the main objective is to capture all structural market changes of a lasting nature resulting from a set of transactions.

The definition of concentration defines the concerned undertakings and consequently their turnover.[97] This determines whether the transaction is notifiable as a single or as separate transactions, having as a result in the former case that that both transactions are notifiable as one and that the failure to notify one of them triggers fines.[98] If the transactions are considered as separate, only part of those transactions would be notifiable. The other consequence is the suspension obligation: if one of the transactions is not considered to be part of the single, notifiable concentration, then this transaction can be closed independently of the outcome of the notification procedure involving the other set of transactions.

The area is complex because it is difficult to establish rules that cover a large number of possible scenarios (Table 6.1). The most appropriate approach is to determine whether the undertakings concerned are the same. The provision only covers two or more transactions between the same undertakings (as buyer, seller or target), not transactions between different undertakings. If such undertakings are the same, Article 4(3) of the MCO will always apply: the parties must notify all transactions. The time frame is 2 years.

The other scenario which is not covered by Article 4 (3) MCO concerns transactions that do not necessarily involve the same parties. Usually such transactions are of a preparatory nature and aim at transferring control from one undertaking to another. Because the control is temporary and not on a lasting basis, it will be considered as a preparatory step to the acquisition of a lasting control if the transactions are linked and take place within 1 year. Two situations have been clarified by the COMCO's Secretariat:[99]

– Acquisition of common control in view of acquisition of exclusive control. There is one single transaction if common control is exercised during a transitional

[95] Article 4 (3) MCO.

[96] Commission Consolidated Jurisdictional Notice under Council Regulation 139/2004 on the control of concentrations between undertakings, OJ 2008, C 95, p. 1, Sects. 1.4 and 1.5.

[97] Articles 4(3) and 9 CartA, Article 1, 2 and 3 MCO.

[98] See Sect. 6.2 above, in particular the discussion of the COMCO decision in SWICA/ProVAG/PROVITA, LPC 2013/2, paras 50–51.

[99] Notice on concentrations from the Secretariat, para 6.

Table 6.1 Interdependent transactions

	Transactions between the same undertakings	Transactions between same or different undertakings
Rule	Article 4 (3) MCO	Practice COMCO
Conditions	Same undertakings involved as buyer, seller or target in different transactions	Same or different undertakings, transitional acquisition of common or exclusive control in view of acquiring subsequent exclusive or common control, and contractual provisions that show the link between transactions
Duration	2 years	1 year
Consequence	Notifiable concentrations	Notifiable concentrations

period of 1 year and a legally binding agreement prepares the transition to exclusive control.[100]

– Acquisition of exclusive control in view of transferring part of the participation to another company, preparing therefore the acquisition of joint control over the same target.[101] In a case were transactions were signed simultaneously, the COMCO's Secretariat considered that the first transaction concerning the acquisition of exclusive control on a target company is not part of the following second set of transactions aiming at transferring a shareholding to two other buyers, in view of exercising joint control over the target company. The turnover of the (exclusive) buyer and of the target in the first transaction did not reach the notification thresholds, and therefore the first transaction was not notifiable, nor would it be subject to the stand still obligation. The second set of transactions whereby the first buyer would transfer some of the shares to the two other buyers reached the notification thresholds and was therefore notifiable and subject to the standstill obligation. The reasoning behind is that from the standpoint of the duty to notify, considering both transactions as a single one would not make a difference.[102] In the scenario submitted for opinion of the COMCO's Secretariat, the ex-ante control over the acquisition of joint control by the three undertakings could be exercised during the notification of the second transaction, however, the opinion of the COMCO Secretariats simply means that there is no standstill obligation for the first transaction, but that if the second transaction is not cleared, the commercial risk is borne by the first buyer who acquires exclusive control.

[100] Notice on concentrations from the Secretariat, paras 5 and 6.

[101] See Advice from the COMCO Secretariat, LPC 2017/3, p. 407.

[102] Idem, p. 409.

6.7 Substantial Assessment

6.7.1 Introduction

According to Article 10 (2) and (3) CartA, the COMCO may prohibit a concentration or authorise it subject to conditions and obligations if the investigation indicates that the concentration:

(a) creates or strengthens a dominant position liable to eliminate effective competition; and
(b) does not improve the conditions of competition in another market such that the harmful effects of the dominant position can be outweighed.

In assessing the effects of a concentration on the effectiveness of competition, the COMCO also takes account of any market developments and the position of the undertakings in relation to international competition.[103]

The dominant position is central to the assessment: the concentration must first create or strengthen a dominant position. However, the dominant position to which the provision refers must be capable of eliminating effective competition. The Federal Supreme Court has confirmed that the condition for intervention is the creation or the strengthening of a "qualified" dominant position, which is a stricter standard for intervention than the concept of dominant position used in abuse of dominance cases.[104] Following the interpretation of the Cartel Act by the FSC, the COMCO may prohibit or impose conditions and obligations only where the concentration creates a "qualified" dominant position on the market, enabling the new entity to eliminate competition. The elimination of competition is a criterion used by the FSC to assess whether there is actual or potential competition in the market: it is only in the event the concentration eliminates all actual or potential competition that the concentration may be prohibited or cleared with remedies.[105] As mentioned above, the Federal Council submitted a bill to parliament in May 2023 to introduce the SLC test.

On the standard of proof, the FSC has clarified that assessment of future market developments necessarily involves assumptions about the future; such hypothetical assumptions and forecasts are by their nature difficult to prove and are partly based on general experience.[106]

[103] Article 10 para 4 CartA.

[104] FSC, judgment of 13 February 2007, 2A.325/2006, *Swissgrid*, pt. 6.3.

[105] FSC, judgment of 13 February 2007, 2A.325/2006, *Swissgrid*, pt. 6.4.

[106] FSC, judgment of 22 February 2007, 2A.327/2006, *Berner Zeitung AG/Tamedia AG*, para 5.4.

6.7.2 *Creation or Strengthening of a Dominant Position*

Market Definition The starting point of the assessment is the definition of a relevant product and geographical market. It is for this reason that Article 11 MCO includes a definition of the product and geographical markets, which is used as a standard definition also in antirust cases. According to the definition, "the product market comprises all those goods or services that are regarded as interchangeable by consumers on the one hand and by suppliers on the other hand with regard to their characteristics and intended use."[107] Both demand side and supply side substitution are taken into account, although the demand side substitution is the decisive factor in defining the relevant product market. The geographic market is defined as "the area in which on the one hand consumers purchase and on the other hand suppliers sell the goods or services that constitute the product market."[108]

Dominant Position According to the Cartel Act, the dominant undertakings are one or more undertakings in a given relevant market which, as suppliers or consumers, are able to behave to an appreciable extent independently of the other participants (competitors, suppliers or consumers) in the market.[109] The reference to "one and more undertakings" allows for the possibility of covering both single and collective dominance.

The additional condition of elimination of competition has led the Federal Supreme Court to acknowledge that the concept of dominant position under Article 10 CartA uses a stricter definition of dominant position compared to Article 7 CartA on abusive conduct,[110] meaning that the threshold would be higher to find a dominant position in view of the merger control. It is even higher than what was the case under the previous EU dominance test of Regulation 4046/89. The path chosen by the Cartel Act is thus differs fundamentally from the common wisdom of merger control as applied in EU and the United States, which aims to prevent the rapid acquisition of market power by means other than the internal growth, and therefore uses a lower threshold for finding dominance in merger control than in abuse of dominance. The acquisition of market power through internal growth is accepted as an efficient growth that is worth preserving, as opposed to selective mergers that can increase market power to the detriment of a well-functioning market.

Such a condition of "qualified" dominance leaves less room for covering situations where the merger does not lead to a prominent market position or where the merger leads to conglomerate or vertical negative effects without adding market shares. Theoretically, the enforcement gap in Switzerland is larger than the gap that existed in the EU prior to the adoption of Regulation 139/2004. The perceived gap did not prevent the prohibition of the merger between the second and third telecom

[107] Article 11 (a) MCO.

[108] Article 11 (b) MCO.

[109] Article 4(2) CartA.

[110] FSC, judgment of 13 February 2007, 2A.325/2006, *Swissgrid*, pt. 6.3.

mobile operators which, without exceeding the market shares of the main operator, increased the risk of collective dominance of the duopoly that would prevail in the market.[111] Similarly, the "qualified" dominance was not an obstacle to the prohibition of the two largest companies in the online ticketing market.[112]

6.7.2.1 Single-Firm Dominance

Single dominance results from the creation of a preeminent market position which, together with other factors such as barriers to entry and low countervailing power of customers, would allow the new entity to behave independently of its competitors and customers. The closer substitutes are the products or services of the parties, the greater the risk of price increases after the merger. Single firm dominance refers therefore to unilateral effects.

The main criteria for the preeminent market position is market shares addition or overlapping of the merging parties. High market shares do not establish a presumption a dominance but are an indication thereof.[113] As established in the case law pertaining to the abuse of dominance, a market share of more than 50% is considered as a critical threshold.[114] Market concentration is also a criterion used to assess actual competition. The COMCO refers regularly to the values and delta of HHI used by the EU Commission. Other factors, such as exclusivity agreements, may strengthen the parties' position in the market. [115] Potential competition can have a disciplining effect on the ability of the new entity to behave independently if there is a certain probability of entry of sufficient scale within a period of 2–3 years. Barriers to entry are another criterion to be considered.

In 2017, the COMCO prohibited the concentration between Ticketcorner and Starticket.[116] The concentration would have combined the main providers of third party online ticketing services, with market shares of approximately 60% and 30%. The two remaining competitors had a market share of approximately 10%. In terms of market concentration, the HHI of approximately 4500 would have increased to at 7500 after the concentration, with a value of the ΔHHI between 3000 and 3500. Starticket was the only complete alternative to Ticketcorner for counterparties, and

---

[111] COMCO, decision of 19 April 2010, *France Télécom SA/Sunrise Communications AG*, LPC 2010/3, p. 499.

[112] COMCO, decision of 22 May 2017, *Ticketcorner Holding AG/Tamedia AG/Ticketcorner AG/Starticket AG*, LPC 2018/3, p. 616.

[113] COMCO, decision of 22 May 2017, *Ticketcorner Holding AG/Tamedia AG/Ticketcorner AG/Starticket AG,* LPC 2018/3, p. 616, para 272.

[114] FSC, judgment of 29 June 2012, 2C_484/2010, Publigroupe, ATF/BGE 139 I 72, para 9.3.3.2. COMCO, decision of 22 May 2017, *Ticketcorner Holding AG/Tamedia AG/Ticketcorner AG/Starticket AG*, LPC 2018/3, p. 616, para 272.

[115] COMCO, decision of 22 May 2017, *Ticketcorner Holding AG/Tamedia AG/Ticketcorner AG/Starticket AG*, LPC 2018/3, p. 616, paras 282 ff.

[116] Idem.

this alternative would have disappeared as a result of the merger. The other players were not able to exert a similar disciplining effect. Although online ticketing has grown in importance and physical stores were not a barrier to entry, there remained other structural and strategic barriers to entry that did not allow for the disciplining effect of new potential entrants.

6.7.2.2 Collective Dominance

Collective dominance has been assessed very early in the practice of the COMCO. [117] In 2010, the COMCO prohibited the merger between the second and third mobile phone operators on the grounds that the merger would create collective dominance with Swisscom, the first mobile phone operator in Switzerland. [118] The lowest retail prices in the market were systematically applied by Sunrise, one of the merging parties. The merger would have created the second largest mobile operator with a market share of 35–40% and the largest operator with a market share of 55–60%. The merger would increase technological and cost symmetries between the two remaining operators in the market, market transparency and the potential for retaliation. Counterparties such as MVNO operators or end-users would not be able to exercise countervailing market power. High investment costs and the availability of spectrum meant that market entry was very high. This made collusion more than likely. In 2019, the merger between Sunrise and UPC, a cable operator, was assessed for collective dominance, which the COMCO rejected. The asymmetries between the new entity and Swisscom were too important to allow collective dominance. [119]

6.7.3 *Elimination of Effective Competition*

It remains contentious to what extent the elimination of competition constitutes a separate and meaningful criterion. The COMCO has always taken the view that the elimination of competition does not bring additional assessment criteria, different from those already taken into account in the dominance assessment. To some extent, the Federal Supreme Court confirms such a position, by stating that the dominant

[117] COMCO, decision of 20 April 1998, *Revisuisse Price Waterhouse/STG-Coopers & Lybrand*, RPW 1998/2, p. 214. COMCO, decision of 20 April 1998, UBS/SBV, LPC 1998/2, p. 278; COMCO, decision of 7 September 1998, *Bell/SEG*, RPW 1998/3, p. 392. COMCO, decision of 3 September 2007, *Migros/Denner*, LPC 2008/1, p. 129. COMCO, decision of 18 Augusts 2008, *Heineken/Eichhof*, LPC 2008/3, p. 422.

[118] COMCO decision of 19 April 2010, *France Télécom SA/Sunrise Communications AG*, LPC 2010/3, p. 499.

[119] COMCO, decision of 23 September 2019, *Sunrise/Liberty Global*, LPC 2020/2, p. 759, paras 575 ff.

position must entail the risk of elimination of competition;[120] the criterion foresees therefore a mere *possibility* to eliminate competition, and not an actual or highly probable elimination of competition:[121] the dominant position should give the *possibility* to the new entity to exclude actual competitors or impede the entry of new ones on the market.[122]

In assessing the case, the Federal Supreme Court confirmed however the detailed assessment of the appeal commission on each (newly defined) relevant markets that resulted in denying the elimination of competition: first, the causality criterion requires that the concentration must have an impact on competition, which is not the case if there was no competition in the market before the concentration.[123] Second, competition is not eliminated if there is a remaining actual competition in the market, or the possibility of potential competition.[124] However, the circumstances discussed by the Federal Supreme Court are not different from those that are already investigated while assessing the creation or strengthening of a dominant position.

Third, the Federal Supreme Court confirmed the distinction between prohibition and approval with conditions and obligations: in the event the conditions and obligations would prevent the elimination of competition, prohibition is not an option. The COMCO does not have the choice between prohibiting and accepting conditions and obligations but should approve the latter. The FSC confirmed the quashing of the prohibition by the appeal entity and the authorisation under certain conditions based on the argument that the conditions ensured that the competition was not eliminated.[125]

The assessment of two subsequent prohibited mergers does not take into account additional factors or other criteria for assessing the elimination of competition. Individual or collective dominance is used to show that competition in the market is likely to be eliminated. [126] The two prohibitions were either not challenged before

[120] FSC, judgment of 13 February 2007, 2A.325/2006, *Swissgrid*, para 6.3.

[121] FSC, judgment of 22 February 2007, 2A.327/2006, *Berner Zeitung AG/Tamedia AG*, para 6.4; FSC, judgment of 13 February 2007, 2A.325/2006 *Swissgrid*, para 6.

[122] FSC, judgment of 22 February 2007, 2A.327/2006, *Berner Zeitung AG/Tamedia AG*, para 6.4.

[123] FSC, judgment of 13 February 2007, 2A.325/2006 *Swissgrid*, paras 6.3 and 8.3 (the case concerned the acquisition of control on the national grid, which was a natural monopoly and consequently the undertakings concerned were not in competition for access to the only available grid).

[124] FSC, judgment of 22 February 2007, 2A.327/2006, *Berner Zeitung AG/Tamedia AG*, para 6.5.

[125] Idem.

[126] COMCO, decision of 22 May 2017, *Ticketcorner Holding AG/Tamedia AG/Ticketcorner AG/Starticket AG*, LPC 2018/3, p. 616, paras 376 ff. COMCO, decision of 19 April 2010, *France Télécom SA/Sunrise Communications AG*, LPC 2010/3, p. 499, paras 382 ff.

the FAC[127] or dismissed because of lack of standing.[128] Consequently, there remain uncertainties on the scope of the condition of elimination of competition.

6.7.4 Competition on Other Domestic or International Markets

Competition on Other Markets The harmful effects resulting from the creation or strengthening of a dominant position liable to eliminate competition can be balanced by improvements of conditions of competition in other markets which have a positive impact in Switzerland.[129] This means that a concentration cannot be prohibited if it improves the conditions of competition in another market such that the harmful effects of the dominant position can be outweighed. The concept of "improvements" is larger than efficiency gains and could encompass in theory any improvement in the bargaining position of the parties or any positive impact on the structure of other markets. Efficiency gains alone are not sufficient to outweigh the creation or strengthening of a dominant position; efficiency gains must lead to an improvement in competition in another market. [130] An improvement of the competitive situation in other markets requires that the efficiency gains also benefit competitors and are passed on upstream or downstream. Economic gains for the merging parties alone (e.g. higher margins) in other markets are not sufficient. [131]

COMCO is generally sceptical in accepting the argument of improvements in other markets.[132] By contrast ACCI, the former appeal commission, has quashed a COMCO decision approving a concentration in electricity markets under conditions and obligations holding that the transaction was able to improve the conditions of concerned undertakings in the international energy trading market, which in turn would have positive effects in Switzerland.[133] Such positive effects would offset any negative effects in the electricity transmission market in Switzerland. The Federal Administrative Court that have replaced ACCI has not had the occasion to opine on the issue.

In 2019, The Commission cleared a merger that would have eliminated effective competition in the market for transhipment services for containers, swap bodies and semi-trailers for rail/rail and ship/rail transhipment in import/export traffic to/from

[127] COMCO, decision of 19 April 2010, *France Télécom SA/Sunrise Communications AG*, LPC 2010/3, p. 499. The appeal was submitted but later withdrawn by the parties.

[128] FAC, judgment of 3 Mai 2018, B-3871/2017, *Ticketcorner Holding AG v COMCO.*

[129] Article 10(1)(b) CartA.

[130] COMCO, decision of 27 May 2019, *SBB/Hupac/Rethmann/GBN*, LPC 2020/2, p. 658, para 678.

[131] Idem, para 681.

[132] See for instance COMCO, decision of 6 March 2006, *Emmi AG/Aargauer Zentralmolkerei AG AZM*, LPC 2006/2, p. 261, paras 169–172.

[133] ACCI, decision of 1 Mai 2006, *Aare-Tessin AG*, LPC 2006/2, p. 310, para 5.

the Rhine basin, because the merger would have improved the competitive situation in the markets for import/export combined transport by rail, import/export wagon-load block trains by rail and import/export container, swap body and semi-trailer operator services by rail. [134]

International Competition In assessing the effects of a concentration on the effectiveness of competition, the COMCO also takes account of any market developments and the position of the undertakings in relation to international competition.[135] The COMCO considers in general that international competition is taken into account in the definition of geographical markets, and therefore no additional assessment is required.[136]

Neither criterion has an equivalent in EU merger control regulations.

6.7.5 *Efficiencies*

The COMCO has considered economic efficiencies resulting from the concentration in several cases. In *Batrec/Recymet*, the COMCO approved a merger to monopoly based on the existence of economies of scale in production, which explained the difficulties of having two companies in the field of battery recycling in Switzerland.[137] Although the merger was cleared by applying the failing company defence theory, the COMCO recognised the merger to monopoly was the most efficient solution in the market given the importance of economies of scale. In *France Télécom/Sunrise*, the COMCO held that efficiency gains may be taken into account in the assessment under Article 10(2)(a) CartA if such efficiencies are liable to avoid the elimination of competition resulting from a dominant position.[138] The efficiency test would assess the trade-off between anti-competitive effects (in the form of price increases) and pro-competitive effects (in the form of prices decrease).

In the case of GBN, efficiencies were taken into account in the assessment of the improvement in other markets. These efficiencies outweighed the elimination of competition. [139]

---

[134] COMCO, decision of 27 May 2019, *SBB/Hupac/Rethmann/GBN*, LPC 2020/2, p. 658, paras 703 ff.

[135] Article 10 (4) CartA.

[136] See for instance COMCO, decision of 7 September 2009, Tamedia/PPSR, LPC 2009/3, p. 245, para 295.

[137] COMCO, *Batrec AG—Recymet SA*, LPC 1999/1, p. 174.

[138] COMCO, decision of 19 April 2010, *France Télécom SA/Sunrise Communications AG*, LPC 2010/3, p. 499, para 409.

[139] COMCO, decision of 27 May 2019, *SBB/Hupac/Rethmann/GBN,* LPC 2020/2, p. 658.

6.7.6 Failing Company Defence

The COMCO has applied very early the theory of the failing company defence.[140] The conditions that were applied follow those used by the EU Commission. As a matter of principle, the economic difficulties of an undertaking cannot justify a merger, unless the circumstances of the case show that the concentration is not the cause of the market share overlap due to the fact that one of the undertakings would disappear from the market regardless of the concentration. There is no causation between the concentration and the overlap if all the following criteria are fulfilled:[141]

1. One of the concerned parties would disappear from the market in the near future;
2. The other party would benefit of all or significant parts of market shares of the undertaking exiting the market;
3. There is no other less anti-competitive solution than the notified merger.

On the first criteria, the exit from the market may have internal or external origins. Internal financial difficulties that could not be overcome by capital injections or internal restructuring measures show the irreversible financial situation.[142] Over indebtedness that arises during the procedure and is the consequence of liquidity problems could also be sufficient.[143] External factors are related to the market conditions, such as a saturation market in decline,[144] the existence of economies of scale which leads to natural monopoly,[145] or a market in transition.[146] All the factual elements must be documented, simple allegations are not sufficient.

Whether the other party to the concentration would be the main beneficiary depends on several factual elements, but it remains an assessment of probabilities. Limited number of competitors in the market and close substitutability[147] between the products of the merging parties indicate a high probability that the customers of the exiting company will be served in the near future by the other notifying party.

The third criteria aim at exploring whether other opportunities exist: other shareholders willing to invest in the company or another buyer capable of maintaining the business of the failing company as an independent force in the

140 See COMCO, decision of 1 December 1997, *Le Temps*, LPC 1998/1, p. 39.

141 COMCO, decision of 1 December 1997, *Le Temps*, LPC 1998/1, p. 39, para 71; COMCO, decision of 6 March 2006, *Emmi AG/Aargauer Zentralmolkerei AG AZM*, LPC 2006/2, p. 261, paras 174 ff.

142 See COMCO, decision of 1 December 1997, *Le Temps*, LPC 1998/1, p. 39, para 74.

143 COMCO, decision of 6 March 2006, *Emmi AG/Aargauer Zentralmolkerei AG AZM*, LPC 2006/2, p. 261, para 180.

144 See COMCO, decision of 1 December 1997, *Le Temps*, LPC 1998/1, p. 39, para 73.

145 COMCO, *Batrec AG—Recymet SA*, LPC 1999/1, p. 174.

146 COMCO, decision of 6 March 2006, *Emmi AG/Aargauer Zentralmolkerei AG AZM*, LPC 2006/2, p. 261, para 181 (on the restructuring of the milk market in view of the abolition of the guaranteed price system).

147 See COMCO, decision of 1 December 1997, *Le Temps*, LPC 1998/1, p. 39, para 77.

market. It will be also assessed whether the production facilities would exit the market in case of no merger.[148] The assessment is factual. Once the assessment shows no other opportunity than the notified merger, it is in the framework of this criteria that the COMCO sees a leeway of imposing remedies to the parties, in order to ensure that the transaction causes as little damage as possible to competition.[149]

The failing division defence was applied in one media merger. The COMCO applied the same criteria but announced that the standard is higher to show that the criteria would be fulfilled.[150] In particular, the parties had to submit substantial documentation to demonstrate fulfilment of the first criteria.

6.7.7 Remedies

The Competition Commission accepts remedies or measures that allow to set off or eliminate negative competitive effects of the merger. Remedies can be accepted during both the preliminary and the in-depth assessment. The Cartel Act provides for an explicit legal basis in the in-depth assessment: conditions and obligations are foreseen as an alternative to prohibition.[151] At the preliminary phase of 1 month, the COMCO will acknowledge the commitments of the parties in its communication of non-opposition notified to the parties.[152] Finally, the COMCO may attach conditions and obligations to decisions that authorise preliminary implementation of the concentration.[153] Remedies must abide to general principles of administrative law, namely they must comply with the public interest and be proportional. The public interest requires not to allow concentrations that create or strengthen a dominant position enabling the new entity to eliminate competition. The measures must remedy such negative effects, no more and no less.

The COMCO has accepted in the past behavioural and structural remedies:

- Structural remedies.
- Measures that ensure the independence of the target or of the joint venture vis-à-vis the buyer or parent entities. In the case Le Temps, to ensure the independence of the president of the board of the joint venture editing a newspaper, the clearance was accompanied with the obligation that such president

[148] COMCO, decision of 6 March 2006, *Emmi AG/Aargauer Zentralmolkerei AG AZM*, LPC 2006/2, p. 261.

[149] See COMCO, decision of 1 December 1997, *Le Temps*, LPC 1998/1, p. 39, para 82.

[150] COMCO, decision of 7 September 2009, *Tamedia/PPSR*, LPC 2009/3, p. 245.

[151] According to Article 10 (2) CartA, the Competition Commission may prohibit a concentration or authorise it subject to conditions and obligations if the investigation indicates that the concentration creates or strengthens a dominant position liable to eliminate effective competition.

[152] See for instance COMCO, decision of 9 September 2016, *PostFinance AG/SIX Payment Services AG/TWINT AG*.

[153] Article 16 para 2 MCO.

should not be a board member of any group company of the buyer.[154] In addition, any change in capital structure and voting shares of the joint venture would be subject to COMCO approval.

- Behavioural remedies. The commitments in the TWINT transaction included open access to the payment system TWINT at all levels (issuing as well as acquiring) on a non-discrimination basis and a commitment not to enter into exclusive agreements at all levels.[155]

6.7.8 Ancillary Restraints

Ancillary restraints (or ancillary agreements) are arrangements that are directly related and necessary to the implementation of the transaction.[156] The parties must identify separately such arrangement in the notification and request that such arrangements be treated ancillary to the notified transaction and therefore covered by the authorisation or clearance.[157] The COMCO follows the EU Commission's approach and refers regularly to the Commission Notice on ancillary restrictions.[158]

The arrangements that are not directly related and necessary to the implementation of the transaction must be assessed separately under Article 5 CartA.[159] In addition, arrangements that are unclear[160] or which effects cannot be assessed *ex ante* will not be considered as ancillary[161] and therefore will not benefit from the privilege of the non-opposition to the transaction. Such arrangements are not covered by the non-opposition communication or decision. However, the fact that such arrangement cannot be covered by the clearance does not mean that they are deemed to restrict competition;[162] it simply means that the COMCO does not give an assurance to companies on their lawfulness. Also, the arrangements for which the

---

[154] See COMCO, decision of 1 December 1997, *Le Temps*, LPC 1998/1, p. 39, paras 87 and 88.

[155] COMCO, communication of 9 September 2016, *PostFinance AG/SIX Payment Services AG/TWINT AG*, paras 127 ff.

[156] See for instance COMCO, communication of 10 August 2010, *HSDG/Maersk Line A/S*, LPC 2017/4, p. 590, paras 294 ff.

[157] COMCO, Note on the notification and evaluation practice of mergers of 21 October 2014, para 7 of Notification Form.

[158] Commission Notice on restrictions directly related and necessary to concentrations, OJ 2005 C 56, p. 24.

[159] See for instance COMCO, communication of 10 August 2010, *HSDG/Maersk Line A/S*, LPC 2017/4, p. 590, paras 294 ff.

[160] See for instance COMCO, communication of 19 February 2016, *Lekkerland (Schweiz) AG/Grosshandelsgeschäft der Contadis AG*, LPC 2016/2, p. 555, para 27.

[161] See for instance COMCO, communication of 9 September 2016, *PostFinance AG/SIX Payment Services AG/TWINT AG*, LPC 2016/4, p. 1062, 1077.

[162] COMCO, communication of 29 July 2015, *Axel Springer Schweiz/Ringier*, LPC 2015/3, p. 430, para 86.

parties have not requested expressly to be considered as ancillary to the notified transaction are not covered automatically by the non-opposition communication or decision. The parties have an interest therefore to clearly identify and describe the scope of the arrangements that they would like to be covered by the notification.

Non-competition obligations on the seller are justified for periods of up to 3 years, when the seller transfers both the business and its related goodwill and know-how. If no know-how is transferred, the non-compete obligations are justified for periods of up to 2 years.[163] Non-compete obligations extending to the purchase or investment in competing products, non-solicitation[164] and confidentiality clauses are assessed similarly.

Geographically, the non-compete clauses must be limited to the area in which the seller has offered the relevant products or services before the transfer, and to territories for which the seller has made investments in order to enter at the time of the transaction. The new products and markets shall be clearly identified in the notification.[165] In relation to products covered, non-competition clauses must remain limited to products and services forming the economic activity of the undertaking transferred, including updates as well as products and services under development. Procurement, delivery and service agreements between the seller and the buyer in the context of acquisition of exclusive control are considered as necessary and therefore ancillary for a limited period of 5 years, aiming to ensure the buyer continues the operations and at the same giving the buyer the incentive to become independent from the seller. Procurement and delivery services of a longer period with the objective of ensuring the same quantity and quality of products to be delivered to final customers will not be considered as necessary and ancillary to the transaction.[166]

For joint ventures, non-competes are accepted for the duration of the joint-venture. Both non-compete obligations on parent companies and on the joint entity can be considered as ancillary to the transaction.[167] Non-compete obligations on the joint entity would be assessed in accordance with the general criteria as well as the conditions applicable to non-compete clauses between parent companies.[168] Procurement, delivery and service agreements between parent companies and the joint entity on existing quantities of products or services are considered as ancillary to the

---

[163] See for instance COMCO, communication of 10 August 2010, *HSDG/Maersk Line A/S*, LPC 2017/4, p. 590, para 299; cf. Commission Notice on restrictions directly related and necessary to concentrations, OJ 2005 C 56, p. 24, para 20.

[164] COMCO, communication of 12 January 2017, *Tech Data/Avnet TS*, LPC 2017/1, p. 110, para 62.

[165] See the discussion in COMCO, communication of 30 June 2017, *Gilden Holding BV/Oel-Pool AG/shop and more AG*, PLC 2017/3, p. 495, para 21.

[166] COMCO, communication of 19 February 2016, Lekkerland (Schweiz) AG/Grosshandelsgeschäft der Contadis AG, LPC 2016/2, p. 555, paras 25ff.

[167] COMCO, communication of 30 June 2017, *Gilden Holding BV/Oel-Pool AG/shop and more AG*, PLC 2017/3, p. 495, paras 20ff.

[168] Idem, para 22.

transaction for a period of 5 years.[169] For instance, the provision of legal, IT and HR services or the facilities enabled the joint venture to focus on the core activities during the initial period of 5 years and therefore ancillary to the transaction, however a much longer duration initially foreseen by the parties was not covered by the clearance.[170] The COMCO clarified that such services could be provided by a parent company for a longer period, but that the clearance of the joint venture under merger control provisions allows only for a limited period assurance.[171]

The creation of a joint team between one of the controlling companies and the joint venture which aim at setting a common strategy was considered as an ancillary restraint to the acquisition of joint control.[172]

Licensing of trademarks and domain names to the joint entity is considered as essential and therefore ancillary to the transaction.[173]

6.8 Timetable and Procedure

6.8.1 Notification and Start of the Review Periods, Preliminary Assessment

Information to be included in the notification are provided at Article 11 MCO and the explanatory note of the COMCO.[174] Upon request by the parties, the Secretariat may accept a simplified notification.[175] The agreed form of the simplified notification will be considered as complete, which will allow the kick off of the review period. This will be the case in the event the COMCO has previously investigated the relevant market concerned by the concentration and has therefore good knowledge thereof or a joint venture is planned to be active in a new market which is in development.[176] Concentrations that are notified to the European Commission or other authorities may also benefit from the simplified notification system. To simplify the exchange of information between the European Commission and the COMCO's Secretariat,

[169] COMCO, communication of 15 March 2017, *Post/SBB/SwissSign*, PLC 2017/2, p. 299, para 164; COMCO, communication of 29 July 2015, *Axel Springer Schweiz/Ringier*, LPC 2015/3, p. 430, para 73.

[170] COMCO, communication of 29 July 2015, *Axel Springer Schweiz/Ringier*, LPC 2015/3, p. 430, para 84.

[171] Idibem.

[172] COMCO, communication of 24 Mai 2017, *BSL AG/Transport Ferroviaire Holding SAS*, PLC 2017/3, p. 469.

[173] COMCO, communication of 29 July 2015, *Axel Springer Schweiz/Ringier*, LPC 2015/3, p. 430, paras 71ff.

[174] Explanatory note on merger notification.

[175] Article 12 MCO.

[176] Explanatory note on merger notification, para 5.

companies may execute a waiver of confidentiality.[177] The Secretariat may nevertheless request at any time other information from the parties, after the confirmation of receipt of complete notification.[178]

The Secretariat confirms the receipt of notification within 10 days, by confirming that the notification is complete or by requesting additional information.[179] The Secretariat will confirm that the notification is complete the moment when the notifying undertakings supplement the notification according to the requests of the Secretariat. The review period of 1 month starts on the day following the receipt of the complete notification.[180] According to a preliminary assessment of the notification, the Secretariat may send questionnaires to customers and competitors of the new entity, however this will not be the case if the concentration clearly is not liable to raise competitive issues.

The duty of the notifying parties to submit information does not end with the complete notification. The notifying parties must provide additional information in two situations. The first case is when material changes have occurred since the notification, either on the transaction itself or of the circumstances surrounding the transaction described in the notification.[181] In this case the notifying parties have an obligation to submit such information without delay. The quality of the changes will be determinant for deciding whether such change will have an effect on the review periods: the Secretariat may consider that the notification was complete from the receipt of the information on the material change and, as a consequence, may start the review period of 1 month on the day after the Secretariat receives the information on the material changes. This means practically that the parties have re-notified the concentration. If the decision is taken after the opening of an in-depth assessment, it is up to the COMCO to take a formal decision to postpone the starting of the 4-month period pertaining to the second phase assessment.

The second situation is when the Secretariat requests additional information and documents.[182] The Secretariat may ask any kind of information which is relevant for the assessment, at any time during the preliminary or in-depth assessment. Such request for information does not have the effect of restarting or postponing the timetable for the assessment of the concentration.

---

[177] Explanatory note on merger notification, para 10; Article 7(3) of the Agreement between the European Union and the Swiss Confederation concerning cooperation on the application of their competition laws, OJ 2014 L 347, p. 3.

[178] Article 15 MCO.

[179] Article 14 MCO.

[180] Article 20 MCO.

[181] Article 21 MCO.

[182] Article 15 MCO.

6.8.2 In-depth Assessment

A special chamber of the COMCO must decide to open an in-depth assessment. This is notified to the parties the last day of the 1-month period at the latest.[183] The in-depth assessment is carried out if the preliminary assessment reveals that the concentration risks creating or strengthening a dominant position.[184] Parties have the possibility to respond to the statement of reasoning (*Beschlussbegründung*) opening of an in-depth inquiry, usually within 10 days, deadline which can be extended.

A short notice on the opening of the in-depth investigation is published in the official journals (FF), and questionnaires are sent to customers and competitors of the new entity. Interested parties may also send unsolicited comments to the COMCO's Secretariat. The COMCO prepares an extended version of the assessment, always in the form of a preliminary assessment which presents the theory of harm and the result of market consultation.[185] During this time, the parties have access to the file and can prepare a response to the assessment of the COMCO.

The in-depth investigation must be completed within 4 months.[186] The COMCO may not suspend the procedure on its own. The term of 4 months can be extended only "for reasons attributable to the undertakings concerned".[187] This is the case where the parties consent to the extension, for example to submit more relevant information for the assessment of the concentration or design remedies. There is no maximum time-limit for the extension.

If no notice is given to undertakings within the 4 months period, the transaction may implement the transaction. The procedure is therefore an opposition procedure, and not an authorisation one. The COMCO usually sends a notice to the parties communicating that it has no objection to the concentration, with the reasoning of the analysis.

6.8.3 Parties to the Procedure and Access to File

In proceedings for the review of concentrations of undertakings, only the undertakings concerned have the rights of parties,[188] and therefore the rights attached to such status. The reason is to allow an efficient and rapid procedure before the COMCO.[189]

The concerned parties have no access to files during the preliminary assessment. The concerned parties have access to file with the opening of an in-depth assessment.

[183] Article 20(2) MCO.

[184] Article 10 (1) CartA.

[185] Vorläufige Beurteilung, évaluation préliminaire.

[186] Article 33 (3) MCO.

[187] Article 33 (3) MCO.

[188] Article 43 (4) CartA.

[189] FSC, judgment of 10 august 1998, *Engel*, ATF/BGE 124 II 499, para 3.a.

The access to file is made electronically if the concerned undertakings consent to it,[190] or physically at the premises of the Secretariat in Bern.

Third parties do not have the status of parties to the procedure and therefore do not have access to file during the assessment of the concentration. After the investigation is closed by the COMCO, third parties may file a request for information on the basis of the Freedom of Information Act.

The Secretariat of the COMCO may exchange information with other competition authorities on the basis of confidentiality waivers given by concerned undertakings. Switzerland has signed two agreements that allow exchange of information: the European Union and Japan. The waiver is a standard practice even for the exchange of information with the European Commission and Japan, even though the COMCO may exchange information without the consent of the parties under certain conditions.

6.8.4 Hearing Before the COMCO

When the COMCO opens an in-depth procedure and the preliminary assessment is confirmed by market participants, the COMCO will send reasons to the parties for comments. The parties have the right to be heard and present their arguments before the COMCO in corpore. This will be also the occasion to explore whether the parties are willing to submit remedies.

6.8.5 Acts Adopted Following an In-depth Assessment

The prior notification system in Switzerland governed by strict deadlines establishes a non-opposition system, in the sense that the concentration is deemed permitted if the COMCO does not communicate or take a decision within the given time frames of respectively one and 4 months. Technically speaking, therefore, the COMCO does not have to authorise the transaction. When the COMCO sends its assessment to the parties before the deadlines by communicating why it doesn't object to the concentration, that communication is commonly considered as an "authorisation" or clearance. Such communisations are not considered as "decisions", which refers to a challengeable act according to APA.

The objection to the concentration is done in two forms: acceptance under conditions and obligations or straightforward prohibition.

[190] Article 26 (1bis) APA.

6.8.5.1 Authorisation Under Conditions and Obligations

Conditions or obligations are ancillary to the main decision and are ordered together with the main decision to authorise the concentration: they are ancillary provisions of the final decision and form part of it.[191] The FSC has clarified that remedies are not the result of a negotiation process, they are not the subject of a public service contract and do not require consensus between the Competition Commission and the concerned undertakings.[192] The parties cannot implement the concentration before fulfilling a condition; the stand still obligations continue to apply until the condition is fulfilled, for example a divestment. Obligations are charges that parties need to fulfil after the implementation of the concentration; the stand still obligation expires with the adoption of the authorisation decision.

However, the fact that conditions and obligations have the status of, and form part of, an administrative order (the decision) does not respond to the question of who is responsible to design the content of the remedies. Contrary to Regulation 139/2004,[193] the Cartel Act does not specify who must design or require the remedies: the COMCO or the notifying parties. This has resulted in difficulties in particular when the parties argue that the proposed concentration will not eliminate competition and, as a consequence, do not submit remedies.

The duty to cooperate of the concerned undertakings cannot form the basis of a duty to submit commitments: indeed, the duty to cooperate exists only insofar as they are obliged to notify their project and to participate in the assessment.[194] However, the FSC goes further by stating that if companies do not want to or are unable to comply with necessary remedies, they must refrain from completing the concentration, just as if the concentration was prohibited.[195] Consequently, by stating the consequences of a failure of the notifying parties to commit to remedies, introduces a duty to proactively find remedies to the issues raised by the Secretariat of the COMCO.

If the notifying parties do not submit or discuss remedies, the question raises whether the COMCO has a duty to find remedies to the transaction and impose them as obligations and conditions, even though the parties do not agree with the suggested remedies prepared by the Secretariat of the COMCO. The Courts have not ruled this issue. The principle of procedural efficiency justifies that the competition authority tries to find out with what conditions the undertakings may live

[191] FSC, judgment of 13 February 2007, 2A.325/2006, *Swissgrid*, pt. 9.2.1.

[192] Idem, pt. 9.2.1.

[193] Cf. Article 6 (2) and 8 (2) of Regulation 139/2002: the expression "following modification by the undertakings concerned" states clearly that remedies must be submitted by the notifying parties. It follows by clarifying that "The Commission may attach to its decision conditions and obligations intended to ensure that the undertakings concerned comply with the commitments they have entered into vis-à-vis the Commission with a view to rendering the concentration compatible with the common market."

[194] FSC, judgment of 13 February 2007, 2A.325/2006, *Swissgrid*, pt. 9.2.1.

[195] Idem, pt. 9.2.2.

with.[196] On the same ground of procedural efficiency, the COMCO must not order remedies that parties are unable or unwilling to implement.

There may be concentrations that eliminate competition and that there are no remedies which can reduce the negative effects on competition. In this case, the COMCO is under no obligation to find or suggest remedies to the parties, to accept the remedies suggested by the parties, or to adopt obligations and conditions in order to allow the merger.

6.8.5.2 Prohibition

Where conditions and obligation are not appropriate, the COMCO may prohibit a concentration. The parties are consequently prohibited to implement the concentration.

6.8.6 Appeals to the Courts

Jurisdiction to Review COMCO Decisions Only the COMCO has the power to review concentrations. The decisions of the COMCO to prohibit or accept a concentration under conditions and obligations may be challenged before the Federal Administrative Court in St Gallen. The rulings of the Federal Administrative Court may be challenged before the FSC in Lausanne.

The Federal Council can grant the concerned parties an exceptional authorisation on grounds of compelling public interests. The request is not an appeal and it can be filed in parallel to the appeal before the Federal Administrative Court.

Acts That Can Be Challenged The following decisions may be challenged separately before the Federal Administrative Court:

- Decision prohibiting the concentration;
- Decision accepting the concentration subject to remedies (conditions or charges);
- Rejection of the request for provisional implementation.

Decisions that refuse access to file, refuse hearing before the COMCO can be challenged together with the final decision.

The opening of an in-depth investigation, the communication of the preliminary assessment of the concentration and the authorisation of the concentration are not considered as individual decisions that affect rights of the concerned undertakings, and therefore cannot be challenged before the Federal Administrative Court.

Parties Who Can Bring an Action Concerned undertakings to a concentration are entitled to bring an action. By contrast, third parties such as competitors,

[196] Idem, pt. 9.2.1.

shareholders, customers or other market participants have no *locus standi* to appeal a COMCO decision. This is because one of the conditions for locus standi before the Federal Administrative Court is that the person should have participated in proceedings before the COMCO,[197] a possibility which is denied to third parties by a special provision in the Cartel Act.[198] Even before the enactment of the ATA, the FSC had denied locus standi to an individual for lack of direct interest, as a shareholder, as a subscriber of one of the newspapers subject to the merger and as the president of the association of friends of such newspaper, holding that in general the case law was strict in requiring an "individual and direct interest" of a third party in a matter.[199] The situation is different in the European Union, where competitors and shareholders have been recognised *locus standi* by EU Courts.

In the case of the prohibition of *Ticketcorner/Starticket* concentration, the Federal Administrative Court denied the interest of the acquirer to bring action alone, because the other notifying party had not joined the appeal. The transaction concerned the acquisition of joint control by the acquirer and the seller to a full function joint venture that would have been created by merging both subsidiaries of the parent companies.[200] The reasoning of the Federal Administrative Court was twofold: on the one hand, the civil consequences of the transaction were suspended by law and an appeal from only one party to the transaction would have the effect of extending the suspension for the other parties, against their will. On the other hand, according to the Federal Administrative Court, the appeal must be raised by all the notifying parties, because they form a community of interests during both the administrative and the appeal procedure. Since the notifying parties have a joint liability to notify, it followed that they have locus standi to appeal a decision only if the appeal is brought by all notifying parties.[201]

Grounds of Appeal In the event a prohibition decision or authorisation on conditions and obligations is successfully challenged before the Federal Administrative Court, the COMCO (SECO) has standing to challenge the FAC judgment before the SFC.[202] The Federal Administrative Court reviews both facts and the points of law. The FSC can review only points of law. Rules of general experience are points of law and can be reviewed by the FSC. Facts on which are based assumptions cannot be

---

[197] According to Article 48 APA on locus standi, "a right of appeal shall be accorded to anyone who: a. has participated or has been refused the opportunity to participate in proceedings before the lower instance; b. has been specifically affected by the contested ruling; and c. has an interest that is worthy of protection in the revocation or amendment of the ruling."

[198] Article 43 para 4 CartA.

[199] FSC, judgment of 10 August 1998, *Engel*, ATF/BGE 124 II 499, paras 3.b and 3.c.

[200] FAC, judgment of 3 Mai 2018, B-3871/2017, *Ticketcorner Holding AG v COMCO*.

[201] FAC, judgment of 3 Mai 2018, B-3871/2017, *Ticketcorner Holding AG v COMCO*, para 54.

[202] See FSC, judgment of 22 February 2007, 2A.327/2006, *Berner Zeitung AG/Tamedia AG*, para 2.6 (on the legitimate interest of the COMCO to bring an action against a decision of the (former) ACCI).

reviewed by the FSC, but it can review whether the consequences drawn by the FAC on such facts are plausible and coherent.[203]

List of Documents

COMCO, Merger notification, notification form and explanatory note of 21 October 2014

Commission Consolidated Jurisdictional Notice under Council Regulation 139/2004 on the control of concentrations between undertakings, OJ 2008, C 95, p. 1

Commission Notice on restrictions directly related and necessary to concentrations, OJ 2005 C 56, p. 24

Council Regulation 139/2004 of 20 January 2004 on the control of concentrations between undertakings, OJ 2004 L 24, p. 1

Federal Act on Administrative Procedure (APA; RS 172.021)

Notice of the Secretariat of the COMCO, Practice regarding the notification and assessment of concentrations of 25 March 2009, para 7 (Notice on concentrations from the Secretariat)

Ordinance on the Control of Concentrations of Undertakings (MCO; RS 251.4)

[203] FSC, judgment of 22 February 2007, 2A.327/2006, *Berner Zeitung AG/Tamedia AG*, para 5.4.

Chapter 7 Sanctions, Leniency and Amicable Settlements

7.1 Introduction

The Cartel Act provides for administrative sanctions against undertakings and criminal sanctions against individuals. The main administrative sanctions are imposed on undertakings for participation in unlawful agreements and abuse of dominant position, as explained in Sect. 7.2 below. This chapter also discusses leniency applications (Sect. 7.2.4), which can lead to immunity from fines, and amicable settlements (Sect. 7.3). Other administrative sanctions can be imposed for failure to comply with the decisions of the COMCO and its Secretariat, and these are presented in Sect. 7.4.1 below. Criminal sanctions concern mainly intentional failure to notify a concentration or to comply with decisions of the COMCO, which are explained in Sect. 7.4.2 below.

7.2 Sanctions for Unlawful Restraints of Competition

According to Article 49a (1) CartA, "any undertaking that participates in an unlawful agreement pursuant to Article 5 (3) and (4) or that is dominant and behaves unlawfully pursuant to Article 7 shall be charged up to 10 per cent of the turnover that it achieved in Switzerland in the preceding three financial years." The use of the word "shall" indicates that the fine is mandatory and that COMCO has no discretion not to fine a company found to have participated in an illegal agreement or conduct covered by the provision, which is very different from the discretion enjoyed by the EU Commission and other competition authorities in imposing fines. [1] However, COMCO does have a margin of appreciation when calculating the fine, in particular

[1] Cf. Article 23 Regulation 1/2003.

P. Këllezi, *Competition Law in Switzerland*,
https://doi.org/10.1007/978-3-031-45117-1_7

when setting the basic amount and the reduction for aggravating or mitigating circumstances.

Intent is not a condition for administrative sanctions against undertakings, unlike criminal sanctions against natural persons. However, fault or misconduct is a prerequisite for the imposition of a sanction under Article 49a CartA. In a recent ruling, the FSC reaffirmed that:

> The abuse of a dominant position constitutes the objective element of an infringement of the Cartel Act, to which a subjective element is added, even if the wording of Art. 49a para. 1 Cartel Act does not expressly state this. This does not necessarily mean that the responsibility for the violation of the Cartel Act has to be attributed to a specific person, but may take the form of a lack of diligence on the part of the undertaking in relation to what could objectively be expected from any undertaking in a similar situation under the law. Thus, when an undertaking engages in established anti-competitive behaviour, it is generally also in breach of its objective duty of care, since undertakings must be aware of and keep themselves informed about the provisions of the Cartel Act, related practice and relevant publications. [2]

The Swiss Federal Council has adopted an ordinance, the CASO, [3] that regulates the assessment criteria for the imposition of sanctions in accordance with Article 49a (1) CartA, the conditions and the procedure for obtaining complete or partial immunity from sanctions in accordance with Article 49a (2) CartA and the conditions and the procedure for notifications under Article 49a (3)(a) CartA. The COMCO Secretariat has published a notice on CASO, [4] an explanatory note on the leniency program [5] and COMCO an explanatory note on the notification of a restriction of competition. [6] The later notices include a form for leniency applications and for the notification of restrictions of competition.

7.2.1 Restraints of Competition and Undertakings Subject to Fines

Only unlawful agreements within the meaning of Article 5(3) and (4) of the Cartel Act are subject to fines, regardless of whether the presumption of elimination of

[2]FSC, judgment of 9 May 2023, 2C_395/2021, *Naxoo*, para 11.1.

[3]Ordinance on Sanctions imposed for Unlawful Restraints of Competition (Cartel Act Sanctions Ordinance, CASO; RS 251.5).

[4]COMCO Secretariat, Remarks on the Ordinance on Fines (Remarks on CASO). Available at https://www.weko.admin.ch/weko/en/home/rechtliches_dokumentation/communications.html. Accessed 18 May 2023.

[5]COMCO Secretariat, Explanatory note and form of the Secretariat of 8 September 2014, Leniency program (voluntary report) (Explanatory note on the leniency program).

[6]COMCO, Explanatory note and form of 21 October 2014, Notification of a restriction on competition.

competition is reversed, as well as conduct that constitutes an abuse of a dominant position within the meaning of Article 7 of the Cartel Act.

Unlawful agreements which substantially restrict or eliminate competition within the meaning of Article 5(1) CartA, without being covered by the scope of Article 5 (3) and (4) CartA, and the abuse of relative market power within the meaning of Article 7 CartA are not subject to direct sanctions or fines. Undertakings participating in such unlawful agreements or abuses of relative market power may be fined only if they do not comply with a final and non-appealable decision of COMCO approving an amicable settlement or prohibiting unlawful conduct, in which case they risk a fine of up to 10% of their turnover in Switzerland in the previous three financial years. [7]

It is therefore crucial to distinguish between agreements that fall within the scope of Article 5(3) and (4) of the CartA and those that do not. Undertakings participating in agreements of the first category risk fines even if the elimination of competition is reversed and the agreement is ultimately assessed under Article 5(1) CartA, unless it is justified on economic efficiency grounds. As of 2022, it will also be important to determine whether the company has relative market power and whether it may ultimately be in a dominant position according to the definition of the relevant market, in which case the undertakings' conduct may be considered abusive and subject to fines.

In *Preispolitik Swisscom ADSL*, [8] the fact that both companies of the group—in the upstream and downstream market—qualify as undertakings within the meaning of Article 49a CartA satisfies the objective constituent element. The subjective constituent element, or fault, is met by the breach of the duty of care in the form of a lack of organization. The proof of a violation of the Cartel Act objectively demonstrates the breach of the duty of care, which is determined by reference to the duties imposed by the Cartel Act on undertakings in a dominant position. [9]

Only legal entities can be fined, not a group of companies or a partnership which does not have legal personality. This is irrespective of the fact that a group of companies is an undertaking within the meaning of Article 2(1) and 49a (1) CartA. Therefore, in the case of a group of companies, only the companies that are constituted as separate legal entities can be the addressees of a COMCO decision and thus be subject to a fine. [10] Formally, the decision should then be communicated to all companies in the group, but this can be a disproportionate burden in the case of proceedings against large groups. [11] The COMCO may therefore address its decision to one or several group companies, generally, to the parent company which has overall control over the group companies involved in the anti-competitive

[7] Article 50 CartA. See Sect. 7.4.1 below.

[8] FSC, judgment of 9 December 2019, 2C_985/2015, ATF/BGE 146 II 217 *Preispolitik Swisscom ADSL.*

[9] See also FSC, judgment of 9 May 2023, 2C_395/2021, *Naxoo*, para 11.1.

[10] FAC, judgment of 16 September 2016, B-581/2012 *Nikon*, para 8.2.6.

[11] FAC, judgment of 4 September 2015, B-7633/2009, *Preispolitik Swisscom ADSL,* paras 69ff.

behaviour. [12] However, a Swiss subsidiary of a foreign group may be the addressee of a decision on a fine, even though it was mainly foreign group companies that restricted imports into Switzerland. [13]

The question has arisen as to whether a fine can be imputed to a successor company that has acquired the infringing company or its assets. COMCO's position is based on a very broad concept of economic continuity, with the consequence that in the case of asset deals, the acquirer of the asset deal could be liable even if the seller is still a company, and that a company could be fined for the whole period before it acquired the assets or shares of another infringing company. The FAC seems to disagree with the broad concept used by the COMCO, stating in one case that "a fine is imputable to an undertaking, but this presupposes that the undertakings are accused of and liable for the imputable conduct. Attribution is based on responsibility - not the other way round. In any event, the imputation criterion of economic continuity is too broad, as it could also be understood as a continuity resulting only from the assets. A complex of assets or individual assets as assets cannot be held responsible for any conduct, and therefore imputability cannot be established in this way". [14]

The FAC confirmed that a fine could be imputed to a new company that had acquired an infringing company because the company that had acquired the infringing company had a shareholding in the new acquirer, [15] and therefore treated it as an internal situation. It had previously refused to extend the acquirer's joint and several liability with the infringing target for the period prior to the acquisition and integration of the group. [16]

To summary, in the case of intra-group restructurings, the situation is rather clear: a broad concept of economic continuity can be applied to share and asset deals, with the consequence that the group is liable to pay the fine and the acquiring company can be imputed the fine or held jointly and severally liable with the former company. The situation is less clear in the case of external corporate restructurings, in particular in relation to asset deals, as not all scenarios have been tested in court, but it can be expected that COMCO will apply the same broad concept of economic continuity to share and asset deals and will seek to impute the entire fine to the acquirer, or at least hold it jointly and severally liable for the entire period.

---

[12] Idem, para 73.

[13] FAC, judgment of 16 September 2016, B-581/2012 *Nikon*, para 8.2.

[14] FAC, judgment of 9 August 2021, B-5130/2019 *Strassenbau Graubünden/Schlub*, para 8.1.3.

[15] FAC, judgment of 9 August 2021, B-5130/2019 *Strassenbau Graubünden/Schlub*, para 8.2.2.

[16] FAC, judgment of 25 June 2018, B-807/2012 *Wettbewerbsabreden im Strassen- und Tiefbau im Kanton Aargau, ERNE*, para 11.4.4.

7.2.2 Legality and ECHR Conformity

Publigroupe [17] was the first occasion on which the FSC considered the imposition of a so-called direct sanction under Article 49a of the Cartel Act, which entered into force on 1 April 2004 and enabled it to lay down certain principles regarding the compatibility of such sanctions with fundamental rights and guarantees. The Court also upheld the imposition of sanctions on an undertaking that had entered into a settlement agreement.

In 2007, the COMCO had imposed a fine of CHF 2.5 million on Publigroupe in 2007 for abuse of a dominant position, while approving an amicable agreement by which Publigroupe, its four subsidiaries and an association of the group companies (ASSP) undertook to amend certain clauses of the ASSP guidelines. The Federal Court upheld the COMCO's decision on the merits. Publigroupe, with a market share of more than 63% and therefore in a dominant position, had abused its dominant position by refusing to commission certain professional intermediaries on the basis of unjustified criteria contained in the ASSP guidelines.

The case is important in that the FSC examined the compatibility of the COMCO's power to impose sanctions with the guarantees of Article 6 (1) and Article 7 (1) ECHR and the corresponding guarantees of Article 30 and 32 of the Swiss Federal Constitution, stating that the direct sanctions of Article 49a para. 1 of the Cartel Act are of a criminal nature. While the COMCO was not an independent and impartial tribunal within the meaning of Article 6 (1) ECHR, the COMCO decisions could be reviewed by the FAC, which has full jurisdiction to review the facts and the law, so that the right to a fair trial is guaranteed at the institutional level in accordance with the *Menarini* case law of the European Court of Human Rights. [18] The FSC therefore confirmed COMCO's power to impose sanctions, although the FAC may exercise some restraint in assessing COMCO's decision on issues requiring technical knowledge.

With regard to the requirements of Article 7 ECHR (*nulla peine sine lega certa*), the FSC held that Article 7 (2) (b) CartA which prohibits discrimination against business partners, taken together with Article 7 (1) CartA, constitute a sufficient legal basis under Article 7 ECHR. In other words, the question of whether a discriminatory practice is abusive must be considered in the light of the general clause of Article 7 (1) Cartel Act, which emphasises the principle that there can only be an abuse of a dominant position if the practice in question has anti-competitive effects on the market (Sect. 5.3.2 above). Furthermore, in reaching its conclusion, the Federal Court indicated that the rule can be clarified on the basis of the criteria developed by case law and doctrine, including the practice in relation to Article 102 TFEU, even though Switzerland is not a member of the EU or the EEA.

[17] FSC, judgment of 29 June 2012, case 2C_484/2010, ATF/BGE 139 I 72 *Publigroupe*.

[18] *Menarini Diagnostics S.R.L. v. Italy*, ECHR judgment of 27 September 2011. See also Notably *Sigma Radio Television v. Cyprus*, ECHR judgment of 21 July 2011.

The case was also an opportunity to confirm that the COMCO may impose a fine on an undertaking after approving the settlement agreement reached between that undertaking and the COMCO Secretariat. The FSC justifies this by taking the view that the settlement agreement only covers, and therefore concerns, the future conduct of the undertaking and not the past unlawful conduct. In 2018, the COMCO Secretariat prepared a note on the purpose and main steps for concluding and approving a settlement agreement with companies (see Sect. 7.3 below). [19]

7.2.3 *Calculation of the Fine*

7.2.3.1 Calculation of the Basic Amount

The first step is to determine the basic amount, which depends on the seriousness and nature of the infringement. [20] The maximum of the basic sanction is set at 10% of the turnover achieved by the undertaking concerned in the relevant markets in Switzerland during the three financial years preceding the end of the infringement. [21]

The turnover for the calculation of the basic amount is the turnover achieved in the relevant market affected by the unlawful restraint of competition, the unlawful agreement, or the abuse of a dominant position. The relevant product or geographic market is the same as the market defined for the assessment of the unlawful conduct, as defined in Article 11(3) MCO. In Naxoo, the FSC implicitly confirmed that the relevant market for the calculation of the basic amount of the fine may be adjacent to the market in which the undertaking is found to be dominant, because such an adjacent market was directly affected by the abusive conduct. [22] If the undertaking had no turnover in the relevant market, e.g. because it made a higher offer without the intention of winning the bid (cover offer), the basic amount will be estimated to reflect a hypothetical turnover in the market. [23]

For the calculation of turnover, Article 9(3) of the Cartel Act refers to the provisions on merger control and thus to the MCO, which apply to the extent

[19] See the COMCO Secretariat's notice of 28 February 2018 on amicable agreements, available at www.weko.admin.ch. Since the entry into force of direct sanctions, the Cartel Act no longer provides for a procedure similar to that of commitments under EU competition law, whereby a company undertakes to change its conduct without the risk of a fine and without the conduct having to be found illegal (see Article 9 of Regulation 1/2003, OJ 2003 L 1, p. 1).

[20] Article 49a (1) CartA and Article 3 CASO.

[21] FAC, judgment of 16 September 2016, B-581/2012 *Nikon*, paras 9.2ff, in particular 9.2.3.

[22] FSC, judgment of 9 May 2023, 2C_395/2021, *Naxoo*, para 11.3.3.

[23] FAC, judgment of 25 June 2018, B-807/2012 *Wettbewerbsabreden im Strassen- und Tiefbau im Kanton Aargau, ERNE*, paras 11.5.4.1 ff, in which the FAC confirmed the sanctioning of those who offered cover in a tender and those who benefited from it.

appropriate, which is also suggested by the word "by analogy". [24] The relevant provisions are Articles 4–8 MCO. For instance, in the case of a price-squeeze involving a group company, the FSC [25] approved COMCO's practice of using turnover of the dominant undertaking on all markets affected by the practice (upstream or downstream markets), without applying Article 5 (2) MCO [26] on the deduction of turnover resulting from transactions between group companies, which was considered irrelevant in the present case as the abuse benefited both entities of the group.

The applicable factor will depend on the seriousness and gravity of the agreement, within a range of up to 10%. For the most serious infringements, in particular agreements within the meaning of Article 5(3) and (4) CartA, the basic amount will normally be in the upper third of the range up to 10%. [27] The basic amount will be higher if the presumption of eliminating competition cannot be reversed. The following cases illustrate the recent COMCO's practice:

- 10% for abuse of a dominant position by an undertaking that is the subject of several fines; [28] in a margin squeeze case, the FAC reduced the 10% factor of the basic amount to 8%; [29]
- 9–10% for a price-fixing and market-sharing cartel under Article 5(3) CartA; [30]
- 7% to the general importer who initiated and arranged a market allocation agreement within the meaning Article 5(3)(c) CartA, 5% to a dealer who has made a significant contribution to the implementation of the agreement, 3% for other dealers who have made a lesser contribution and 1% to a company who has made a minimal contribution to the agreement; [31]
- 7% for a market allocation agreement within the meaning Article 5(3)(c) CartA; [32]

[24] FSC, judgment of 9 December 2019, 2C_985/2015, *Preispolitik Swisscom ADSL,* ATF/BGE 146 II 217, para 9.2.2.3.

[25] Idem.

[26] Article 5(2) MCO reads "In calculating the total turnover of an undertaking concerned, the turnover from business activities between the undertakings mentioned in paragraph 1 shall not be taken into account."

[27] Remarks on CASO, Article 3.

[28] COMCO decision of 21 September 2015, *Swisscom WAN-Anbindung*, LPC 2016/1, p. 128, para 594.

[29] FAC, judgment of 4 September 2015, case B-7633/2009, *Preispolitik Swisscom ADSL,* paras 747–748, LPC 2015/3, p. 561. The FAC highlighted the fact that Swisscom had acted with gross negligence by failing to consider the explicit indications of the COMCO Secretariat regarding the application of the margin squeeze to the facts at hand, the apparent disproportion between the wholesale and retail prices for broadband products and the significant impact of its practice on the competitiveness of competitors in the retail market for broadband products.

[30] COMCO decision of 23 February 2015 *Tunnelreinigung*, LPC 2015/2, p. 193, para 296; COMCO decision of 19 August 2019 *Bauleistungen Graubünden*, LPC 2020/4a, p. 1721, para 585.

[31] COMCO decision of 23 May 2022 *Concessionari Volkswagen*, para 608.

[32] COMCO decision of 29 January 2018 *Gerätebenzin*, LPC 2018/2, p. 347, para 100.

- 4–6% for the restriction of parallel imports in vertical agreements within the meaning of Article 5(4) CartA; [33] FSC upheld a factor of 5% for Gaba and BMW. [34]
- 4–6% for resale price maintenance within the meaning of Article 5(4) CartA; [35]
- 5% for price recommendations amounting to a vertical price fixing within the meaning of Article 5(4) CartA; [36]
- 3–7% for various abuses of dominant position under Article 7 CartA.

Two cases illustrate the Supreme Court's evolving approach to the gravity of misconduct in abuse of dominance. In *Preispolitik Swisscom ADSL*, the basic amount of the fine of 8%, reduced by the FAC from 10% to 8%, was considered proportionate to the seriousness of the abuse. [37] As explained in Sect. 5.2.2, the price squeeze was caught by Article 7(1) CartA without the need to apply any of the cases of paragraph 2. The FSC rejected the dominant undertakings' argument that only the practices listed in Article 7(2) CartA should be considered serious, arguing that there was no qualitative difference between the practices covered by either of the two paragraphs of Article 7 CartA. In discussing the gravity or seriousness of the abuse in relation to the amount of the fine, the FSC refers to the EU Commission's Guidance on Enforcement Priorities in the Application of Article 102 TFEU [38] and considers that the abusive conduct listed in that guidance must be considered serious. The FSC states that:

> The fact that margin squeezes as such are particularly problematic from a competition law perspective is also reflected in the fact that the EU Commission has included them in its Communication on Enforcement Priorities. With the Communication on Enforcement Priorities, the European Commission has announced its priorities with regard to anti-competitive practices. In this sense, both the abstract potential threat and the degree of competitive harm are very high. Overall, all competitors of the complainants on the final product market were harmed in the years 2001–2007. [39]

[33] COMCO decision of 27 May 2013 *Marché du livre écrit en français*, LPC 2018/2, p. 245, paras 732 ff.

[34] FSC, judgment of 28 June 2016, 2C_180/2014, *Gaba*, ATF/BGE 143 II 297, para 9.7.3. FSC, judgment of 24 October 2017, 2C_63/2016, *BMW*.

[35] COMCO decision of 20 August 2012 *Altimum*, LPC 2016/2, p. 384, para 334. The fine in this case was set aside by the FSC on procedural grounds.

[36] COMCO decision of 2 November 2009 *Hors-Liste Medikamente: Preise von Cialis, Levitra und Viagra*, LPC 2010/4, p. 649, para 371.

[37] FSC, judgment of 9 December 2019, case 2C_985/2015, *Preispolitik Swisscom ADSL*, ATF/BGE 146 II 217, para 9.2.3.2. The COMCO had applied a basic amount of 10%, and the FAC had reduced it to 8%.

[38] EU Commission, Guidance on the Commission's enforcement priorities in applying Article 82 of the EC Treaty to abusive exclusionary conduct by dominant undertakings, JO 2009 C 45, p. 7.

[39] FSC, judgment of 9 December 2019, case 2C_985/2015, *Preispolitik Swisscom ADSL*, ATF/BGE 146 II 217, para 9.2.3.3 (free translation, references omitted). The FSC refers here to "die abstrakte Gefährdungspotential", which we have translated as "abstract potential threat".

In SIX DCC, the FSC again refers to the EU Commission's Guidance on Enforcement Priorities in the Application of Article 102 TFEU in relation to tying and bundling to demonstrate the seriousness of the abuses listed in the EU Commission's Guidance. [40] The FSC goes one step further and considers the tying and bundling of two products as a "risk-based conduct". This would mean that the conduct of tying and bundling itself poses a risk to competition which qualifies it as serious for the purpose of setting the basic amount of the fine (see Sect. 5.3.3.6).

According to Article 49a Cartel Act, the fine must consider the likely profit that has resulted from the unlawful behaviour. The basic amount is considered to include a normal profit of around 15–20%, and therefore no investigations or calculations are normally carried out to determine the level of profit. [41] If the infringement has resulted in an unusually high profit, this will not be taken into account in the basic amount but will be considered as an aggravating circumstance. Exceptionally, if no profit was made, this could be considered as a mitigating circumstance.

7.2.3.2 Increase in Function of the Duration

The basic amount is increased by up to 50% for infringements that have been ongoing for between 1 and 5 years. The first year is comprised in the basic amount and therefore there is not increase if the infringement does not exceed 12 months. For longer infringements, the basic amount is increased by an additional sanction of up to 10% for each additional year. [42] The basic amount of the fine is increased by 0.8333% per month for periods of less than 1 year. [43]

7.2.3.3 Increase for Aggravating Circumstances and Reduction for Mitigating Circumstances

The basic amount is increased for aggravating circumstances and reduced for mitigating circumstances. Aggravating circumstances include repeated violations of the Cartel Act, [44] obtaining a profit from the violation that is particularly high by objective standards, or refusing to cooperate with the authorities or otherwise

[40] See Sect. 5.3.3.6, referring to FSC, judgment of 2 November 2022, case 2C_596/2019, *SIX DCC*, para 10.2.3. As explained above, we have translated 'Gefährdungstatbestand' as 'risk-based conduct'.

[41] Remarks on CASO, Article 2 paragraph 1 and Article 3 paragraph b).

[42] Article 4 CASO.

[43] FSC, judgment of 9 May 2023, 2C_395/2021, *Naxoo*, para 11.3.

[44] COMCO decision of 23 May 2023 Concessionari Volkswagen, paras 528.

attempting to obstruct the investigation, [45] for example by destroying evidence. [46] Mitigating circumstances include, in particular, the fact that the undertaking terminates the restraint of competition after the first intervention of the Secretariat of the Competition Commission, but at the latest before the initiation of proceedings pursuant to Articles 26–30 of the Cartel Act, [47] enters into an amicable settlement agreement or acknowledge the facts of the case. [48] The FAC appears to be more conservative than COMCO in applying reductions, stating that a 20% reduction for admission of facts would be excessive, although it could not reduce the fine because the conditions for reformatio in peius were not met. [49]

Additional aggravating or mitigating circumstances apply to agreements that are presumed to eliminate competition within the meaning of Article 5(3) and (4) of the Cartel Act: the basic amount will be increased if the undertakings played an instigating or leading role in the restriction of competition or ordered or carried out retaliatory measures against other undertakings that participated in the restriction of competition in order to enforce the agreement affecting competition. [50] Retaliation may be used to force other cartel members to comply or to dissuade them from leaving the cartel (see Article 5(3) CartA) or to force retailers to stop parallel imports or to respect resale prices by threatening termination or boycotts (see Article 5 (4) CartA). [51] The basic amount will be reduced if the undertaking played a strictly passive role in the restriction of competition and did not carry out retaliatory measures that were agreed upon to enforce the agreement affecting competition. [52]

There is no limit to the percentage increase or decrease. The increase or decrease is applied to the interim amount obtained after the increase of the basic amount for the duration of the agreement.

7.2.3.4 Reduction for Partial Immunity

The reduction for partial immunity (Sect. 7.2.4.2 below), if any, is applied at the end of the calculation to the second intermediate sum obtained after the increase or reduction for aggravating or mitigating circumstances. The reduction is applied to the second interim amount which results from the increase or decrease for aggravating or mitigating circumstances of the first interim amount.

---

[45] Article 5(1) CASO.

[46] Remarks on CASO, Article 5 paragraph 1 lit. c).

[47] Article 6(1) CASO.

[48] COMCO decision of 23 May 2023 *Concessionari Volkswagen*, paras 542 et 543.

[49] FAC, judgment of 5 June 2023, B-4596/2019 *CA Auto Finance Suisse SA*, para 9.6.27.

[50] Article 5(2) CASO.

[51] Remarks on CASO, Article 5 paragraph b).

[52] Article 6(2) CASO.

7.2.3.5 Absolute Ceiling on the Amount of Fines

Article 49a (1) CartA and Article 7 CASO provide for an absolute ceiling of fines of 10% of the turnover the undertaking achieved in Switzerland in the preceding three financial years. The three financial years are the financial years prior to the year in which COMCO takes a decision on the fine and not the period prior to the end of the infringement as when determining the basic amount. The turnover here covers all activities of the undertakings, not only those concerned by the infringement. [53] The turnover is the group's total turnover in Switzerland, not just that of a Swiss branch, as this corresponds to the concept of an undertaking. [54]

In general, the ceiling is not applied because the fine calculated based on the turnover in the relevant market in which the infringement takes place is in any case lower than the ceiling. [55] However, the ceiling could be useful for instance for a company that is the instigator of a long-term cartel—and therefore not eligible for immunity—that lasts for more than 10 years and covers the whole industry, for which a 10% factor is applied to the basic amount because the presumption of competition is not reversed. The second example in Sect. 7.2.3.6 below illustrates such a case.

If the undertaking has no turnover in the three financial years preceding the year in which the COMCO decides on the fine, the ceiling would be zero, which would risk undermining the effectiveness of the fines. This could be the case if the company ceases its activities or withdraws from the Swiss market. In this case, the ceiling could be calculated, as for the basic amount, on the basis of the turnover in the three financial years preceding the end of the infringement. The turnover for the calculation of the basic amount may be lower if the undertaking is active in other relevant markets in Switzerland, or the same as for the calculation of the ceiling if the infringement concerned all the undertaking's activities.

7.2.3.6 Sample Calculation (Tables 7.1 and 7.2)

Table 7.1 Sample calculation in general

Description		Calculation of the fine (CHF)	Explanation
Year of decision Y			
Turnover Y-1		10,000,000	Turnover of all activities in Switzerland in Year Y-1
Turnover Y-2		10,000,000	Idem

(continued)

[53] Cf. Sect. 7.2.3.1 above on the basic amount.

[54] FAC, judgment of 16 September 2016, B-581/2012, *Nikon*, para 9.2.2.

[55] Remarks on CASO, Article 3 paragraph c).

Table 7.1 (continued)

Description		Calculation of the fine (CHF)	Explanation
Turnover Y-3		10,000,000	Idem
Total turnover		30,000,000	
Ceiling 49a CartA (10%)		3,000,000	The limit of 10% of total turnover is calculated on the basis of the sum of the undertaking's turnover in Switzerland from all its activities. Here 10% of CHF 3,000,000 = CHF 300,000.
Year of termination of infringement YN = (Y-N)			
Market turnover YN-1	A	1,000,000	The basic amount is calculated on the basis of the undertaking's turnover in the relevant market where the infringement took place.
Market turnover YN-2	B	1,000,000	Idem
Market turnover YN-3	C	1,000,000	Idem
Total market Turnover	D	3,000,000	D = A + B + C The basic amount is calculated on the basis of the undertaking's total turnover over the last 3 years in the relevant market in which the infringement took place.
Basic amount 5%	E	150,000	D × (basic amount in %) The basic amount is calculated by applying a percentage of between 1% and 10% of the undertaking's total turnover over the last 3 years in the relevant market in which the infringement took place. Here 5% of CHF 3,000,000 = CHF 150,000.
Increase for 11-year duration (110%)	F	165,000	10% × (number of years) × E Here 110% of CHF 150,000 = CHF 165,000
First intermediate sum	G	315,000	G = E + F Basic amount plus increase for duration. Here CHF 150,000 + CHF 165,000 = CHF 315,000.
Increase for aggravating circumstances 10%	J	31,500	G × (increase in %) 10% of CHF 315,500 = CHF 31,500
Reduction for mitigating circumstances 20%	H	(63,000)	G × (reduction in %) 20% of CHF 315,500 = CHF 63,000
Second intermediate sum	I	283,500	I = G + J − H CHF 315,000 + 31,500 − 63,000 = CHF 283,500
Reduction as partial immunity 50%	K	(141,750)	K = I × (reduction in %) 50% of CHF 283,500 = CHF 141,750
Final amount of the sanction	L	141,750	L = I − K CHF 283,500 − 141,750 = CHF 141,750

Table 7.2 Sample calculation in the case of an instigator of a horizontal cartel

Case of an instigator of a cartel in all its activities, no reversal of the presumption of elimination of competition			
Description		Calculation of the fine (CHF)	Explanation
Year of decision Y			
Turnover Y-1		10,000,000	Turnover of all activities in Switzerland in Year Y-1
Turnover Y-2		10,000,000	Idem
Turnover Y-3		10,000,000	Idem
Total turnover		30,000,000	
Ceiling 49a CartA (10%)		3,000,000	The limit of 10% of total turnover is calculated on the basis of the sum of the undertaking's turnover in Switzerland from all its activities. Here 10% of CHF 3,000,000 = CHF 300,000.
Year of termination of infringement YN = (Y - N)			
Market turnover YN-1	A	10,000,000	The basic amount is calculated on the basis of the undertaking's turnover in the relevant market where the infringement took place.
Market turnover YN-2	B	10,000,000	Idem
Market turnover YN-3	C	10,000,000	Idem
Total market turnover	D	30,000,000	D = A + B + C The basic amount is calculated on the basis of the undertaking's total turnover over the last 3 years in the relevant market in which the infringement took place.
Basic amount 10%	E	3,000,000	D × (basic amount in %) The basic amount is calculated by applying a percentage of between 1 and 10% of the undertaking's total turnover over the last 3 years in the relevant market in which the infringement took place. Here 10% of CHF 30,000,000 = CHF 3,000,000.
Increase for 11-year duration (110%)	F	3,300,000	10% × (number of years) × E Here 110% of CHF 3,000,000 = CHF 3,300,000
First intermediate sum	G	6,300,000	G = E + F Basic amount plus increase for duration. Here CHF 3,000,000 + CHF 3,300,000 = CHF 6,300,000.
Increase for aggravating circumstances 10%	J	630,000	G × (increase in %) 10% of CHF 6,300,000 = CHF 630,000
Reduction for mitigating circumstances 20%	H	(1,260,000)	G × (reduction in %) 20% of CHF 6,300,000 = CHF 1,260,000

(continued)

Table 7.2 (continued)

Case of an instigator of a cartel in all its activities, no reversal of the presumption of elimination of competition			
Description		Calculation of the fine (CHF)	Explanation
Second intermediate sum	I	5,670,000	I = G + J − H CHF 6,300,000 + 630,000 – 1,260,000 = CHF 5,670,000
No immunity	K	(0)	K = I × (reduction in %) K = 5,670,000 × (0) = 0
Amount of the sanction	L	5,670,000	L = I – K CHF 5,670,000 – 0 = CHF 5,670,000
Ceiling and total amount of the fine		3,000,000	L > ceiling, therefore ceiling applies

7.2.4 Leniency Application and Immunities

According to Article 49a (2) CartA, the fine may be waived in whole or in part if the undertaking assists in the discovery and elimination of the restraint of competition. The leniency programme is described in detail in Articles 8–14 CASO, with Articles 8–11 CASO providing for full immunity from fines and Articles 12–14 CASO providing for reduction of fines or partial immunity. [56] The following sections outline the conditions for full immunity and partial immunity.

7.2.4.1 Complete Immunity

Pursuant to Article 8 CASO, the COMCO grants full immunity to an undertaking if the undertaking is the first to report its own participation in a restraint of competition within the meaning of Article 5 (3) and (4) CartA. This covers one of the following situations:

– the undertaking provides information that enables the COMCO Secretariat to initiate in-depth investigations pursuant to Article 27 CartA and it does not already have sufficient information to initiate proceedings pursuant to Articles 26 and 27 of the Cartel Act in respect of the reported restraint of competition. [57] This information should be enough to enable the COMCO Secretariat to act, such as organising inspections [58] and open an in-depth investigation: the evidence and statements are intended to show that a suspected infringement of the Cartel Act exists. General assertions which are not supported by any evidence are not sufficient for a company to benefit from total immunity from fines. If the

[56] Cf. Commission Notice on Immunity from fines and reduction of fines in cartel cases, OJ 2006, C 298, p. 11.

[57] Article 8(1)(a) and 3 CASO.

[58] Explanatory note on leniency program, para 9. Remarks on CASO, Article 8 paragraph 1 lit. a).

information provided to the COMCO Secretariat is only for the purpose of opening a preliminary investigation (Article 26 CartA), the COMCO Secretariat states that "there can be no question of total immunity from fines". [59] However, such information may be considered in the context of partial immunity.

- the undertaking provides conclusive evidence that enables the COMCO to establish a competition infringement pursuant to Article 5 (3) or (4) of the Cartel Act, no other undertaking already fulfils the conditions for full immunity and the COMCO Secretariat does not already have sufficient evidence to prove an infringement. [60] The information to be provided by an applicant must be of a much higher standard than in the previous case: information enabling an investigation to be opened only has to provide sufficient grounds for suspicion, while the evidence disclosed to enable the authority to establish an infringement must provide proof of an unlawful practice. [61]

General information is not sufficient, the undertaking must provide information not only on the nature and form of the cooperation, but also on the purpose of its conduct and how it was implemented. [62] It must admit that it participated in the conduct in a prescribed manner, which means that leniency applications that provide evidence without admitting that the cooperation amounted to an agreement or concerted practice will not be accepted. Similarly, the leniency application must not contain statements that cast doubt on undertakings participation in a cartel or on the fact that it was an agreement or concerted practice, or statements that deny that the conduct had any effect on the market. On the contrary, the undertaking must "demonstrate the ends pursued by the infringement of competition and the effects the infringement produced on the market." [63] The undertaking will be asked to admit that its participation fulfilled the objective and subjective elements of, for example, an agreement to fix prices or share markets. On the other hand, the undertaking is not obliged to admit that it has infringed the Cartel Act or to provide a legal assessment of the facts.

There are four additional conditions for the grant of full immunity, [64] and the exclusions from immunity go beyond the case of coercion as set out in the EU guidelines. [65]

First, the undertaking must not have coerced another undertaking to participate in the infringement and must not have played the role of instigator or leader in the infringement in question. This is presumably why full immunity does not apply to conduct by dominant undertakings, but they can still apply for partial immunity. [66]

---

[59] Ibidem.

[60] Article 8(1)(b), (3) and (4) CASO.

[61] Explanatory note on leniency program, para 14.

[62] Explanatory note on leniency program, para 5. Remarks on CASO, Article 8 paragraph 1.

[63] Explanatory note on leniency program, para 6.

[64] Article 8(2) CASO.

[65] COMCO Secretariat, Remarks on CASO, Article 2 paragraph 2 lit. a).

[66] Explanatory note on leniency program, para 21a.

Second, the undertaking must voluntarily provide the COMCO Secretariat with all available information and evidence relating to the infringement within its sphere of influence. Voluntary means without being asked by the COMCO Secretariat. Sphere of influence means making its employees and governing bodies available for questioning and interviews and producing documents and other evidence located on the company's premises or where employees and governing bodies are domiciled. [67]

Third, the undertaking must cease its involvement in the infringement upon submission of the voluntary report or upon order of COMCO. The COMCO Secretariat may, in certain circumstances, ask the company to continue its participation in order not to jeopardise the investigation, such as house searches of other cartel members. [68] It is therefore advisable for companies involved in ongoing cartels to contact the COMCO Secretariat as soon as possible in order to obtain a "marker" for their leniency application, but also to seek advice as to what their obligations are with regard to their continued involvement in the cartel.

Fourth, the undertaking must cooperate fully and promptly with the COMCO Secretariat throughout the proceedings. This goes beyond the general obligation to cooperate in administrative procedures that applies to all companies. The leniency applicant must cooperate fully with the authorities throughout the procedure. This means that if the company denies its participation in an agreement, raises doubts, modifies or softens its statements in the leniency application in written replies to the COMCO or during the oral hearing, this will be considered as a withdrawal of the leniency application and immunity will not be granted again. [69] Counsel and company representatives should therefore pay careful attention to their written submissions and their pleadings at the hearing.

Only one undertaking may submit an application for leniency, which means that there can be no joint applications for immunity. [70] Leniency applications are submitted in writing or orally at the premises of the COMCO Secretariat. The leniency application must contain all necessary information concerning the undertaking itself, the nature of the reported competition infringement, the other undertakings involved in the competition infringement and the affected or relevant markets. [71] Leniency applications can also be submitted during searches. [72] In this case, the inspected undertakings will be informed of their right to submit a leniency application and to make a declaration to that effect, which they will be encouraged to do as a matter of priority by email and which they can complete at a later stage. The "marker" is less demanding than a full leniency application. [73]

---

[67] COMCO Secretariat, Remarks on CASO, Article 2 paragraph 2 lit. b).

[68] Idem, Article 2 paragraph 2 lit. d).

[69] Idem, Article 8 paragraph 1 lit. c).

[70] Explanatory note on leniency program, para 23.

[71] Article 9(1) CASO. Explanatory note on leniency program, para 5.

[72] Explanatory note on leniency program, para 13.

[73] For the content of the Marker and other practical advice applicable to searches and inspections, see Explanatory note on leniency program, paras 26 and 30.

The "marker" can be submitted in any case and is not limited to searches and inspections. However, the marker is not a requirement and undertakings may submit a full leniency application from the outset. [74]

The leniency application may be submitted anonymously. The COMCO Secretariat will determine on a case-by-case basis the modalities and the time limit within which the undertaking must disclose its identity. A member of the COMCO Presidency is informed. [75] An anonymous submission may be used by a company representative to inquire about the chances of success in obtaining immunity before deciding whether or not to submit a full, nominative leniency application. [76]

The COMCO Secretariat will acknowledge receipt of the leniency application, indicating the date and time of receipt. The COMCO Secretariat will inform the applicant whether its application is complete or of any additional information that the reporting undertaking needs to provide. [77] The COMCO Secretariat will also notify the undertaking whether its leniency application fulfils the conditions for complete immunity, but this notification is subject to the undertaking continuing to fulfil the four conditions set out above, in particular the condition of continued cooperation. [78]

In the case of multiple leniency applications, the COMCO Secretariat will not consider any subsequently received application until it has taken a decision on previously received leniency applications pursuant to Article 9(3) CASO. [79]

The final decision on full immunity will be taken by COMCO together with the final decision on the infringement. COMCO will not depart from a notification made by the COMCO Secretariat pursuant to Article 9(3)(a) CASO that the conditions for immunity are met, unless it subsequently receives information that precludes the granting of immunity from sanctions. [80] This may be the case if it is found that the undertaking concerned was in fact the instigator or principal actor of the infringement, [81] or if the undertaking withdraws its admission of participation in an agreement or concerted practice in written replies to the COMCO or during the oral hearing.

7.2.4.2 Partial Immunity

Undertakings that fail to qualify for full immunity may qualify for partial immunity, which means that they will benefit from a reduced fine. Article 12(1) CASO provides that the sanction may be reduced if an undertaking cooperates voluntarily in the

[74] Explanatory note on leniency program, para 34.
[75] Article 9(2) CASO.
[76] COMCO Secretariat, Remarks on CASO, Article 9 paragraph 2.
[77] Article 9(3) CASO.
[78] Explanatory note on leniency program, para 41.
[79] Article 10 CASO.
[80] Article 11 CASO.
[81] Remarks on CASO, Article 11 paragraph 2.

proceedings and terminates its involvement in the infringement at the latest at the time when it submits its evidence.

There are two types of reduction: a regular reduction, which can amount to up to 50% of the fine, and an additional reduction of up to 80% of the fine (or Bonus Plus). For the first type of reduction, the undertaking's contribution to the success of the proceedings will be decisive. [82] The second type of reduction, or bonus plus, is granted when an undertaking voluntarily provides information or evidence on other competition law infringements pursuant to Article 5(3) or (4) or Article 7 [83] of the Cartel Act, which allows the COMCO Secretariat either to open an in-depth investigation or to establish an infringement. [84]

Undertakings shall submit the same type of information as in the case of total immunity (Sect. 7.2.4.1), namely information on the notifying undertaking itself, the nature of the reported competition infringement, the undertakings involved in the competition infringement and the affected or relevant markets. [85] Submission should allow evidence that would have remained hidden to come to light and help reduce the cost of investigations. [86]

The procedure is also the same, i.e. the COMCO Secretariat acknowledges receipt of the evidence, stating the date and time of receipt. Partial immunity may be granted to several undertakings. Finally, COMCO takes the final decision on partial immunity and on the amount by which the sanction imposed on the cooperating undertaking should be reduced. [87]

If the cooperating undertaking submits evidence containing information on a longer duration of the competition infringement which was not known to the COMCO Secretariat, COMCO will not increase the sanction for this additional period which the undertaking itself has contributed to discovering by submitting new evidence. [88] This is to encourage the voluntary submission of new evidence in the context of leniency applications.

7.2.4.3 Confidentiality and Access to Leniency Documents

Access to the leniency application and statement of the undertaking is limited to the premises of the Secretariat and the other parties to the proceedings may not make copies or photos, but they may take notes. The other parties will have access to the evidence and exhibits submitted with the leniency application, also in electronic form, but will have to undertake in writing to use the document only in the

[82] Article 12(2) CartA.

[83] Explanatory note on leniency program, para 21a.

[84] Article 12(3) CartA. See Explanatory note on leniency program, para 20.

[85] Article 13 CASO.

[86] Remarks on CASO, Article 12 paragraph 2.

[87] Article 14 CASO.

[88] Remarks on CASO, Article 14 paragraph 2.

proceedings before the COMCO and its Secretariat and in appeal courts, but not in civil or criminal courts in Switzerland or before other authorities or courts abroad. The conditions of confidentiality and access to the file are explained in detail in the Explanatory Notice. [89]

Third parties, such as competitors and business partners, who are not parties to the proceedings do not have access to the file, neither to the leniency statement nor to the documents. Cantonal authorities that were victims of public procurement cartels were granted access to the documents of the cartel proceedings based on the administrative assistance provisions of the Data Protection Act, [90] and Article 25 (2) of the Cartel Act on the protection of business secrecy was not considered sufficient to oppose such a request. [91] Access was granted because of the Canton's important interest in pursuing civil claims and obtaining damages, but disclosure of the documents was limited to the examination of civil claims. [92] Business secrets and personal data of third parties were not disclosed.

In the case of multiple leniency applications in other countries, the COMCO Secretariat will ask the undertaking to sign a waiver of the confidentiality of its leniency application in Switzerland, covering the disclosure to other competition authorities, so that the Secretariat can exchange information and coordinate investigative measures with them. [93]

According to Article 7(6) of the Agreement between the European Union and the Swiss Confederation, [94] "the competition authorities of the Parties shall not discuss or transmit to each other information obtained under the Parties, leniency or settlement procedures, unless the undertaking which provided the information has given its express consent in writing." Article 42b (f) CartA expressly excludes the exchange of confidential information with foreign authorities, even based on an international agreement such as that with the European Union, in the context of an amicable settlement or an application for complete or partial immunity. Although there have been no cases to date, a refusal by a leniency applicant to provide confidential information or documents to the European Union may be considered a lack of cooperation under Article 8(2)(c) CASO.

[89] Explanatory note on leniency program, paras 47ff.

[90] The Data Protection Act applied to moral persons until the entry into force of the new Data Protection Act in September 2023.

[91] SFC, judgment of 18 March 2021 in cases 2C_1040/2018 and 2C_1051/2018, ATF/BGE 147 II 227, para 7.4.2.

[92] Idem, para 7.5.2.

[93] Explanatory note on leniency program, para 46.

[94] Agreement between the European Union and the Swiss Confederation concerning cooperation on the application of their competition laws, OJUE L 347, 3.12.2014, p. 3; RS 0.251.268.1.

7.2.5 Inability to Pay

Excessive fines and procedural costs can have an impact on a company's cash flow and worsen its liquidity situation, thus weakening its market position and even contributing to its exit from the market, which is not the objective of the Cartel Act. The Confederation cannot initiate bankruptcy proceedings to collect fines, [95] and therefore fines cannot cause bankruptcy, but the COMCO considers the impact of its fines even before they are imposed, if the undertaking is facing liquidity difficulties at that time. The company facing a fine can request a reduction on the grounds that it is unable to pay, and the COMCO will assess its inability to pay (ITP) according to transparent and equal criteria applied in all cases.

Inability to pay is considered under the principle of proportionality. [96] The SFC has ruled that a sanction is proportionate only if it preserves the company's competitiveness, which implies its existence. [97] Sanctions are intended to hurt, but not to drive a company into bankruptcy, as this would ultimately not serve competition. In setting the fine, the principle of proportionality means that the amount of the fine should be in reasonable proportion to the undertaking's performance, but the financial disadvantage must be such that it is not economically worthwhile to participate in the infringement.

The COMCO Secretariat will assess the financial situation at the time when the decision on the fine is taken to determine whether a fine will lead to an acute inability to pay or to over-indebtedness. The COMCO Secretariat will assess the financial situation to determine whether a fine will result in acute insolvency or over-indebtedness by examining both liquidity and debt-to-equity ratios. [98] The insolvency risk is tested by checking the company's ability to pay short-term liabilities with cash, then with cash and short-term receivables, then with current assets (e.g. inventories), using various common liquidity ratios. The company's difficulties are considered serious if the debt and liquidity ratios indicate that the company is at risk of being forced into bankruptcy by its creditors. In addition, the COMCO Secretariat will consider whether there are other refinancing options, such as a capital injection from shareholders. Fines are usually reduced for companies with serious liquidity and indebtedness concerns. The fine will be reduced to the level at which the reduction will enable the company to avoid being the subject of bankruptcy proceedings by creditors.

---

[95] Article 43(1) DEBA.

[96] Article 5 (2) Cst and Article 2 (2) CASO.

[97] FSC, judgment of 28 June 2016, 2C_180/2014, *Gaba*, ATF/BGE 143 II 297, para 9.7.2.

[98] For a situation discussed by courts, see FAC, judgment of 2 April 2020, B-823/2016, *Music Hug*, para 6.

7.2.6 Recovery of Fines, Default Interest and Tax Deduction

A COMCO decision on the amount of the fine is not enforceable if the company appeals to the FAC. Neither the COMCO nor the FAC can revoke the suspensive effect of the appeal on the fine itself. [99] However, an appeal to the FSC has no suspensive effect in general, including on the amount of the fine, unless the FSC grants it upon the request of the appealing undertaking. The COMCO decision becomes enforceable if upheld by the FAC and becomes a title that can be enforced in debt collection proceedings if the undertaking objects to the summons to pay. [100]

There is no case law on default interests. The Cartel Act does not regulate the issue. COMCO does not provide for a default interest in its decision, and therefore the amount of interest does not become enforceable upon entry into force of the decision. The summons to pay should therefore in principle include the applicable default interest, which is legally set at 5% per annum. [101] Undertakings must pay default interest as a rule from the date of the summons to pay. [102]

In 2016, the FSC ruled that fines imposed by the European Commission on the basis of EU competition law are not deductible as they are of a criminal nature, and that in principle only the part of the fine used to deduct undue profits, which is not of a criminal nature, remains deductible. [103] The same principle applies to COMCO sanctions. The case concerned a fine of EUR 348,000 imposed by the European Commission on a Zurich-based consultancy firm responsible for administering the meetings, statistics and minutes of a quantity and market sharing cartel agreement between companies in the EU. [104] As the consultant was not active in the markets affected by the cartel, the company did not "collect" the illicit profits of the cartel from its clients. The fine was upheld by the EU courts. The tax authorities of the canton of Zurich refused to allow the provision for the fine to be deducted from taxable profits. The FSC upheld the decision, clarifying that fines and other financial penalties of a criminal nature imposed on legal entities for their own liability do not constitute expenses justified by commercial usage and are therefore not deductible. The situation is different only in the case of sanctions aimed at reducing profits, insofar as they do not pursue a criminal objective: the part of the fine corresponding to the disgorgement of profits is considered an expense justified by commercial

[99] Article 55(2) APA.

[100] Article 80 (2)(2) DEBA.

[101] Article 104 (1) CO (applicable by analogy). Compound interest for default is prohibited in Switzerland.

[102] See for instance in other areas of enforcement of administrative decisions FSC, judgment of 18 May 2016, case 5D_13/2016, para 2.3.3; FSC, judgment of 31 March 2022, 5A_825/2021, ATF/BGE 148 III 225, para 4.2.1.

[103] FSC, Judgment of 26 September 2016, 2C_916/2014 and 2C_917/2014, ATF/BGE 143 II 8, paras 7 and 8.

[104] See CJEU of 22 October 2015, *AC-Treuhand*, C-194/14 P, ECLI:EU:C:2015:717.

usage and is therefore tax deductible, but the company must provide evidence of any part corresponding to the deprivation of unjustified profits.

7.2.7 Prior Notification of Restraints of Competition

According to Article 49a (3)(a) CartA, there will be no fine if the undertaking submits notification of the restraint of competition before it takes effect. Notification will not exempt an undertaking from the fine if the agreement or conduct of a dominant undertaking has already been implemented before the notification, or begins to be implemented after the notification, and the undertaking continues to do so after notification of the opening of proceedings within 5 months. [105] The 5-month period begins on the day following receipt of the notification by the COMCO Secretariat. This is also known as the "objection procedure", as COMCO has 5 months to respond or object.

If the undertaking is informed of the opening of a procedure under Articles 26–30 within 5 months of submitting its notification but continues to implement the restraint of competition, the charge is not waived. If, on the other hand, the undertaking is not informed of the initiation of proceedings pursuant to Articles 26–30 of the Cartel Act within 5 months of receipt of the notification, there will be no sanction in respect of the facts notified. [106] Notification does not confer immunity from future investigations and prohibitions or measures. COMCO may investigate and prohibit the conduct if it finds an unlawful restriction of competition, but it will simply not impose a fine. The purpose of the notification is therefore not to obtain a document comparable to a comfort letter for the notified conduct, but only for the sanctions. The Swiss Cartel Act does not provide for comfort letters on the legality of agreements or conduct of undertakings in a dominant position. The FSC has held that a notification under Art. 49a (3) (a) Cartel Act is a special procedure which does not lead to a decision on the lawfulness of the notified agreement or practice. It is a preliminary, sui generis procedure which is intended to enable the notifying parties to make their own assessment of the legality of the agreement or conduct. [107]

The notification or objection procedure is an option, not an obligation. The introduction of direct sanctions in 2003 was considered permissible only thanks to the possibility for undertakings to notify their projects before their implementation, to compensate for the legal uncertainty resulting from the low normative density of Articles 5 and 7 CartA. If the parties consider that they can bear the risk and do not need to reduce their legal uncertainty, they are free not to notify. Furthermore, undertakings that notify an agreement or conduct may choose to implement their

[105] COMCO Secretariat, Remarks on the Ordinance on Fines, Article 15.

[106] Article 19 CASO.

[107] FSC, judgment of 12 December 2008, ATF/BGE 135 II 60, para 3.4.

project unchanged even if the Secretariat initiates proceedings, since the proceedings may ultimately find no infringement. The risk is carried by the undertakings, and this is the meaning of the FSC judgment cited above.

The scope and content of the notification may be agreed in advance with the Secretariat. This may include a form of simplified notification. [108] The Secretariat will confirm whether the notification is complete or whether more information is required on any material point. [109] It is very important to describe the facts and the intended conduct or project in detail, as only what is described in the notification is covered by the immunity. [110]

In complex cases, one way of obtaining an initial opinion from the COMCO Secretariat on the proposed agreement or behaviour is to submit a request for advice under Article 23(2) CartA, which is not binding and does not trigger the 5-month deadline. The opinion can be used by the companies to adapt their projects in such a way as to meet specific concerns expressed by the Secretariat in its opinion, thus increasing the chances that the COMCO will not open an investigation.

The notification may be made by one undertaking or jointly by several participating undertakings, but a joint notification is not required. [111] A participating undertaking may also act on behalf of the other participating undertakings. For example, a trade association may notify an agreement on behalf of its members. The notification must clearly indicate on whose behalf it is made and to which undertakings or categories of undertakings it applies, for example whether it applies to all distributors in a selective distribution system. Where a large number of undertakings are involved, as in the case of distribution systems, the notification must identify the known distributors and define the criteria for future distributors. This is important to define the circle of undertakings that benefit from immunity.

Foreign companies may file a notification filed in another jurisdiction if the notification contains the information required in the form published by the COMCO and if it is drafted in German, French or Italian, which are official languages in Switzerland. Foreign notifications in English may be attached to the filing. Foreign companies or their representatives domiciled abroad must select an address for service in Switzerland. [112]

---

[108] Article 17 CASO. See Explanatory note on notifications of a restriction on competition, para 5.

[109] Article 18 CASO.

[110] See Explanatory note on notifications of a restriction on competition, para 22.

[111] See Explanatory note on notifications of a restriction on competition, paras 11 ff.

[112] See Explanatory note on notifications of a restriction on competition, paras 14 et 29.

7.2.8 *Time-limitation Applicable to Administrative Sanctions*

According to Article 49a (3)(a) CartA, the fine is waived if "the restraint of competition has not been exercised for more than 5 years by the time an investigation is opened."

The period to be taken into account starts with the end of the restraint and ends with the opening of an in-depth investigation pursuant to Article 27 CartA against at least one, but not necessarily all, of the undertakings involved in the infringement. [113] In other words, the opening of an investigation is in relation to the facts which are restrictive of competition and not in respect of a specific company. [114] If an investigation is opened within this period, the COMCO may impose a fine on the participants for the entire duration of the infringement [115] back to 1 April 2004, the date of entry into force of Article 49a CartA.

COMCO can still open an investigation after the 5-year period has expired. It can prohibit the restrictive practice but cannot impose a fine. The FSC has confirmed that there is no statute of limitations for COMCO proceedings, [116] with the exception of Art. 49 (3) (b) CartA, which only applies to the possibility of imposing sanctions.

7.3 Amicable Settlements

According to Article 29 CartA on amicable settlements, "if the Secretariat considers that a restraint of competition is unlawful, it may propose an amicable settlement to the undertakings involved concerning ways to eliminate the restraint. The amicable settlement is formulated in writing and approved by the Competition Commission."

Amicable settlements are frequently used, and the COMCO Secretariat published a notice in 2018. [117] The amicable settlement is discussed and concluded between the COMCO Secretariat and the company under investigation but must be approved by COMCO. The COMCO can therefore refuse to approve the amicable settlement and send the case back to the Secretariat. The amicable settlement may be requested by the Secretariat or by the undertaking itself, although the latter has no right [118] to initiate discussions on an amicable settlement and the Secretariat has discretion as to which cases will be subject to an amicable settlement. Before entering into discussions on a possible amicable settlement, the undertaking must sign a document

[113] This is for instance the case when a global and lasting agreement is found.

[114] FAC, judgment of 9 August 2021, B-5119/2019 *Strassenbau Graubünden/Centorame*, para 5.2.4. Cf. Article 25 (3) Regulation 1/2003 which contains a similar rule.

[115] See Remarks on CASO, Article 4.

[116] FSC, judgment of 2 November 2022, 2C_596/2019, *SIX DCC*, para 6.4.1.

[117] COMCO Secretariat, Note of 28 February 2018 on Amicable Settlements (Note on amicable settlements).

[118] Note on amicable settlements, para 13.

setting out the general terms and conditions under which the discussions will take place. An English translation is attached to this section.

The subject matter of the amicable settlement is very different from the subject matter of the commitments procedure conducted in the EU under Article 9 of Regulation 1/2003. The commitments procedure concludes that there are no longer grounds for action by the European Commission in view of the undertaking's commitments to change its behaviour, whereas the amicable settlement under Article 29 Cartel Act does not affect the finding of an infringement and the principle that there must be a sanction, but only makes the agreed measures binding for the future. Therefore, while there will be no fine in the EU commitment procedure, undertakings will be subject to a fine in Switzerland, albeit a lower one. The amicable settlement procedure is closer to the settlement procedure for cartel cases in the EU. [119] The legality of the imposition of fines in the context of an amicable settlement has been confirmed by the FSC in the Publigroupe case. [120] The final decision of COMCO will find an unlawful agreement or abuse of a dominant position and impose a (lower) fine, but instead of a prohibition it will make binding the measures agreed by the parties in the operative part of the decision.

The facts, their qualification and the sanction are decided by the COMCO on a proposal from its Secretariat The facts and their qualification are not negotiable, but the decision will be shorter and therefore not all the facts will be disclosed to the public. This also means that the undertakings are not obliged to confess or admit to having violated the Cartel Act in the amicable settlement. The sanction is also decided by the COMCO, but the parties will know the range of the sanction proposed by the Secretariat before signing the settlement and will therefore know what to expect. The COMCO usually does not exceed the upper end of the range, although it is not bound by the Secretariat's proposal.

Undertakings have an interest in reaching an amicable settlement because the fine will be lower, the duration of the procedure will be shorter and therefore the costs to be paid to the COMCO and their counsel will be lower, the final decision will also be shorter with less factual development and a shorter legal assessment.

Companies are expected to cooperate during the investigation, not to engage in dilatory conduct, not to request additional investigative measures, to waive, in principle, their right of access to the file and their right to be heard in person by the COMCO, to submit short statements and replies, and not to appeal against the final decision of the COMCO. The waiver of the right to appeal does not prevent the companies from appealing against the COMCO decision approving the amicable settlement, since under Swiss law any waiver of the right to appeal before the

[119] Commission Notice on the conduct of settlement procedures in view of the adoption of Decisions pursuant to Article 7 and Article 23 of Council Regulation 1/2003 in cartel cases, OJ 2008, C 167, p. 1.

[120] FSC, judgment of 29 June 2012, 2C_484/2010, *Publigroupe*, ATF/BGE 139 I 72. See also Sect. 5.3.1.

decision is notified is ineffective. [121] However, if the COMCO decision does not deviate from the Secretariat's proposal and the amicable settlement, the companies have no interest in appealing and any appeal, while admissible, would have little chance of success.

The conclusion of an amicable settlement is considered as good cooperation in determining the level of the fine. The Note of the COMCO Secretariat on Amicable Settlements has clarified and standardised the level of reduction of fines in different scenarios.

The level of reduction depends on the stage of the procedure at which the settlement is reached: the earlier the settlement, the higher the reduction. [122] If a settlement is signed at the beginning of the investigation, during the fact-finding phase, the fine will be reduced by 20%, which is the maximum reduction for amicable settlements. A signature at the intermediate stage of drafting the proposal to be submitted by the Secretariat to the COMCO will result in a reduction of 15%. At the end of the fact-finding and investigation, when the draft proposal is substantially drafted by the Secretariat, the reduction will not exceed 10%. An amicable settlement may be reached even after the proposal has been notified to the undertaking, but the reduction in the fine will not exceed 5%.

The reduction may be higher if the company voluntarily provides evidence or acknowledges the facts outside a leniency procedure, which is called particularly good cooperation. In this way, the maximum reduction of 20% for good cooperation within the meaning of Article 6(1) CASO can be combined with the maximum reduction of 20% for signing an amicable settlement, resulting in a combined reduction of 40%. [123]

The reduction for signing an amicable settlement is also possible in the case of total or partial immunity, although only the undertakings benefiting from partial immunity will benefit from an additional reduction, as the fine is fully waived in the case of total immunity in any event. The main benefit for undertakings that have applied for full immunity is a shorter decision and procedure.

A reduction for signing an amicable settlement combined with a 50% reduction for partial immunity results in a reduction of up to 60%. [124] In the case of bonus plus, signing an amicable settlement result in a combined reduction of up to 84%. The reductions are not combined or added, but the reduction for an amicable settlement and for immunity are applied in stages to various intermediate amounts in the calculation of the fine. The reduction for an amicable settlement is applied first as a mitigating circumstance (Sect. 7.2.3.3), and the reduction for partial immunity is then deducted from the interim amount.

[121] FAC, judgment of 5 June 2023, B-4596/2019 *CA Auto Finance Suisse SA*, para 1.2.

[122] Note on amicable settlements, para 11.

[123] Note on amicable settlements, para 12.

[124] Note on amicable settlements, para 12.

7.4 Other Sanctions

7.4.1 Administrative Sanctions to Undertakings

In addition to the sanctions for an illegal agreement or abuse of a dominant position pursuant to Article 49a of the Cartel Act, the Cartel Act provides for other administrative fines that may be imposed on undertakings by the COMCO. Intent is not a condition for administrative sanctions against undertakings, unlike criminal sanctions against natural persons.

The heaviest fine, which is equivalent to the fine under Article 49a of the Cartel Act, is imposed if an undertaking violates an amicable settlement or a final and non-appealable decision of the COMCO. Pursuant to Article 50 CartA, an undertaking which infringes an amicable settlement, a final and non-appealable decision of the COMCO or a decision of an appeal body may be charged up to 10% of its turnover in Switzerland in the previous three financial years. In determining the amount, due account shall be taken of the likely profit made from the unlawful conduct. In 2005, COMCO imposed a fine of CHF 248,000 on Zurich Airport for failure to comply with an interim order (LPC 2006/1, p. 141). No other fines have been imposed since then.

Article 51 of the Cartel Act provides for fines of up to CHF 1,000,000 for undertakings that implement a concentration that should have been notified without filing a notification, fail to comply with a suspension obligation, fail to comply with a condition attached to an authorisation, implement a prohibited concentration, or fail to implement a measure intended to restore effective competition. In the event of repeated failure to comply with a condition attached to the authorisation, a fine of up to 10% of the total turnover in Switzerland of all the undertakings concerned may be imposed. There were some cases of failure to notify reported in Sect. 6.2.2, which resulted in fines of between CHF 30,000 and 70,000, and of gun-jumping, which resulted in a fine of CHF 60,000 fine for each of the notifying undertakings (Sect. 6.3.3).

Finally, a fine of up to CHF 100,000 may be imposed on any undertaking, whether a party to the proceedings or not, which does not fully comply with its obligation to provide information or submit documents. [125] In 2021, the COMCO fined a group of companies a total of CHF 40,000 for two breaches of the duty to inform committed by two of its subsidiaries. [126] The group had an estimated turnover of around CHF 10 million and about 100 employees. The subsidiaries failed to respond to several requests from the COMCO Secretariat to complete a questionnaire in connection with investigations in the watchmaking sector. The Secretariat had warned the companies that if they failed to respond, it would issue a decision requiring them to provide the information requested in the questionnaire. The

[125] Article 52 Cartel Act.

[126] COMCO decision of 28 June 2021, LPC 2021/3, p. 688. The procedural costs of approximately CHF 19,000 were shared equally between the two subsidiaries.

companies still did not respond to the Secretariat's decision ordering them to respond, nor did they appeal against that decision. The Secretariat and COMCO initiated sanction proceedings and issued a fine to the group company. The FAC confirmed the sanctions but reduced the fine after correcting the way in which two separate infringements were counted for a group of companies: instead of applying the same sanction to each company in the group and then allocating the amount to the group, the FAC requires that the first amount be fixed and then increased it for the second infringement of the sister company. After confirming the fine of CHF 20,000 for the first company, the FAC increased it by CHF 15,000 for the second infringement, resulting in a total fine of CHF 35,000. The FAC also took the opportunity to clarify that the principle of proportionality, the gravity of the infringements and the mitigating and aggravating circumstances within the meaning of Articles 2, 3, 5 and 6 CASO also apply by analogy to the application of other administrative sanctions pursuant to Articles 50–52 CartA. [127]

7.4.2 *Criminal Sanctions to Individuals*

The Cartel Act provides for several criminal sanctions against natural persons, such as directors, managers, or employees. These sanctions are not imposed for participating in a restriction of competition, but only for failing to comply with an order or decision of the COMCO or for intentionally failing to notify a concentration. Unlike administrative sanctions against undertakings, criminal sanctions can only be imposed on natural persons if their conduct is intentional. The fines are issued by the COMCO. The prosecution and adjudication of such offences is not governed by the APA but by the Administrative Criminal Law (ACL). [128]

Anyone who intentionally violates an amicable settlement, a final and non-appealable decision of the competition authorities or a decision of an appeal court is liable to a fine of up to CHF 100,000. [129] Prosecution and the imposition of penalties are subject to a limitation period of 5 years, which may not be suspended for more than half of its original duration. [130]

Anyone who intentionally fails to comply with a decision of the COMCO concerning the obligation to provide information or fails to do so in full, or who implements a concentration that should have been notified without filing a notification, or who violates decisions concerning concentrations of undertakings, is liable to a fine of up to CHF 20,000. [131] In this case, criminal prosecution and the imposition of a fine are subject to a shorter limitation period of 2 years. [132]

[127] FAC, judgment of 16 February 2023, B-3882/2021, LPC 2023/1, p. 163.

[128] Article 57 CartA.

[129] Article 54 Cartel Act.

[130] Article 56 (1) CartA.

[131] Article 55 CartA.

[132] Article 56 (2) CartA.

To our knowledge, no criminal sanctions have been applied to natural persons.

List of Documents

COMCO Secretariat, Explanatory note and form of the Secretariat of 8 September 2014, Leniency program (voluntary report) (Explanatory note on the leniency program)

COMCO Secretariat, Remarks on the Ordinance on Fines (CASO)

COMCO Secretariat, Remarks on the Ordinance on Fines (Remarks on CASO). Available at https://www.weko.admin.ch/weko/en/home/rechtliches_dokumentation/communications.html. Accessed 18 May 2023

COMCO Secretariat's notice of 28 February 2018 on amicable agreements

COMCO, Explanatory note and form of 21 October 2014, Notification of a restriction on competition

Guidelines on the method of setting fines imposed pursuant to Article 23(2)(a) of Regulation No 1/2003, OJ C 210, 1.9.2006, p. 2

Ordinance on Sanctions imposed for Unlawful Restraints of Competition (Cartel Act Sanctions Ordinance, CASO; RS 251.5)

Index

P. Këllezi, *Competition Law in Switzerland*,
https://doi.org/10.1007/978-3-031-45117-1

MIX
Papier aus verantwortungsvollen Quellen
Paper from responsible sources
FSC® C105338

If you have any concerns about our products,
you can contact us on
ProductSafety@springernature.com

In case Publisher is established outside the EU,
the EU authorized representative is:
Springer Nature Customer Service Center GmbH
Europaplatz 3, 69115 Heidelberg, Germany

Printed by Libri Plureos GmbH
in Hamburg, Germany